Technology, Innovation and Access to Justice

Future Law

Series Editors
Burkhard Schafer, Professor of Computational Legal Theory,
University of Edinburgh
Edina Harbinja, Senior Lecturer in Media/Privacy Law, Aston University

Books in the series are critical and topic-led, reflecting the global
jurisdiction of technology and culture interacting with law. Each title
responds to cutting-edge debates in the field where technology interacts
with culture to challenge the ability of law to react to frequently
unprecedented scenarios.

Available or forthcoming titles

Buying Your Self on the Internet: Wrap Contracts and Personal Genomics
Andelka M Phillips

Future Law: Emerging Technology, Regulation and Ethics
Lilian Edwards, Burkhard Schafer and Edina Harbinja (eds)

Technology, Innovation and Access to Justice:
Dialogues on the Future of Law
Siddharth Peter de Souza and Maximilian Spohr (eds)

edinburghuniversitypress.com/series/ful

Technology, Innovation and Access to Justice

Dialogues on the Future of Law

Siddharth Peter de Souza and
Maximilian Spohr

EDINBURGH
University Press

Edinburgh University Press is one of the leading university presses in the UK. We publish academic books and journals in our selected subject areas across the humanities and social sciences, combining cutting-edge scholarship with high editorial and production values to produce academic works of lasting importance. For more information visit our website: edinburghuniversitypress.com

Edinburgh University Press Ltd
The Tun – Holyrood Road
12(2f) Jackson's Entry
Edinburgh EH8 8PJ

First published in hardback by Edinburgh University Press 2021

Typeset in 11/13pt Adobe Garamond by
Servis Filmsetting Ltd, Stockport, Cheshire,
and printed and bound by CPI Group (UK) Ltd, Croydon, CR0 4YY

A CIP record for this book is available from the British Library

ISBN 978-1-4744-7386-6 (hardback)
ISBN 978-1-4744-7387-3 (paperback)
ISBN 978-1-4744-7388-0 (webready PDF)
ISBN 978-1-4744-7689-8 (epub)

Contents

Contributors

Alistair Alexander was project lead for The Glass Room at Tactical Tech July 2016–May 2020. He now works with companies and organisations around the world on data, privacy, technology and sustainability.

Maurits Barendrecht Research Director Hague Institute for Innovation of Law; Professor of Innovation of Justice Systems, Tilburg University

Ana Paula Camelo Researcher and Project Manager, Center for Education and Research on Innovation, Getulio Vargas Foundation, São Paulo Law School

Siddharth Peter de Souza PhD Candidate, Humboldt University of Berlin; Founder of Justice Adda

Christian Djeffal Assistant Professor for Law, Science and Technology, Technical University of Munich

Angelo Dube Associate Professor of International Law, Department of Public, Constitutional and International Law, College of Law, University of South Africa

Özgür Kahale Director of Pro Bono for Europe, DLA Piper

Suzanna Kalendzhian Co-founder and CEO of Legal Advice Middle East

Odunoluwa Longe Co-founder and Lead Counsel at The Longe Practice; Co-founder of DIYlaw; Regional Head, West Africa–Justice Accelerator, Hague Institute for the Innovation of Law

Maeve Lavelle Data Analyst, Thriva

Cláudio Lucena Head of the International Office and Professor of Law, Paraíba State University; Advisor, INOVATEC; Researcher, Foundation for Science and Technology in Portugal

Lyria Bennett Moses Director, Allens Hub for Technology, Law and

Innovation; Professor, Faculty of Law and Justice, University New South Wales Sydney

Dory Reiling Independent Court Reform and IT Expert; Former Senior Judge

Aviva Rotenberg Director Strategic Initiatives (National), Canadian Bar Association

Roger Smith OBE Visiting Professor, London South Bank University; Honorary Professor, University of Kent

Gianluca Sgueo Research Associate, Center for Social Studies of the University of Coimbra; Global Media Seminar Professor, New York University (Florence); Policy Analyst, European Parliament

Maximilian Spohr Legal and Policy Advisor, Friedrich Naumann Foundation for Freedom in Berlin

Mira Suleimenova International Lawyer

Cedric Vanleenhove Post-Doctoral Researcher, Faculty of Law and Criminology, Ghent University; Professor, HEC Management School, University of Liège

Astrid Wiik Post-Doctoral Researcher (Habilitand), Institute for Constitutional Law, Constitutional Studies and Philosophy of Law, Faculty of Law, Heidelberg University

George Williams AO Deputy Vice-Chancellor, Planning and Assurance; Anthony Mason Professor and Scientia Professor, Faculty of Law and Justice, University New South Wales Sydney

Monika Zalnieriute Senior Lecturer and Australian Research Council DECRA Fellow, Faculty of Law and Justice, University New South Wales Sydney

Illustrations

Figures

Table

Table of Cases

Table of Legislation

Acknowledgements

This volume has been possible due to the enthusiasm of the contributors, and we would like to thank them for their engagement and support with putting together this book.

The academic inspiration, exchange and contributions for this book emerged during an international conference on 'The Future of Law: Technology, Innovation and Access to Justice', held 28–29 November 2018 at Humboldt University Berlin. Thank you to Prof. Philipp Dann, Humboldt University Berlin for his support in organising the conference. Our special thanks to Freya Schramm who provided great editorial assistance on the project and to the team at Edinburgh University Press, Laura Williamson, Sarah Foyle and Fiona Conn.

The conference was generously funded by the Friedrich Naumann Foundation for Freedom.

Foreword

Maurits Barendrecht

This book is recommended for anyone studying the ways to improve access to justice. It starts from a clear challenge: the justice gap, as identified and quantified by the Task Force on Justice. Instead of addressing this challenge as a national issue, caused by the flaws of national laws, courts and practices, the book takes access to justice as a challenge for humanity.

What strikes me most when reading the chapters is the independent thinking and analysis. The authors (mostly from the Millennial generation) easily switch between disciplines and develop their own frameworks. Many technologies and options for bridging the justice gap have a place in their thinking. According to them, we face a future with automated government decision-making, new ways of serving documents, gamification of legal services, plain language writing, outcome-focused court procedures, new forms of education and promising innovations.

The chapters present a menu of options, rather than a clear unified framework. This is amazing for a book on law. Interestingly, the logic of the legal system is mostly absent from these pieces. The reader will find no ultimate authority being looked for in a constitution or in the rulings of a supreme court. The starting point is the need to deliver justice. The authors then look for the people and the solutions responding to this need.

All writers seem to feel comfortable with this. They accept the legitimacy of expertise, helped by reports such as the ones published by the Task Force on Justice, the OECD and the Elders. They follow the user perspective or write about the possible contribution of a certain technology.

It is interesting to reflect on this freedom of thought. Is this the free-thinking of a younger generation, not looking for clear careers towards a professorship or a partnership in a law firm? Do they see life as a series of ever-deeper experiences?

The language of law, as expressed in these pieces, is building on local capacities, which are similar in multiple locations. The approach is not so much the one of an academic paper. These papers are more interacting, emerging, user-centred.

The underlying urge and sense of direction is strong, though. Somehow this all feels like one programme. The authors want to do something about the justice gap. Better outcomes for people. The flow of new ideas, technologies, innovations and free-thinking people will bridge the justice gap.

Underneath, I see a few ideas about organisation and structure. Some chapters address the structural issues of how to ensure sufficient innovation. Here we find the need for legal systems to focus on what works, on sustainability, on legal empowerment, on R&D and on market structures that may or may not be helpful. One of the defining issues is how this movement will relate to the existing structures and power relations in the justice sector. We see some movement here: bar associations opening up in the US, pressured by innovators and younger lawyers; innovative new procedures in many countries, competing with traditional court processes that are adversarial and assuming lawyers are there to help clients navigate the process.

Governments are urged to rethink their policies by landmark reports. Research is lining up. Will this movement gain momentum and finally improve access to justice? Or is more needed, because this is a new paradigm, which requires a fundamental change in how we think about and manage justice sector institutions? The readers of this volume will surely have their views on this after turning the final page.

1

Introduction

Making Access to Justice Count: Debating the Future of Law

Siddharth Peter de Souza & Maximilian Spohr

A. Introduction

Over 5 billion people do not have meaningful access to the justice delivery system, according to a recent report produced by a network of international development organisations (Pathfinders 2019). The magnitude of the gap is further understood where over 253 million people live in conditions of extreme injustice such as slavery, conflict and statelessness; 1.5 billion have justice problems they cannot solve, and over 4.5 billion people are excluded from protections of the law that provide for socio-economic and political security (Pathfinders 2019). Addressing this justice gap is of critical importance and is central to the imagination of the Sustainable Development Goals, which aspire to build inclusive societies and protect vulnerable populations (United Nations Sustainable Development Goals 2015).

While the justice gap continues to grow, we are also living in an age where the scale of technological innovation has resulted in developments such as document automation, e-discovery, predictive analytics and online dispute resolution increasingly being adopted in the delivery of legal services. The influx of new services that are engineered around improving efficiency, productivity and quality review are influencing changes in the ways of working in the legal sector. These factors are also leading to the development of alternative business models for law firms, new models of legal education, and new expectations and demands from public services.

These new technologies are beginning to deeply impact the ordinary functioning of law and the everyday life of its users. In an age of digital change, it is crucial to understand what these changes mean for the resolution of common legal problems that result in social, economic and cultural challenges for citizens. How do we place people first, and understand their challenges and difficulties and ensure they find a solution for their justice problems?

Debating about the future of law and of the justice sector requires a mapping of the changes to different actors and institutions in the legal sector whether lawyers, judges, firms and most of all, ordinary citizens. While there is much work emerging in terms of trends around 'legal tech', 'artificial intelligence and law' in the commercial law space, there is less scholarly and policy attention on the use of such technologies in terms of its implications for ensuring access to justice and addressing the needs of the ordinary citizen. This book seeks to mainstream discussions on access to justice into discussions on the future of law. In doing so, it seeks to examine what changes in technology mean for the end user, whether an ordinary citizen, a client or a student. In this way, it looks at the everyday practice of law through a sector-wide analysis of law firms, universities, start-ups and civil society organisations. It argues that a lack of access to justice is not a concern limited to civil society organisations alone but requires collaboration and synergies between different actors and institutions in the legal sector.

We propose a three-step approach towards investigating how to build a strategic roadmap for meeting the challenges of the justice gap in the context of dynamic innovation and technological changes. The first is to provide broad insights and trends into what technology changes have been introduced in the private sector, public sector, civil society and in legal education by conducting a mapping exercise to survey the field. The second is to locate what these changes mean for the concerns of a digital divide, for legal empowerment and for access to justice. For example, do these technologies enable individuals to understand procedures better? Does it render justice more cost-effective? Or does it result in less transparency and accountability because technological solutions are more opaque? And the third is to plug the gap by examining how to address sector-specific access to justice questions and learn as we go forward.

By analysing the technological changes taking place in the legal sector, this book seeks to explore where the developments have taken place, the types of actors and institutions driving these developments, and the impact and lessons they have had for the future of law.

In the next section of this chapter, we examine the significance of the scale of change, taking place, how this has been forecasted, and why we are living in particularly dynamic times. Thereafter, we look at the importance of emphasising these changes on debates around access to justice, and the value of a sector-wide approach. Finally, we examine the key lessons in order to make justice count and provide an outline of the volume.

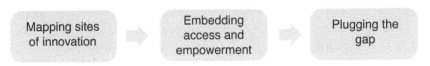

Figure 1.1   Scheme of chapter

B. Mapping Sites of Innovation: Examining Trends and Identifying Points of Change

The debate on 'The future of the law' has been around for some time with Richard Susskind, a reference point in almost all related publications, publishing a book under this title as early as 1996 (Susskind 1996). A good ten years later his seminal 2008 publication 'The end of lawyers?' then sparked a euphoric legal tech debate and made a very self-confident profession wonder if it, too, could one day be replaced by intelligent machines (Susskind 2008).

Apart from this, other factors regularly cited for the emergence of 'legal tech' in the past decade include the 2008 global economic downturn that forced legal service providers to become more cost-efficient and the technological development such as the take-up of cloud computing (Goodman 2018: 70). Furthermore, market liberalisation, such as through the UK Legal Services Act 2007 allowed for new business models in the field and fuelled entrepreneurship (Goodman 2018: 67). The Covid-19 pandemic has also seen a accelerated push towards digital transformation with more multi-disciplinary perspectives needed to be able to respond to rapidly changing market and client needs (Cohen 2020).

A good decade after the Susskind prophecies, the ever-accelerating development of technology has opened the door to new exciting possibilities. While the legal services industry had been somewhat of a latecomer in adopting new means of technology, the rise of artificial intelligence and machine learning have now given us an idea of what the future of the law might look like. Predictive analytics, today, allows forecasting the outcome of US Supreme Court decisions with over 70 per cent accuracy – far better than expert legal analysts (Katz, Bommarito, Blackman 2017). Furthermore, it plays an increasing role in predictive policing, tax evasion and tax outcomes, recurrence rates of criminal defendants and even lawsuit financing (Vogl 2018: 57). Intelligent machines can even forecast the enactment of legislation, as demonstrated by Skopos Labs in 2017 (Hutson 2017).

This new technology is increasingly included in the everyday practice of the law. While initially this was with respect to making the job of a (human) lawyer easier through faster and more effective file and knowledge management, billing or other administrative tasks, it has now started to impact the very heart of rendering legal advice (de Souza 2017). Examples include automated contract analysis tools such as eBrevia, Kira, Luminance or Leverton. E-discovery tools such as Relativity, legal expert systems like Neota Logic or prognostic tools like Ravel, LexPredict or IBM Watson (Wenzler 2018: 78). McKinsey has predicted that 35 per cent of a law clerk's job will be rendered redundant while 22 per cent of a lawyers job will be replaced by these technologies (Winick 2017).

With their access to large financial resources, it is the big law firms that are the early adopters of these new technologies (Goodman 2018: 70). Additionally, with the rise of AI-powered programs, the development and training of these intelligent machines becomes more and more important, and many law firms find themselves in a race to also succeed as legal tech investors and developers (Goodman 2018: 72). This competition has now intensified considerably with the big accountancy firms, who have a head start in adopting technology, muscling their way in on the market wherever possible (Derbyshire 2018).

Apart from the big firms, a vibrant legal tech start-up scene has emerged in the past few years, particularly in places that saw market liberalisation such as the UK. In part, this was also fuelled by the fact that many of the big firms are investing in start-ups rather than applying the technology to their own business (Dipsham and Strom 2018; Goodman 2018: 72). In 2015, leading law firm Dentons created Next Law Labs, a wholly-owned business accelerator that aims to support and invest in legal tech ventures while Allen & Overy in 2017 launched a legal and regulatory tech incubator called Fuse to support tech companies who are innovating in the work that they do (Dipsham and Strom 2018). 2018 also marked a breakthrough year with a record-setting $1.6 billion of total investments in the legal tech sector, which constituted a 713 per cent growth over the previous year (Dolm 2019). Today, Stanford's CodeX Techindex lists over 1,300 legal tech start-ups, currently across nine categories of 'Marketplace', 'Document Automation', 'Practice Management', 'Legal Research', 'Legal Education', 'Online Dispute Resolution', 'E-Discovery', 'Analytics' and 'Compliance' (Stanford Law School n.d.). While initially offering niche services, these technologies are increasingly influencing the legal services industry as a whole. Alternative legal service providers, such as Axiom, are growing rapidly and have a considerable impact on the market as they contribute to the unbundling of legal services and give more options and hence bargaining power to clients (Vogl 2018: 64).

Apart from the purely commercial interests, social motives of legal aid and legal assistance improvement played an important role early on in legal tech, as Roger Smith describes in Chapter 5 of this volume. Small claims and class action, from the beginning, were interesting fields for innovation and soon start-ups like DoNotPay in the UK or MyRight and FlightRight in

Germany helped clients to fight their parking tickets, receive damages for delayed flights or bring a class action against Volkswagen in the context of the "Clean Diesel" scandal (Gnirke 2019). Entrepreneurs have also been driven by the idea that technology could improve access to justice around the world. Since 2007, online platforms in the Netherlands, Canada and the UK have helped to solve marriage, landlord-tenant and other disputes through projects like Rechtwijzer by HiiL, MyLawBC or Relate (Smith, R. 2017; Smith, R. 2017a). Innovators like Joshua Browder of DoNotPay soon turned to more social ventures by supporting homeless people in finding accommodation (Cresci 2016). Through platforms such as Haqdarshak in India, legal tech is also helping people claim benefits by assisting community-level advisers to assess individuals' eligibility for benefits and then supporting those individuals to apply (Walker and Verhaert 2019: 62). Common good lawsuits can today be financed through platforms like Crowd Justice that was recognised as the 2018 Financial Times top innovative lawyer (Boulton 2018). Since 2016 the mobile app PLP 2.0 (Promotoras Legais Populares) from Brazil that won the 2014 Google Social Impact Award helps women in situations of domestic, sexual or family violence translating twenty years of legal empowerment experiences into the digital age (Walker and Verhaert 2019: 32). Legal Geek, one of the world's most influential legal tech conferences in October 2019, held its first own Law for Good conference in London (Law For Good n.d.).

The Public sector has followed more slowly and is only beginning to embrace the new means of technology. While digitisation holds the great promise to make the entire state administration more effective, accessible and transparent, recent years have demonstrated that making this a reality is a far greater challenge than imagined. Digitising our chronically overburdened courts, for example, is a far more complex endeavour than many expected as Dory Reiling insightfully illustrates in Part II of this volume. Often, limited public resources are one of the challenges. However, a certain exclusivity of lawyers running our justice systems, which tend to be more reluctant to innovate than others are, seems to be part of the problem (HiiL 2019: 7). Nevertheless, governments are increasingly trying to tap into the potential of legal tech beyond the digitisation of the administration. An example of this development is the growing number of initiatives of online dispute resolution mechanisms that are being integrated into court or tribunal processes. These include initiatives in Canada (British Columbia), and pilots in the US (Utah, Ohio, California), Australia (Victoria), and England and Wales (Walker and Verhaert 2019: 18). These mechanisms, like the British Columbia Civil Resolution Tribunal, help individuals diagnose a problem, provide them with legal information and lead them through a guided online dispute resolution process, followed by links to a formal tribunal process (Walker and Verhaert

2019: 18). In India, the government has also introduced a number of technology-based platforms, which aim at improving the technological aspects of courts, creating better access to lawyers for clients and improving the delivery of pro bono services. However, much remains to be done to recognise and improve the scale and impact of these services (de Souza and Aithala 2018).

These technological developments will change the legal profession. Ultimately, the demand on the labour market will follow, which will not allow for legal education to remain the same. However, as multiple authors in this book find, the legal profession is rather conservative when it comes to adopting change. Legal education is no exemption here as Aviva Rotenberg illustrates in Chapter 15, describing a reluctant profession that needs to be engaged in its own future. Canada, as demonstrated by Ryerson Law School, offers interesting examples of innovation in legal education. It attempts to train the lawyers of the future, taking into account that graduates today make their way into practice in an ever-widening range of ways (Holloway 2019). Just in April 2019, the Law Society of Ontario unanimously approved Ryerson's application to have its JD programme designated as an Integrated Practice Curriculum (IPC). A broad overview of innovation in legal services and particularly in legal education is offered by the Law School Innovation Index (Legal Services Innovation Index n.d.). Responding to growing criticism over the past years that law schools failed to update their curricula, this prototype index collects and lists schools that drive innovation. Some examples of law schools embracing the future also come from Michigan State University College of Law or the Massachusetts Institute of Technology (MIT) which collaborates with Georgetown Law School. Addressing these examples, Ana Paula Camelo and Cláudio Lucena, in Part IV, describe what a roadmap for legal education, on its path to the future, could look like.

In addition to the law firms setting up accelerators, there are also innovation clusters emerging around the world. Singapore, with its Future Law Innovation Programme by the Singapore Academy of Law, is seeking to create a space for legal innovation and collaboration to create solutions for the changing legal services market. The Innovating Justice Accelerator by The Hague Institute for Innovation of Law (HiiL), on the other hand, has been a pioneering programme that supports entrepreneurs particularly from the Global South. Projects span a wide range including family law, criminal law, legal aid and technical project support.

C. Embedding Access and Empowerment in Technology and Innovation

What we see from this mapping exercise is that the legal sector is at a crucial moment in its history. It seems clear that with technology and innovation, legal institutions are changing. Whether it be law firms who are looking at alternative ways of working by investing and transforming into technology enterprises, legal tech firms boosted by an influx of capital to scale their services or others who are strategically merging; courts, and public institutions like the police who are increasingly using technology for predictive analytics or creating more IT-based infrastructures; civil society organisations that are helping people diagnose problems and also using technology for spreading legal literacy; and education where law schools are innovating and offering new courses to meet the demands of the market. These institutional changes are at differing levels of speed, scale and with different levels of success. While the previous section has included examples to present a picture of the changes taking place, this section focuses more on asking what it means to the different sectors to embed questions of access to justice and empowerment in their work.

Access to justice is understood as the ability for people to address their everyday legal problems, either through recourse to law, courts or other forums (Cappelletti and Garth 1981; UNDP 2004). The challenges of access to justice can emerge in multiple ways, such as where courts and legal institutions are out of reach of litigants because of costs, distance, or even a lack of knowledge of rights and entitlements. It can also be because many judicial institutions are under-funded and as a result there is poor judicial infrastructure, inadequate staff, and limited resources to meet the needs and demands of litigants who require such services. In many instances, the text of the law itself is riddled with complexities, and that makes it difficult for ordinary litigants to understand and use it effectively.

As legal needs surveys have shown over the years, some of the major challenges that confront legal systems concern everyday justice problems from matters concerning property rights, securing ownership or paying rent, to family matters including on matters related to inheritance, divorce or domestic violence and abuse and even matters of employment or joblessness (Pleasance and Balmer 2018; Barendrecht, Kamminga and Verdonschot 2008). What is apparent from these different surveys within these different data sources is that major challenges within the law are emerging from the most routinised matters.

For this, what becomes important is to find a way to empower people to use the law and increase their agency in the use and delivery of legal services. Golub has described legal empowerment as the agency people have to make choices and take control over their lives (Golub 2003). This concept is echoed by the Commission for Legal Empowerment of the Poor which in 2008, argued that ensuring the recognition of identity and also ensuring that people have a voice were central to thinking of empowerment.

Each of these three concepts of access to justice, legal needs and legal empowerment overlap and interact in different ways because they are related to understanding the challenges of justice sector reform from a demand perspective. This entails asking how providers of justice, such as courts or law firms, can adapt based on what the user needs. It inverts the approach from one which has traditionally revolved around deciding from the top-down regarding what innovations and changes are needed to make the law work inclusively, efficiently and productively for everyone.

This emphasis on people-centred approaches to justice requires making sense of how justice is realised, based on the needs and desires of people (Gramatikov, Barendrecht and Verdonschot 2011; de Souza 2019). A recent report by OECD on inclusive growth and access to justice examined people centricity of justice by focusing on understanding legal needs by examining what the needs are, when and where they are experienced, who experiences them and what works to meet these needs and how must they be assessed (OECD 2019). What we find relevant in exploring these different concepts is that they place emphasis on building the agency of people.

By placing importance on the agency of people and examining the ways in which justice is realised, there is a renewed focus on outcomes. As a recent HiiL report argues, it aims at ensuring that a solution is achieved, a dispute is resolved, or harm is prevented (HiiL 2019), and in doing so, we are able to understand the material implication of how technology can be adapted and used to meet the needs of people.

The Engine Room in their report on Tech for Legal Empowerment provided useful insights on implementing projects in an access to justice context (Walker and Verhaert 2019). Among the key findings of the report was that technology was a supplement and not a substitute for support in-person, so it is essential to have a clear idea of the problem that needs to be solved. In developing a solution, it was also important to continuously test with user feedback and iterate if necessary. Further, ensure that you open dialogue with other comparable projects across jurisdictions to learn from their experiences and finally measure the impact of the intervention.

Mainstreaming aspects of empowerment and access into debates on technology, we argue, provides a vocabulary to ask (1) whether the technological product is increasing the agency of a justice user, whether this is a client, a student, a judge or someone else, (2) whether the product resulted in improving the outcomes for the user and resulted in solutions for their dispute, and (3) whether the product is responsive and reflexive such that it is able to adapt and iterate to the needs of users.

D. Plugging the Gap

While thinking in terms of empowerment and access providing an important lens to investigate the potential of technology, in this section, we explore some of the factors that can create an environment that will enhance innovation while also meeting the needs of the justice gap.

As we have demonstrated through the first section of mapping different sites of innovation – what is clear is that the scale and funding of innovation has resulted in the development of particular clusters around the world. While the US is still a pioneer in terms of scale and reach, Singapore and Hong Kong are also emerging as legal tech hubs with active involvement from the State and law societies (Pickup 2018). HiiL in the Netherlands through their work with a Justice Accelerator has focused on innovation from Africa. In particular, they have funded projects that work on matters related to criminal law, employment, legal advice and land-related problems. Each of these clusters has its own particularities and priorities and comparatively examining their frameworks offers an opportunity to understand the diversity in the contexts within which innovation is taking place. Equally, it is important to recognise the different kinds of expertise that are required in order to foster innovation. While each of these clusters has lawyers who can provide domain expertise, they also require business consultants to examine questions of funding and strategy, they require technologists to build products, and they require communicators who can market and build a user base for these technologies. In this book, we have also brought together a variety of voices to show how it is important to have a diversity of perspectives in order to tackle the complex challenges of access to justice.

Coupled with bringing expertise from across the board is the idea of introducing collaboration. As we will demonstrate in the overview of the different sectors addressed in the book, innovation cannot take place in silos but rather where there is more interaction and exchange between different sectors. HiiL in a recent report argues for how the public sector must use their convening power and create an enabling environment for innovation, the private sector which has the capacity to be agile and innovative in their ways of working must look at ways to scale their impact, civil society can provide perspectives of people's needs and wants, while academia can provide the knowledge on how to connect these different strands (HiiL 2019). Collaboration offers the opportunity to pool resources, but more importantly it is the advancement of a mindset that recognises that the challenges of a justice gap can only be resolved through cross-sectoral partnerships. Technology-based solutions can only work if they are able to get buy-in from different stakeholders (de Souza and Aithala 2018). Thus an outcome of a collaborative approach is one where there is fundamental change in the mindsets (Zent 2018).

Another aspect of plugging the gap is to address how to scale innovation. In this regard, the challenges can emerge from issues with respect to economic infrastructure that does not provide the apparatus or climate to grow. It can also arise from regulation that makes it difficult to experiment and take risks which in turn is also influenced by more conservative mindsets and finally the question of financing that is required for implementing different kinds of innovations. Scaling innovation also builds on the other aspects mentioned previously because in order to scale you need to have diversity of expertise and experience that can provide the contextual knowledge that helps address multifaceted challenges of access to justice. Additionally, scaling also requires more collaborative enterprise because it involves creating an atmosphere and mindset driving collective ownership and clear outcomes, it requires the distribution of responsibility, as well as the authority and regulation to implement solutions (O'Reilly 2018).

E. Finding Relations Between Sectors: Ideas from the Book

Innovation is impacted by several factors from capital, which allows for experimentation, to regulation and regulatory institutions that create climates for a culture of change, to different kinds of mindsets that allow for risk taking (Cohen 2017; Cohen 2018). As a trans-disciplinary project, this volume brings together leading authors from different parts of the legal sector such as judges, academics, practitioners, policy makers and entrepreneurs from all parts of the world, including countries like Brazil, Nigeria, United Arab Emirates, Germany, Netherlands, Belgium, Italy, India, Canada, United Kingdom, South Africa, and Australia.

By doing so, it seeks to widen the conversation by introducing comparative experiences to understand the manner and implications in which changes are taking place. Adopting a sector-wide approach provides insights into where and how innovation is taking place, who is driving it, and how it is developing. Further by seeking to look at change across different regions and geographies, this book also pluralises the conversation by introducing contextual understandings of innovation.

The design and choices of the sectors also reflect on the impact of technology in the law. For reasons of capital, capacity and competencies, innovation has had a larger impact in the private sector first. With a growing availability of capital and market liberalisation, a vibrant start-up scene is evolving, too. At the same time, though traditionally a bit slower, the public sector follows. It is driven by the promise that technology holds the key to build cost-effective administrations such as, for example, that it will solve the problem of chronically overburdened courts with technology-driven solutions. As described above, legal aid and the improvement of access to justice is an objective for many law innovators, which makes civil society an important sector to look at. Ultimately, legal education has to adopt technology and to produce tomorrow's lawyers they might have to include multi-disciplinary skills in their curricula.

However, the discussion on the future of the law is still highly fragmented along country borders, jurisdictions and legal systems, just as the law itself. Hence, internationalisation of the debate is highly expedient. The authors in this volume from around the world engage with the different protagonists and stakeholders and attempt to find reasons and meanings for the latest developments. They offer evidence that the drivers of technological change are emerging from beyond the private sector, and it is important to understand how conversations among different stakeholders can help think about questions of access to justice in the age of the future of law.

Accordingly, this volume looks at the private sector first. Leading innovators, entrepreneurs and experts from law firms, legal tech start-ups and the legal aid sector share their view on current changes in the industry, its challenges and opportunities.

Özgür Kahale starts us off, giving an insight to innovation at one of the world's biggest law firms, focusing particularly on the role of pro bono work and how it is evolving with technology. From this, it becomes clear that the sector is at a defining moment and will face considerable change and disruption in the near future. A growing number of indicators foreshadow this development already today, but we are barely scratching the surface of future change, as Suzanna Kalendzhian points out. She further maps out the most relevant technologies that are currently changing the law.

Odunoluwa Longe argues that the abundance of newly evolving possibilities will only allow those lawyers that are innovative and open to change to keep up. Roger Smith, too, takes a closer analytical look and describes how differently innovation drives the for-profit and not-for-profit sector forward. Apart from identifying the key challenges and opportunities, he is convinced that, since technology is transnational, there are lessons learnt from international comparison, comparative research and global benchmarking.

The second part turns to the public sector with leading academics and practitioners assessing the potential but also the risks and challenges of digitising the law in the public sphere. Automating governmental decision-making, however promising it is, has turned out not to be without risks where applied, as comprehensively illustrated by Monika Zalnieriute, Lyria Bennett Moses and George Williams. A lack of transparency, consistency and predictability of such automated decisions or human bias that translates into such programs, they find, could have a severe impact on the rule of law. All of these factors have to be taken into account if technology is to develop its full potential in this sector. In light of the complexities of the technological revolution of the public sector of the law, Christian Djeffal proposes a sustainable AI development framework to think about the impacts of the use of AI systems at a social, technical and governance level. From practice, Dory Reiling then shares her professional experiences in bringing a court into the digital age, a goal worth pursuing but not easy to achieve. Lastly, Cedric Vanleenhove analyses the potential role of social media in legal proceedings, a technology that might help solve some typical problems of the analog world.

In the third part of the book, we learn about some of the multiple ways that technology influences the law in civil society. Gianluca Sgueo explores the potential of gamification as a tool for digital advocacy. Siddharth Peter de Souza then shows us that we can re-shape legal communication taking into account inter-disciplinary influences of design and visualisation. However, the promise of technology fixing the global access to justice crisis will not come true all too easily. Alistair Alexander and Mira Suleimenova demonstrate how privacy issues play a key role in all levels of the legal tech revolution. They present practical solutions and an artistic approach to engage stakeholders and raise their awareness. Lastly, Astrid Wiik illustrates how potential solutions always need to be based on a firm understanding of how law and technology operate in the specific socio-cultural context of the target community. Hence, she argues, development cooperation needs to directly engage with communities for interventions to be effective and meaningful.

In the final part of the book, we look at legal education. Since fundamental change and disruption in one sector of the law is unlikely to leave the others untouched, we ask the question if the education sector is changing too. One thing seems clear: Law schools and universities have to start producing tomorrow's lawyers today if they want to satisfy future demand on the labour market. As Maeve Lavelle describes, legal education, together with the whole profession seems to be caught up in an identity crisis. Similarly, Aviva Rotenberg observes a reluctance of the profession to engage in its own future and offers concrete strategies of promoting change. Cláudio Lucena and Ana Paula Camelo offer concrete solutions by presenting a roadmap for the future of legal education. They further engage, among many others, in the key question of how much coding skills future lawyers will need. In some cases, however, progress is made with no plan or strategy at all as we learn from Angelo Dube. He tells the story about how technology helped keep up legal education despite university shutdowns in the context of the 2015–2016 FeesMustFall protests in South Africa.

F. Conclusion

By drawing on both scholars and practitioners reflecting on debates around the future of law and the changes that are taking place due to technological innovation, this book seeks to embed and mainstream discussions on access to justice into discussions on the future of law. It begins by mapping innovations taking place around the world and identifying the different locations for innovation, next it examines what embedding access and empowerment can mean for a technological innovation and lastly it examines ways to plug the gap through focusing on aspects of diversity, users and scale. In order to do this, it provides an analysis of how questions of access to justice can be addressed in different parts of the legal industry; second, it draws from conversations in both the Global North and Global South, to showcase the diversity in experiences and expertise in addressing technological innovation in the legal sector; and third, offers a dialogue between theory and practice that allows for both practical and reflective essays on the nature of changes in the legal sector.

There is now further impetus among legal tech entrepreneurs to apply legal technologies for the common good, which is evident through the first Law for Good conference in London in October 2019 as a spin-off from Legal Geek. The time is now ripe to fuel and structure the debate on legal tech for access to justice. As innovation is driven by the big law firms and technology is developed and applied by them first – could pro bono work be a space for translating some of the technology into access to justice solutions? Can the public sector and regulators incentivise different players to contribute to the field by encouraging and developing innovation policies? Can legal education which, is gearing up to address the need for new skill sets, also spearhead a responsibility revolution among new lawyers? Or must such change be driven by civic tech enterprises who can act as effective power brokers? We have seen that while technology can help address social challenges, it is important to ensure that to actually achieve something, there is an infrastructure that supports such innovation. This is to ensure that we are not just left with techno-fixes, which do not have a long-term impact. Technology can address barriers to access to justice – however, it needs a concerted and systematic effort to amplify, structure and translate its impacts to be relevant in different contexts.

Bibliography

Barendrecht, M., P. Kamminga, and J. H. Verdonschot (2008), 'Priorities for the Justice System: Responding to the Most Urgent Legal Problems of Individuals', *TISCO Working Paper*, 5 February 2008, <https://papers.ssrn.com/abstract=1090885>, (last accessed 12 March 2020).

Boulton, L. (2018), 'Top 10 innovative lawyers: the legal profession embraces the future', *Financial Times*, October 2018, <https://www.ft.com/content/c3a5c736-9faa-11e8-85da-eeb7a9ce36e4>, (last accessed 12 March 2020).

Cappelletti, M., and B. Garth (1981), 'Access to Justice as a Focus of Research Foreword', *Windsor Yearbook of Access to Justice* 1: ix–2.

Cohen, M. A. (2017), '"Legal Innovation" Is Not An Oxymoron – It's Farther Along Than You Think', *Forbes* (blog), 2017, <https://www.forbes.com/sites/markcohen1/2017/03/14/legal-innovation-is-not-an-oxymoron-its-farther-along-than-you-think/>, (last accessed 12 March 2020).

———— (2018), 'Legal Innovation Is the Rage, But There's Plenty of Resistance', *Forbes* (blog), 2018, <https://www.forbes.com/sites/markcohen1/2018/08/30/legal-innovation-is-the-rage-but-theres-plenty-of-resistance/>, (last accessed 12 March 2020).

———— (2020), 'Covid-19 Is Transforming The Legal Industry: Macro And Micro Evidence', *Forbes* (blog), 2020 <https://www.forbes.com/sites/markcohen1/2020/09/15/covid-19-is-transforming-the-legal-industry-macro-and-micro-evidence/#6156504e3269> (last accessed 31 October 2020).

Cresci, E. (2016), 'Creator of Chatbot That Beat 160,000 Parking Fines Now Tackling Homelessness', *The Guardian*, August 11, 2016, sec. Technology. <https://www.theguardian.com/technology/2016/aug/11/chatbot-lawyer-beat-parking-fines-helping-homeless-do-not-pay>, (last accessed 12 March 2020).

Derbyshire, J. (2018), 'Big Four circle the legal profession', *Financial Times*, 15 November 2018 <https://www.ft.com/content/9b1fdab2-cd3c-11e8-8d0b-a6539b949662>, (last accessed 12 March 2020).

Dipsham, R., and R. Strom (2018), 'Law Firms Are Investing in Tech Before It Overtakes Them', *Daily Business Review* (blog), 2018, <https://www.law.com/dailybusinessreview/2018/03/26/law-firms-are-investing-in-tech-before-it-over takes-them/>, (last accessed 12 March 2020).

Dolm, N. (2019), '713% Growth: Legal Tech Set An Investment Record In 2018', *Forbes*, 15 January 2019 <https://www.forbes.com/sites/valentinpivovarov/2019/01/15/legaltechinvestment2018/#5260b52c7c2b>, (last accessed 12 March 2020).

Golub, S. (2003), 'Beyond Rule of Law Orthodoxy: The Legal Empowerment Alternative', 41, Rule of Law Series, <https://carnegieendowment.org/2003/10/14/beyond-rule-of-law-orthodoxy-legal-empowerment-alternative-pub-1367>, (last accessed 12 March 2020).

Gramatikov, M., M. Barendrecht, and J. H. Verdonschot (2011), 'Measuring the Costs and Quality of Paths to Justice: Contours of a Methodology', *Hague Journal on the Rule of Law* 3 (2): 349–79.

Goodman, J. (2018), 'The UK legal tech scene', in M. Hartung (ed.), *Legal Tech*, München: C. H. Beck, pp. 67–74.

HiiL (2019), 'Innovating Justice: Needed and Possible. The Report of the Innovation

Working Group of the Task Force on Justice', <https://www.hiil.org/news/innovating-justice-needed-and-possible-report-of-the-innovation-working-group-of-the-task-force-on-justice/>, (last accessed 12 March 2020).

Holloway, I. (2019), 'Ryerson, Reform and the Pessimistic Lawyer', 2019, <https://www.canadianlawyermag.com/news/opinion/ryerson-reform-and-the-pessimistic-lawyer/276163>, (last accessed 12 March 2020).

Hutson, M. (2017), 'Artificial intelligence can predict which congressional bills will pass', *Science*, June 2017 *doi*:10.1126/science.aan7003.

Katz, D. M., M. J. Bommarito II, J. Blackman (2017), 'A general approach for predicting the behavior of the Supreme Court of the United States', *PLOS ONE*, 12(4): e0174698. <https://doi.org/10.1371/journal.pone.0174698>, (last accessed 12 March 2020).

Law For Good n.d., 'Law For Good | Using Technology to Improve Access to Justice', <https://www.lawforgood.org.uk/> (last accessed 7 August 2019).

Legal Services Innovation Index n.d., 'Law School Innovation Index', <https://www.legaltechinnovation.com/law-school-index/> (last accessed 31 July 2019).

OECD (2019), 'Equal Access to Justice for Inclusive Growth – Putting People at the Centre' <https://www.oecd.org/governance/equal-access-to-justice-for-inclusive-growth-597f5b7f-en.htm>, (last accessed 12 March 2020).

Pickup, O. (2018), 'Legal Tech around the World: Top Three Innovative Global Hubs', Raconteur, 28 November 2018, <https://www.raconteur.net/risk-management/legal-tech-global-hubs>, (last accessed 12 March 2020).

Pleasance, P., and N. Balmer (2018), 'Legal Needs Surveys and Access to Justice', OECD, <https://iris.ucl.ac.uk/iris/publication/1620815/1>, (last accessed 12 March 2020).

Smith, R. (2017) 'The decline and fall (and potential resurgence) of the Rechtwijzer', September 2017 <http://legalvoice.org.uk/decline-fall-potential-resurgence-rechtwijzer/>.

—— (2017a) 'The Fate of Rechtwijzer's English Daughter: Relate Suspends Online Family Dispute Resolution Project', September 2017, <https://law-tech-a2j.org/odr/rechtwijzers-english-daughter-relate-suspends-online-family-dispute-resolution-project/>, (last accessed 12 March 2020).

De Souza, S. P. (2017), 'Transforming the Legal Profession: The Impact and Challenges of Artificial Intelligence', Digital Policy Portal, 16 November 2017, <http://www.digitalpolicy.org/transforming-legal-profession-impact-challenges-artificial-intelligence/>, (last accessed 12 March 2020).

De Souza, S. P., and V. Aithala (2018) 'Can Technology Finally Deliver on India's Legal Aid Promise? (SSIR)', *Stanford Social Innovation Review*, <https://ssir.org/articles/entry/can_technology_finally_deliver_on_indias_legal_aid_promise>, (last accessed 12 March 2020).

Stanford Law School n.d., 'CodeX Techindex', <https://techindex.law.stanford.edu/companies?category=4>, (last accessed 31 July 2019).

Pathfinders (2019) 'Task Force on Justice ¦ Justice for All Report', <https://www.justice.sdg16.plus/report>, (last accessed 12 March 2020).

United Nations Development Programme (2004), 'Access to Justice Practice Note', 2004, <http://www.undp.org/content/undp/en/home/librarypage/democratic-governance/access_to_justiceandruleoflaw/access-to-justice-practice-note.html>, (last accessed 12 March 2020).

United Nations Sustainable Development Goals (2015) 'Peace, Justice and Strong Institutions – SDG 16', <https://www.un.org/sustainabledevelopment/peace-justice/>, (last accessed 12 March 2020).

Vogl, R. (2018), 'Changes in the US Legal Market Driven by Big Data/ Predictive Analytics and Legal Platforms', in M. Hartung (ed.), *Legal Tech*, München: C. H. Beck, pp. 53–65.

Walker, T. and P. Verhaert (2019) 'Technology and Legal Empowerment around the World', *The Engine Room*, <https://www.theengineroom.org/tech-and-legal-empowerment-around-the-world/>, (last accessed 12 March 2020).

Wenzler, H. (2018), 'Big Law & Legal Tech', in M. Hartung (ed.), *Legal Tech*, München: C. H. Beck, pp. 77–91.

Winick, E. (2017), 'Lawyer-Bots Are Shaking up Jobs', *MIT Technology Review*, 2017, <https://www.technologyreview.com/s/609556/lawyer-bots-are-shaking-up-jobs/>, (last accessed 12 March 2020).

Zent, M. (2018), 'Why Every Lawyer Should Adopt An Innovation Mindset', *Evolve the Law* (blog), <https://abovethelaw.com/legal-innovation-center/2018/04/12/why-every-lawyer-should-adopt-an-innovation-mindset/>, (last accessed 12 March 2020).

PART I:

Mapping the Private Sector

2

How Can Law Firms Contribute to Access to Justice in an Age of Technology and Digitalisation? Pro Bono, Law Firm Innovation and Ideas for the Legal Community

Özgür Kahale

A. Introduction

Advancements in technology are reshaping our world. By analysing the needs of people living in this era, we are inventing new products and new services every day to meet those needs and always questioning how to improve our experience of this world and our interactions using technological inventions. Justice actors, although coming from a traditionally conservative approach, are not immune to this change. Recently, they also have started getting curious about the promises of technology for the justice system. This chapter highlights one of these justice actors, international law firms, to investigate how they are using or can use technology in order to improve access to justice for vulnerable people.

The World Bank reports that approximately 5.1 billion people around the world today – about two-thirds of the global population – lack meaningful access to justice (The World Bank 2019). This traps people (especially the most vulnerable) in vicious cycles of poverty, inequality and marginalisation. (The World Bank 2019). United Nations Rule of Law Unit says that access to justice is a basic principle of the rule of law and underpins the full and free enjoyment of all other rights. In the absence of access to justice, people are unable to have their voices heard, exercise their rights, challenge discrimination or hold decision-makers accountable. (United Nations Rule of Law Unit 2019).

In welfare states, governments are the main actors in the access to justice space. They provide free legal aid services in criminal and civil matters in order to ensure that their indigent citizens can access justice. In instances where legal aid falls short or in non-welfare states, provision of free legal assistance (pro bono) by volunteer lawyers or international law firms come into play.

All around the world (welfare and non-welfare states alike) resources being devoted to legal aid is dwindling. Major changes in the eligibility for both civil and criminal legal aid are evidenced in the increased public use of pro bono (MacPartholán 2018: 27) Although pro bono could and should not replace legal aid, all the actors in the legal aid space are feeling the strain and they are looking for solutions which can provide efficiency, cost cutting and speed. Can the use of technology be the solution they are looking for?

Governments, legal aid lawyers funded by governments, charities and international law firms have all an interest in benefiting from technological advances in order to close the justice gap. This chapter will focus on pro bono's contribution to access justice and how this can be enhanced using technology. Before delving into pro bono and technology, the chapter will briefly touch upon access to justice and technology in order to place the discussion in the broader picture and present what barriers exist in the access to justice realm. After the general analysis of access to justice and technology, the following section will put a highlight on international law firms' pro bono programmes to try to explain what pro bono is, who uses it and why international law firms invest a great deal of resources to provide it. The following section will do needs and resources based analysis for pro bono and technology and pose the following questions: what are the needs of the pro bono world which can be met by technology and what opportunities new technologies used in law firms create for pro bono?

As one of the prominent actors in the access to justice space, international law firms can make a meaningful contribution to solving the access to justice problem using pro bono and this proposal can be enhanced even more using technology. The chapter will try to draw a road map in order to arrive at this premise.

B. The Promise of Technology for Access To Justice

In order to understand what technology can do for access to justice, we need to identify what prevents people from accessing justice. In other words, what are the barriers to access to justice? The results of this investigation will point us in the direction of the technological solutions that can be proposed to remove those barriers. However, our needs analysis needs to be comprehensive, connected, long-lasting and holistic. Without a strong needs analysis and long-term planning, we run the risk of creating technological solutions that will not to be used or will provide temporary solutions. Margaret Hagan from Legal Design Lab at Stanford Law School labels disconnected technological solutions as the 'my brilliant app' model. She suggests that together our aim should be to move towards a more integrated journey for the user and in order to do that we need to understand where they are coming from and what obstacles they are grappling with (Hagan 2019).

To answer the question of what impediments exist for access to justice we can look into several studies investigating a number of challenges. An OECD study categorises the factors which hinder access to justice as economic, structural and institutional factors (OECD and Open Society Foundations 2016). The Bingham Centre for the Rule of Law in its report, prepared with the International Bar Association, categorises the barriers as societal and cultural barriers (such as poverty, discrimination, language, literacy and education); institutional barriers (such as legal assistance and representation, fairness, openness, enforcement and compliance); and social and institutional intersections (such as distrust of justice systems and corruption) (Beqiraj and McNamara 2014). The Fundamental Rights Agency identifies the barriers to access to justice within the European member states as statutory limitation (time limits) for bringing a claim, legal standing, length of proceedings, legal costs, procedural formalities and complexity of legislation (European Union Agency for Fundamental Rights 2011).

The categorisation of barriers might prompt our thinking on whether we want to make improvements in a particular area or think about redesigning it entirely. For the sake of illustration, let us take the procedural formalities as an example: How can we use technology to improve people's experience of dealing with procedural formalities? We need to be cautious when answering this question as improving processes are not always derisible when the procedure itself became a barrier to access to justice in the first place. In other words, as emphasised by Richard Susskind, we should not digitise a bad system for the sake of using technology.[1] In these cases we need to think about how to use technology to innovate in the justice system. Technology is not a goal in itself but rather a tool to prompt critical thinking about the way systems are designed.

Therefore, when governments are digitising their justice systems and their procedural law, caution must be taken to make sure the new system does not become a barrier. In order to do that we need to understand what purpose the procedure was serving and whether we can achieve the same purpose more efficiently using technology. For example, in order to ensure that children are less traumatised when giving testimony against people who abused them, we can take their testimonials via video while they are talking

---

[1] This has been emphasized during a talk given by Richard Susskind during the Access to Justice and Technology Summit on 17 June 2019 in London. Recording of the talk is available at <https://youtu.be/R9NtpEVLHNk> (last accessed 11 November 2019).

to a psychologist instead of putting them in front of the judge and the perpetrator. If the procedural law does not allow for this, we may think about changing the law instead of trying to find a technological solution to work with the current procedural law. In order to adapt this line of thinking, we need to look at our justice system from the point of view of who is vulnerable, how do these people interact with the justice system, what their experience is, how to protect them and how to ensure justness is served.

Following this line of thinking, the Global Network for Public Interest Law and DLA Piper organised a summit on 17 June 2019 in London to examine the possibilities that technology may provide to improve access to justice around the world, and to find innovative and workable solutions so that people in need have access to effective remedies, regardless of ability to pay (the Summit).[2] The framework of four pillars the Summit introduced follows a person's interaction with the justice system and the questions posed prompts our thinking about the axis of access to justice and technology.

- The Digital Divide: Economic and social inequality in access to technologies is causing a digital divide between the most vulnerable in the society and the rest of people. Is access to justice using technology a remote possibility for those vulnerable people?
- Legal Empowerment: How can technology increase people's ability to understand and make use of the law?
- Access to advice and assistance: How do legal aid lawyers, boards, pro bono lawyers, bar associations, government legal aid providers, etc., use technology to improve their impact and reach more people?
- Online dispute resolution: How can technology break down the barriers and provide faster, cheaper and more transparent access to dispute resolution for all?

The first pillar, even before thinking about using technology, ponders about the experience of people who cannot use technology. One Summit speaker, Dame Hazel Genn, a law professor at UCL suggested we set up partnerships in order to reach those people such as the health-justice partnerships in the UK. Genn's students from law school set up a legal clinic in a GP clinic in order to help patients who come to the GP's clinic with their legal problems such as filling in online forms for them to launch claims.

During the legal empowerment pillar, the Summit participants discussed

---

[2] A list of participants, speaker bios, photos and video recordings of the morning and closing sessions can be found at <https://www.dlapiper.com/en/uk/insights/events/2019/06/access-to-justice-and-technology-summit/17-june-2019/> (last accessed 16 November 2019).

where people look for legal advice (mostly on Reddit and Google) and how to make those tools more efficient so that they give the right type of information to the right people.

The third pillar which discussed how justice actors use technology to increase their impact is the discussion which is relevant to this chapter and I will expand on it in the coming section during a discussion on pro bono. While pro bono has been a spontaneous effort in the past, it is more organised and professionalised now thanks to international law firms investing a great deal in it.

C. What is Legal Pro Bono and Who Does It?

The free provision of legal services by individual lawyers rather than the state has its roots in Ancient Greece. When we research the history of the legal profession, we see that the earliest people who could be described as lawyers were probably the orators of ancient Athens. Orators were noble people who excelled in public speaking, logic and ethics. In Athens, individuals were supposed to plead their own cases but they were also allowed to ask a friend (usually someone who is better at speaking than them) for assistance. The friends could not take a fee to plead the cause of another as they were merely an ordinary citizen generously helping out another (Bonner 1927). After the establishment of the legal profession, for many years lawyers practiced pro bono as a charitable duty and perhaps even as a mark of chivalry or honour of the legal profession (Khadar 2016: 9).

The first organised law firm pro bono practice emerged in the 1960s in the US and by 1973, at least twenty-four large US law firms had formalised pro bono programmes (Khadar 2016: 12). The American Bar Association's 2013 Report on the Pro Bono Work of America's Lawyers documents "the legal profession's longstanding and on-going commitment to pro bono legal services as a core value". Today it is widely accepted all over the world that the legal profession has an ethical obligation to provide pro bono legal representation. American Bar Association's Model Rules of Professional Responsibility states that "Every lawyer has a professional responsibility to provide legal services to those unable to pay" (American Bar Association 2018).

Many large law firms encourage pro bono work, employ pro bono professionals to run the pro bono practice and set up executive committees and even legal arms to support it. More recently, corporations also encourage their legal departments to deliver pro bono legal work. Although starting as a charitable activity, today there are a multitude of reasons why most big international law firms develop large pro bono programmes. Performing pro bono work often yields substantial practical economic benefits for law firms and the profession as a whole (Ginsburg 2014).

One of the many business cases for pro bono is recruitment. In the

1960s in the United States, a number of public interest law firms were set up to defend the civil rights movement and it inspired law students across the country to take up public interest law. These firms began to attract the best students, thus reducing the talent pool available to large commercial law firms. Commercial law firms recognised this trend and responded by establishing pro bono programmes (replete with managers, committees, and policies) to attract top law graduates (Khadar 2016: 9). Today pro bono continues to be even a greater pull to attract talented law graduates. A 2016 study by Cone Communications says that 75 per cent of millennials would take a pay cut to work for a socially responsible company and 76 per cent of millennials consider a company's social and environmental commitments before deciding where to work (Cone Communications 2016).

Pro bono also provides opportunities to lawyers to learn new skills and improve their legal knowledge in areas where they would otherwise not have a chance to encounter. This can help people link different practices and develop niche areas of expertise.

A strong pro bono practice helps a law firm build a solid reputation among clients and the public. When the pro bono work is communicated effectively, it can create a competitive advantage vis-à-vis other law firms. Pro bono strengthens a firm and its brand and it also gives the firm an opportunity to develop its relationship with its clients. Most in-house legal teams of corporations at the moment are also in the process of developing pro bono practices and they look up to the law firms they work with for support and inspiration. The law firms invite their clients to collaborate with them on different pro bono projects and it gives both client and law firm lawyers an opportunity to get closer.

Some very large firms use also pro bono as an integration tool. They set up multinational pro bono projects where lawyers from different countries work together. This, in turn, helps the firm create close working relationships between its lawyers located in different parts of the world.

As law firms organise and professionalise pro bono they are also engaging more with concepts of responsible business practices, human rights and business and social impact measurement. These law firms run their programme in accordance with their pro policies and generally work with six types of pro bono clients:

- individuals who cannot afford a lawyer and cannot access legal aid;
- non-governmental organisations such as associations, charities, foundations, and etc.;
- UN agencies;
- social entrepreneurs;

- academic institutions; and
- least developed or (in some cases) developing countries.

Individuals who cannot afford a lawyer and cannot access legal aid can approach law firms in order to seek pro bono help. 'Access to legal aid' criteria is set here because law firms maintain that it is the government's responsibility to ensure citizens can access justice. Pro bono is not there to take the place of legal aid but it is there to catch people who fall through the cracks. Since legal aid is organised differently in different countries, individual pro bono clients differ from country to country.

For example, in the US, state legal aid is only available for criminal cases for defendants under criminal prosecution who cannot afford to hire an attorney. Civil legal aid is not guaranteed under federal law but is provided by a variety of public interest law firms and community legal clinics for free or reduced cost (George 2006: 293). Therefore there is a greater need for pro bono to provide support to individuals in the US compared to Western Europe. Generally speaking, in Western Europe, civil and criminal legal aid is freely available to individuals who earn below a certain wage. In those countries, pro bono support for individuals goes to people who are at the margins of the society and cannot even provide documents to apply for legal aid such as stateless people.[3]

International law firms are not only interested in doing pro bono themselves, but also they try to contribute to the growing pro bono culture in the world. They do this by organising pro bono weeks, holding events for law students to promote pro bono, training other lawyers and working with bar associations to raise awareness. UK Collaborative Plan for Pro Bono (the Collaborative Plan) is a good example of such initiative. Today the Collaborative Plan has fifty-four participating law firms, and they work together in order to improve access to justice through pro bono in the UK and to develop the systems and infrastructure to allow pro bono services to

---

[3] Statelessness is a big problem among the Roma population in Italy. The conflicts and the fall of ex-Yugoslavia triggered a migration among the Roma population, and a big number of them ended up in Italy. Some did not have any documents and were stateless while living in their country of origin; others lost their nationality after their ex-Yugoslavia collapsed, and they did not associate themselves with any of the new countries. International law firm DLA Piper with United Nations High Commissioner for Refugees (UNHCR) and the Italian Refugee Counsel set up a pro bono legal clinic in Italy for stateless people. Through the clinic, DLA Piper lawyers start civil legal proceedings before Italian Courts on behalf of stateless people so that they can get recognition as stateless or further down the line, obtain Italian citizenship.

be effectively delivered to address unmet legal need.[4] One of the systems mentioned above is technology as there is a great interest and motivation among the pro bono lawyers to innovate in the pro bono space.

D. Law Firm Innovation and Pro Bono

In order to be able to talk about how to further develop pro bono using technology, we can adapt two lines of analysis. I will entitle the first line as 'the needs based analysis' and the second one as 'the resource based analysis'.

I. Needs Based Analysis

Needs based analysis focuses on which areas in the pro bono realm need improving and how we can do it using technology. For the sake of illustrating the analysis, I will list below a few questions and answer them recounting the technological tools put in place by pro bono clearinghouses and international law firms. However, please bear in mind that this list is by no means exhaustive. The pro bono community will have other issues to tackle using technology, and this is a point of ongoing discussion.

a. How Can We Use Technology to Increase the Volume of Pro Bono Support Given to Individuals and Non-profits?

One way to answer this question would be to look at how pro bono connections are made. That way we can aim to use technology to ensure individuals and non-profits reach pro bono more easily. One successful example using technology for this purpose is Justice Connect's Pro Bono Portal in Australia. Justice Connect is a legal clearinghouse which connects people or organisations in need of pro bono with law firms or lawyers which provide pro bono legal advice. Recently, Justice Connect went through a vigorous investigation process in order to identify the way help-seekers find, connect with and enter Justice Connect and its services; the way legal advice providers find and interact with Justice Connect; the way Justice Connect interacts with its network of pro bono lawyers and the way it pulls together insights regarding supply and demand to create a more efficient pro bono marketplace.[5]

The research which started in 2017 showed that for help-seekers the legal system is confusing and difficult to navigate – that people looking for free legal help regularly have a poor experience of finding and connecting with relevant services. Justice Connect furthermore found that lawyers want to do

---

[4] Information obtained from the website of the UK Collaborative Plan available at <http://probonoplan.uk/> (last accessed 16 November 2019).
[5] Information obtained from Justice Connect website at <https://justiceconnect.org.au/about/digital-innovation/gateway-project/pro-bono-portal/> (last accessed 17 November 2019)

more pro bono work, but that matching up unmet need with relevant expertise is time-consuming and labour intensive. Following a rigorous design process, they launched an online Pro Bono Portal, and today Justice Connect reports that since the launch, the number of pro bono referrals to pro bono lawyers has doubled with no increase in resourcing.

This successful digitalisation project demonstrates that use of technology can increase efficiency and therefore augment the volume of pro bono done by law firms. Following the successful launch and implementation in Australia, Justice Connect announced on 9 November 2019 that it will collaborate with PILnet to implement the same model worldwide. They observe that appetite in the legal profession to undertake pro bono work is steadily increasing year on year and they hope that the Pro Bono Portal they will develop together will apply sophisticated technology to unlock latent pro bono legal capacity and match it with unmet legal need in an efficient manner. In their press release which announced the launch of the Pro Bono Portal, Justice Connect and PILnet say that

'Over 5 billion people globally have a legal problem each year, with the majority missing out on any legal assistance. Currently, around 2.3 million hours are contributed pro bono by lawyers to access to justice projects each year across the world. A recent survey undertaken by PILnet and Justice Connect showed that 76% of organizations that match lawyers with pro bono opportunities (clearinghouses) would likely use the platform. PILnet and Justice Connect anticipate that their global platform could double the number of hours contributed by lawyers for free over the next five years.'

b. How Can We Use Technology to Increase Collaboration Between Law Firms?
The organisation which uses technology effectively to achieve this purpose is the Association of Pro Bono Counsel (APBCo), a mission-driven membership organisation of over 200 attorneys and practice group managers who run pro bono practices in over 100 of the world's largest law firms.[6] APBCo uses a tool called Salesforce Chatter which provides an online forum where APBCo members can discuss all aspects of their pro bono practices and access to justice issues. The Chatter has a general group, as well as many sub-groups (for example, by office location, by theme) through which members freely ask for and receive advice on practice points and professional development. Through the tool, members regularly share knowledge on diverse subjects, find or pass opportunities to each other and discuss matters of concern to the

---

[6] Information obtained from APBCo website. For more information on APBCo and its mission, please see their website at <https://apbco.org/> (last accessed 16 November 2019).

group. This, in turn, increases the collaboration between pro bono lawyers so that they can provide better and more pro bono support to those in need.

c. How Can We Use Technology to Analyse the Impact of the Pro Bono Work Law Firms Do?

Sine qua non for impact measurement is data collection. Relevant and accurate data can help us make precise analyses, informed decisions and good choices. Data collection discussion for the pro bono community is in its infancy at the moment. The only organisation which collects data consistently is the American Lawyer where its chart ranks the 200 top law firms by their pro bono score for work performed by US-based lawyers. It collects data on the average number of pro bono hours per lawyer per year and the percentage of lawyers who perform more than twenty hours of pro bono work.[7] However, when clearinghouses such as Justice Connect and PILnet start implementing their global Pro Bono Portal, it will not only serve to find and place pro bono matters more efficiently but also serve the purpose of collecting good quality data which can be used for measurement afterwards.

II. Resource based Analysis

The second analysis which we can do in order to be able to talk about how to develop pro bono using technology is called resource based analysis. In this analysis we ask what kind of legal tech tools law firms are using for their commercial clients and discuss how we can use them for the benefit of pro bono clients. Law firms invest a significant amount of money in technology for commercial clients and using these tools for the benefit of pro bono would be an efficient way of making use of available resources.

One example of such technology is called KIARA, a machine learning software that identifies, extracts and analyses text in contracts and other documents.[8] It helps corporate lawyers working in the field of mergers and acquisitions with their due diligence tasks. A lawyer can upload, for example, 200 contracts on the system and ask the software to compare all the governing law clauses or indemnity clauses in all contracts.

Multijurisdictional research requests from NGOs is an area where a number of law firms often get pro bono requests. For example, a pro bono client may ask a law firm to run a study in twenty countries to find out which

[7] For more information on the 2018 rankings, please visit <https://www.law.com/american-lawyer/2019/06/26/the-american-lawyers-2019-national-pro-bono-rankings/> (last accessed 16 November 2019).

[8] For more information on KIRA, please visit <https://kirasystems.com/how-it-works/> (last accessed 16 November 2019).

counties have laws that require immigration officers confiscate passports of asylum seekers. When a law firm runs this study manually, they contact each country where they have an office and ask their lawyers to answer a questionnaire. A typical exercise of this sort can easily take 500 hours of research and fifty hours of management time for the pro bono team. Today, provided that the language barrier is overcome, we can upload all immigration laws in twenty countries to KIARA and ask the software to run the research in a matter of minutes. In order to develop this line of thinking, pro bono teams in international law firms need to be on top of the technology their firms are using and ready to create links whenever an opportunity presents itself.

One firm which followed this line of thinking is Gilbert + Tobin, a Sydney-based commercial law firm which had a pro bono collaboration with the Refugee Advice and Casework Service (RACS), a charity offering legal support to asylum seekers in Australia. Caseworkers at RACS used to manually fill in hundreds of asylum application forms for the tens of thousands of asylum seekers who travel by boat to Australia each year. The time-consuming process of filing asylum papers attracted the attention of lawyers from Gilbert + Tobin who were providing pro bono support to fill in the forms, and they developed an automated platform to process asylum requests. The new system no longer requires caseworkers to fill in three separate forms and saves approximately forty-five minutes per application. Gilbert + Tobin using their firm's resources provided the software licensing to RACS at no charge (Feng 2018).

E. Conclusion

Technology has fundamentally reshaped the way in which we live our lives. We have access to huge amounts of information at our fingertips through the Internet, we can shop without ever needing to leave the house, and email has revolutionised the way in which we communicate. However, access to justice remains a protracted process for many. Although governments and bar associations put in place legal aid programmes in order to ensure everyone can access justice, there are still people who fall through the cracks. Who is falling through the cracks and how we can catch them is a question which motivates many international law firms to set up pro bono programmes.

International law firms, by way of doing pro bono, contribute a great deal to furthering the access to justice agenda. Today the depth, professionalism, enthusiasm and strategic thinking put behind building pro bono practices in each and every international law firm is remarkable. With dedicated public interest lawyers invested in access to justice coupled with management support grows pro bono activities of all law firms by the year. By using technology, law firms will have a chance to make even a bigger difference.

Justice Connect and PILnet recently organised a panel entitled

'Redesigning Pro Bono for a Digital Future' during the Global Pro Bono Forum in Singapore. They noted that

> 'the international pro bono ecosystem has reached a critical stage in its maturation. An increasingly global and technologically enabled ecosystem presents significant opportunities to more effectively direct pro bono effort. This current pivotal moment presents an opportunity to implement a common system, protocols, and a shared data standard that can deliver significant benefits for access to justice and create the conditions for the strategic use of pro bono legal support.'[9]

Using technology as a tool to fill the access to justice gap is an exciting and stimulating journey. It will give us an opportunity to improve our processes and even redesign our justice system by getting rid of the procedures which were designed for a different era and replacing them with the ones that are more suited to the era we are living in now. However, when using the technology for access to justice, our starting point always needs to be the constituency we are trying to help. We need to listen to their needs, understand their point of view, put ourselves in their situation, go where they are and work with them hand in hand. Technology is a tool to prompt us to embark on the journey of rethinking and redesigning. In order to get it right, we always need to be mindful of what exactly we are trying to achieve, move away from silo mentality and collaborate more effectively with a view to push the agenda altogether. By doing a needs and resources analysis and also identifying points where we can make even a bigger difference when we collaborate, law firms can augment their impact. As Margaret Hagan points out, we need to move away from 'my brilliant app' model to an 'our strategic blueprint' model where we do not build the same thing over and over again but build on each other's work and build it together.

Bibliography

American Bar Association (2018), *Model Rules of Professional Conduct, Rule no 6.1*, available at <https://www.americanbar.org/groups/professional_responsibility/publications/model_rules_of_professional_conduct/model_rules_of_profesional_conduct_table_of_contents/> (last accessed 11 November 2019).

Beqiraj, J., and McNamara, L. (2014), *International Access to Justice: Barriers and Solutions*, Bingham Centre for the Rule of Law Report 02/2014, available at <https://www.biicl.org/documents/485_iba_report_060215.pdf?showdocu

---

[9] For more information on the panel and the speakers, please see the PILnet Global Forum website at<https://www.pilnetevents.org/globalforum/sessions/redesigning-pro-bono-for-a-digital-future/> (last accessed 17 November 2019).

ment=1> (last accessed 11 November 2019).

Bonner, R. J. (1927), *Lawyers and Litigants in Ancient Athens: The Genesis of the Legal Profession*, New York: Benjamin Blom.

Cone Communications (2016), *Millennial Employee Engagement Study*, available at <https://static1.squarespace.com/static/56b4a7472b8dde3df5b7013f/t/5819e8b303596e3016ca0d9c/1478092981243/2016+Cone+Communications+Millennial+Employee+Engagement+Study_Press+Release+and+Fact+Sheet.pdf> (last accessed 14 November 2019).

European Union Agency for Fundamental Rights (2011), 'Access to Justice in Europe: an overview of challenges and opportunities', available at <https://fra.europa.eu/sites/default/files/fra_uploads/1520-report-access-to-justice_EN.pdf> (Last accessed 11 November 2019).

Feng, E. (2018), 'Pro bono is no side project for law firms', *The Financial Times*, available at <https://www.ft.com/content/3e1105cc-4dfc-11e8-97e4-13afc22d86d4> (last accessed 16 November 2019).

George, J. (2006), 'Access to Justice, Costs, and Legal Aid', *American Journal of Comparative Law*, vol. 54, p. 293–316.

Ginsburg, R. (2014), *Pro Bono Makes Cents: The Business Case for Pro Bono* (Blog Post), available at <https://www.royginsburg.com/published-articles/pro-bono-makes-cents-business-case-pro-bono/> (last accessed 11 November 2019).

Hagan, M., talk given during the 'Access to Justice and Technology Summit' on 17 June 2019 in London, a recording of the talk is available at <https://youtu.be/C_M2_-OYMtw> (last accessed 14 November 2019).

Justice Connect, 12 November 2019, Press Release 'A global pro bono portal to increase access to justice', available at <https://justiceconnect.org.au/launch-global-pro-bono-portal/> (last accessed 16 November 2019).

Khadar, L. (2016), *The Growth of Pro Bono in Europe: Using the Power of Law for the Public Interest*, available at <https://www.pilnet.org/public-interest-law-resources/163-the-growth-of-pro-bono-in-europe.html> (last accessed 11 November 2019).

MacPartholán, C. (2018), 'Access Denied? Pro Bono and the Truncated Right to Justice' *Criminal Law & Justice Weekly*, Vol. 182, 13 January 2018, p. 27.

OECD and Open Society Foundations (2016), 'Leveraging the SDGs for Inclusive Growth: Delivering Access to Justice for All', available at <https://www.oecd.org/gov/delivering-access-to-justice-for-all.pdf> (last accessed 11 November 2019).

United Nations Rule of Law Unit, 11 November 2019, 'What is Rule of Law', available at <https://www.un.org/ruleoflaw/what-is-the-rule-of-law/> (last accessed 11 November 2019).

The World Bank (2019), 'A Tool For Justice: A Cost Benefit Analysis of Legal Aid', available at <file:///C:/Users/KAHALEO/Downloads/ToolforJustice-CBAsoflegalaid.pdf> (last accessed 11 November 2019).

3

How Technology is Changing the Nature of Work and Altering the Practice of Law

Suzanna Kalendzhian

A. Introduction

Since the start of the First Industrial Revolution in the eighteenth century, the global economy has grown exponentially, driven by a series of advancements in technology. Each new wave of technology, from steam engines to electricity, telephones, automobiles, aeroplanes, computers, and the Internet, has enabled efficient new methods for performing existing tasks and given rise to entirely new types of businesses, bringing about surges in productivity and economic growth (McKinsey 2013).

Certain technologies, particularly general-purpose ones that could be applied across economies, have had massive and disruptive effects. For instance, over the past decades, advances in information technology and widespread penetration of the Internet have been the main drivers of changes across all spheres of our lives. We have adopted these changes into our lives so swiftly that now for most people, it is impossible to imagine their world without personal computers, mobile electronic devices and round-the-clock access to the information they need.

Information technology has changed the way business is conducted, it has disrupted and transformed almost every industry, and the legal one is no different, although it is renowned for its lagging behind technology[1] innovations. Lawyers resist changes, resist new technologies, and do not want to fix

[1] Technology is a broad term which can be used in different contexts. Oxford Dictionary, for example, defines it as 'the application of scientific knowledge for practical purposes, especially in industry'. To avoid any misinterpretation, the use of the term 'technology' will be equal to use of the term 'information technology' in this article.

what they do not see as broken. Of course, they recognise that their way of doing business will inevitably evolve in accordance with technology trends, but in reality, the path for legal professionals in many aspects is less clear than for other sectors.

The legal profession, while seemingly untouched by the impact of technology, is undergoing its own changes. More and more exciting changes are already underway in the day-to-day operations of law firms across the world. So, what will the law firm of the future be like? How is the legal industry set to change in the following years? This article is an attempt to address these questions.

Part I briefly examines enabling technologies making the most impact on the legal industry. Part II examines legal applications of technology, compares existing classifications, and introduces eight key legal tech categories with related subcategories indicating specific technology applications. Part III focuses on how technology is changing the practice of law. It identifies eight emerging trends which are affecting the legal industry and examines each of them. Finally, this article concludes with key findings.

I. Technologies Making the Most Impact on the Legal Industry

When discussing the influence of technology on the legal industry in general and practice of law in particular, it is worth agreeing on some terminology as a starting point:

- Enabling technologies
  General-purpose technologies that (1) can be applied across economies, (2) are able to drive radical change in the capabilities of their users or culture of the society in general, and (3) are characterised by the rapid development of subsequent derivative technologies, often in diverse fields (Wikipedia 2019).
- Legal technology (legal tech)
  The application of enabling and subsequent derivative technologies to the legal industry. That includes technology catered to consumers of legal services, individual lawyers, law firms, in-house legal departments, judicial authorities and other key stakeholders in the legal industry.

It is expected that the following four enabling technologies have the most potential to impact the legal profession and delivery of legal services, namely:

- The Internet
  A global computer network, providing a variety of information and communication facilities, consisting of interconnected networks using

standardised communication protocols (Oxford 2019). The Internet is a fundamental technology layer enabling virtually free and unlimited exchange of information.

- Cloud Services
  Any services made available to their users on-demand over the Internet from servers of the cloud computing provider as opposed to being provided from a local computer used to access the service (Beal 2019). Cloud computing technology can be defined as software or services that can be accessed and used online using a browser or an app, where the software itself is not installed locally on the device being used to access the service (Kennedy 2017). Cloud technology creates almost endless possibilities for data storing, sharing, processing, and management. The cloud is a fast and scalable way to use sophisticated technology tools without substantial upfront investment in hardware, software, and support services.
- Artificial intelligence (AI) and machine learning (ML)
  AI is the quest to build software running on machines that can think and act like humans. As such, AI is used as an umbrella term that encompasses more specific approaches to machine intelligence, including machine learning and deep learning. ML is a subset of AI focused on using algorithms that learn and improve rather than being explicitly programmed. The algorithms take data as input, output predicted data or actions, and improve as they are exposed to more data (451 Research 2018). AI and ML create possibilities for the automation of knowledge work involving unstructured commands and subtle judgments.
- Blockchain
  The near equivalent of a database that is synchronised, public, distributed and protected (Cole 2017). It can be used to record a wide variety of information. The information in the blockchain is held on a universally accessible register that is regularly updated and is considered incorruptible. While benefits of the Internet, cloud technology and AI/ML are obvious, the possible applications and benefits of blockchain technology for the legal industry are not so apparent. Nevertheless, many legal technology enthusiasts and think tanks consider that blockchain has the potential to change the business of law even more dramatically than artificial intelligence (Ambrogi 2017; Global Legal Blockchain Consortium 2019).

II. Legal Applications of Technology

The legal profession, like other industries, is being disrupted by technological advancements that are changing the way legal work is performed. While still lagging behind other professions in the adoption of new technologies, lawyers are increasingly engaging with product offerings designed to enhance their productivity and efficiency. There is a clear emerging trend for technology to address increasingly more issues in how lawyers run their practice.

Although new legal tech start-ups are appearing everywhere and delivering a growing range of services, the legal tech ecosystem remains fragmented and diverse, as the industry it serves has some inherent limitations, such as:

- Weak Research and Development component
  The legal industry, by and large, has no R&D sector. It is just not in the nature of lawyers to pursue technological innovation.
- Ageing of the legal profession
  The legal profession is ageing at a dramatic pace (American Bar Association 2014a; American Bar Association 2014b; Solicitors Regulation Authority 2017; Law Society of New South Wales 2017). According to the 2017 ABA Survey, 75 per cent of respondent lawyers were over 50 years old, and 51 per cent were over 60 years old (American Bar Association 2017). This data means that more than half of US lawyers started practising back in the 1980s. This creates a real obstacle and is one of the reasons why the legal profession is so conservative and does not like change.
- Law industry is not that big
  The global legal services market is estimated at around $700 billion (Business Wire 2017). That is, for example, ten times less than the travel and tourism industry. On top of that, the legal market is itself very fragmented, making each segment even smaller.
- Legal markets are jurisdiction-specific
  Every country has its own regulations and its own peculiar legal industry. Building scale across jurisdictional boundaries in the legal market is difficult.
- Law is highly regulated
  In many countries, regulators discourage innovation through different regulatory restrictions, for instance, a ban on non-lawyer ownership of legal practices or a ban on the unauthorised practice of law.

However, even with the limitations mentioned above, legal tech entrepreneurs still see that there are significant needs and problems in the industry that can be addressed with the right mix of technology, business model adaptation and execution. Today, it is hard to overstate the tremendous economic and technological ferment of the legal ecosystem growing up within and around the traditional legal services market. So, what are these emerging technology applications, what issues are they solving, and how are they helping to make the legal industry more efficient?

Due to the emergent nature of legal tech market, there is little shared understanding of what categories constitute the legal technology, as currently there is no commonly accepted classification. In the comparative table below are presented some existing classifications of legal tech (Susskind 2017; Linnar, et al. 2019; LawGeex 2018). Similar categories in different classifications are marked in different shades.

Table 3.1 Existing classifications of legal technology (comparative table)

Thomson Reuters (Curle 2016)	CodeX (Stanford Centre for Legal Informatics 2019)	CB Insights (CB Insights 2016)
E-Discovery	E-Discovery	E-discovery
Practice Management	Practice Management	Practice Management
Legal Research	Legal Research	Legal Research
Business Development / Marketplaces	Marketplace	Lawyer Search
Document Automation	Document Automation	Artificial Intelligence Legal Tech
Legal Education	Legal Education	Intellectual Property/ Trademark Software Services
Online Dispute Resolution	Online Dispute Resolution	Online Legal Services
Case Management Analytics	Analytics	Notarization Tools
Litigation Funding	Compliance	Litigation Finance
Contract Management / Analysis		
Consumer		

As can be observed from the table above, existing classifications are inconsistent, and lack desired details. To address this gap, further suggested a new classification of key areas of legal technology. It consists of eight broad legal tech categories with related subcategories indicating specific technology applications.

Based on the assessment of current product offerings, legal applications of technology appear to fall into the following categories:[2]

---

[2] This is a 'beta' classification under further development and refinement. The suggested categories may be somewhat arbitrary, and the classification itself may be a little imprecise and blurred.

Key areas of legal technology[3]

- **Practice management**
  - Matter management
  - Case management
  - Knowledge management
  - Timekeeping, Billing & Accounting
  - Expertise automation
  - Task management
  - Scheduling & Calendaring
  - Communication
  - Collaboration
- **Document automation**
  - Drafting
  - Review
  - Due diligence
  - Extraction
  - Analytics
  - Digital signature
- **Analytics and Search**
  - Legal research
  - Investigation & Intelligence
  - Due diligence
  - Electronic discovery
  - Prediction
  - Litigation analytics
- **Marketplace**
  - B2C marketplace (end users)
  - B2B marketplace (outsourcing)
  - Talent marketplace (HR)
- **Online Legal Services**
  - Online delivery
  - Alternative services
  - Alternative service bundling
  - Automated rendering
- **E-learning**
  - Legal education
  - Technology competence
  - Client education

---

[3] The order of categories is irrelevant.

- **Automation of judicial procedures**
  - Docketing
  - E-filing
  - E-service of process
  - E-payments
  - Document management
  - Case management
  - Statutory information
  - Scheduling & Calendaring
  - Evidence and media presentation
  - Video conferencing
  - Digital recording
  - Publication of judgments
  - Alternative dispute resolution
  - Online dispute resolution
- **Other**
  - Litigation financing
  - Digital notarisation
  - IP/Trademark services

III. How Technology is Changing the Practice of Law

The legal market is far from efficient, and there are great opportunities for offering legal services in new, less costly, more client-friendly ways. Powerful market forces drive the increasing penetration of technology in the legal industry. While these fundamental shifts and further advancements in technology are encouraging innovation and efficiency, the very nature of the practice of law is changing too. And to maintain a competitive advantage, lawyers must understand the trends and embrace these changes. Now more so than at any other time in history, the industry is in the transition from a traditional model of one-to-one consultative legal services to one where technology enables one-to-many legal solutions (Henderson 2018).

a. Automation of Legal Work
Advances in information technology, especially artificial intelligence and machine learning, are making it possible to automate knowledge worker tasks that have long been considered impossible or impractical for computers to perform. This opens up possibilities for sweeping change in how legal work is organised and performed (McKinsey 2017a).

Sophisticated practice management, document automation, analytics and prediction tools can be used to augment the talents of legal professionals, and as machines can do more their tasks, it is possible that some types of legal jobs could soon become fully automated. As the delivery of legal services will shift online, automated cloud-based services will more and more displace human lawyers unless complex legal judgment is necessary.

Minor activities that were once time-consuming are now made much faster and easier by machines, allowing legal professionals to streamline the legal process and spend more time on crucial tasks. For instance, searching for a particular case in a legal library now can be done almost instantly in the electronic database (Harvard Law School 2019).

According to the authoritative British lawyer and futurist Richard Susskind, routine legal tasks will be increasingly automated, and more and more jobs in the legal industry will involve managing legal processes and applying technological solutions to achieve maximum cost-effectiveness. As technological capabilities evolve, legal professionals will be pressed to either use their expertise for designing tomorrow's legal machines or perform complex non-trivial tasks where human involvement comes at a premium (Susskind 2017).

Currently, in the legal profession, technology is replacing low-level work typically done by junior legal staff and paralegals on the one hand and helps legal professionals perform more complex and knowledge-intensive tasks more efficiently, on the other. Technology-enabled services for both high-volume and more complex work are expected to deliver value that will drive future growth.

A study by McKinsey Global Institute determined that up to 44 per cent of paralegal work and up to 22 per cent of lawyer-level work can be automated in the period to 2030 (McKinsey 2017b).

North Carolina School of Law reveals an estimated 13 per cent reduction in lawyer work hours caused by the automation of legal work within the next five years (Remus, Levy 2016).

One of the recent examples of big-scale automation of legal processes is a restructuring of the entire system of back-office support services by DLA Piper, a top-five Global 100 law firm (Ambrogi 2018). They use technology to better delegate support tasks and manage support workflows. They have done this using a tool designed to simplify the capture and transfer of legal tasks from lawyers to support staff and to give managers a thorough under-standing of workloads and capacities so that they can adjust assignments and staffing levels to stay within deadlines.

b. Teleworking

Thanks to the benefits offered by broadband Internet access, cloud technol-ogy and personal computing devices, remote working or teleworking is being made increasingly possible, bringing greater flexibility and mobility within the legal industry. These technologies empower a new age of collaboration and increased productivity as lawyers are no longer limited by their location when conducting legal work. Thus, a growing number of legal professionals are working remotely (Zaretsky 2017).

For years now, lawyers have been working more and more frequently from places other than their law office. Many lawyers work from home, their client's office, co-working offices, or from a courthouse. Even lawyers with traditional offices frequently do legal work from home, while travelling, or anywhere else they are with their laptop, tablet or smartphone. It is common now for lawyers to do online legal work (like checking email, working on documents, or scheduling appointments) away from their office as much as from their desk.

According to the American Bar Association's 2017 Legal Technology Survey Report, 16 per cent of US lawyers primarily work from home and 17 per cent work in shared offices. Even among lawyers who have private offices, 77 per cent regularly work from home, 33 per cent while travelling, and 20 per cent regularly work from clients' or opposing counsel's office or from court.

The amount of time lawyers do their work remotely seems to be increasing too, with almost 85 per cent of lawyers working remotely at least 10 per cent of the time, over a third of lawyers working remotely at least 25 per cent of the time, and more than 10 per cent of lawyers working remotely more than half the time. Over 30 per cent of lawyers say they telecommute at least once per week. Essentially everybody uses a smartphone at least occasionally to do legal work. At close to 100 per cent smartphone adoption, it is fair to say that all lawyers are now remote workers (Street 2017).

Technology is a crucial component of working remotely, so the flexibility offered by practice management systems, virtual legal libraries, conferencing and collaboration software, along with other technologies serving the legal industry, means that legal professionals will have an increased opportunity to work from virtually anywhere, changing the infrastructure of the average law practice and giving the rise for the phenomenon of virtual law firms.

c. Virtual Law Firms

Technology has long been a driver for change, empowering whole industries to increase productivity and adopt new progressive business models. In the legal industry, virtual law firms, stemming from the concept of teleworking, and thanks to the same technology that makes remote work possible, are redefining how legal practices operate and the services they offer.

A virtual law firm (sometimes also referred to as *mobile* or *cloud-based* law firm) is a law practice that does not have a traditional brick-and-mortar practice office. In this set-up, office space is leveraged where and when needed but is secondary to delivering legal services. A virtual law firm usually operates from the homes or satellite offices of its lawyers and delivers services to clients using technological means of communication. Virtual law firms are regulated in the same way as traditional law firms, but the lawyers working for a virtual firm may be self-employed consultants rather than partners or employees.

Running a virtual law firm is just another way of practising law outside the traditional brick-and-mortar setting. It means leveraging technology to work from any geographic location securely and efficiently, and to interact more effectively with clients and co-workers at a distance, so that proximity to them becomes far less critical. Also, it supposes using a business model that allows being more flexible with fee structures due to the absence of a large-scale infrastructure that would typically come with a brick-and-mortar law firm's office (Burton 2017).

While some virtual firms conduct all business online including the delivery of legal services, others employ a hybrid approach. Such law firms use the term 'virtual' mostly to describe their adoption of the technology allowing their employees to work remotely or their clients to communicate with lawyers through an online client portal.

According to statistics from the American Bar Association, virtual law firms are on the rise. In 2014, 7 per cent of US lawyers described their practice as a virtual law practice, compared with 5 per cent in 2012, and 3 per cent in 2011. In the 2017 ABA Survey, 33 per cent of respondents (mostly solo practitioners) said that they do not have a traditional private law office and are primarily working from home or in a shared office space. The same trends can be seen all over the world. For example, LexisNexis reported that over 800 lawyers were working for virtual law firms in the United Kingdom (LexisNexis 2017).

Although in many jurisdictions there are regulatory limitations on such a method of practicing law, the number of virtual law firms is set to increase. It is predicted that virtual law firms will offer mostly legal services that can be effectively delivered online to satisfy consumer demands for cheaper and more flexible options.

d. Online Delivery

Given the rapid pace of change fuelled by technology, the delivery of legal services will inevitably shift online. Consumer demands for efficiency and their expectations are increasingly shaped by their experiences across other industries. Today, consumers tend to utilise the legal resources available online, including the services of virtual law firms and other non-traditional legal service providers, to manage their general needs when it comes to the law. The increase in the availability of these online services, especially unbundled[4], is driving the fundamental shift in the way legal services are bought, sold and delivered.

Before the Internet age, obtaining specific information about a legal topic was challenging, giving legal professionals an advantage and keeping the asymmetry of knowledge between lawyers and unsophisticated clients. Laypeople could not easily get the information and answers they needed, so the public had little choice but to consult lawyers to answer even relatively simple legal questions. Nowadays, the Internet is facilitating the dissemination of expert knowledge, making it considerably easier for non-experts to access the information they need. When combined with technological advances that allow the automated delivery of that knowledge and related services, there is no surprise that legal services now are generally perceived by consumers to be more fungible than bespoke (Cohen 2017).

The days when the only way to receive legal assistance was meeting lawyers at their office have long been a thing of the past. Today, legal help, particularly for routine matters that require little or no legal judgment, is only a few clicks away. Searching for and hiring a lawyer can now be done online in a matter of minutes. In a digitised world, clients have the ability to self-navigate like never before, and buying decisions are less relationship- and more procurement-driven. Now, more than ever, consumers of legal services can make more informed, less subjective, and more cost-effective buying decisions.

Online legal service providers, so-called 'NewLaw' companies, like LegalZoom and Rocket Lawyer leverage technology to expand access to law for millions of underserved individuals and small and medium businesses. Such providers can offer round-the-clock availability and, although they usually offer only a few niche services, they perform those very efficiently. As a result, not only is access to legal solutions expanded and the cost of services reduced, but also the speed of service delivery is aligned to the demands of the modern world.

Even dispute resolution goes online. According to Colin Rule[5], online dispute resolution platforms (ODR), such as Modria, now resolve more than

---

[4] Unbundled legal services, also known as limited scope representation, is a method of legal representation when the lawyers provide only the agreed-upon services (usually for a fixed price), rather than the whole 'bundle', leaving responsibility for other aspects of the case to the client.

[5] Colin Rule is a co-founder of ODR provider Modria and vice president for online dispute resolution at Tyler Technologies (acquired Modria in 2017).

a billion e-commerce disputes a year globally (The Digital Edge 2018). The ODR technology is now moving into courthouses. Court-annexed ODR platforms are emerging, and more are likely to appear in the near future. The European Union, for example, has already implemented an ODR for all its consumer and online trading disputes (European Commission 2019).

These developments have allowed sophisticated clients to demand more from traditional law firms. Clients now require from their lawyers not only quality work, but greater transparency, better communication, and faster delivery than ever before, all at a lower price. The traditional law firm business model, developed in a bygone era, needs to be updated to address the changing market. To be successful and competitive tomorrow, lawyers must carefully consider how they will meet the needs of tomorrow's clients. Adopting online delivery models will result in more access to legal services to the public on the one hand, and more business to the lawyers on the other, as they will be able to reach a much broader clientele over the Internet.

e. Alternative Billing Models

Since the middle of the twentieth century, the predominant way that law firms have charged for their work has been through the use of billable hours. In recent years, however, there has been a shift in terms of the clients' expectations regarding the billing models used by their lawyers. Nowadays, consumers are increasingly expecting predictability and transparency from their legal providers on both timelines and fees. Hourly billing based on how much time it took to complete a certain task is coming under pressure, as such fee agreements incentivise lawyers to spend more time on matters. Clients, especially corporate ones, are under increasing pressure to operate within tight budgets and keep legal costs low while requiring the provision of high-quality legal services.

Therefore, alternative billing models (or alternative fee arrangements – AFAs), which may be defined as fee agreements between a lawyer and client using a structure other than hourly billing, are gaining momentum and becoming more and more popular with both lawyers and their clients. AFAs include, but are not limited to fixed, capped, contingency or retainer fee arrangements (Law Technology Today 2014; Crawford, et al. 2017).

Essentially, a well-crafted AFA should provide realistic expectations for both the lawyer and client on the scope of the work, costs and timing. Although, law is uncertain enough, the more a legal service provider can manage potential outcomes and expectations, the greater client satisfaction in the end. Reducing uncertainty, essential to overcoming buyer reluctance, is a key feature of alternative billing practices. This requires providers of legal services to sell their work with a clearly stated budget, which, in turn, can be accomplished by leveraging legal technology to better manage quality and the risk of cost overruns through effective project management and process improvement.

The concept of alternative fee arrangements is not new; it has been around for quite some time. However, recent advances in legal technology make the adoption of alternative billing models by legal service providers increasingly common. Automation of legal processes, use of litigation analytics and prediction tools not only improve the productivity of lawyers but allow them to be more transparent with clients and use AFAs to build sustainable business models, reach scale and gain a long-term competitive advantage.

In the 2015 Altman Weil survey of large and midsize law firms, more than 93 per cent of firms reported that they use some form of AFA (Clay and Seeger 2015). In terms of law firms' revenue, according to 2018 Report on the State of the Legal Market, the percentage accounted for by alternative fee arrangements reached almost 25 per cent (Thomson Reuters Legal Executive Institute 2018).

f. Alternative Legal Service Providers

In the last few decades, a new delivery model for legal services has evolved and transformed the industry. The new model, known as legal process outsourcing, transfers the work typically performed in-house by lawyers and other legal professionals to external vendors. Legal process outsourcing involves the performance of discrete legal projects or tasks by typically less expensive third-party providers. Often such providers are located in onshore or offshore geographic areas where the outsourced legal work can be performed at a decreased cost (American Bar Association Commission on the Future of Legal Services 2016).

Traditionally, clients hired law firms to get a full-range service, so that their lawyers handled every aspect of a matter, often including those activities that did not require expensive legal professionals and could be more effectively performed by third-party providers. Today, a growing number of Alternative Legal Service Providers (ALSPs) are changing the way legal work is getting done. ALSPs usually rely upon three central concepts as they relate to the delivery of the legal work (Dzienkowski 2014):

- First, initial analysis of the matter to determine how it can be unbundled
- Second, the division of the individual tasks of the entire representation into legal work and nonlegal work
- Third, execution of nonlegal work by the client or a related entity to save costs.

The innovation that lies at the core of most ALSPs involves a sophisticated unbundling of the legal project. Through the use of technology, business management practices, and sophisticated judgment, these ALSPs break down a representation into (1) highly-automated routine work (commodity), and (2) work that requires complex legal judgment. They present the client with a detailed plan on the most efficient way to deliver high-quality legal services through the use of different lawyer and non-lawyer service providers (Dzienkowski 2014).

Today, the most common use of ALSPs is low-risk or standardised, high-volume tasks, such as document review or e-discovery support services. For corporate clients, the ability to reduce costs and to handle high-volume transactional processes provides an incentive to look to ALSPs. Law firms are utilising ALSPs mainly in a reactive manner as a way to deliver more cost-effective solutions for their clients. Those law firms that partner with ALSPs proactively and act as their clients' general contractor have all chances to win the competition and grow their business. According to the 2018 Report on the State of the Legal Market, more than half of law firms and corporations report using ALSPs in at least some capacity today. The number of customers using ALSPs and the number of tasks done through ALSPs is expected to grow in the near future (Thomson Reuters Legal Executive Institute 2018).

The study conducted by Thomson Reuters Legal Executive Institute, Georgetown University Law Center, and the Oxford Saïd Business School, identified five separate categories of ALSPs (Thomson Reuters Legal Executive Institute 2017):

1. Accounting and audit firms;
2. Captive LPOs/law firm affiliates;
3. Independent LPOs, e-discovery, and document review providers;
4. Managed legal services;
5. Contract lawyers, in-sourcing, and staffing services.

These alternative providers comprise a relatively new sector of the legal market. This sector is emerging and evolving rapidly but is still very much in its infancy. The study estimated the overall revenues of ALSPs at $8.4 billion, which comprise only a bit more than 1 per cent of total global legal spending (Thomson Reuters Legal Executive Institute 2017). It must be noted, however, that ALSP revenues have been growing rapidly, and that virtually all of the growth comes at the expense of traditional law firms, representing the revenue from services once provided by law firms. Undoubtedly, ALSPs represent one of the most dynamic segments of the legal services industry, and they are likely to remain a growing and competitive part of the legal marketplace for years to come.

While the use of alternative providers today mainly involves the performance of standardised tasks, better technology and increasing sophistication of the delivery models, as well as growing familiarity of law firms and corporations with such new models, will lead to ALSPs playing a more significant role in increasingly complex legal services and tasks. Whether coming from start-ups or the Big Four accounting firms, the emergence of such a wide variety of new alternative providers, which includes companies like Axiom, UnitedLex, Integreon, QuisLex, Elevate, Counsel On Call and many others, has given clients a plethora of new vendors from whom they can receive services and further flex their buying power. At the same time, the dynamic development of the ALSP market presents both challenges and opportunities for law firms, increasing competition, but also enabling new ways for growth.

g. Skills Shift

In today's complex, fast-changing world, legal professionals require a bigger toolbox that includes the ability to collaborate effectively across multiple disciplines. With clients increasingly demanding outcome-based solutions, legal professionals must complement their traditional legal skills with a breadth of knowledge across other disciplines, such as technology, process design, data analytics, accounting, marketing and finance.

Client demands and external pressures will primarily determine the business strategies of law firms; yet, with employee expectations also changing, organisations will be forced to develop a new talent strategy if they are to remain competitive in the future. Fewer law school graduates will have traditional careers, but there are expanding opportunities for so-called 'T-shaped' legal professionals who will create a more diverse pool for the benefit of the industry and consumers. The future of law is profoundly multidisciplinary, as the complexity of problems facing the industry requires close collaboration between lawyers, legal technologists, process design experts, and data scientists (Cohen 2018).

According to Deloitte, the legal profession will be radically different in ten years. Changing client demands, employee expectations, technology and other external factors will alter the nature of jobs and skills required in the future (Deloitte 2016). Richard Susskind, in his *Tomorrow's Lawyers*, also points out that in the future, more and more legal jobs will involve managing legal processes by applying technological solutions rather than traditional lawyering (Susskind 2017).

Fewer traditional lawyers will be needed as the adoption of technology increases. However, more roles in the transient talent pool will be required. These include project managers, sales executives, dealmakers, data and technology experts as well as non-traditional lawyers. Traditional lawyers must also be able to understand data, deal with sophisticated technology and manage risk in addition to utilising their traditional knowledge and technical skills.

For this, for example, in 2012, the American Bar Association formally approved a change to the Model Rules of Professional Conduct which pertains to technology competence of lawyers. It clearly states that lawyers must be competent not only in the law and its practice but also in technology. Since then, thirty-eight US states have adopted the duty of technology competence (Ambrogi 2019). The Federation of Law Societies of Canada is considering a similar technology competence amendment to its Model Rules of Professional Conduct (Federation of Law Societies of Canada 2017). As the number of jurisdictions adopting the new competence rules continues to grow, lawyers no longer have an excuse for their incompetence in technology.

h. New Legal Marketing

In the modern world, consumers empowered by technology want to get legal help the same way they hail a taxi, book a stay or manage a bank account – online and from any device. According to the Legal Trends Report 2018,

> 'Client perceptions of technology are changing. Those who have experienced a legal issue in the past two years – who are more familiar with modern practices and newer technologies – show more openness to working with virtual lawyers, working with lawyers remotely, and using tools such as artificial intelligence and chatbots to handle their legal issues. Those who prefer not to hire lawyers are even more open to these alternative formats, suggesting that there are those who may be looking for a different type of legal experience entirely' (Clio 2018).

A new digital marketplace is changing the way legal services are bought and sold. And as the delivery of legal services is shifting online, legal marketing should follow the trend.

Digital marketing is not a new concept, it has been around for more than two decades, but as with many other aspects of technology adoption, the legal industry is lagging behind. While the science of online marketing has advanced rapidly in recent years, the template for most law firm websites has evolved little since firms first began employing the Internet as a marketing channel, although simply having an attractive website in a crowded marketplace is no longer a significant differentiator (Getman, et al. 2014). More and more consumers of legal services start their search for lawyers using online resources, but, by some estimates, nearly 40 per cent of all small US law firms still do not have websites (Rocketmatter 2014)[6].

A modern approach to legal marketing involves generating interest of consumers through demonstrating knowledge and expertise and developing relationships through building trust. The goal of new legal marketing is not just to advertise, but to engage a lawyer's target clients, prospective clients, referral sources and the influencers of those groups. To stay above the crowd, lawyers must carefully listen to the questions and concerns of consumers and respond to such concerns in a way that demonstrates their skill, experience, and care as a professional. Of course, such an approach requires time and effort, but mere dissemination of information limits lawyers' visibility and reach, which in turn limits referrals (Rocketmatter 2014).

Attracting new clients and building referral networks takes up a significant amount of time for law firms, so being more efficient in finding and retaining clients will open up more time for billable work. Knowing more about what clients are looking for can help lawyers attract more clients while also helping them show how to get the most value from their services (Clio 2018).

Advances in technology and shifts in consumer behaviour fuel development of online legal marketplaces like Avvo, FindLaw and others, that help lawyers address their marketing pain point. They leverage technology to provide legal practitioners with sophisticated digital marketing solutions, allowing lawyers not only to be found by their target clientele but also to interact with them online effectively.

Aggregation of available offerings in an online marketplace as a way for lawyers and clients to reach each other works for big corporate clients as well. For example, General Electric has an internal website called 'GE Select Counsel' for its in-house legal team that enables users to search the database of more than 200 law firms that are GE preferred providers. Each firm posts its profile which GE counsels can access for reviews, rates, discounts, and a range of other information relevant to buying decisions (Cohen 2017).

Since the early days, most lawyers obtain new business from word of mouth referrals. Even with the proliferation of the Internet, that has not changed. What has changed, is how people exchange word of mouth, where they go to seek referrals, and whom they listen to. Today, more and more consumers ask for recommendations online for everything from restaurants

---

[6] The similar situation can be observed in other countries as well. For example, a research of the UAE legal market conducted in May 2016 by the online legal services marketplace Legal Advice Middle East (https://legaladviceme.com) revealed that 46 per cent of UAE law firms do not have websites.

and hotels to legal services. As Kevin O'Keefe, founder of LexBlog, says, 'The Internet and social media serve as accelerators of relationships and a lawyer's word-of-mouth reputation' (Shields 2017).

C. Conclusions

Technology has swept through the legal industry, dictating a fast pace of innovation for legal professionals. As has been examined in this Article, four key technologies are making the most impact on the legal industry, namely (1) the Internet, (2) cloud services, (3) artificial intelligence and machine learning, and (4) blockchain. These four technologies enable the development of subsequent derivative technologies for application in the legal industry. Such applications of technology form legal technology. According to the suggested formal classification of the legal tech, all legal applications of the technology can be grouped into eight key categories and forty-eight subcategories (see Part II).

The new reality lawyers are facing, and the future of the legal industry determined mostly by eight emerging interconnected trends empowered by the development of legal technology. These trends include (1) increasing automation of legal work, (2) the ability to work remotely, (3) the emergence of virtual law firms, (4) the global shift towards online delivery of legal services, (5) the wide adoption of alternative fee arrangements, (6) the rapid growth of alternative legal service providers, (7) the shift in skills required for legal professionals, and (8) the new approach to legal marketing.

Although we can see the trends, we are barely scratching the surface of future change. The potential is staggering, but ultimately, innovation in law practice may not look like how we envision it. Technology is rapidly changing the way legal services are delivered, but it remains early days, and the potential to disrupt is enormous.

Bibliography

451 Research (2018), 'Why Machine Learning is Important for Lawyers', in 451 Research, Global Digital Infrastructure Alliance Report.

Ambrogi, B. (2018), 'DLA Piper Uses Tech to Restructure Support Services Across All U.S. Offices', *LawSites,* 23 October 2018, available at <https://www.lawsitesblog.com/2018/10/dla-piper-uses-tech-restructure-support-services-across-u-s-offices.html> (last accessed 13 June 2019).

Ambrogi, R. (2017), 'In Legal, Blockchain Is The New Black', *Evolve the Law,* 28 August 2017, available at <https://abovethelaw.com/legal-innovation-center/2017/08/28/in-legal-blockchain-is-the-new-black/> (last accessed 13 June 2019).

Ambrogi, R. (2019), *Tech Competence,* Law Site, availabe at <https://www.lawsitesblog.com/tech-competence> (last accessed 9 December 2019).

American Bar Association (2014a), *Lawyer Demographics,* available at <https://

c.ymcdn.com/sites/www.inbar.org/resource/resmgr/Conclave/new_Lawyer_D emographics_Tabl.pdf> (last accessed 13 June 2019).

American Bar Association (2014b), NOBC-APRL-CoLAP second joint committee on aging lawyers: Final Report, April 2014, available at <http://aprl.net/wp-content/uploads/2016/07/APRL_Web_NOBC-APRL-CoLAP_Joint-Report-on-Aging_04-2014_w-Appendix.pdf> (last accessed 13 June 2019).

American Bar Association (2017), *ABA Techreport 2017*, availabe at <https://www.americanbar.org/groups/law_practice/publications/techreport/2017/> (last accessed 13 June 2019).

American Bar Association Commission on the Future of Legal Services (2016), 'Report on the Future of Legal Services in the United States', August 2016, available at <http://abafuturesreport.com/2016-fls-report-web.pdf> (last accessed 18 June 2019).

Beal, V. (2019), 'cloud service', *webopedia*, available at <https://www.webopedia.com/TERM/C/cloud_services.html> (last accessed 13 June 2019).

Burton, C. (2017), '2017 Virtual Law Practice', in American Bar Association, *Techreport 2017,* available at <https://www.americanbar.org/groups/law_practice/publications/techreport/2017/virtual_law_practice/> (last accessed 13 June 2019).

Business Wire (2017), *Global Legal Services Market Report 2017 – Research and Markets*, available at <https://www.businesswire.com/news/home/20170504005920/en/Global-Legal-Services-Market-Report-2017--> (last accessed 13 June 2019).

CB Insights (2016), 'Legal Tech Market Map: 50 Start-ups Disrupting The Legal Industry', *Research Briefs*, 13 July 2016, available at <https://www.cbinsights.com/research/legal-tech-market-map-company-list/> (last accessed 13 June 2019).

Clay, S. and E. A. Seeger (2015), 'Law firms in Transition', *Altman Weil Inc.*, availabe at <http://www.altmanweil.com/LFiT2017/> (last accessed 18 June 2019).

Clio (2018), *Legal Trends Report*, available at <https://www.clio.com/wp-content/uploads/2018/10/Legal-Trends-Report-2018.pdf> (last accessed 18 June 2019).

Cohen, M. A. (2017), 'It's Time For A Digital Legal Marketplace', *Forbes*, 7 January 2017, available at <https://www.forbes.com/sites/markcohen1/2017/01/07/its-time-for-a-digital-legal-marketplace/#4e1fe3af1%20f3e> (last accessed 13 June 2019).

——— (2018), 'Legal Delivery at the Speed of Business – And Why it Matters', *Forbes*, 25 June 2018, available at <https://www.forbes.com/sites/markcohen1/2018/06/25/legal-delivery-at-the-speed-of-business-and-why-it-matters/#25bcc37d5e53> (last accessed 18 June 2019).

Cole, S. (2017), 'Breaking Down Blockchain for Lawyers', *Legal Talk Network*, 8 November 2017, available at <https://legaltalknetwork.com/blog/2017/11/breaking-down-blockchain-for-lawyers/> (last accessed 13 June 2019).

Crawford, J., E. L. Davis (2017), 'Show Me the Bill: Alternatives to the Hourly Rate', *Michigan Bar Journal*, June 2017, available at <http://www.michbar.org/file/barjournal/article/documents/pdf4article3144.pdf> (last accessed 13 June 2019).

Curle, D. (2016), 'Legal Tech Startups: Not Just For Silicon Valley Anymore', *Thomson Reuters*, availabe at <http://www.legalexecutiveinstitute.com/legal-tech-startups/> (last accessed at 13 June 2019).

Deloitte (2016), 'Developing Legal Talent: Stepping into the future of Law firm', *Deloitte Insight Report*, February 2016, available at <https://www2.deloitte.com/content/dam/Deloitte/uk/Documents/audit/deloitte-uk-developing-legal-talent-2016.pdf> (last accessed 18 June 2019).

The Digital Edge (2018), 'Expanding Access to Justice through Online Dispute Resolution', Legal Talk Network, 13 February 2018, 122nd edition, available at <https://legaltalknetwork.com/podcasts/digital-edge/2018/02/expanding-access-to-justice-through-online-dispute-resolution/> (last accessed 13 June 2013).

Dzienkowski, J. (2014), 'The Future of Big Law: Alternative Legal Service Providers to Corporate Clients', *Fordham Law Review 2995*, 82:6.

European Commission (2019), *Online Dispute Resolution*, available at <https://ec.europa.eu/consumers/odr/main/index.cfm?event=main.home2.show&lng=EN> (last accessed 13 June 2019).

Federation of Law Societies of Canada (2017), *Model Code of Professional Conduct Consultation Report*, 31 January 2017, available at <https://flsc.ca/wp-content/uploads/2014/10/Consultation-Report-Draft-Model-Code-Amendments-for-web-Jan2017-FINAL.pdf> (last accessed 18 June 2019).

Getman, A., M. O. Hill and M. Jacobsen (2014), 'Why Most Law Firms Websites are Designed to Fail: Logic, Emotion and Today's Legal Consumer', *FindLaw*, March 2014, available at <https://www.lawyermarketing.com/white-papers/why-most-law-firm-websites-are-designed-to-fail/> (last accessed 18 June 2019).

Global Legal Blockchain Consortium (2019), available at <https://legalconsortium.org> (last accessed 13 June 2019).

Harvard Law School (2019), *Caselaw Access Project*, available at <https://case.law> (last accessed at 13 June 2019).

Henderson, B. (2018), 'Confusing conversations about clients (048)', *Legal Evolution*, 6 May 2018, available at <https://www.legalevolution.org/2018/05/confusing-conversations-about-clients-048/> (last accessed 13 June 2019).

Kennedy, D. (2017), 'Cloud Computing', in American Bar Association, 1 December 2017, available at <https://www.americanbar.org/groups/law_practice/publications/techreport/2017/cloud_computing/> (last accessed 13 June 2019).

Law Society of New South Wales (2017), *National Profile of Solicitors 2016 Report*, 24 August 2017, Urbis, available at <https://www.lawsociety.com.au/sites/default/files/2018-04/NATIONAL%20PROFILE%20OF%20SOLICITORS%202016.compressed.pdf> (last accessed 13 June 2019).

Law Technology Today (2014), *What Is, and Is Not, an Alternative Fee Arrangement*, 10 December 2014, available at <https://www.lawtechnologytoday.org/2014/12/what-is-and-is-not-an-alternative-fee-arrangement/> (last accessed 13 June 2019).

LawGeex (2018), *The Legal Tech Buyer's Guide*, available at <https://www.lawgeex.com/resources/buyersguide/> (last accessed 13 June 2019).

LexisNexis (2017), 'Law firms of the future—virtual lawyers', *The Future of Law*, availabe at <https://www.lexisnexis.co.uk/blog/future-of-law/law-firms-of-the-future-virtual-lawyers> (last accessed 13 June 2019).

Linnar Jr., D. W., J. Galvin, S. E. Acosta, A. M. Burgess, J. C. Joyce, S. Reid and A. Western (2019), *Legal Services Innovation Index*, available at <https://www.legaltechinnovation.com> (last accessed 13 June 2019).

McKinsey (2013), *Disruptive technologies: Advances that will transform life, business, and the global economy,* May 2013, available at <https://www.mckinsey.com/~/media/McKinsey/Business%20Functions/McKinsey%20Digital/Our%20Insights/%20Disruptive%20technologies/MGI_Disruptive_technologies_Full_report_May2013.ashx> (last accessed 13 June 2019).

McKinsey Global Institute (2017a), *A Future That works: Automation, Employment, and Productivity,* January 2017, available at <https://www.mckinsey.com/~/media/McKinsey/Featured%20Insights/Digital%20Disruption/Harnessing%20automation%20for%20a%20future%20that%20works/MGI-A-future-that-works_Full-report.ashx> (last accessed 13 June 2019).

——— (2017b), *Jobs Lost, Jobs Gained: Workforce Transitions In a Time of Automation,* available at <https://www.mckinsey.com/~/media/McKinsey/Featured%20Insights/Future%20of%20Organizations/What%20the%20future%20of%20work%20will%20mean%20for%20jobs%20skills%20and%20wages/MGI-Jobs-Lost-Jobs-Gained-Report-December-6-2017.ashx> (last accessed 13 June 2019).

Oxford (2019), *Dictionary Entry: Internet,* available at <https://en.oxforddictionaries.com/definition/internet> (last accessed at 13 June 2019).

Remus, D. and F. S. Levy (2016), *Can Robots Be Lawyers? Computers, Lawyers, and the Practice of Law,* 27 November 2016, available at <https://papers.ssrn.com/sol3/papers.cfm?abstract_id=2701092> (last accessed 13 June 2013).

Rocketmatter (2014), *10 Surprising Stats on Law Firm Websites (Infographic),* available at <https://www.rocketmatter.com/law-firm-websites-infographic/> (last accessed 18 June 2019).

Shields, A. (2017), 'Social Media and Blogging', *American Bar Association,* 1 December 2017, available at <https://www.americanbar.org/groups/law_practice/publications/techreport/2017/social_media_blogging/> (last accessed 18 June 2019).

Solicitor Regulation Authority (2017), *How diverse are law firms?,* available at <https://www.sra.org.uk/sra/equality-diversity/key-findings/law-firms-2017.page> (last accessed 13 June 2019).

Stanford Centre for Legal Information (2019), *CodeX Techindex,* available at <http://techindex.law.stanford.edu> (last accessed 13 June 2019).

Street, A. (2017), '2017 Mobile Technology', in American Bar Association, *Techreport 2017,* 01 December 2017, available at <https://www.americanbar.org/groups/law_practice/publications/techreport/2017/mobile/> (last accessed 13 June 2019).

Susskind, R. (2017), *Tomorrow's Lawyers: An Introduction to Your Future,* Oxford: Oxford University Press, chapter 5.

Thomson Reuters Legal Executive Institute (2017), 'Alternative Legal Service Providers: understanding the Growth and benefits of these New Legal Providers', Georgetown University Law Centre and Oxford Säid Business School, 19 February 2017, available at <https://www.2civility.org/wp-content/uploads/Georgetown-Law-Alternative-Legal-Service-Providers.pdf> (last accessed at 18 June 2019).

——— (2018), '2018 Report in the State of the Legal Market', The Center for the Study of the Legal Profession at the Georgetown University Law Center, *Peer Monitor,* 10 January 2018, available at <http://www.legalex

ecutiveinstitute.com/2018-legal-market-report/> (last accessed 18 June 2019).

Wikipedia (2019), *Enabling Technology*, available at <https://en.wikipedia.org/wiki/Enabling_technology> (last accessed 13 June 2019).

Zaretsky, S. (2017), 'More Biglaw Firms Join the Future of Law: Practice By Offering telecommuting Programs', *Above the Law,* 20 march 2017, available at <https://abovethelaw.com/2017/03/more-biglaw-firms-join-the-future-of-law-practice-by-offering-telecommuting-programs/> (last accessed 13 June 2019).

4

Future of Law – Increasing Access to Justice through technology

Odunoluwa Longe

A. Introduction

Sustainable Development Goal (SDG) 16.3, which borders on strengthening the rule of law and increasing access to justice for all, is one of the SDG targets that has recorded the slowest progress, globally, and even more so in Africa (The United Nations Statistics Division 2018).

Access to justice is a basic principle of the rule of law. In the absence of access to justice, people are unable to have their voices heard, exercise their rights, challenge discrimination or hold decision-makers accountable. (The United Nations and the Rule of Law).

Lack of access to justice not only results in injustice and inequality but also has an effect on economic empowerment. With many African countries having high poverty rates, it comes as no surprise that lack of access to justice is a pressing and urgent problem in many African countries as people who are more vulnerable to social exclusion typically report more justice problems than other groups.

The Organisation for Economic Cooperation and Development (OECD) reports that countries with trusted justice systems report higher levels of GDP per capita, property protection rights and national competitiveness. Costs of unresolved legal and justice needs are borne by citizens, business and society. It further states that when citizens' legal needs remain unmet, it can have adverse effects on other areas of their everyday life, for example, income, housing loss, health, or employment issues, and that the inability to resolve legal problems diminishes economic opportunity, reinforces the poverty trap and undermines human potential and inclusive growth.

To address this urgent situation, the Future of Law for Africa is one that must encompass all the elements of innovation, particularly scalability and efficiency. In addition, it must be affordable, simple and easily accessible.

This Paper will consider the justice needs of Nigeria and a few other African countries. It will consider the solutions currently in place, new innovative solutions that are being introduced and suggest solutions that can potentially address these needs. In addition to Nigeria, Uganda and South Africa will be used as case studies.

B. Legal Innovations and Access to Justice

I. A Nigerian Perspective

In June 2018, Nigeria reportedly overtook India as the country with the most extremely poor people in the world, with about 91.7 million Nigerians living in extreme poverty (World Poverty Clock 2019). Considering that Nigeria has the highest number of people living in extreme poverty in the world, it comes as no surprise that the country is faced with enormous access to justice challenges. According to a report by the Hague Institute for the Innovation of Law (HiiL), in 2018, many Nigerians reported more than one situation of need for justice encountered in the previous four years (HiiL 2018).

The report states that about 73 per cent of Nigerians have to deal with legal problems; most of which are related to disputes with neighbours, crimes, disputes over lending money, land disputes and employment disputes. Based on the report, only two out of ten Nigerians engage formal institutions to solve their justice problems, with the police being the most frequently used and the courts and lawyers being rarely used. This has been closely linked to the fact that legal aids and traditional justice systems are not adequately visible to meet the increasing justice needs of Nigerians; the ancillary financial pressures that come with seeking recourse from formal justice institutions; and the negative perceptions of many Nigerians with respect to the formal justice system. (HiiL 2018).

While the solutions to an average Nigerian's lack of access to justice are numerous, justice innovators in Nigeria have played a major role in bridging this gap.

Below is a synopsis of some legal innovations founded in Nigeria that have influenced the legal practice in Nigeria in a positive way and are building bridges for Nigerians to access justice easily.

a. Law Padi

LawPadi is an online platform that educates individuals and businesses about the law in Nigeria by providing well-researched legal information in a clear and concise manner. It was founded by Tunde Ibidapo-Obe in 2015 and exists to educate the average Nigerians about their rights and duties by giving clear and simplified answers to legal questions and how it affects their daily lives. To use the online platform, users submit their legal question or issue, and a member of the LawPadi team would review and respond within a 24-hour window.

The platform recently launched a number of legal chatbots on its platform. These chatbots are designed to relate with users on subject matters such as Divorce, Employment Law, Intellectual Property (IP) Law and Property Law. The divorce chatbot was the first to be launched and the chatbots relating to general legal issues was launched about a year after, and more is to come.

Tunde Ibidapo-Obe, the founder, stated that the choice to launch the first chatbot was a response to user behaviour fuelled by cultural nuances. In Nigeria, getting a divorce is still considered a taboo and many people would rather not approach a lawyer for this service to avoid being perceived as going against societal norms. For this reason, the Internet, LawPadi in this case, provided a cloak of anonymity, which made it possible for users to make inquiries they were typically reluctant to ask a lawyer, most of the inquiries being how to get a divorce. LawPadi also enables users to subscribe to SMS services to receive weekly content on various topics, explaining the rights in the circumstances in the featured topic(s).

b. DIYlaw

DIYlaw founded by Bola Olonisakin, Funkola Odeleye and Odunoluwa Longe in response to the growing start-up and entrepreneurship ecosystem in Nigeria seeks to help Nigerian entrepreneurs access legal services ranging from, registration of their businesses, to getting template legal documents, registering their intellectual property, engaging a lawyer and provision of simple legal information.

Founded in 2015, it is one of the leading legal-tech start-ups on the continent and has recently begun to offer additional business support services in what it describes as 'Human-supported SaaS'.

Human-supported SaaS is a concept DIYlaw has developed in response to its experience over the past three years in providing services to entrepreneurs in Africa, taking into context the peculiarities of African society. Below are the three key factors fuelling this direction:

1. While Nigeria has an Internet penetration of about 51.1 per cent, most devices are mobile devices, specifically feature phones with Internet usage mostly limited to low-data apps like WhatsApp. (Internet World Stats 2017)

2. Financial inclusion in Nigeria is still at its infancy with only about 39.7 per cent of Nigerians having bank accounts or mobile money (The World Bank Report 2017).
3. Many entrepreneurs still carry on their businesses offline.

The Human-supported SaaS combines the efficiency of technology with the trust factor that comes with the human touch. An example is subscribing to a fixed legal bouquet that includes automated legal documents and 2 lawyer-attended meetings with pre-fixed duration at a fixed price.

While many tech-enabled solutions continue to be founded in the Nigerian legal service-delivery and litigation space, innovating for in-house counsel is slow and almost non-existent, as non-Nigerian solutions like practical law are still being used by many Nigerian in-house counsel, and only a small number of in-house solutions have in-house tech developers.

c. LawPavilion

LawPavilion, a forerunner and arguably the first legal technology company in Nigeria has developed software solutions for the legal industry through an array of products that include electronic law reports, case management software and court management software.

Founded by Ope Olugasa in 2007, its electronic law reports include decisions of the Supreme Court of Nigeria and Court of Appeal of Nigeria from 1970 to date, a smart search function, Rules of all the Courts in Nigeria, Court Forms and Judgments of the Supreme Courts of England and America for International/Global comparison.

When LawPavilion was founded in 2007, adoption of its products was met with much hostility. Ope Olugasa has recounted his battle tales many times on how he was ridiculed by many lawyers saying no judge will accept law citations from an electronic law report in their courtrooms (LawPavilion 2014). The turning point for LawPavilion was bench-driven when Ope Olugasa convinced a few judges to let him install the software on their computers. Having experienced its efficiency, the judges started to accept the citation of LawPavilion's electronic law reports in their courts.

Beyond electronic law reports, Law Pavilion has forayed into case management, court management and will be launching an artificial intelligence powered software in the coming months. Ope Olugasa has expressed that this artificial intelligence powered software is not intended to make lawyers jobless but rather to assist them in focusing on high-level tasks such as advising clients, negotiating deals and appearing in court, thereby being productive and doing much more in less time (LawPavilion 2014).

II. A South African Perspective

The post-apartheid government in South Africa introduced various measures to enhance access to justice for the most vulnerable communities in the country (Noleen 2018). However, South Africa still remains one of the legally under-serviced countries in the world. A study conducted in 2016 by the Department of Justice and Constitutional Development in South Africa pointed out that only about 51 per cent of South Africans are aware of their constitutional rights (Nagtegaal 2019).

Over the years, however, various legal innovations such as Creative Contracts and Legal Legends are improving South Africans' access to justice.

a. Creative Contracts

The scope of access to justice not only entails access to lawyers and courts but encompasses a recognition that everyone is entitled to the protection of the law. In this context, there is no access to justice where citizens, especially marginalised groups, conceive the system as frightening or alien (Shittu 2015).

With the aim of making legal contracts easily understandable for people with low literacy skills, Robert de Rooy through his company, Creative Contracts Pty Ltd, produced the world's first Comic Contracts. Robert de Rooy, a lawyer and professional mediator, while recognising the efficacy of mediation as a dispute resolution tool was inspired to find a solution that goes beyond resolving disputes amicably to even preventing such disputes from happening in the first place.

Comic Contracts, also known as visual contracts, are visually dominant contracts written in pictures. Parties to the contracts are represented by illustrated characters; the terms of the agreement are captured as comics, and the parties sign the comic as their contract (Hutchinson 2018). These comic contracts are premised on the ideology that written agreements still lead to disputes for many reasons including the fact that words can be interpreted subjectively, but with pictures and visualisation, we all see what we mean with little or no grey areas.

In an interview with the Justice Hub at the Innovating Justice Forum 2019 organised by the HiiL, Robert in highlighting the rationale behind the creative contracts innovation said,

> 'Often illiterate people are vulnerable. They are poor and don't have access to resources and contracts are such a fundamental part of our market economy that it's wrong for illiterate people not be able to participate on their own. They don't have access to resources, they don't have ways to advise them on the content of the contracts . . . what we do is we create

contracts using pictures which is a language which everyone understands so that illiterate people can independently understand their contracts'. (De Rooy 2019)

While no Comic Contract has been subjected to tests in the courts of law, they appear to meet the basic requirements of a contract (offer, acceptance, consideration and are also in writing). (Creative Contracts 2019).

b. Legal Legends

Popularly known as Africa's first e-commerce website for legal services, Legal Legends is another legal innovation that is meeting legal needs in South Africa.

Legal Legends was developed by Andrew Taylor and Kyle Torrington in 2015. Legal Legends was borne out of the frustration both founders saw in the corporate legal world, which was plagued with ambiguous hourly billing rates, exorbitant legal fees and difficulty in accessing lawyers.

In an interview with Disrupt Africa, Kyle Torrington said that 'The average South African consumer is unable to access high-quality legal services as a result of, among others, the uncertainty attached to hourly legal fees, unscalable resources, and a characteristic reticence to adopt technological efficiencies, all of which are unavoidably passed on to an unwitting consumer' (Torrington, in Jackson 2016).

Through Legal Legends, entrepreneurs, start-ups and small businesses in South Africa are able to access quality and affordable legal services at fixed upfront prices. Orders made through the platform are distributed among a panel of highly-rated freelance lawyers who have primarily practised at big law firms in the past but are currently running boutique-sized practices.

The platform offers a range of services ranging from company registration, intellectual property (IP) registration, drafting of company incorporation documents and agreements, and online video legal consultations. Though only operating in South Africa for now, the start-up has plans to expand into the rest of Africa, as well as to India and Australia.

III. A Ugandan Perspective

The Ugandan government has reportedly ratified a number of international and regional legislative instruments that seek to guarantee access to justice as an absolute right for Ugandans, and is continuously making efforts to curtail the lack of access to justice by encouraging and supporting various legal aid schemes in Uganda. Nonetheless, a substantial percentage of the Ugandan population still struggles to access justice. (Legal Aid Service Providers Network [LASPNET] 2015)

In a 2016 study conducted by HiiL in Uganda, it was discovered that in a four year period, close to 90 per cent of Ugandans experienced one or more serious justice need that proved difficult to resolve, with the most prevalent justice needs being premised on land, family and crime matters (HiiL 2016).

Based on the study, majority of Ugandans prefer to seek information and advice from their social networks and the Local Council Courts (LCCs), as opposed to going through the formal legal procedures of obtaining justice, when faced with justice problems. The more vulnerable people (poor people in the rural areas and the less educated) on the one hand, tend to seek less information and advice due to lack of knowledge and the negative perception of the Justice, Law and Order Sector (JLOS) of Uganda. (HiiL 2016)

Study into the causes of the limited access to justice in Uganda have shown that it is imperative for key stakeholders in the Ugandan government, legal sector and society to deploy and implement 'people-focused' innovations which will focus on satisfying to a large extent the justice needs of Ugandans.

Barefoot Law is a good example of one of the recent 'people-focused' innovations that is perceived to be doing commendable work in Uganda by bridging the gap between Ugandans and their access to justice.

Barefoot Law, a leading online legal service in Uganda and East Africa, was founded by Gerald Abila, in response to the ignorance of the law identified among Ugandan citizens. Gerald started Barefoot Law as a Facebook group in 2012 as a law student at Kampala International University. In an interview with Inter Press Service, Gerald stated: 'I'd be in class but at the same time I was Tweeting and on Facebook. So many legal questions would come up so I thought let me start a Facebook group. It was just me giving free advice' (Fallon 2014).

What began as a Facebook group with just 100 members, whom Gerald helped every Saturday from three pm to four pm, has now grown into Barefoot Law, a not-for-profit organisation with over 16,000 online followers and an Android app (Fallon 2014). Barefoot Law provides free legal information and consultation to the general public using technology such as Facebook, Twitter, Skype and other traditional methods such as SMS, radio and television. It also educates individuals on laws, their legal rights and remedies.

Barefoot Law works in partnership with other individuals and organisations, including justice enforcement organisations, law firms, medical personnel and others. It is also in the process of setting up offices in neighbouring countries like Kenya and hopes to expand to other East African countries in the near future.

C. The Future of Law and Access to Justice

It is impossible to do justice to a discussion on the future of law without referencing Richard Susskind, one of the first voices on the modernisation of the practice of law; his writings have become a bible of sorts to many legal innovators worldwide. Susskind predicts a world of online-courts, AI-based global legal business, liberalised markets, commoditisation and outsourcing, Internet-based simulated practice, and new legal jobs (Susskind 2017).

Below are some of the ways by which technology is currently shaping and will potentially shape access to justice and justice delivery in the coming years:

I. Service Delivery

In the book, *The Future of Professions, How Technology Will Transform the Work of Human Experts*, Daniel and Richard Susskind observe that, prior to this current digital age, information was difficult to obtain, giving professionals a monopoly of sorts – an exclusive and critical role which gave them a 'business' advantage. People could not access the information they needed by themselves to help themselves when it came to issues relating to professional services like law, medicine, or accounting, so clients had little or no choice but to consult professionals in these fields to answer even routine queries. (Susskind 2017).

With the advent of Internet and technology, information is free and available to all, and people can now access information on any topic without having to consult a lawyer or an expert in any professional field.

Though the tables have not entirely turned, lawyers need to rethink how they deliver legal services, as the beneficiaries of legal services are becoming smarter and can easily access legal information by a simple Google search. Hence, law firm services need to be delivered with client satisfaction as the major focus. Changing trends in the legal profession show a continuous shift from clients being consumers of law firm services to also being consumers of legal services as a whole, with legal services including do-it-yourself services, automated document generators, online legal marketplaces etc.

II. Work Environment

The traditional work environment of many law firms, especially in Nigeria is a large expanse of office space with different cubicles and/or rooms where lawyers and paralegals work with their desktop computers, numerous shelving units, fireproof and tamper-proof safes and so many papers strewn around.

This work environment design is based on a model that has been around for almost 100 years. The allocation of space comes from a mentality that legal work is individual and that the private office is a symbol of status and success even though legal work and legal culture are changing rapidly (Archer, et al. 2012). New technologies and new ways of working are placing a demand on the legal work environment to be more flexible and adapt to new working realities. In recent times, there has been an emergence of powerful mobile devices, software, and secure, web-based technology that allows legal professionals to work from virtually anywhere. As a result, more legal professionals are working remotely from home or a virtual law office and are having virtual consultations and meetings. Virtual law offices provide an alternative method of practising law that permits flexible work hours and fosters a better work/life balance for legal professionals (Kane 2018).

These changes are also promoting cost-efficiency as lawyers can divert their investments in setting up and running massive law offices to other meaningful things. For instance, an Australian legal practitioner designed and launched a law firm staffed solely by artificial intelligence (AI) providing tax and estates law services (Davies 2017).

What this means for the future lawyer and law firms is that there needs to be an adaptation of these changes in the legal work environment. While not eliminating the need to set up law offices with human lawyers, law offices can be structured as a hybrid of a physical work environment and a virtual work environment to give room for remote lawyers and ease of collaboration where the need arises.

III. Automation and Standardisation of Legal Documents

As opposed to spending long hours drafting and reviewing legal documents, and managing correspondences of parties to legal contracts, legal practice is witnessing the automation of these services. Providers of legal services such as DIYlaw, LegalZoom, and Rocket Lawyer are providing automated legal documents. Some law firms are subscribing to SaaS applications that also allow them to generate legal document to increase efficiency in service delivery. Nigerian law firms are yet to be purveyors of such SaaS applications but it is only a matter of time before such applications become the order of the day.

Smart Contracts using blockchain technology is also one innovation to watch out for, though adoption is still in its very early stages and its enforceability appears debatable.

IV. Social Media

In order to remain competitive and relevant, lawyers and law firms are taking their digital engagements more seriously. Social media engagement and content creation have even become more important to law firms in jurisdictions like Nigeria, where advertising is prohibited.

Lawyers use social media tools such as LinkedIn, Facebook, Twitter and Instagram to engage with clients, reach a broad audience network, and establish themselves as thought leaders in various topics. Blogging and writing have also become important for the same reasons as well.

Legal innovations like Barefoot, DIYlaw and LawPadi are also using social media as a tool for creating legal awareness to the public on legal issues affecting their lives and businesses hereby enabling people to access legal information easily.

Naturally, as lawyers are inclined to do, these same tools have become legal weapons and are used to locate and discredit witnesses.

V. Cloud Computing

Though there has been a shift from storing data on client's transactions in paper files to computers, the future of legal practice will witness and is currently witnessing law firms investing in either customised cloud storage solutions or SaaS cloud solutions such as Dropbox, OneDrive and Google Drive to:

(a)   organise client data and information per transaction;
(b)   easily store and retain client data; and
(c)   easily share information.

Cloud computing software offers preventive care for legal documents as fire, and other natural disasters that may affect these documents if stored in law offices are avoided. They also aid better data retention and help preserve evidence for e-discovery of electronically stored information.

VI. Online Dispute Resolution

While the legal profession has witnessed litigation being gradually replaced with alternative dispute resolution (ADR), the future of ADR is online dispute resolution.

Online dispute resolution (ODR) is a branch of dispute resolution which uses technology to facilitate the resolution of disputes between parties. It primarily involves negotiation, mediation or arbitration, or a combination of all three. In this respect, it is often seen as being the online equivalent of ADR. ODR provides the ability for two (or more) disparate parties to settle their dispute using the Internet. Sometimes this involves lawyers and mediators, and sometimes it does not. It depends on the vehicle/provider that the parties agree to use to resolve their claim (Ahalt 2009).

In addition to the aforementioned forms of online dispute resolution, there is a new form of online dispute resolution which is currently being developed: blockchain arbitration – a dispute resolution mechanism for disputes arising from smart contracts.

Adopting ODR for commercial and transactional disputes will likely one day become the norm. However, a country like Nigeria with congested prisons as a result of most of the inmates awaiting trial should look to adopting ODR for criminal cases to facilitate speedy administration of justice. Such adoption will be subject to reforms, amendments and policies.

VII. Artificial Intelligence

The creation of Artificial Intelligence (AI) has witnessed a prediction that robot lawyers will replace human lawyers. AI is the term used when machines are able to complete tasks that typically require human intelligence (Marr 2018). The goals of AI include learning, reasoning and perception, and machines are wired using a cross-disciplinary approach based in mathematics, computer science, linguistics, psychology and more. AI tools such as ROSS Intelligence, Case Cruncher Alpha, Luminance and LawGeex are changing the way in which legal research is being conducted, aiding faster document review, due diligence, analysing data and making accurate predictions of the outcomes of legal proceedings (Thompson 2017).

D. The Potential Pitfalls

In taking advantage of the myriad advantages technology offers, lawyers must avert their minds to the potential pitfalls these innovations may cause in view of the foundational ethics of the legal profession and the state of the societies in which these innovations are being recommended for. Jurisprudential discourse continues to go on around some of these issues while some Bar Associations have released white-papers addressing some concerns.

I. Technology Literacy Level

In a study conducted by the Hague Institute for the Innovation of Law (HiiL) in 2018, less than 10 per cent of Nigerians seek and receive legal information from electronic or printed media sources (including the Internet). About 5 per cent of Nigerians who encountered a problem obtained information from a radio broadcast. Social media and websites are not widely used by Nigerians to access legal information. (HiiL 2018).

Though this statistic represents a fraction of the populace, the reality is that with all the innovations being introduced to aid efficient legal service delivery, the end users of these innovations are not well skilled in the intricacies of these technologies. This then begs the question of how these technologies are being suited to increase access to justice for those who have no access to technology or lack the literacy skills to understand these innovations.

II. Fiduciary Obligation

The relationship between a lawyer and a client is one that is built on trust and a lawyer owing his client a duty of care to act in his best interest at all times.

With the creation of artificial intelligence software like ROSS Intelligence and legal chatbots, the question of who delivers legal services and has the responsibility to protect this duty arises. In other words, which legal person can be sued in the event where this duty is breached?

III. Cybersecurity – Confidentiality

Legal ethics require that lawyers treat certain information that is disclosed to them as confidential, that is the lawyer-client privilege. It ensures that the client's information on a legal matter or legal dispute is well protected and not disclosed to third parties (save for legal exceptions). Changes in the nature of work such as LPO and technology innovations such as cloud computing are eroding this moral duty. Lawyers and law firms have an increased duty to ensure cybersecurity where clients information are shared in collaborative applications like Dropbox and Google Documents.

IV. Intellectual Property

With collaboration and legal process outsourcing, legal work can now be done by a variety of lawyers with expertise in different fields. Where ten different lawyers in different jurisdictions are involved in legal research for an international journal, this begs the question of who owns the intellectual property rights in the work and where the work was created?

V. Data Retention & Records

The cloud is now being considered as the safest place to retain data and records on various client transactions. While this solves the problem of organisation and preservation of this data as opposed to storing them in physical law offices that could be damaged by fire or water and personal computers that could crash, the level of trust being reposed in cloud storage providers like Google and Dropbox is very daunting. Let's not forget that these cloud storage programs are being managed by companies that have the potential of being wound up.

E. Conclusion

The continued surge of new technologies in the world and the legal space is inevitable as change is forever constant. Its potential in increasing access to justice is undoubtedly immense. However, these technologies should have the potential of increasing justice for all; both the rich and the poor and should not only address big corporate challenges but everyday legal problems ranging from housing disputes, employment disputes, crime and debt recovery disputes. In increasing access to justice, these technologies, to be impactful and scalable, have to be simple and easy to use.

Only lawyers that are innovative, open to change, willing to grow, willing to take advantage of the opportunity change presents rather than make themselves obstacles of change and growth, can keep up with the future. 'In a traditionally risk-averse profession, lawyers who do not adapt to change are making the riskiest move of all.' (Thomson Reuters n.d.)

Bibliography

Ahalt, A. M. M. (2009), 'What You Should Know About Online Dispute Resolution' *The Practical Litigator,* March 2009, available at <https://www.virtualcourt house.com/index.cfm/feature/1_7/what-you-should-know-about-online-dis pute-resolution.cfm> (last accessed 30 March 2019).

Archer, M., B. Dunn, S. Martin, J. Simet and D. Zucker (2012), 'The trends in the legal workplace', available at <https://www.gensler.com/research-insight/gensler-research-institute/trends-in-the-legal-workplace> (last accessed 30 March 2019).

Bay, M. (2017), '5 ways to adopt technology and improve access to justice', *Legal talk network,* 21 April 2017, available at <https://legaltalknetwork.com/podcasts/law-technology-now/2017/04/5-ways-to-adopt-technology-and-improve> (last accessed 30 March 2019).

Creative Contracts (2019), 'Frequently Asked Questions about Creative Contracts and Comic Contracts', available at <https://creative-contracts.com/faq/> (last accessed 19 May 2019).

Davies, A. R. (2017), 'Rage against the machines: Artificial Intelligence and the future of legal Practice', *Thomson Reuters,* December 2017, available at: <http://insight.thomsonreuters.com.au/posts/artificial-intelligence-future-legal-practice> (last accessed 30 March 2019).

De Rooy, R. (2019), 'The Justice Innovation is giving illiterate workers a stake in the economy' *The Justice Hub,* 12 February 2019, available at <https://justicehub.org/article/this-justice-innovation-is-giving-illiterate-workers-a-stake-in-the-economy/> (last accessed 30 March 2019).

Fallon, A. (2014), 'Ugandan lawyer revolutionises access to justice with just an iphone and facebook', *inter-press Service News Agency,* available at: <http://www.ipsnews.net/2014/05/ugandan-lawyer-revolutionises-access-justice-iphone-facebook/> (last accessed 30 March 2019).

HiiL (2016), 'Justice needs in Uganda', available at <https://www.hiil.org/wp-content/uploads/2018/07/Uganda-Mini-Folder_2016-1.pdf> (last accessed 30 March 2019).

HiiL (2018), 'Justice Needs and Satisfaction in Nigeria', available at <https://www.hiil.org/wp-content/uploads/2018/07/HiiL-Nigeria-JNS-report- web.pdf> (last accessed 29 March 2019).

Hutchinson, A. (2018), 'Legal contracts drawn up as comic strips are being used in

South Africa', *Quartz Africa,*9 August 2018, available at <https://qz.com/africa/1352015/legal-contracts-drawn-up-as-comic-strips-are-being-used-in-south-africa/> (last accessed 30 March 2019).

Internet World Stats (2017), *Internet Usage and Telecommunication Reports Nigeria,* available at <https://legal.thomsonreuters.com/en/insights/articles/overcoming-lawyers-resistance-to-change> (last accessed 19 May 2019).

Kane, S. (2018), 'Trends that are reshaping the legal industry', September 2018, available at <https://www.thebalancecareers.com/trends-reshaping-legal-industry-2164337> (last accessed 30 March 2019).

LawPavilion (2014), 'The LawPavilion Chronicles: Unveiling our Decade of Achievements – Part One', available at <https://lawpavilion.com/blog/the-lawpavilion-chronicles-unveiling-our-decade-of-achievements-part-one> (last accessed 19 May 2019).

Legal Aid Service Providers Network [LASPNET] (2015), 'Access to Justice for the Poor, Marginalised, and Vulnerable people in Uganda', available at <https://namati.org/wp-content/uploads/2015/12/Access-to-Justice-for-the-Poor-Marginalised-and-Vulnerable-> (last accessed 30 March 2019).

Marr, B. (2018), 'How AI and Machine learning are transforming law firms and the legal sector', *Forbes*, 23 May 2018, available at <https://www.forbes.com/sites/bernardmarr/2018/05/23/how-ai-and-machine-learning-are-transforming-law-firm> (last accessed 30 March 2019).

Nagtegaal, J. (2019), 'Justice for all: why South Africa should invest in legal Technology', *Daily Maverick,* 8 March 2019, available at <https://www.dailymaverick.co.za/opinionista/2019-03-08-justice-for-all-why-south-africa-should-invest-in-legal-technology/> (last accessed 30 March 2019).

Noleen, L. (2018), 'The Paralegal and the right of access to justice in South Africa', available at <http://etd.uwc.ac.za/xmlui/handle/11394/5801> (last accessed 29 March 2019).

Ope, O. (2017), 'Electronic Law reporting has enhanced justice administration', *Punch Newspaper,* 27 July 2017, available at <https://punchng.com/electronic-law-reporting-has-enhanced-justice-administration-olugasa/> (last accessed 30 March 2019).

Perlman, D. A. (Chair ABA Center for innovation) 'Predicting the future of legal service', available at <http://abacenterforinnovation.org/predicting-the-future-of-legal-services> (last accessed 30 March 2019).

Shittu, W. (2015), 'The challenges of access to justice', *The Guardian*, 21 July 2015, available at <https://guardian.ng/opinion/the-challenges-of-access-to-justice/> (last accessed 30 March 2019).

Susskind R. (2017), *Tomorrow's Lawyers*, Oxford: Oxford University Press.

Thompson, A. (2017), 'AI beats Human Lawyers at Lawyering', *Popular Mechanics*, 27 February 2017, available at <https://www.popularmechanics.com/technology/robots/a18839164/ai-beats-human-lawyers-at-lawyering/> (last accessed 19 May 2019).

Thomson Reuters n.d., 'Overcoming lawyers' resistance to change', available at <https://legal.thomsonreuters.com/en/insights/articles/overcoming-lawyers-resistance-to-change> (last accessed 29 March 2019).

The World Bank Report (2017), *The Global Findex database,* available at <https://globalfindex.worldbank.org/> (last accessed 29 March 2019).

Torrington, K. (2016), in T. Jackson, 'SA's Legal Legends is an e-commerce plat-form for legal Services', *Disrupt Africa*, 7 December 2016, available at <http://disrupt-africa.com/2016/12/sas-legal-legends-is-an-e-commerce-platform-for-legal-services/> (last accessed 19 May 2019).

United Nations, 'United Nations and the Rule of Law', available at <https://www.un.org/ruleoflaw/thematic-areas/access-to-justice-and-rule-of-law-institutions/access-to-justice/> (last accessed 18 May 2019).

United Nations Statistics Division (2018), *The Sustainable Development Goal Report* available at <https://unstats.un.org/sdgs/report/2018/overview/> (last accessed 29 March 2019).

World Poverty Clock (2019), 'People living in extreme poverty', available at <https://worldpoverty.io> (last accessed 18 May 2019).

5

The Future of Law:
Technology, Innovation and Access to Justice
in Legal Services Around the World

Roger Smith

A. Introduction

Technology is improving the provision of legal and judicial services for poor people around the world. This paper ends with a sketch of recent global developments set out by location. But, advancing though it may be, digital's impact on access to justice is nowhere near as powerful as its influence in the legal commercial market. And, we should recognise that there are reasons for this. These should not limit our ambitions and willingness to explore digital in the drive for greater access to justice but may well mean that digital could – perhaps should – never attain the kind of impact which we can begin to see in commercial markets.

In commerce, you can see various indicators of interest, finance and change. For example, over 4,000 recently attended the technology ILTACON conference in the US and more than 2,000 attended last year's LegalGeek equivalent in London. One estimate of the current US spend on legal tech is $1.5 billion on software alone (Friedmann 2016). A further stab at the value of 'the global LegalTech market is . . . $15.9 billion, and growing.' (The Legal Festival 2018). The Stanford University, as at 13 November 2018, listed 1,093 legal start-ups 'changing the way legal is done' (Stanford University 2018). All this frenetic action and expenditure could not avoid being a source of inspiration, not to say jealousy, in the legal aid, legal services and access to justice sector of the legal market. But it is not reflected in a comparable fever of activity. Most providers of basic legal services are just struggling to provide services in conventional ways under increasing funding pressures.

The relative lack of impact is, to some extent, surprising. A few years ago, it appeared that a number of developments might kickstart a major engagement with tech among access to justice providers. First, de-regulation of the legal profession in England and Wales looked likely to encourage providers like Co-operative Legal Services (Co-op Legal Services 2018) to link web-led firms with DIY unbundled legal services in cheap fixed fee packages in areas like divorce. Second, led by the Rechtwijzer (HiiL 2015) project funded by the Dutch Legal Aid Board, it seemed there might be internationally marketed products that combined user-focused guided pathways with online assistance in court proceedings – funded by legal aid authorities. Third, judicial reports (for example Briggs 2015) in England and Wales suggested that small claims courts might develop an initial 'front end' that would link DIY assistance with court proceedings in ways which followed the innovative approach of British Columbia's Civil Resolution Tribunal (British Columbia Civil Resolution Tribunal 2018a). Finally, the United States Legal Services Corporation, building on an existing technical initiatives programme, had developed a coherent plan for the use of technology among its grantees – those delivering legal services to those on low incomes in individual states – which was agreed at a summit in 2013 (Legal Services Corporation 2013). The potential full promise of each has not yet been met.

B. The US Plan

It is worth, perhaps, beginning with the US plan. It identified a five-point strategy which was a prescient statement of key issues.

I. A Vision of an Integrated Service-Delivery System

Technology can and must play a vital role in transforming service delivery so that all poor people in the United States with an essential civil legal need obtain some form of effective assistance. Technology can and must play a vital role in transforming service delivery so that all poor people in the United States with an essential civil legal need obtain some form of effective assistance.

The strategy for implementing this vision has five main components:

1. Creating in each state a unified 'legal portal' which, by an automated triage process, directs persons needing legal assistance to the most appropriate form of assistance and guides self-represented litigants through the entire legal process;
2. Deploying sophisticated document assembly applications to support the creation of legal documents by service providers and by litigants themselves and linking the document creation process to the delivery of legal information and limited scope legal representation;

3. Taking advantage of mobile technologies to reach more persons more effectively;
4. Applying business process/analysis to all access-to-justice activities to make them as efficient as practicable:
5. Developing 'expert systems' to assist lawyers and other services providers.

The plan has had a major influence in the US, not least because it influenced funding decisions. The annual conference which the LSC holds every year to discuss technology has become an important force in inspiring people within the US legal services movement and a smattering of others around the world. But, the LSC itself could only have a limited effect even within the US – it funds only some of the civil legal services for those on low incomes in the US; its grants programme necessarily has to be spread around the country; $4million a year (the budget for its technology grant programme) is tiny when compared to the levels of commercial spend; services are under enormous pressure in all directions; and the corporation itself is subject to a hostile President who wishes to defund it.

II. The Importance of the Basic

There was one element which was perhaps not entirely captured by the US list of priorities. The US principles stated:

> 'All access-to-justice entities will employ a variety of automated and non-automated processes to make the best use of lawyers' time to assist requesters with their cases, including:
>
> ⊕ conducting business process analyses to streamline their internal operations and their interactions with all collaborating entities
>
> ⊕ having clients/litigants perform as much data entry and handle as many of the functions involved in their cases as possible (given the nature of the case and the characteristics of the client/litigant)
>
> ⊕ having lay staff perform a broad range of assistance activities not requiring the expertise of a lawyer
>
> ⊕ having expert systems and checklists available to assist and save time for lawyers and lay service providers
>
> ⊕ maximizing the extent to which services are provided remotely rather than face-to-face, to save the time of both the clients/litigants and the service providers.' (Legal Services Corporation 2013)

Goals like these are very much dependent on basic office productivity tools that would now be routinely expected in a commercial environment. Installation of these is a continuing work in progress for many organisations and is the source, around the world, of an enormous amount of effort.

In particular, legal aid/services organisations have sought to install modern customer relationship management programs developed originally in a commercial context. This is Kate Fazio of Justice Connect in Australia: 'We are in the process of implementing a new customer relationship management (CRM) system that will bring together the functions of several fragmented databases. This work is being led by our operations team. We undertook a six months search process and involved a team of ten staff to examine products. We've settled on Microsoft Dynamics.' (Fazio 2018). Greater Boston Legal Services in the US, a legal service programme not funded by the LSC, is going through a similar process (Smith 2018a) : 'An early, and very practical, challenge was to design a new intake system': it then moved on to other elements of client management.

In many organisations, a major effort is going into upgrading the basic 'productivity tools' that surround an operational customer management system. An example is the grant by the Legal Education Foundation of members of the Law Centres Network in England and Wales to implement a digital vision which included:

'. . . a minimum standard for digital equipment and systems across the network . . . [followed by]
- phased rollout of desktop computers to Law Centres,
- move from office systems to cloud based services such as Office 365,
- migration of data to secure cloud-based storage,
- upgrading broadband where required,
- establishing national IT support,
- developing a national Law Centre data set and standardised set of forms,
- distributing digital tools being developed for Law Centre specific use as they become available, such as, tools to assist with client reception, client feedback and document generation.' (Legal Education Foundation 2018)

A related innovation, linked to making use of established commercial applications for technology, is the exploration of the use of Skype or video to leverage scarce resources. A number of legal services organisations are experimenting with video links from their home base to remote locations in a variety of different ways – sometimes involving pro bono advisers in the package. Thus, just as examples, we have a legal clinic in Ontario which is using a link with a neighbouring community:

'Technically, the requirements are simple. We first started doing this with lawyers and paralegals using their laptops in their offices. When we moved into new office space, we included in the plans two video-conferencing rooms. These have a 55" computer monitor mounted on the wall and a computer under a table. When seated at the table in the room, the images on the screen are at the same level – effectively sitting across the table from us. A webcam is mounted just above the monitor, so that when the clinic caseworker and client are looking at the monitor, they are also facing the webcam. A control on the table allows the direction of the webcam to be moved if necessary. We also have a polycom conference phone on the table as some video conferencing solutions use telephone audio. A softbox light in the room boosts the lighting, showing the client and caseworker more favourably than overhead fluorescent lighting. Finally, an "on air" light outside the room warns others that it is in use, so the door should not be opened.' (Fleming 2018)

Two English projects, funded by the Legal Education Foundation, have undertaken similar projects (Smith 2017a): one in Brighton and the other linking the Legal Advice Centre (University House) in London with an advice centre in Cornwall in the far west of the country.

Kate Fazio summarises the position:

'Technology is exciting when it comes to access to justice, however, a lot of basic stuff is not being done well in the legal assistance sector (and the legal sector more broadly). Search engine optimisation is a good example. Not-for-profit and government agencies are not coming up in google search results when common search queries are made. Overseas, non-reputable sites like Wikihow often outrank them. The sector needs to focus on getting some basic things right – their websites and data management systems, and then move into really innovative spaces. Once the sector has a stronger digital foundation, there are really exciting collaborative possibilities.' (Fazio 2018)

The importance of the basic is also shown in the undramatic but invaluable improvement of websites providing legal information. A good example of that is citizensadvice.org.uk (Citizens Advice 2019). This is being revamped to take into account the lessons on presentation learnt from the government's own websites (which have significantly improved) and technology that, for example, can show which content readers spend time on and which they gloss over.

C. The Dutch Lead the World – for a Time

The US may have been the best for domestic analysis, but it was the Dutch who led a global advance with a practical product. Staff from what is now known as the Hague Institute for Innovation of Law or HiiL fanned out across the world to promote the Rechtwijzer (HiiL 2015), a product that they had designed in collaboration with the Dutch Legal Aid Board and an American developer, Modria (now subsumed into Tyler Technologies (Tyler Technologies 2019).

The Rechtwizjer was important for two reasons – it was both a unique product, and it was also uniquely promoted. HiiL was always an internationally as well as technologically focused organisation. Indeed, it has now reorientated towards justice innovation in the legal system, particularly in the developing world. It is run by a charismatic leader, Sam Muller (The Hague Institute for Global Justice 2019), who comes from an international criminal justice background. As one instance of HiiL's international reach, its Jin Ho Verdonschot addressed the LSC's annual technology conference in 2015.

The Rechtwijzer was largely focused on family problems, though it was intended to expand to others. Part of its uniqueness was the way in which it used 'guided pathways'. Instead of static screens of information, users interacted with the program and received bite-size answers to structured questions. In addition, it allowed online third-party mediation and, indeed, structured communication between the parties. So, mediation could take place asynchronously in a considered way – with or without third party assistance – and with the parties aware of the likely results of court intervention.

The Rechtwijzer was designed to increase the number of settlements which could be presented to the court for approval. It was not in itself an online dispute resolution (ODR) platform where the online process itself resolved conflicts: agreements were drafted for submission to a judge in a conventional way for final approval. The hope was that it would become financially self-sufficient with user payments from private litigators and contributions for legally aided parties. The Dutch Legal Aid Board pulled the plug when they considered that it was running at too much of a loss. The reasons for its collapse have been contested. One of those involved in the project thought the reason for failure was that 'The Dutch legal aid board and Ministry of Justice did not actively market the platform' (Barendrecht 2018). But there may be other reasons. This was a good product, but it faced particular difficulties: its main champion within the Legal Aid Board retired; the financial goals were too difficult to meet; not enough time was given; the organisational structure of three organisations trying to work together was unwieldy. Some support for the view that the reasons were contingent rather than structural is given by the fact that the Rechtwijzer has been reincarnated as a more limited product with easier financial constraints and more a national focus (Smith 2017b).

Internationally, some of the Rechtwijzer's influence, however, continues. Specifically, the principles of the guided pathway can still be seen in MyLawBC.com (Legal Service Society 2019) – originally developed by the

Rechtwijzer team for the Legal Services Society of British Columbia. London-based Relate is also about to launch a product originally developed with help from the Rechtwijzer team. A number of advice websites – such as Victoria Legal Aid's Legal Checker (Code for Australia 2017) – now incorporate interactive elements to narrow down relevant areas of information which are then given in familiar linear fashion – as a form of hybrid guided pathway/conventional information site.

The overall failure of the Rechtwijzer is, however, highly significant. It indicates the difficulty of any one national legal aid funder putting its weight and resources behind one solution to the use of technology to provide access to justice. The US Legal Services Corporation has, perforce, operated in a different way – funding a set of individual initiatives. It has assumed the role of encourager and pump primer rather than a mainstream provider. England and Wales have traditionally spent the most per head of the population on legal aid but its role has been eroded by the swingeing cuts to legal aid introduced from 2012. Legal aid spending is under pressure in most jurisdictions. And, as a further problem, many legal aid schemes – like that in England and Wales – rely on a mix of private and public provision to deliver basic level provision which makes it hard centrally to find the resources to invest either in technology or even to develop the kind of coherent technology strategy possible for the Legal Services Corporation.

D. Enter the Courts

If legal aid is not to be a major central funder of government-led technological reform, there is probably only one other credible candidate other than the commercial market or a few foundations with, overall, very marginal funds: the courts. Around the world, governments and judges are being drawn to the possibilities of delivering their services online. Where the focus is on small civil court or tribunal claims, there may be opportunities for increased access to justice.

The leader in this field is the Civil Resolution Tribunal in British Columbia. This was created by legislation in 2012. The really innovative part of this tribunal has been its front end: the 'Solution Explorer' which it explains as follows:

> 'The Solution Explorer is the first step in the CRT process. We'll give you free legal information and self-help tools. If necessary, you can apply to the CRT for dispute resolution right from the Solution Explorer.' (British Columbia Civil Resolution Tribunal 2018b)

The explorer leads you to refine your issue and to ways of resolving it short of court action before you may make an online application. The CRT has not been independently evaluated but by July 2018 (British Columbia Civil Resolution Tribunal 2018c) 23,971 people had used its small claims solution explorer and 40,865 for 'strata dispute', a type of housing dispute.

The CRT has been influential around the world. Lord Briggs, asked to write a report (Briggs 2015) to commence the digital court programme in England and Wales, visited British Columbia to see it. He placed high importance on the replication of something similar in the small claims court that he was recommending for his jurisdiction:

> 'success will be critically dependent upon the painstakingly careful design, development and testing of the stage 1 triage process. Without it, it will offer no real benefits to court users without lawyers on a full retainer, beyond those inadequately provided by current practice and procedure. Pioneering work in British Columbia suggests that it will be a real challenge to achieve that objective by April 2020, but one which is well worth the effort, and the significant funding budgeted for the purpose.' (Briggs 2015).

The first tier of the process was also explained in the report of a committee chaired by Professor Richard Susskind (Online Dispute Resolution Advisory Group 2015) that preceded Briggs 2015:

> 'The function of Tier One of HMOC [the Online Court] will be to help users with grievances to evaluate their problems, that is, to categorize their difficulties, and understand both their entitlements and the options available to them. This will be a form of information and diagnostic service and will be available at no cost to court users. This part of HMOC will be shared with or will work alongside the many other valuable online legal services that are currently available to help users with their legal problems. For example, systems developed by charitable bodies or provided by law firms on a pro bono basis will either sit within HMOC or be linked to the service. The broad idea of online evaluation is that the first port of call for users should be a suite of online systems that guide users who think they may have a problem. It is expected that being better informed will frequently help users to avoid having legal problems in the first place or help them to resolve difficulties or complaints before they develop into substantial legal problems.'

The court modernisation programme has proceeded apace, funded largely and controversially by the sale of existing physical courts. Much has amounted to an improvement, particularly for professional users of the court – the judiciary and lawyers. However, in the rush for rapid implementation, the Briggs/Susskind initial stage has largely been forgotten. A respected mediator reported (infolaw 2018) his profoundly underwhelming experience of using the beta version of the small claims online procedure. There were no guided pathways; no built-in assistance for users (who increasingly will be acting with help from legal aid); and the system effectively leaves it all to potential litigants to make their own claim; there are no checks or structure to assist them:

> 'Apart from a series of questions designed to identify the basic information about the parties you are given a blank box in which to explain the case. . . . I was left with the impression that I could have answered with information that my case was totally devoid of merit with just a series of rambling random sentences and the case would have issued on payment. This is not how an online justice system should operate.'

The limitation of domestic English thinking is particularly concerning because a wave of jurisdictions is now poised to implement online small claims courts – from Utah and Ohio in the United States to Victoria in Australia. A choice is opening up between the British Columbian and the English approach. Some jurisdictions will regard simple digitalisation of existing procedures plus perhaps the addition of some degree of online mediation as the required solution – as in England and Wales. Others will follow the British Columbian model.

E. One Aim, Many Routes

In the absence of a comprehensive approach made possible by one major funder, technological advances are split into a wider number of discrete projects in different jurisdictions which do not really hang together in a coherent fashion beyond perhaps productivity tool improvements. Put at its best, we are in an age of disparate experiment funded by occasional foundations and various market initiatives.

A major inhibitor in the access to justice field as compared with the commercial is not only the absence of the level of funding but also the prevalence of large numbers of small providers unable to provide the large levels of 'clean data' to be expected from large commercial practices. The emphasis on installing basic productivity tools is an illustration of this. In addition, the commercial sector deals with processes such as due diligence in company mergers and acquisitions which are essentially the same across many jurisdictions. That creates an international market, independent of jurisdictional peculiarities, of enough size to attract considerable commercial interest. The problems of 'poverty law' tend to involve much fewer internationally valid principles and far fewer documents.

Initial optimism about web-based providers, like Co-operative Legal Services (CLS) able to harness fixed fee services with various packages of assistance for clients and resourced by de-regulated possibilities of funding has evaporated. CLS has pulled back its ambitions and focused more on probate than family. It is looking for a tie-in with its national funerals business. Even in England and Wales, with its loose rules as to the practice of law, online legal retailers like Rocket Lawyer or LegalZoom have made little dent in the market for legal services in the areas of 'poverty' or 'social welfare law' from which legal aid has been withdrawn. There are examples of virtual legal practice in the UK – as in the US – but there are surprisingly few and, in any event, there is little inherently innovative in simply practising through a website rather than an office.

F. Portals

The US principles from the 2013 summit do provide the beginning of a grid against which we can place developments in different jurisdictions. Many jurisdictions are, for example, concerned to provide some version of an advice 'portal'. These differ in their emphasis but have some or all of the same elements. There is the provision of general information (for some jurisdictions, the distinction between advice and information is important, as in the US, and others, such as the UK, it is not); referral to providers – who, in many jurisdictions, may be predominantly pro bono services (which in an increasingly accepted jargon, may be managed at levels that are often described as cold, warm or hot depending on how much assistance is given to the person being referred); and intake for specific services on clearly demarcated grounds of scope, merit (sometimes) and financial eligibility. The Legal Services Corporation is working on two demonstration projects in Alaska and Hawaii (Legal Services Corporation 2017). These have assistance in kind from Microsoft.

Justice Connect has just developed its Gateway project. With help from Google, Justice Connect is developing a suite of linked programmes:

> 'Our online intake tool, already launched, helps people quickly and easily understand whether they are eligible for our services, and make a full application online. Our referral tool will help our sector colleagues understand when we can help, and easily warm-refer clients deep into our system, reducing referral drop-out. Our pro bono portal will revolutionise the way we work with our network of 10,000 pro bono lawyers, ensuring we're making the most of their capacity, and matching them with the rights clients.' (Smith 2018b)

An important element of a full portal is the provision of information which will potentially allow a user to deal with their own problem or, at the least, to understand it better. England and Wales has two of the best examples of general information websites: that of the citizens advice service (Citizens Advice 2019) and one by an organisation called Law for Life (Advice Now

2018). Historically, these did not have to be so good at referral because legal aid was widely available from lawyers in private practice. That position is now changing and there may well be a move to sites more like that of Illinois Legal Aid Online (Illinois Legal Aid Online 2019) whose origins are in the pro bono movement and which combines the provision of information, some self-help material, referral and intake.

G. Self-help Document Assembly

The LSC's second objective related to self-help document assembly. In the US, the LSC has rather shrewdly funded a project called A2J Author which is (Access to Justice Author 2018)a cloud-based software tool that delivers greater access to justice for self-represented litigants by enabling non-technical authors from the courts, clerk's offices, legal services organisations, and law schools to rapidly build and implement user friendly web-based document assembly projects.

This allows organisations to use a basic template to draw up a simple guided interview that generally takes a user through half a dozen steps to a courthouse where their objective is achieved – for example to issue proceedings of some kind. A2J Author is supplemented by the work of an NGO, LawHelp Interactive (Pro Bono Net 2019), a Pro Bono Net project, which provides assistance both to users and to lawyers. One of its products, a motion to modify child support of spousal maintenance in Minnesota won recognition (Self Represented Litigants Network 2017) as the 'best automated form' in 2017 from the Self Represented Litigants Network. That reflects a move toward the provision of self-assembly documentation.

The UK has followed into the self-assembly field with caution. CourtNav (Court Nav 2019), however, is very similar to projects fuelled by A2J author – without the visuals. It is an online tool developed by a specialist Citizens Advice Service office in the Royal Courts of Justice (the central civil courts of England and Wales). The system has now been taken up by the whole Citizens Advice service and can be accessed from local offices. It relies on pro bono lawyers to check the self-assembled documents.

There has also been some exploration in England and Wales of the possibility of interactive self-assisted letters rather than court interventions for example for a disability payment known as PIP where an app will help the users with a letter of claim and another provider (seAp 2017; Advice Now 2018) will produce a similarly interactive request for a mandatory reconsideration. A user can be guided to complete a standard letter with information that is relevant to the matter in hand – and given 'just in time' resources to help them understand what is required.

The interactivity enabled by the Internet offers a number of ways in which provision may be tailored to an individual user and services leveraged. The guided pathway framework for advice is one example. Another more specific use has been in digitalising 'legal health check-ups'. This idea has been around for some time and, before the Internet, it consisted of offering people a questionnaire to check on their legal needs. This is an obvious candidate for digitalisation and the newly created ABA Centre for Innovation has announced that

> 'Currently in development is a free, online legal check-up tool that is being created by a working group led by the ABA Standing Committee on the Delivery of Legal Services. The checkup will consist of an expert system of branching questions and answers that helps members of the public to identify legal issues in specific subject areas and refers them to appropriate resources.' (American Bar Association Centre for Innovation 2018)

Actually, Canada has already got there in the form of Halton Community Legal Services in Ontario (Smith 2018c). Since it published an online legal aid check-up in 2014, around 3,000 have been completed leading to over 1,000 requests for more legal advice and another 1,000 for more information.

H. Expert Systems, AI and Chatbots

Additionally, the LSC identified the importance of expert systems. This takes us into the world of artificial intelligence and its little sister, the Chatbot. Indeed, guided pathways are a move towards the kind of branching logic required by AI and, ultimately, its application must be able to help in the presentation of information and advice. In its turn, that leads to a question which can be articulated as 'should we plan to sleep with Google' – that is, should the aim of information providers in legal services ultimately be to be taken with a suite of services provided by one of the big commercial providers – most likely Facebook or Google. Or is it important for independent advice agencies to maintain their own identity? Luckily, this dilemma is some way off and may even be too much of a diversion to raise. For the moment, a person seeking advice on the law in their own jurisdiction will look to provision provided by organisations like Illinois Legal Aid Online in the US or Citizens Advice in the UK.

Chatbots have been the subject of enormous hype. At the centre of their use in an access to justice context has been Joshua Browder, onetime Stanford University student. He has developed a number, most famously grouped under the DoNotPay name and available as an app (Browder 2018). These began with assistance in challenging parking tickets and have now moved into the field of (US) small claims. They do help and the interactivity of the bot is an advance but many of the applications are actually still quite simple, not to say simplistic. They may well assist well informed users with fairly good technical and language skills. Those more disadvantaged are likely to need more of a combination in which the technology supplements rather than replaces individual assistance.

I. Serendipity

There is a high degree of serendipity in current exploration of technology. This is a new field and new opportunities are opening up for innovators in all sorts of enterprising and unexpected ways – of which these are three examples. *rightsnet* (Lasa Charity UK Ltd. 2019) in the UK provides an Internet platform on which rights workers can build up a community; be updated on new cases and legislation; and mutually assist each other to answer questions. In the US, Project Callisto (Callisto 2019) is developing totally innovative ways using technology to combat sexual harassment on university campuses by facilitating the reporting of sexual harassment in a way, which allows the automatic matching of records if users report the same perpetrator. Similar, but slightly different use of the confidential recording possibilities of the Internet is made by JustFix.nyc (JustFix.nyc 2019) which facilitates the recording of housing disrepair in New York City. This has plans to expand into other cities both in the US and elsewhere. And, finally, the crowd funding movement is a good example of an initiative which is, in practice but not theory, dependent on the Internet. Technology is just a tool that brings potential funders together with opportunities. But crowdfunding is beginning to have an impact. British-based crowdjustice.com (Crowdjustice 2019) has funded challenges to Brexit in the UK and Stormy Daniels in her US litigation against President Trump. Finally, AI itself can have unexpected uses. One UK family law practitioner uses his subscription to IBM Watson to predict costs on cases so that he can better meet the challenge of fixed fees (IBM 2018).

J. Conclusion

So, what are the takeaways? As far as legal tech and poor people are concerned, there is no 'killer app'. There are, however, a myriad of small-scale advances. And, there is the continued spur of the froth on the commercial legal tech bubble. So, who knows what is to come? But there are some conclusions which might shape further endeavour.

I. Most Value may Come from the Implementation of 'Productivity Tools' Which Have Become Standard in Commercial Fields

The use of SMS or texts for short communications, particularly reminders of appointments have become standard in many health or commercial organisations. The adoption of customer management systems which will allow those in the access to justice to do the same could be a major advance – as could the basic core of a system that marshals dealings with clients in the same way as is becoming routine in commercial law – linking documents, appointments, diaries and court appearances. Commercial firms are increasingly using video to communicate about their product, and this too would be helpful in the access to justice sector.

II. The Importance of Experiment, Evaluation, Research, Monitoring, International Benchmarking and Leadership

All round the world people are grappling with much the same general problems – albeit with very local particularities. Given that technology is transnational even if most law is not, then it would be surprising if there were not lessons to be learnt from international comparison, comparative research and global benchmarking. Increasingly, the need for these becomes overwhelming.

We need to start benchmarking similar projects against each other – particularly because of the almost universal shortage of funds. In some jurisdictions, there are national bodies that might undertake this role: for example, in the United States the Legal Services Corporation, the ABA Centre for Legal Innovation or the various court-based research groups. Academics have a role and there is a particular need for European collaboration which might help to overcome the current English-speaking bias to what comparative coverage there is. There is also a language barrier to overcome. It is easier to keep track of developments around the world which are articulated in English than it is in other languages.

We need to continually monitor, research, and discuss evaluations of ongoing projects. There is too much 'fire and forget' – the running of IT projects without rigorous evaluation of the results and without any sharing on a national and international basis.

III. Identification of 'What Works' – Segmenting Users

The reason for more international benchmarking and comparison is to identify what works in the context of legal services and access to justice. It seems likely that the section of the population is in need of legal services but unable to access them is not homogenous in terms of its digital and legal capacity. There will be groups among those on low incomes who have the requisite language, technical and other skills to use digital tools. We need to be able to identify and to encourage them. To do this, we need to pool experience but also to recognise that, within all our societies, there will be groups for whom digital is not appropriate.

IV. Sustainability

The Holy Grail of technology projects in the access to justice field is sustainability – the idea that they can reach a steady financial state through uncovering a stream of funding that will keep them going after the initial seed corn investment. There are projects where this might be possible. Crowdfunding is an obvious one where money might come in on what is effectively a commercial basis. Project Callisto is an example where technology for access to justice might provide a route to other funds as educational institutions are encouraged to invest in protection of their students. Generally, however, the notion that website-based provision can raise significant funds is pretty fanciful. After all, poor people do not actually have much money: that is their fundamental problem. We will need governments to provide the resources.

There is another aspect to sustainability. Digital is probably best seen as supplement the work of agencies and organisations rather than substituting for them – though this will be a temptation for governments. For example, seAp developed its interactive disability claim as a way of providing some level of help which used the expertise that it had built up from its work for clients for those outside its catchment area (seAp Advocacy 2017).

V. The Digital Divide

The question of the digital divide still hangs over the use of technology in the provision of access to justice. Where technology is used on a voluntary basis to supplement face to face to provision – such as by the Citizens Advice Service in England and Wales – that is not really a problem. A non-digital route remains. To the extent that systems go 'digital by default', as is the (English and Welsh) Government's mantra, this raises difficulties. These can be seen in the field of Universal Credit where the intention is to move the whole system to a digital basis. The *Observer* newspaper reported that 'According to data released under the Freedom of Information Act, which analysed applications for universal credit over one month, a fifth were turned down because of "non- compliance with the process"'. We will see in due course how this compares with figures for digital courts and digital exclusion has to be born in mind even by the great enthusiasts for digital expansion. We need more evidence about this crucial factor.

It is too early to accept fixed limitations on the reach of digital in a legal setting, but we need more research and experience of whatever the limitations actually are which are imposed by lack of the appropriate technical, cultural, linguistic, social and cognitive skills. There will be a percentage of every population in every country which will not be able to take advantage of digital means of communication and, for them, there need to be alternatives. It may well be that we should accept that, say, 20 per cent of the population will be unable to use digital means of communication effectively. That is sizeable enough to require addressing and retaining face to face channels of communication.

VI. Legal Empowerment

Technology has the capacity to aid the legal empowerment of those currently unable to obtain the information that they need. However, we have to bear in mind that many disputes between those on low incomes and those in powerful positions require not only information but advocacy support. Government departments and powerful corporations may, for example, remain obdurate in refusing the rights of an individual. Information may not be enough: some form of assistance may be required to succeed. Technology is only a tool: it will not, by itself, be a solution. However, one value possibility that technology can accentuate is the collection of data so that agencies in the field can better bring together similar classes of case in order to demonstrate problems and, indeed, solutions.

VII. Interactivity

Ultimately, it is the Internet's capacity for interactivity which offers the best prospect to combat access to justice. Digital can increase the information to which people have access, but it can also provide myriad ways in which users can interact with that information either through chatbots or AI or guided pathways or audio or video connection or by using the data collection capacities of the net.

VIII. 'Sleeping with Google'

As the experience of the sector increases, the question will arise about whether the best way forward is for the various organisations involved is – in whatever way becomes available – to hand over their expertise in basic information and signposting to a major commercial player. There is an argument that the only way in which that basic 'portal' function can be properly universalised is through Amazon, Facebook or Google. The benefits of being able to ask Siri or Alexa about your benefit entitlement or housing status are obvious. There would have to be a commercial rationale, but the provider might be able to make money on referrals. Would we want this to happen? Could a commercial provider keep the information up to date and why would it want to? This is the issue that sometimes goes by the description of 'sleeping with Google'. No offer has been made as yet but we need to prepare ourselves for the appropriate answer.

Bibliography

Access to Justice Author (2018), available at <https://www.a2jauthor.org> (last accessed 13 November 2018).

Advice Now (2018), *PIPI Mandatory Reconsideration Request Letter Tool,* available at <https://www.advicenow.org.uk/pip-tool> (last accessed 13 November 2018).

American Bar Association Centre for Innovation (2018), available at <https://www.americanbar.org/groups/centers_commissions/center-for-innovation/> (last accessed 13 November 2018).

Barendrecht, M. (2018), 'Rechtwijzer: why online supported dispute resolution is hard to implement', *Law, Technology and Access to Justice,* 20 June 2017, available at <https://law-tech-a2j.org/odr/rechtwijzer-why-online-supported-dispute-resolution-is-hard-to-implement/> (last accessed 13 November 2018).

Briggs, M. (2015), 'Civil Courts Structure Review: Interim Report', available at <https://www.judiciary.uk/wp-content/uploads/2016/01/ccsr-interim-report-dec-15-final1.pdf> (last accessed 1 June 2019).

British Columbia Civil Resolution Tribunal (2018a), available at <https://civilresolutionbc.ca> (last accessed 13 November 2018).

———— (2018b), *What is the strata Solution Explorer?*, available at <https://civilresolutionbc.ca/how-the-crt-works/getting-started/strata-solution-explorer/> (last accessed 13 November 2018).

———— (2018c), *CRT Statistics Snapshot: July 2018*, available at <https://civilresolutionbc.ca/crt-statistics-snapshot-july-2018/> (last accessed 13 November 2018).

Browder, J. (2018), *DoNotPay App,* available at <https://itunes.apple.com/app/id1427999657> (last accessed 3 June 2019).

Callisto (2019), *by survivors, for survivors*, available at <https://www.projectcallisto.org> (last accessed 3 June 2019).

Citizens Advice (2019), available at <https://www.citizensadvice.org.uk> (last accessed 3 June 2019).

Co-op Legal Services (2018), available at <https://www.co-oplegalservices.co.uk> (last accessed 13 November 2018).

Code for Australia (2017), *Victoria Legal Aid*, available at <http://lac.vla.vic.gov.au> (last accessed 3 June 2019).

CourtNav (2019), available at <http://courtnav.org.uk> (last accessed 3 June 2019).

Crowdjustice (2019), available at <https://www.crowdjustice.com> (last accessed 3 June 2019).

Fazio, K. (2018), 'Activists Speaking 4: Kate's Story – Kate Fazio of Justice Connect', *Law, Technology and Justice*, 27 September 2018, available at <https://law-tech-a2j.org/digital-strategy/activists-speaking-4-kates-story-kate-fazio-of-justice-connect/> (last accessed 13 November 2018).

Fleming, J. (2018), 'In Praise of Video in a Legal Clinic', *Law, Technology and Access to Justice*, 9 September 2018), available at <https://law-tech-a2j.org/video/in-praise-of-video-in-a-legal-clinic/> (last accessed 13 November 2018).

Friedmann, R. (2016), 'Legal Tech Market: sizing and Opportunities', *Prism Legal*, available at <https://prismlegal.com/legal-tech-market-sizing-and-opportunities/> (last accessed 13 November 2018).

The Hague Institute for Global Justice (2019), *Dr. Sam Muller*, available at <http://

www.thehagueinstituteforglobaljustice.org/people/dr-sam-muller/> (last accessed 3 June 2019).

HiiL (2015), *Rechtwijzer at the 'Crystal Scales of Justice' price,* 4 November 2015, available at <https://www.hiil.org/news/rechtwijzer-at-the-crystal-scales-of-justice-prize-ceremony/> (last accessed 3 June 2019).

———— (2018), *#JustInnovate18 taking on the global tech scene one startup at the time,* available at <https://www.hiil.org/news/justinnovate18-taking-on-the-global-legal-tech-scene-one-startup-at-a-time/> (last accessed 13 November 2018).

IBM (2018), *Family Law Partners,* available at <https://www.ibm.com/case-studies/family-law-partners> (last accessed 13 November 2018).

Illinois Legal Aid Online (2019), available at <https://www.illinoislegalaid.org> (last accessed 3 June 2019).

Infolaw (2018), *Developments in ODR and the online court,* available at <https://www.infolaw.co.uk/newsletter/2018/05/developments-odr-online-court/> (last accessed 13 November 2018).

JustFix.nyc (2019), available at <https://www.justfix.nyc> (last accessed 3 June 2019).

Lasa Charity UK Ltd. (2019), *rightsnet,* available at <https://rightsnet.org.uk> (last accessed 3 June 2019).

Legal Education Foundation (2018), *Law Centres Network,* available at <http://www.thelegaleducationfoundation.org/grantee/law-centres-network> (last accessed 13 November 2018).

The Legal Festival (2018), available at <https://www.legalfestival.com/blog/the-rise-of-the-legaltech-market> (last accessed 13 November 2018).

Legal Service Society (2019), *MyLawBC,* available at <https://mylawbc.com> (last accessed 3 June 2019).

Legal Services Corporation (2013), *Report of The Summit on the Use of Technology to Expand Access to Justice,* available at <https://www.lsc.gov/media-center/publications/report-summit-use-technology-expand-access-justice> (last accessed 13 November 2018).

———— (2017), *The Legal Service Corporation Announces Pilot States for Innovative Program to Increase Access to Justice,* 24 April 2017, available at <https://www.lsc.gov/media-center/press-releases/2017/legal-services-corporation-announces-pilot-states-innovative> (last accessed 13 November 2018).

Online Dispute Resolution Advisory Group, Civil Justice Council (2015), *Online Dispute Resolution: for Low Value Civil Claims,* February 2015, para 6.2, available at <https://www.judiciary.uk/wp-content/uploads/2015/02/Online-Dispute-Resolution-Final-Web-Version1.pdf> (last accessed at 1 June 2019).

Pro Bono Net (2019), *Legal Help Initiative: Legal Documents made simpler,* available at <https://lawhelpinteractive.org> (last accessed 3 June 2019).

seAp (2017), *Disability and Work Capacity Benefits Support,* available at <https://www.seap.org.uk/services/c-app/> (last accessed 13 November 2018).

Self-Represented Litigants Network (2017), *SRLN 2017 Form Competition: 2017 SRLN Forms and Technology Working Group – Best Forms Contest,* available at <https://www.srln.org/node/1247> (last accessed 13 November 2018).

Smith, R. (2017a), 'Video boosts the radio star: the possibilities of Skype in delivering legal advice', *Law, Technology and Access to Justice,* 15 November 2017, available at <https://law-tech-a2j.org/advice/video-boosts-the-radio-star-the-possibilities-of-skype-in-delivering-legal-advice/> (last accessed 13 November 2018).

———— (2017b), 'The Rechtwijzer Rides Again', *Law technology and Access to Justice*, 7 December 2017, available at <https://law-tech-a2j.org/odr/the-rechtwijzer-rides-again/> (last accessed 13 November 2018).

———— (2017d), 'Victoria Legal Aid's online triage tool: a small step with large implications', *Law, Technology and Access to Justice*, 23 February 2017, available at <https://law-tech-a2j.org/guided-pathways/victoria-legal-aids-new-online-tool-early-steps-to-an-interactive-future/> (last accessed 13 November 2018).

———— (2018a), 'Beyond the rhetoric: the practical challenges of implementation of new case management system', *Law technology and Access to Justice*, 24 September 2018, available at <https://law-tech-a2j.org/case-management/beyond-the-rhetoric-the-practical-challenges-of-implementation-of-a-new-case-management-system/> (last accessed 13 November 2018).

———— (2018b), 'Justice Connect: Gateway to a new Digital world', *Law, Technology and Access to Justice,* 23 August 2018, available at <https://law-tech-a2j.org/odr/justice-connect-gateway-to-a-new-digital-world/> (last accessed 13 November 2018).

———— (2018c), 'Access to Justice and interactive digital provision', *Law, Technology and Access to Justice,* 23 April 2018, available at <https://law-tech-a2j.org/advice/access-to-justice-and-interactive-digital-provision/> (last accessed 13 November 2018).

Stanford University (2018), *CodeX Techindex*, available at <http://techindex.law.stanford.edu> (last accessed 13 November 2018).

Tyler Technologies (2019), *Modria: Increase access to Justice with online dispute resolution*, available at <https://www.tylertech.com/products/modria> (last accessed 3 June).

Part II

Smart Government: Building Responsive Future Ready Institutions

6

Automating Government Decision-making: Implications for the Rule of Law

Monika Zalnieriute, Lyria Bennett Moses and George Williams

A. Introduction

Automation promises to improve a wide range of processes. The introduction of controlled procedures and systems in place of human labour can enhance efficiency as well as certainty and consistency. It is thus unsurprising that automation is being embraced by the private sector in fields including pharmaceuticals, retail, banking and transport. Automation also promises like benefits to government. It has the potential to make governments – and even whole democratic systems – more accurate, more efficient and fairer. As a result, several nations have become enthusiastic adopters of automation in fields such as welfare allocation and the criminal justice system. While not a recent development, automated systems that support or replace human decision-making in government are increasingly being used.

This chapter assesses the benefits and challenges to the rule of law posed by automation of government decision-making. In this regard, reference should be made to a few short commentaries which call for more attention to be paid to the governmental context: see, for example, Mikhaylov, Esteve, and Campion 2018; Kennedy 2017; and Perry 2017. It adopts the rule of law as a standard because it is accepted worldwide as providing normative guidance on the appropriate conduct and operation of governments. The rule of law is a ubiquitous, yet elusive concept, at the heart of which lies a widely held conviction that society should be governed by law. However, in this chapter, our goal is not to provide yet another account of the rule of law (modern accounts include Lord Bingham 2007: 69; Tamanaha 2004: 2; and Gowder 2016). Instead, we critically investigate how principles of the rule of law are affected by the increasing use of two kinds of automation:

human-authored pre-programmed rules (such as expert systems) and tools that derive rules from historic data to make inferences or predictions (often using machine learning).

We focus narrowly on aspects of the rule of law that have the widest acceptance across political and national systems, notably that it requires governance in which the law must be predictable, stable, accessible and everyone must be equal before the law (International Congress of Jurists 1959: para. 1). In applying these principles, our focus is upon the formal and procedural aspects of the rule of law, rather than its capacity to encompass a broader set of human rights, including free speech and privacy. Hence, we limit our analysis to the following core components: transparency and accountability; predictability and consistency; and equality before the law.

These rule of law values are applied to four case studies: automated debt-collection in Australia, data-driven risk assessment by judges in the United States, social credit scoring in China, and automated welfare in Sweden. The case studies have been selected to provide a diverse range of viewpoints from which to assess the benefits and risks to the rule of law posed by the use of automated decision-making by governments around the world. We do not provide a detailed consideration of jurisdiction-specific constitutional, administrative and statutory requirements constraining decision-making in these nations. For example, in the United States, this would include due process protections in the Administrative Procedure Act, Pub L 79–404, 60 Stat 237, 5 USC §§ 551–559. Our aim instead is to analyse developments at the conceptual level of how they impact upon the rule of law, rather than seeking to develop a detailed prescription for the design or implementation of such systems.

B. Automation of Decision-Making

Automation in government decision-making is not a new phenomenon, nor is it linked to a single technology. Automation can vary from partial to full – that is from decision support (for example, a facial recognition tool that helps humans make decisions) to human-in-the-loop (decisions are made with some human involvement), to the disappearance of humans from the decision-making process entirely.

While it is not always easy to strictly categorise the degrees of automation, in analysing the impact of automation on the rule of law, we look at two classic types. The first type, known as expert systems, is a process that follows a series of pre-programmed rules written by humans, and has been used in a variety of government contexts such as child protection and the calculation of welfare benefits since the 1980s (for example, Schuerman, et al. 1989; Sutcliffe 1989). The Robo-debt and the Swedish welfare system are more modern examples of expert systems, sometimes described as the first wave of artificial intelligence ('AI') (see generally Tyree 1989; Susskind 1987: 114–15). The second type, supervised machine learning, deploys rules that are inferred by the system from historic data. It is deployed in the judicial sentencing in US and is widely known as a 'second wave' AI (Launchbury 2017). Machine learning describes a variety of data-driven techniques that establish processes by which a system will 'learn' patterns and correlations so that it can generate predictions or reveal insights. Unlike standard statistical methods, machine learning is generally iterative (capable of continually 'learning' from new information) and capable of identifying more complex patterns in data.

Despite automating the decision-making process to varying extents, neither of the approaches to automation considered in this chapter remove humans from the process entirely. At least at this stage of technological development, most of the automation comes after humans have designed and built the system. This means that the human aspect of these technologies can never be discounted. This is apparent in each of the following case studies, which we apply as the reference point for our analysis in this chapter.

I. Robo-debt in Australia

Robo-debt is a nickname given by the media to a controversial programme, announced by the Australian government in 2015, to calculate and collect debts owed because of welfare overpayment. The program was introduced as part of a 2015–16 Budget measure, 'Strengthening the Integrity of Welfare Payments' and a December 2015 Mid-Year Economic Fiscal Outlook announcement. The system combined data matching (possibly employing machine learning), such data matching being authorised by the *Data Matching Program (Assistance and Tax) Act 1990* (Cth), and automated assessment through the application of human-authored formulae, and automated generation of letters to welfare recipients.

Under the system, data on annual income held by the Australian Tax Office (ATO) was automatically cross-matched with income reported to the government welfare agency Centrelink. To understand how it worked, it is important to know that income is reported to the ATO as an annual figure but to Centrelink as a fortnightly figure. The first step was to check the two annualised income figures against each other. Where the ATO annual income was greater than the Centrelink annualised income, individuals were sent a letter giving them an opportunity to confirm their annual income through an online portal. Those who accessed the online portal were given an opportunity to state their fortnightly income (with evidence), whereas those who did not access the portal were assumed to earn a fortnightly figure calculated as the annual ATO figure divided by the number of weeks in a year (Commonwealth Ombudsman 2017: 1, 4). However, the letter sent to individuals did not explain that recording variation in income over the year was important to an accurate calculation of welfare entitlements (Commonwealth Ombudsman 2017: 9). Concerns about Robo-debt range from poorly worded correspondence, inaccuracy of the formula in a percentage of cases, issuing debt notices to those not owing money (Carney 2018), shifting the burden of proof (Hanks 2017: 9–11), and leaving individuals to the mercy of debt collectors.

II. Data-driven Risk Assessment in US Sentencing Decisions

In some jurisdictions in the United States, judges use an automated decision-making process called COMPAS (Correctional Offender Management Profiling for Alternative Sanctions) that draws on historic data to infer which convicted defendants pose the highest risk of re-offending, particularly where there is a risk of violence. Reliance on COMPAS in judicial sentencing has been endorsed by a Conference of US Chief Justices (CCJ/COSCA Criminal Justice Committee 2011) and by the Supreme Court of Wisconsin in *State of Wisconsin v. Loomis*, 881 N.W.2d 749 (Wis. 2016) ('*Loomis*') where it was found to be permissible so long as the decision was not fully delegated to machine learning software. For example, a judge will still need to consider a defendant's arguments as to why other factors might impact the risk they pose (*Loomis* at [56]). The United States Supreme Court denied certiorari on 26 June 2017.

Concerns have been raised that African Americans are generally more likely than whites to be given a false positive score by COMPAS (Angwin, et al. 2016). This is not necessarily because race is used as a variable in modelling relative dangerousness of the offender population; differential impact can result where race correlates with variables that are themselves correlated with risk classification. In *Loomis*, data on gender was included in the set on which the algorithm was trained, the reason being that rates of re-offending, particularly violent re-offending, differ statistically between men and women. The Supreme Court of Wisconsin held that this kind of differential treatment did not offend the defendant's due process right not to be sentenced based on his male sex. Its reason was that because men and women have different rates of recidivism, ignoring gender would 'provide less accurate results' (*Loomis* at [77] and [86]). This highlights a fundamental question about the logic employed in drawing inferences using rules derived from historic data – if the goal is to maximise predictive accuracy, does it matter from a rule of law perspective whether individuals are classified differently based on inherent characteristics?

III. Automated Student Welfare in Sweden

The Swedish National Board of Student Finance (CSN) manages financial aid to students in Sweden for their living costs, which includes grants and various loans (see the website of CSN, n.d.). The CSN automated rule-based decision-making system is mandated by national legislation, and the role of professional officers is to guide customers through the e-service in accordance with an ethical code (Wihlborg, Larsson and Hedström 2016). Numerous e-services provided by CSN are partially or fully automated. For example, an e-service that allows people to apply for a reduction in repayments is used to support decision-making processes (partial automation), while all decisions on loan repayments based on income over the last two years are fully automated. The automated decision-making system combines data from CSN with publicly available information, including tax information (which is publicly available in Sweden) (Swedish Tax Agency 2016). Whenever an individual applies for a reduction, an officer enters any relevant information into the system manually before letting the automated system take over again, meaning that the system is partially automated. While it is the system that 'makes' decisions, the officers are obliged by law to take responsibility for them and to communicate the decisions to the customers by editing the default formulation and signing it.

IV. Social Credit System in China

A fourth case study of automation is the Social Credit System (*shehui xinyong tixi* – 'SCS') developed by the central government of China and implemented by forty-three 'demonstration cities' and districts at a local level. (A linguistic note made by Creemers [2018] is useful in this context: 'the Mandarin term "credit" [*xinyong*] carries a wider meaning than its English-language counterpart. It not only includes notions of financial ability to service debt, but is cognate with terms for sincerity, honesty, and integrity.') According to the government planning document that outlines the system, translated by Creemers, 'its inherent requirements are establishing the idea of a sincerity culture [sic], and carrying forward sincerity and traditional virtues, it uses encouragement to keep trust and constraints against breaking trust as incentive mechanisms, and its objective is raising the honest mentality and credit levels of the entire society.' (State Council 2014 in Creemers 2018 [ed.]). In accordance with such goals, the SCS provides rewards or punishments as feedback to individuals and companies, based not just on the lawfulness of actions, but on their morality, and covers economic, social and political conduct (see Creemers 2018 [ed.] for a detailed analysis of the thinking and design process behind the SCS).

From a technological perspective, the SCS resembles a straight-forward, pre-programmed rule-based system, however each of the forty-three 'model cities' implement the programme differently. For example, under the Rongcheng City model (Junwei 2017), everyone is assigned a base score of 1,000 points on a credit management system, which connects four governmental departments. Subsequent points are then added or deducted on the system by (human) government officials for specific behaviour, such as, for example, late payment of fines or traffic penalties. There are, in total, 150 categories of positive conduct leading to additional points on the system, and 570 categories of negative behaviour leading to point deductions for individuals. The implications of the SCS cover a wide range of economic and social repercussions. For instance, those with low social credit rating scores may not be eligible for loans and certain jobs and could be denied the ability to travel on planes or fast trains. In contrast, those with high scores enjoy benefits such as cheaper public transport, free gym facilities and priority for waiting times in hospitals.

The SCS is still in its early stages and the Chinese government has been forming partnerships with private companies with sophisticated data analytics capacities. For example, the central government has been cooperating with Chinese tech giant Alibaba in a Sesame Credit system, which includes, among other things, an automated assessment of potential borrowers' social network contacts in calculating credit scores (Hvistendahl 2017). This means that those with low-score friends or connections will see a negative impact on their own scores because of an automated assessment (Zhong and Mozur 2018). Sesame Credit combines information from the Alibaba database with other personal information, such as individual online browsing and transaction history, tax information and traffic infringement history, to automatically determine the trustworthiness of individuals.

C. Benefits and Challenges to the Rule of Law

I. Transparency and Accountability

Automation offers many potential benefits in enhancing the transparency and accountability of governmental decision-making. Whereas a human may come up with justifications for a decision ex post that do not accurately represent why a decision was made (Nisbett and Wilson 1977: 231), a rules-based system can explain precisely how every variable was set and why each conclusion was reached. It can report back to an affected individual that the reason they were ineligible for a benefit was that they did not meet a criterion that is a requirement of a legislative or operational rule that is pre-programmed into the logic of the system. It is important to note here that such feedback is not necessarily provided for rules-based expert systems. The designer decides what the output of the system will be and whether it will include reasons for its conclusions or decisions. In the case of robo-debt, individuals were not provided with clear information as to how the debts were calculated in general or in their individual case. The opposite is true for the Swedish system, where decisions are made based on clear, public rules and a human confirms and takes responsibility for each decision.

To understand the barriers to transparency, it is helpful to understand Burrell's three 'forms of opacity' (Burrell 2016: 1). The first form is intentional secrecy, which arises when techniques are treated as a trade or state secret, or when data used in the process contains personal information which cannot be released due to privacy or data protection laws. This form of opacity can apply to systems based on rule-based logic and systems that derive rules from data using techniques such as machine learning. In the case of the Chinese Social Credit system, only limited information is made public. For example, the details of the cooperation between the central government and the private sector in the Sesame Credit system are not clear. While it is known that the system will use machine learning and behavioural analytics in calculating credit scores (Hvistendahl 2017), individuals have no means to know what information from their social network contacts was used or its precise impact on their scores (Zhong and Mozur 2018).

A government agency may also outsource the building of or licence the use of an automated system and will then be bound by contractual terms that prevent further disclosure (see Noto La Diega 2018: 11–16 for a discussion of intellectual property rights limiting the transparency of algorithms; in the context of outsourcing, there are additional considerations [beyond non-transparency] that may have legal implications that are beyond the scope of this paper). In the case of COMPAS, Northpointe Inc (now 'equivant' (Equivant, n.d.)), which built the tool, has not publicly disclosed its methods as it considers its algorithms trade secrets (this is noted in *Loomis* at 144). While the risk assessment questionnaire and thus the input variables have been leaked (see Angwin, et al. 2016), there is insufficient information available about methods and datasets used in training. While trade secret rights may legitimately be claimed by private corporations and enforced against contracting parties who agree to confidentiality provisions, there are important questions from the perspective of the rule of law about whether secret systems can be used in government decision-making in contexts that directly affect individuals. In at least some circumstances, rule of law considerations should favour open source software.

The second form of opacity identified by Burrell (Burrell 2016: 4), again potentially relevant to both kinds of automation considered here, is technical illiteracy. Here, the barrier to greater transparency is that even if information about a system is provided (such as a technique used in training a machine learning algorithm or the formal rules used in an expert system), most people will not be able to extract useful knowledge from this. A system may accordingly be transparent to a technical expert, while remaining opaque to the majority of the governed, including those affected by particular decisions. In contexts where the consequences of a decision are severe, the lack of access to expert advice in understanding and challenging a decision effectively reduces the extent to which the decision itself can be described as transparent and accountable in practice.

Whereas the second form of opacity involved limitations of expertise, the third form of opacity recognises human limitations in truly understanding or explaining the operation of complex systems. It relates specifically to machine learning and stems from the difficulty of understanding the action of a complex learning technique working on large volumes of data, even equipped with the relevant expertise (Burrell 2016: 10). Because humans reason differently to machines, they cannot always interpret the interactions among data and algorithms, even if suitably trained. This suggests that the transparency necessary for the rule of law may decrease over time as machine learning systems become more complex.

There are some possible and partial solutions to this challenge. Some researchers are working on 'explainable AI', also known as XAI, which can explain machine learning inferences in terms that can be understood by humans – for example, there is an XAI programme at the Defence Advanced Research Projects Agency in the US that aims to develop machine learning systems that 'will have the ability to explain their rationale, characterise their strengths and weaknesses, and convey an understanding of how they will behave in the future.' (Gunning, n.d.). It is also possible to disclose key information about a machine learning system, such as the datasets that were used in training the system and the technique that was used. Machine learning systems can also be made transparent as to aspects of their operation. However, some machine learning techniques cannot be rendered transparent, either generally, in particular circumstances or to particular people. The three challenges identified by Burrell, taken together, mean that it will rarely be possible for public transparency as to the full operation of a machine learning process, including understanding reasons for the decision, understanding limitations in the dataset used in training (including systemic biases in the raw or 'cleaned' data), and accessing the source code of the machine learning process.

An alternative solution lies in the fact that decision-making systems only need to be transparent and accountable as a whole, which does not necessarily imply visibility of the entire operation of automated components of that system. For example, in the Swedish student welfare example, a human remains accountable for the decision, even though the logic itself is first run through an automated system. Ultimately, the success of this strategy depends on its implementation. If the human can be called on to provide independent reasons for the decision, so that the automated system is essentially a first draft, then the decision-making system as a whole is as accountable and transparent as it would have been in the absence of decision-support software. If, however, the human can rely on the output of the system as all or part of their reason for decision, then accountability for the decision remains flawed despite assurances. This goes back to the question of the degree of automation in the decision-making process and the influence of outputs over the ultimate decision. A decision-making system as a whole can be made transparent and accountable by marginalising automated components (at the cost of efficiency and other benefits) and ensuring human accountability in the traditional way or by rendering transparent and accountable those automated components.

As is evident from above, the degree of transparency inherent in an automated system is a question of human design choices. Professionally, there has been a move to the development of standards, frameworks and guidelines to ensure that decision-making and decision-support systems are ethical (for example, the Artificial Intelligence, Ethics and Society (AIES) conference, the IEEE's (Institute of Electrical and Electronics Engineers) Global Initiative on Ethics of Autonomous and Intelligent Systems, the International Standards Organisation's JTC1/SC42 standardisation programme, and the 'Artificial Intelligence Roadmap and Ethics Framework' project at Australia's Data61). This suggests another potential way forward for the rule of law, writing it into the language of technical specifications for decision-making and decision-support systems deployed by government. However, it is achieved, the need for greater transparency about automated decision-making software is one of the most frequently emphasised issues by both technical and legal experts (Carlson 2017: 303; Diakopoulos 2016). Citron and Pasquale have advocated for a 'technological due process', which would enable individuals to challenge automated decisions made about them (Citron and Pasquale 2014: 20). In particular, they argue that people should have a 'right to inspect, correct, and dispute inaccurate data and to know the sources (furnishers) of the data' (Citron and Pasquale 2014: 20). Furthermore, they argue that an algorithm that generates a score from this data needs to be publicly accessible – rather than secret – so that each process can be inspected (Citron and Pasquale 2014: 22). However, where automated components of systems cannot be made transparent, accountability needs to be assured by humans. Ensuring a human is responsible for independently justifying the decision and that humans are involved in appeal processes, as is the case is Sweden, is one way in which accountability can be preserved. In these situations, it will be important to ensure that such humans feel able to act independently of the outputs of the automated system. Finally, it may be the case that, because of the inherent opacity, certain decision-making by the governments, such as criminal sentencing, should not be partially or fully delegated to software with whose logic cannot be rendered transparent and comprehensible to defendants and their representatives. This ensures that factors that ought to be irrelevant in the sentencing process remain so.

II. Predictability and Consistency

Automation can also improve the predictability and consistency of government decision-making. Unlike humans, computer systems cannot act with wanton disregard for the rules with which they are programmed. As such, the systems in our examples generally enhance the predictability and consistency of decision-making, even where they are otherwise problematic. The social credit system in China works as a tool of social control because people can predict the consequences of engaging in particular activities that the government wishes to discourage. Australia's robo-debt programme and Sweden's social welfare system perform the same calculation for everyone.

However, automation also poses many challenges for the rule of law principles of predictability and consistency. A first challenge arises when the rule that is applied in an automated decision-making process does not correspond with statutory or common law requirements. The inconsistency in such case is not in the application of the rule in different cases, but between the rule as formulated and the rule as applied in every case. An example of such inconsistency is robo-debt. The formula failed to produce the legally correct result for many people. There is some dispute about the rate of error and how these should be characterised; approximately 20 per cent of people who received debt notices succeeded in providing additional information that demonstrated that no debt was owed (Senate Community Affairs References Committee, Parliament of Australia 2017: para. 2.88). The problem was not that there was an error rate, which also exists for decisions made by humans, but that the processes in place to manage the error were insufficient. There was no human checking of the decision to issue a debt notice. The online portal in place to deal with challenges to debt notices was also hard to use (Senate Community Affairs References Committee, Parliament of Australia 2017: para. 2.110), with human alternatives inadequate to meet the demand (Senate Community Affairs References Committee, Parliament of Australia 2017: paras. 3.98, 3.106, 3.107 and 3.119). The rate of errors also potentially exceeded the capacity of institutions designed to deal with appeals. This compares unfavourably with the automated Swedish system, where humans edit and take responsibility for each decision, with usual processes in place for appeal (CSN decisions can be appealed to the National Board of Appeal for Student Aid [Överklagandenämnden för studiestöd, 'OKS'], see OKS' [n.d.] website). The result in Australia is a far higher likelihood that the law is being misapplied in ways that are unpredictable and inconsistent.

When moving from pre-programmed rules to rules derived from data (for example, through supervised machine learning), the predictability and consistency of decision-making may be reduced. This is not because the computers are acting contrary to programming but because, like human children who 'learn', it is hard to predict the outcomes in advance and behaviour will change as 'learning' continues. Consider what is known about the COMPAS tool (which is limited due to the transparency issues discussed above). Those developing the tool did not necessarily know in advance what criteria would be found to correlate, alone or in combination, with particular behaviours (such as reoffending). The rules allocating scores to individuals were derived, likely through a supervised machine learning process, from a large set of data (namely data recording historic re-offending behaviour). The behaviour of the system is thus difficult, and sometimes impossible, for a human to predict in advance.

Machine learning raises another issue for predictability and consistency because it continues to 'learn' from new data fed into it over time. If it gives a low score to an individual, thereby contributing to a decision to grant parole, but the individual reoffends, that will be fed back into the algorithm in order to improve its predictive accuracy over time. In that way, a new individual who was relevantly 'like' the earlier false negative will have a different outcome, namely a higher risk score and lower chance of parole. This means that the system treats identically situated individuals differently over time which, as discussed below, is a problem not only for consistency but also for equality before the law.

Moreover, the fact that COMPAS relies on variables that would not have been considered relevant by a human judge (such as whether their parents are divorced, Angwin (Angwin 2018) showing the question '[i]f you lived with both parents and they later separated, how old were you at the time?') creates an inconsistency between decisions made by judges under the law and decisions suggested by algorithmic inferencing. The lack of transparency about the data relied on in the machine learning process in a particular case, as well as opacity of the algorithm itself, makes it more difficult for judges to adjust their expectations of the tool to ensure appropriate use.

Automation according to human-crafted rules (derived from statute or judge-made law) can ensure that the correct decision is made every time and can overcome issues with human error and corruption. Rules derived from data raises more complex challenges, particularly in ensuring predictability and consistency with the 'law on the books'. Supervised machine learning and other iterative systems also struggle with consistency over time. However, these are matters that can be controlled from the perspective of predictability and consistency, in the first case through design of the system as well as independent testing and evaluation, and in the latter by moderating continual learning. Hence, a system that combines both types of automation by using explicit programming to automate the application of a fixed rule (originally derived from data, for example through machine learning) can ensure consistency over time. Automation can thus prove beneficial for predictability and consistency, although the evidence suggests that may not be achieved in practice.

III. Equality before the Law

Automation can enhance the principle of equality before the law by reducing arbitrariness in the application of law, removing bias and eliminating corruption. For instance, automation in China's social credit system could, through the use of cameras and face recognition technology, be deployed to ensure consequences apply to everyone who breaches certain rules (such as jaywalking or parking illegally) without exception. By contrast, without such automation, systems in place for minor infringements of this kind require a person to be 'caught', with the severity of the penalty often depending on the discretion and 'generosity' of the officials in question. Moreover, the enhanced consistency discussed above, particularly of the expert systems, such as the Swedish welfare or robo-debt, that give the same answer when presented with the same inputs, helps to ensure that similarly situated individuals are treated equally. These examples demonstrate how certain kinds of automation can remove the capacity for biased humans to discriminate against unfavoured groups. A properly designed system could do so by eliminating both conscious and unconscious bias by only applying criteria that are truly relevant to making the decision.

The benefits that automation can provide to equality before the law are however qualified by two main interrelated challenges. First, automation in government decision-making might compromise due process rights and the extent to which the laws apply to all equally; and second, it might undermine the extent to which people, irrespective of their status, have equal access to rights in the law.

Firstly, automation can compromise individual due process rights because it may undermine the ability of that person to influence or challenge a decision affecting them. For instance, in robo-debt, the right to review and rectify information was undermined because the letter sent to individuals by the government did not explain the importance of the income variation over the year for an accurate calculation of welfare entitlements (Kehl, Guo and Kessler 2017: 9). By contrast, the involvement of a case officer in the Swedish student welfare example enables explanation of the process and provides an immediate opportunity for those affected to rectify information or exercise a right of review. Moreover, the process is strengthened by a relatively straight-forward appeal procedure to challenge the CSN decisions. For example, a student who had been prevented from joining the job market due to their disability had the initial CSN decision reversed after examination by the Swedish National Board of Appeal for Student Aid (OKS 2014). Decisions by the Board which are deemed to be of fundamental importance and in the public interest are available on OKS' website (OKS n.d.).

Similarly, under Shanghai Municipality's SCS model, individuals have a right to know about the collection and use of their social credit information and can access and challenge the information contained in their credit reports (Shanghai Development and Reform Commission 2017: art 34; article 36 fur-ther states, '[w]here information subjects feel that there was error, omissions, and other such circumstances . . . they may submit an objection to the munici-pal Public Credit Information service center, credit service establishments, and so forth'). The municipal Public Credit Information services centre will deter-mine whether to rectify the information within five working days of receiving the objection materials. These rights were tested in practice by Chinese citizen Liu Hu, who was blacklisted on the SCS and unable to purchase a plane ticket after he accidentally transferred the payment for a fine to the wrong account (Mistreanu 2018). After a court learnt that Liu Hu had made an honest mis-take, the information on his social credit report was rectified.

In the case of machine learning, lack of transparency, which is common for the reasons discussed above, is the primary reason why due process rights may be compromised. In *Loomis*, the Supreme Court of Wisconsin held that due process was preserved because a COMPAS score was only one among many other factors to be considered by the judge. (It is likely significant that the judge told Loomis at the sentencing hearing that the COMPAS score was one of multiple factors that his Honour weighed when ruling out probation and assigning a six-year prison term: '[i]n terms of weighing the various factors, I'm ruling out probation because of the seriousness of the crime and because your history, your history on supervision, and the risk assessment tools that have been utilised, suggest that you're extremely high risk to re-offend.': *Loomis* at 755.) However, the extent to which an individual decision is based on the outputs of COMPAS is difficult to assess – the Court simply added that while COMPAS cannot be determinative in sentencing decision, the risk scores can be considered a *relevant* factor in several circumstances, including: '(1) diverting low-risk prison-bound offenders to a non-prison alternative'; (2) assessing the public safety risk an offender poses and whether they can be safely and effectively supervised in the community rather than in prison; and (3) to inform decisions about the terms and conditions of probation and supervision (see *Loomis* at 767–72 [Bradley, J.], 772 [Rogennsack, C. J., concurring], and 774 [Abrahamson, J., concurring]). The Court also added that the right to review and rectify was satisfied because the defendant had a degree of control over relevant input data: he could review the accuracy of public records and offer other data directly through completion of the COMPAS questionnaire (*Loomis* at 765). However, there is a difference between the ability to review and rectify separate pieces of information which are fed into the software and the ability to review or challenge how the score is calculated.

Further, a defendant lacks an effective opportunity to challenge the idea that factors outside of his control (for example, the fact that his parents divorced when he was three, asked in the COMPAS questionnaire) influence the length of his sentence. Indeed, it would be impossible for a defendant to even know whether such a factor did influence his score, as the lack of transparency prevents a defendant from knowing the extent to which any given data (in public records or the questionnaire) has proved to be material. A defendant is therefore only given an opportunity to argue against a score in the absence of any real understanding of the basis for its calculation. Similar due process concerns because of lack of transparency also arise in parts of the SCS system.

Further challenges to equality before the law and due process safeguards can arise in some cases of automated decision-making due to what could be described as a 'reversal' of the burden of proof or lowering of the 'evidence threshold'. (On the importance of the burden of proof and 'evidence threshold' in the context of social welfare in the US, see Kaplow 2012: 738. In Australia, see, for example, Gray 2012: 13. In the context of the European Court of Human Rights, see Ambrus 2014. On due process implications of shifting the burden of proof in the US legal context, see McCauliff 1982: 1293; Petrou 1984: 822.). For example, in the robo-debt case, debt notices were issued for money that was not in fact owed by some welfare recipients, and the fact-finding burden for debt that previously rested on the Department was reversed, arguably contrary to the enabling legislation (Hanks 2017). While debts issued under this automated decision-making process can be challenged, it has been argued that the government failed its responsibility to ensure that it has established the existence of the debt before initiating the claim (Carney 2018).

Finally, the use of automated decision-making by governments poses a further challenge to the idea that all individuals irrespective of their status must have equal access to rights in the law, and that in accessing these rights 'like cases be treated alike'. This includes the notion that governments should not treat individuals differently due to their demographic group or an immutable trait. (People have particularly strongly objected to courts systematically imposing more severe sentences on defendants who are poor or uneducated or from a certain demographic group: see Kleck 1981: 783; Wacquant 2001: 401; Hsieh and Pugh 1993: 182.) Automated decision-making systems, such as COMPAS and Sesame Credit, can undermine this principle because they may: a) explicitly incorporate and rely on various static factors and/or immutable characteristics such as socio-economic status, employment and education, postal codes, age or gender; or b) take such matters into account indirectly, for example by 'learning' the relevance of variables that correlate with these. For example, in *Loomis*, the defendant had argued that the judge's consideration of the COMPAS score also violated his constitutional rights because COMPAS software used 'gendered assessments' (*Loomis* at 757) and, in turn, undermined his right to an individual sentence.

The greatest challenge to equality before the law comes from the fact that automation can infer rules from historical patterns and correlations. Even when variables, such as race, are not used in the learning process, a machine can still produce racially or otherwise biased assessments (Angwin, et al. 2016). This unequal treatment before the law results because many other factors can correlate with race, including publicly available information such as, for example, Facebook 'likes' which are not excluded from the machine learning process (see especially Kosinski, Stillwell, and Graepel 2013: 5802; finding that easily accessible digital records such as Facebook 'likes' can be used to automatically and accurately predict highly sensitive personal information, including sexuality and ethnicity). Further, the data from a pre-sentencing questionnaire (from which the COMPAS tool draws inferences) records the number of times and the first time a defendant has been 'stopped' by police. Given historical profiling practices of law enforcement in the United States, status as an African-American is likely to correlate with higher numbers and earlier ages in response to this question (O'Neil 2016: 25–26; 'so if early "involvement" with the police signals recidivism, poor people and racial minorities look far riskier'). Racial differentiation is thus built into the data from which correlations are deduced and inferences are drawn.

Unlike the risk assessment tool COMPAS, decisions in Swedish student welfare management system are made solely on factors that are legally relevant. The pre-programmed nature of the system ensures that those factors play a role in the decision precisely in the circumstances in which they are relevant. Decisions are made consistently with the law, with students treated equally under that law. In Chinese SCS, diversity of implementation means that equality before the law is affected differently. For example, decisions in the Rongcheng City model of the SCS system are made solely with reference to clearly defined categories of behaviour which leads to either a point deduction or addition – there is no room to consider any other factors in the pre-programmed system. In contrast, however, the Sesame Credit system in the SCS relies on variables that are irrelevant from a rule of law perspective, such as the rankings of an individual's social network contacts, which could lead to differential treatment in effect based on social status, sex or ethnic origin (see Kosinski, Stillwell, and Graepel 2013).

As our examples demonstrate, in understanding the benefits and challenges of automating government decisions, it is crucial to consider both the context of the decision and the type of system deployed. A system with pre-programmed rules can ensure that decisions are made based on factors recognised as legally relevant and hence avoid or minimise the risk of corruption or favouritism by officials. However, procedural rights and opportunities to check and rectify data on which the decision relies are crucial, as is ensuring that the logic of the system accurately reflects the law. As our case studies demonstrate, the challenges posed by systems based on rules inferred from data are different. Here, the role of humans is limited to setting parameters, selecting data (possibly biased due to flawed human collection practices), and deciding which variables to use as a basis for analysis. Unless the humans involved in these processes who have a deep understanding of the legal context in which a decision is made, systems may fail in practice to meet the standard of equality before the law. The COMPAS system is an example of software that does not meet the needs of a fair criminal justice process – lack of transparency in a tool that relies on a large set of often legally irrelevant inputs prevents a defendant from having sufficient opportunity to participate in the court's findings on dangerousness, which is a crucial component of the ultimate decision.

This does not imply that machine learning techniques can never be used in government decision-making in ways that do comply with equality before the law. It can be used in the development of high-level policies, from traffic flow management to modelling interventions in the economy. Even at the level of decisions affecting individuals, machine learning is sometimes consistent with or even of benefit to equality before the law. For example, facial recognition, if designed to recognise the faces of diverse individuals accurately, could be used to identify individuals where that is an aspect of the system, and if programmed correctly may even overcome conscious and unconscious bias on the part of humans. While concerns about privacy and surveillance may counter its benefits, the use of machine learning in such a system can improve equality before the law by reducing arbitrariness.

D. Conclusion

Automation can improve government decision-making. The benefits include cost savings and greater speed, as well as a capacity to enhance the rule of law. Properly designed, implemented and supervised automation can help government decision-making better reflect the values of transparency and accountability, predictability and consistency, and equality before the law.

What is apparent, though, is that three of the four studies of automation considered in this chapter fail to live up to this ideal. In some cases, such as robo-debt, this failure results from poor design and implementation of the automated system. Indeed, one consistent theme is that human choices, and often error, at the design and implementation stage of automation can cause a system to fail to meet rule of law standards. A contrast is the Swedish student welfare system, which involves high levels of automation, but does not raise the same concerns. The Swedish model, which puts a strong emphasis on compliance with national legislation, officers' ethical codes, and publicity of the rules, demonstrates how a carefully designed system integrating automation with human responsibility can realise many benefits, while remaining sensitive to the values expressed in the rule of law.

It would nonetheless be a mistake to suggest that effective human design and implementation can ensure a particular automation technique will enhance or at least meet the minimum standards of the rule of law. It is clear from our study that even with active human engagement, some forms of technology raise intractable problems. This may be because the form of automation is inappropriate for its context. For example, machine learning offers many benefits, but some techniques or software products come at the price of transparency and accountability. This may be tolerable in particular circumstances, such as in the distribution of low-level welfare benefits (with appeal mechanisms), assisting with tasks such as optimising the traffic flow in a city, or conducting facial recognition for identification purposes. In such cases, testing and evaluation of accuracy and disparate impact may be sufficient from a rule of law perspective.

On the other hand, machine learning that cannot be rendered transparent and comprehensible may not be appropriate where it is used to make decisions that have greater effects upon the lives and liberties of individuals. It can also be inappropriate where a machine learning system may be influenced by criteria that ought not to be relevant, such as a person's race or even variables that have not traditionally been used to discriminate, such as the credit rating of one's friends. Such problems are exacerbated, as in the case of

COMPAS, when the system operates according to undisclosed, proprietary algorithms. These problems would be compounded if COMPAS were used not only to assist judges, but to replace them.

From the perspective of the rule of law, these problems may become more acute over time. As technology develops, and machine learning becomes more sophisticated, forms of automation used by governments may increasingly become intelligible only to those with the highest level of technical expertise. The result may be government decision-making operating according to systems that are so complex that they are beyond the understanding of those affected by such decisions. This raises further questions about the capacity of voters in democratic systems to evaluate and so hold to account their governments, including in respect of compliance with rule of law values. Ignorance in the face of extreme complexity may enable officials to transfer blame to automated systems, whether or not this is deserved. The result may be an increasing tension between automation and the rule of law, even where humans design such systems in ways that seek to respect such values.

Ultimately, humans must evaluate each decision-making process and consider what forms of automation are useful, appropriate and consistent with the rule of law. The design, implementation and evaluation of any automated components, as well as the entire decision-making process including human elements, should be consistent with such values. It remains though to be seen whether these values can be fully integrated into automated decision-making and decision-support systems used by governments. Converting rule of law values into design specifications that can be understood by system designers, and enforced through regulation, professional standards, contracts, courts or other mechanisms, represents a formidable technical and legal challenge. This chapter highlights a number of common themes in this respect, including the need for an awareness of the link between tools and design, transparency and accountability, the need to consider consistency and predictability not only over time but also as between automated and human systems, the importance of embedding procedural due process rights, and the tension between deriving rules from historic data and equality before the law. Resolving these issues in the automation of government decisions will be critical for any nation that claims to uphold the basic ideals of the rule of law.

Bibliography

Administrative Procedure Act, Pub L 79–404, 60 Stat 237, 5 USC §§ 551–559.
Ambrus, M. (2014), 'The European court of human rights and standards of proof: an evidential approach toward the margin of appreciation', in Gruszczynski, L. and W. Werner, (eds.), *Deference in international courts and tribunals: standard of review and margin of appreciation*, Oxford: Oxford University Press.

Angwin, J. (2018), 'Sample-COMPAS-Risk-Assessment-COMPAS-"CORE"', available at <https://www.documentcloud.org/documents/2702103-Sample-Risk-Assessment-COMPAS-CORE.html> (last accessed 16 August 2018).

Angwin, J., J. Larson, S. Mattu and L. Kirchner (2016), 'Machine bias', *ProPublica*, 23 May 2016, available at <https://www.propublica.org/article/machine-bias-risk-assessments-in-criminal-sentencing> (last accessed 16 August 2018).

Bingham, T. H. (2007), 'The rule of law', *CLJ* 66, p. 67.

Burrell, J. (2016), 'How the machine "thinks": understanding opacity in machine learning algorithms', Big Data & Society 3: 1, p. 1.

Carlson, A. M. (2017), 'The need for transparency in the age of predictive sentencing algorithms', *Iowa Law Review*, 103, p. 303.

Carney, T. (2018), 'The new digital future for welfare: debts without legal proofs or moral authority?', *UNSW Law Journal Forum*, May 2018, available at <http://www.unswlawjournal.unsw.edu.au/wp-content/uploads/2018/03/006-Carney.pdf> (last accessed 16 August 2018>.

CCJ/COSCA Criminal Justice Committee (2011), 'In support of the guiding principles on using risk and needs assessment information in the sentencing process', 3 August 2011, available at <http://ccj.ncsc.org/~/media/Microsites/Files/CCJ/Resolutions/08032011-Support-Guiding-Principles-Using-Risk-Needs-Assessment-Information-Sentencing-Process.ashx> (last accessed 15 August 2018).

Citron, D. K. and F. Pasquale (2014), 'The scored society: due process for automated predictions', *Washington University Law Review* 90, p. 1.

Commonwealth Ombudsman (2017), 'Centrelink's automated debt raising and recovery system: a report about the department of human services' online compliance intervention system for debt raising and recovery', Investigation Report, available at <https://www.ombudsman.gov.au/data/assets/pdf_file/0022/43528/Report-Centrelinks-automated-debt-raising-and-recovery-system-April-2017.pdf> (last accessed 27 November 2018).

Creemers, R. (2018), 'China's social credit system: an evolving practice of control', available at <https://papers.ssrn.com/sol3/papers.cfm?abstract_id=3175792> (last accessed 16 August 2018).

CSN n.d., available at <https://www.csn.se/languages/english.html> (last accessed 6 November 2018).

Data Matching Program (Assistance and Tax) Act 1990 (Cth).

Diakopoulos, N. (2016), 'We need to know the algorithms the government uses to make important decisions about us', *The Conversation*, 24 May 2016, available at <http://theconversation.com/we-need-to-know-the-algorithms-the-government-uses-to-make-important-decisions-about-us-57869> (last accessed 16 August 2018).

Equivant n.d., 'Software for Justice', available at <http://www.equivant.com/> (last accessed 10 September 2018).

Gowder, P. (2016), *The rule of law in the real world*, Cambridge: Cambridge University Press. Gray, A. (2012), 'Constitutionally protecting the presumption of innocence', *University of Tasmania Law Review*, 31: 1, p. 13.

Gunning, D. n.d., 'Explainable artificial intelligence (XAI)', Defense Advanced Research Projects Agency Project Information, available at <https://www.darpa.mil/program/explainable-artificial-intelligence> (last accessed 16 August 2018).

Hanks, P. (2017), 'Administrative law and welfare rights: a 40-year story from *Green v Daniels* to "robot debt recovery"', *AIAL Forum*, 89, p. 1.

Hsieh, C. and M. D. Pugh (1993), 'Poverty, income inequality, and violent crime: a meta-analysis of recent aggregate data studies', *Criminal Justice Review*, 18, p. 182.

Hvistendahl, M. (2017), 'Inside China's vast new experiment in social ranking', *Wired*, 14 December 2017, available at <https://www.wired.com/story/age-of-social-credit/> (last accessed 10 September 2018).

International Congress of Jurists (1959), 'The rule of law in a free society', Report of the International Commission of Jurists, New Delhi.

Junwei, T. (2017), 荣成：建信用体系 创" 示范城市 [Rongcheng: the making of a demonstration city for the social credit system], 新 华 社 [Xinhua News Agency], 13 July 2017, available at <http://xinhua-rss.zhongguowangshi.com/13701/6003014383535113117/2049163.html> (last accessed 10 September 2018).

Kaplow, L. (2012), 'Burden of proof', *Yale Law Journal*, 121, p. 738.

Kehl, D. L., P. Guo and S. A. Kessler, (2017), 'Algorithms in the criminal justice system: assessing the use of risk assessments in sentencing', *Berkman Klein Center for Internet & Society, Harvard Law School*, available at <http://nrs.harvard.edu/urn-3:HUL.InstRepos:33746041> (last accessed 16 August 2018).

Kennedy, R. (2017), 'Algorithms and the rule of law', *Legal Information Management*, 17, p. 170.

Kleck, G. (1981), 'Racial discrimination in criminal sentencing: a critical evaluation of the evidence with additional evidence on the death penalty', *American Sociological Review*, 46, p. 783.

Kosinski, M., D. Stillwell and T. Graepel (2013), 'Private traits and attributes are predictable from digital records of human behaviour', *Proceedings of the National Academy of Sciences of the United States of America*, 110, p. 5802.

Launchbury, J. (2017), 'A DARPA perspective on artificial intelligence', DAPRAtv, YouTube, available at <https://www.youtube.com/watch?v=-O01G3tSYpU> (last accessed 20 August 2018).

Mathiesen, T. (1998), 'Selective incapacitation revisited', *Law and Human Behaviour*, 22, 455.

McCauliff, C. M. A. (1982), 'Burdens of proof: degrees of belief, quanta of evidence, or constitutional guarantees', *Vanderbilt Law Review*, 35, p. 1293.

Mikhaylov, S. J., M. Esteve and A. Campion (2018), 'Artificial intelligence for the public sector: opportunities and challenges of cross-sector collaboration', *Philosophical Transactions of the Royal Society A*, 376: 2128, available at <https://doi.org/10.1098/rsta.2017.0357> (last accessed 10 September 2018).

Mistreanu, S. (2018), 'Life inside china's social credit laboratory', *Foreign Policy* (online), 3 April 2018, available at <https://foreignpolicy.com/2018/04/03/life-inside-chinas-social-credit-laboratory/> (last accessed 10 September 2018).

Nisbett, R. E. and T. D. Wilson (1977), 'Telling more than we can know: verbal reports on mental processes', *Psychological Review*, 84, p. 231.

Note (1982), 'Selective incapacitation: reducing crime through predictions of recidivism', *Harvard Law Review*, 96, p. 511.

Noto La Diega, G. (2018), 'Against the dehumanisation of decision-making: algorithmic decisions at the crossroads of intellectual property, Data Protection and Freedom of Information', *JIPITEC* 9, p. 3.

O'Neil, C. (2016), *Weapons of math destruction: how big data increases inequality and threatens democracy*, New York: Broadway Books.

OKS (2014), 'Dnr: 2014-03172', 13 October 2014, available at <https://oks.se/wp-content/uploads/2016/03/2014-03172.pdf> (last accessed 6 November 2018).

OKS n.d., 'Avgöranden (rulings)', available at <https://oks.se/avgoranden/> (last accessed 6 November 2018).

Perry, M. (2017), 'iDecide: administrative decision-making in the digital world', 91 *Australian Law Journal*, 91, p. 29.

Petrou, P. (1984), 'Due process implications of shifting the burden of proof in forfeiture proceedings arising out of illegal drug transactions', *Duke Law Journal* 822.

Schuerman J. R., E. Mullen, M. Stagner and P. Johnson (1989), 'First generation expert systems in social welfare', *Computers in Human Services*, 4, 111.

Senate Community Affairs References Committee (2017), 'Design, scope, cost-benefit analysis, contracts awarded and implementation associated with the better management of the social welfare system initiative', Parliament of Australia.

Shanghai Development and Reform Commission (2017), '上海市社会信用条例 [Shanghai social credit regulations]', 29 June 2017, available at <http://www.shdrc.gov.cn/gk/xxgkml/zcwj/zgjjl/27789.htm> (last accessed 10 September 2018).

State Council (2014), 'Planning outline for the construction of a social credit system (2014–2020)', 14 June 2014, in Creemers, R. (ed.) (2015), *China Copyright and Media*, 25 April, available at <https://chinacopyrightandmedia.wordpress.com/2014/06/14/planning-outline-for-the-construction-of-a-social-credit-system-2014-2020/> (last accessed 16 August 2018).

'State of Wisconsin v. Loomis' (2016), 881 N.W.2d 749.

Susskind, R. E. (1987), *Expert systems in law: a jurisprudential inquiry*, Oxford: Clarendon Press.

Sutcliffe, J. (1989), 'Welfare benefits adviser: a local government expert system application', *Computer Law & Security Review*, 4: 6, p. 22.

Swedish Tax Agency (2016), 'Taxes in Sweden: an English summary of tax statistical yearbook of Sweden', available at <https://www.skatteverket.se/download/18.361dc8c15312eff6fd1f7cd/1467206001885/taxes-in-sweden-skv104-utgava16.pdf> (last accessed 10 September 2018).

Tamanaha, B. Z. (2004), *On the rule of law: history, politics, theory*, Cambridge: Cambridge University Press.

Tyree, A. (1989), *Expert systems in law*, Sydney: Prentice Hall.

Wacquant, L. (2001), 'The penalisation of poverty and the rise of neo-liberalism', *European Journal on Criminal Policy and Research*, 9, p. 401.

Wihlborg, E., H. Larsson and K. Hedström (2016), '"The computer says no!" A case study on automated decision-making in public authorities', 49th Hawaii International Conference on System Sciences.

Zhong, R. and P. Mozur (2018), 'Tech giants feel the squeeze as Xi Jinping tightens his grip', *New York Times* (online), 2 May 2018, available at <https://www.nytimes.com/2018/05/02/technology/china-xi-jinping-technology-innovation.html> (last accessed 10 September 2018).

7

Sustainable AI Development (SAID):
On the Road to More Access to Justice

Christian Djeffal

A. Introduction

Artificial intelligence (AI) impacts society and our lives. Yet, there are very different ways to frame it. AI poses ethical, political, societal, organisational and economic questions. Scholars, politicians and other observers often use one of the frames to support or criticise AI. Fewer observers engage in the discussion what the right frame should be and why we choose a specific frame. Therefore, this chapter looks into the potential of sustainable development as a frame for AI (Djeffal 2019b). Sustainable development is a framework that has not yet been in the centre of discussions surrounding AI, despite the fact that there is a huge potential to consider the transformative potential of digitisation and calls for a transformation for a sustainable future.

B. Sustainable AI Development

I. Artificial Intelligence

Artificial intelligence is a research question and area that is today dealt with by a whole subdiscipline of computer science. It aims to create intelligent systems, i.e. those which, according to Klaus Mainzer's working definition, can 'solve problems efficiently on their own'(Mainzer 2019: 3). Even the inventors of the computer had systems in mind that were supposed to perform intelligent actions; one of their first projects could be described as a big data project for predicting the weather (Dyson 2014). The term artificial intelligence itself was coined by a group of computer scientists in a proposal to the Rockefeller Foundation to fund a seminar. They described their central research concern as follows:

'We propose that a 2-month, 10-man study of artificial intelligence be carried out during the summer of 1956 at Dartmouth College in Hanover, New Hampshire. The study is to proceed on the basis of the conjecture that every aspect of learning or any other feature of intelligence can in principle be so precisely described that a machine can be made to simulate it. An attempt will be made to find how to make machines use language, form abstractions and concepts, solve kinds of problems now reserved for humans, and improve themselves. We think that a significant advance can be made in one or more of these problems if a carefully selected group of scientists work on it together for a summer.' (McCarthy, et al. 1955)

In its origins, the concept of artificial intelligence was thus broad and reflected the intention to replace human intelligence with machines. Alan Turing foresaw that such projects would be criticised in his epochal essay 'Computing Machinery and Intelligence' (Turing 1950). In this essay, he dealt with the question of whether machines can think. His hypothesis was that humans will no longer be able to distinguish between human and machine intelligence after a certain point in time and that the question will thus lose relevance. So far, this has not happened; instead, two camps have formed. Some have pursued the so-called 'strong AI thesis', according to which AI can and will match and surpass human intelligence, while others, supporters of the 'weak AI thesis', have denied this and referred to the capacity of machines to solve certain problems rationally. This shows the fundamental disagreement in computer science about the goals and possibilities of this branch of research.

However, if the goals of the technologies are controversial, their development and eventual areas of application are likewise not predetermined. This is reflected in the dispute on whether AI should serve to automate human tasks or augment humans. This was already discussed in the early years of the AI debate (Grudin 2017: 99). One of the technologies that has brought artificial intelligence back on the map are so-called deep neuronal networks. These are adaptable non-linear mathematical models that are able to 'learn'. Since 2011, there have been several improvements that have led to an increasing hype around artificial intelligence.

II. The Impact of a General-purpose Technology

Like other technologies, one could describe AI as 'multistable'. This means that the scope and meaning of a technology in a society is only developed over time and in the process of application and that these are not defined by the technology itself (Ihde 2012). What's more, AI is a general-purpose technology (Djeffal 2019a). By its nature, its purposes and its societal and individual consequences are contingent and dependent on its use.

Since AI technologies are flexible per se, they open up a new dimension of technical possibilities for action and reaction. It is not for nothing that the system is highlighted as an 'agent' from a computer science point of view (Poole and Mackworth 2011). As mentioned above, you could say that AI gives computers eyes, ears, arms and legs. Conversely, you could also say that cameras, microphones, loudspeakers and machines receive a brain.

If seeking to contrast AI with other fundamental innovations, one might meaningfully compare it with the 'invention' of iron. Iron is not a tool itself, but it is the basis for many different tools. Humans can forge swords or ploughshares from it. Iron also forms the basis for other technologies, be it the letterpress or steam engines. It is precisely for this reason that it is very difficult to speak in a general manner of the opportunities and risks of artificial intelligence. For what is seen as an opportunity and what as a risk often depends on how AI is specifically developed and used.

C. Sustainable Development as a Framework for AI

I. The Meaning of Sustainable Development

The notion of sustainable development was famously defined by the World Commission on Environment and Development (Brundtland Commission) as 'development that meets the needs of the present without compromising the ability of future generations to meet their own needs' (World Commission on Environment and Development 1987: 43). This is a vague but all-encompassing concept that forms the basis of a worldwide political process of setting goals and implementing them. Sustainable development has come to be a frame for agreeing on good policies in the international sphere. It is not in itself a goal but a meta-principle balancing several considerations in a specific way (Lowe 2001: 31). The concept of sustainable development is today universally referred to in international, national and local relations. The clearest expressions of that trend are the sustainable development goals of the United Nations. The Agenda 2030 describes seventeen goals the international community should work towards. The Agenda 2030 describes 169 targets in order to ensure the implementation of the goals.

The concept of sustainable development was rooted in specific discourses in the 1970s and then proliferated substantially after that (Fukuda-Parr 2018). The discourse on sustainability was rooted in rising concerns about impacts on the environment. Environmental protection was one major driving factor. This was due to the fact that the consequences of environmental harm became increasingly evident. Furthermore, it also became clear that certain natural resources were limited and potentially running out. Another important concern was the desire of less developed parts of the world to meet the needs of their populations and give them a good life. Decolonised states in particular called for justice and their right to development. They felt disadvantaged. Environmental and development concerns both raised questions of justice and equity in different temporal regards. First, sustainable development relates to intragenerational justice, which means justice considerations between different people within one generation. Second, intergenerational justice concerns the justice between generations. This applies particularly to resources, but also to the behaviour of previous generations, particularly in the colonial context.

In a succession of activities at the United Nations, sustainable development became a major concept encompassing aspects and goals. Today, the goals laid down in the 2030 Agenda for Sustainable Development apply to different aspects transcending the categories of development and environment. The concerns included in the concept of sustainable development are represented by three pillars, namely the economic, the social and the environmental pillar. By tracing the different resolutions and declarations, the proliferation of the concept of sustainable development can be clearly mapped and we can see how it addressed an ever-increasing number of issues such as gender equality and access to justice. Sustainable Development Goal (SDG) 16 aims to 'promote peaceful and inclusive societies for sustainable development, provide access to justice for all and build effective, accountable and inclusive institutions at all levels'. While commentators have criticised this aspect of sustainable development and stressed its contingency, sustainable development has become a governance mechanism encompassing the whole world in a comparable manner. While the concept has no ascertainable fixed core, its content is fixed through a deliberative process.

This feature of being contingent but ascertainable could also be described as a major advantage. It conveys the understanding of a general process of balancing different considerations in a general conflict between maintaining and changing a status, between development and sustainability, between stasis and evolution. While different considerations might be relevant over a period of time, the principle of sustainable development can be a concept that offers room for all considerations if they are relevant for the general tension between sustainability and development.

II. The Case for SAID as an AI Framework

SAID is a very apt framework for designing, assessing and governing AI. The potential of the relation between artificial intelligence and sustainable development is sometimes touched upon but has not yet been fully explored.

Figure 7.1   Principles of digital development, derived from https://digital principles.org/principles/

In reflections upon AI, it is often stated that AI ought to be in compliance with human rights and ethical considerations. Commentators and policy makers stressed that stakeholders can use artificial intelligence to attain SDGs (United Nations Development Group 2017; Riegner 2016: 22; IEEE 2018). It is emphasised less frequently that AI applications can be used to further human rights and ethical principles (Djeffal 2018: 18). Development agencies have drawn up the 'Principles for Digital Development' in order to guide their development efforts.

The interesting aspect of these principles is that they directly relate to the assessment of technical artefacts. They provide for principles and criteria in order to make research and development sustainable (Principles for Digital Development 2017).

The same holds true for another framework published by the German Advisory Council on Global Change (WGBU – German Advisory Council on Global Change 2019). The report generally recommends using the digital transformation for a transformation towards sustainability. The report outlines many ways in which digital technologies can be used to achieve the goals of sustainability. It also outlines general requirements for digital technologies that also apply to AI.

Linking sustainable development goals to AI development has several advantages. There seems to be a huge potential to understand and guide the process of research and development (R&D) of AI through the lens of sustainable development. The term development is part of sustainable development and of R&D. Furthermore, the underlying conflict addressed by the notion of sustainable development is also present in processes of introducing AI applications. Development is done in order to meet certain needs, but from a perspective of sustainability there ought to be limits due to a holistic view of other needs, be it of peers or of future generations. Most importantly, in the process of development, certain needs are in the foreground and sustainable solutions bring other less visible needs to the forefront. This general way of thinking (*Denkbewegung*) translates very well to the development of AI applications. They are often developed to fulfil certain tasks, whereas their unintended consequences and long-term impacts are not taken into consideration. This general fit might have its root causes in the fact that sustainable development was born out of the industrial revolution and is, therefore, translatable to what is today called the digital revolution.

Different considerations can play a part in this process of balancing the needs. While the 2030 Agenda for Sustainable Development addresses the digital divide in particular, other considerations such as data protection or cybersecurity could also be included in the framework of the SDGs. Its history shows the adaptability of the principle of sustainable development. The knowledge and the questions that have been so far produced in the discourse around AI could very well also help to update the SDGs with new considerations and needs that will have importance for future generations.

One major advantage of using SAID as a framework is the inclusiveness of SD. The generic nature of sustainable development also leads to an all-encompassing design of the principle. The needs considered are not limited to certain categories such as human rights, societal interests or group rights. Sustainable development can account for all kinds of needs. This allows a more complete picture than would, for example, be garnered by focusing on human rights. Sustainable development is not a specific goal in itself, but a mission for continued awareness of the social, political and environmental consequences of our actions (Mulder, et al. 2011: 242). Another advantage is that environmental concerns have a self-standing value irrespective of whether they have immediate value to human beings. Sustainable development goals also set out positive goals that promise a better life on earth. Instead of framing questions in negative terms, such as discrimination or arbitrariness, sustainable development goals envisage positive ideals that should either not be impaired or furthered, such as equality and access to justice. These objectives are formulated in a manner that makes it possible to support them by specific measures and make progress visible by indicators. This verifiable and specific approach is very apt especially when it comes to processes of design. The specificity of the discourse and the general visions underlying them could help bridging communication gaps especially in multidisciplinary groups engaged in developing AI.

Sustainable development is always thought of in terms of the dimension of governance. This is expressed in the 17th SDG, addressing strengthening the means of implementation and setting out specific targets concerning governance. Reports and declarations on AI have seldom touched upon governance issues and even more rarely on international governance mechanisms.

SDG 17 could have a very important impact here. This is also due to the fact that the governance of AI could be situated in existing fora that have an inclusive setting, allowing all states, along with different stakeholders, to enter the discussion. The governance mechanisms are well established and are constantly developed. They are forming on the international as well as on the national plane. This leads to a final decisive advantage of sustainable development as a framework for AI. SDGs are goals that are widely accepted in the international community. In many instances, they already provide guidance for AI development processes; in other instances, the development of the SDGs is necessary but also possible. It is very important to discuss the ethics of AI. Yet, an international agreement on the right international ethical standards on AI at the green table might be a long-lasting endeavour. In contrast, it is much easier to draw on work that has already been done in previous years and that resulted in actionable goals and an agenda that gives clearer guidance.

III. Layers of SAID

Commentators often denote sustainable development as a multi-dimensional concept. In order to arrive at a SAID framework, it will be important to address all applicable dimensions and implement the lessons the sustainable development process has learnt so far. Yet learning from AI discourses should also feed into the future of SDGs. Considering that AI-systems gain an ever-increasing importance, the future development of those systems might have a big impact on sustainable development. This would also serve as an active attempt to update the discussion on sustainable development, which dates from the industrial age, to the digital age, which is where we are heading. As a first attempt to map these dimensions, I propose three layers that should be addressed by SAID: the technology layer, the social layer and the governance layer.

a. Technology Layer

The technology layer translates issues of sustainable development to the level of specific applications. The goal here is to build 'sustainable technologies' (Mulder, et al. 2011). In line with this, technological design choices ought to be identified, highlighted and analysed. The important aspect is to link the design of technology to the goals pursued by SD. In that regard, SDGs can play different roles: the first role is to use technology for the realisation of the SDGs. In the case of AI, it would be to use different AI technologies in order to achieve sustainable development goals. The technology layer guides design choices. At the moment, there are several initiatives looking at what good design choices could mean. Examples pertaining to the technical layer relate to choices such as datasets and the architecture and design of algorithms. One issue is, for example, whether datasets to train algorithms are representative of all the people who will use the system later. If a speech recognition system is trained only with people with one particular accent, it will not understand people who speak differently. The choice of specific algorithms can make a big difference concerning their functionality but also their transparency. With deep neural networks with many layers, for example, the decision structures become increasingly blurred and harder to understand. This can have a big impact on access to justice, especially when the basis of a decision is blurred. These design choices have an effect on how the system operates and how it can be understood.

b. Social Layer

The social layer looks at the consequences of the use of AI systems in the social sphere. The focus of the sustainability analysis here looks at the impacts of the systems on individuals, groups and society as a whole. The dual effect of sustainable development also plays out in this field. On the one hand, AI can be used as a tool to achieve the goals set out in Agenda 2030. On the other hand, it should not be used to impair or contradict the SDGs. Regarding access to justice, there are applications facilitating citizens to make specific claims. Yet, microtargeting, for example, could aim at barring access to justice in certain situations. The social layer looks at the socio-technical reality of an AI system. This goes beyond a mere analysis of how the technology works. Especially the way in which AI systems are embedded in processes and the way their outputs are recognised socially are also looked into in this layer of analysis. In the case of algorithmic decision systems, one question would be whether there is a person able to exercise meaningful oversight over the system. Another question would be at which stage of a decision human oversight is possible or necessary. Therefore, the social layer looks at the design choices beyond technology. There are plenty of possibilities for how to embed technology socially. SAID is based on a focus and reflection process on how technology is embedded in real life.

c. Governance Layer

The governance layer looks at all the ways of influencing systems of artificial intelligence irrespective of the level (national, international, transnational). Together with sustainable development goals, a specific governance structure was drawn up in order to realise the goals. As previously mentioned, SDG 17 addresses this very issue as it looks at and questions governance and implementation. In the discourse on artificial intelligence, governance issues are raised on the national level (Tutt 2017) as well as on the international level (Gasser, et al. 2018). The governance level of SAID might complement the previous stocktaking and governance models in that it addresses specific governance challenges and problems more clearly. Naturally, it sees governance from a multi-level perspective, allowing for differences on the ground while stressing comparability between the different layers of governance.

d. Socio-technical Comparison

Together, the three layers give an account of what good design of artificial intelligence could mean. They are not to be perceived as existing in clinical isolation from each other but as different nodes in an active interaction. There is constant feedback and adjustment in order to improve design choices, social-technical settings and the right governance. If one looks at the layers as a choice architecture, one could compare it to a mixing console with three general areas and many ways to adjust the sound. There might be different possibilities to arrive at a good mix. Nevertheless, a requirement for a good mix is to understand the different layers and the attached choices.

Considering the many ways to achieve or not to achieve certain goals, a mere impact assessment will not be enough. If one approaches the implementation of an AI system from a perspective of equity, the impact assessment can only be made if taking into account also the current state of affairs. The proposal made here is to make a socio-technical comparison that not only focuses on positive and negative impacts, but also assesses the current situation (Djeffal 2018: 14). An analytical framework comprising different layers allows for socio-technical comparisons.

D. Use Cases Concerning Access to Justice

In the following, I will present two cases in which automated systems were developed over time and impacted on access to justice in different ways. The framework of sustainable development suggests looking at cases not only as being one point in time but also at their changes over time.

I. The Chatbot DoNotPay

In 2015 Londoner Joshua Browder programmed a chatbot *DoNotPay*. The idea was sparked when Browder received thirty unjustified parking tickets at the age of eighteen. He wondered how he could help people who wanted to take action against a parking ticket. He then successfully programmed a chatbot which asked people simple questions in order to obtain the knowledge necessary for making their case.

a. Description

After an automated conversation, the bot advises people on the right course of action and potentially even returns a letter that they can use to send to their local authorities. In order to understand the administrative process and the relevant criteria, Browder filed several freedom of information requests. He programmed two versions for London and New York, which became a huge success. According to Tech Insider, 3,000 people used the service, 250,000 parking tickets were appealed, with 160,000 successful appeals, saving the appellants a combined $ 4 million.

The chatbot was based on a decision tree and an automated document that resulted in a letter at the end of the procedure. With this relatively simple technical setup and sufficient background knowledge, Browder was able to help many people. The first development entailed a proliferation of the service. The chatbot was subsequently rolled out to all states of the US in 2017. What is even more remarkable is the fact that RoboLawyer was subsequently extended to ever more and more issue areas. With the chatbot having so much success, people contacted Browder to make him aware of other problems where a chatbot could be needed. This is when he discovered the problem of evictions and looming homelessness.

Collaborating with lawyers and several non-profit organisations, he went on to extend his chatbot to cover this topic as well. This new area revealed the limitations of such automation projects: while there was an enforceable right to housing in the UK, the situation in the US varied from one city to another. After the so-called Equifax scandal, in which sensitive data about many US citizens were stolen, a chatbot was created to help citizens to claim damages up to $25,000. Other chatbots were created to provide basic information and advice to asylum seekers, to help pursue charges because of unexplained bank charges or disputes between landlords and tenants. After further calls for help, Browder reconsidered his model of operation and implemented several changes. In order to assist people effectively, he aimed to include new issue areas. Therefore, he offered his technology as an infrastructure for people to develop their own chatbots. With this method, the RoboLawyer managed to extend to about 1,000 functions. They include the following:

- Sue anyone in small claims court for up to $25,000 without the help of a lawyer.
- Fight unfair bank, credit card and overdraft fees.
- Overturn your parking tickets.
- Claim hidden government and class action settlement money.
- Earn refunds from Uber and Lyft when a driver takes a wrong turn.

- Fix errors on your credit report.
- Save money on over 20,000 prescription and over the counter drugs.
- Scan your McDonalds, Jack In The Box, KFC and Carl's Junior receipts for free fast food.
- Find a California DMV Appointment in days rather than months.
- Apply for a United States B2 Tourist Visa extension or Family Based Green Card.
- Dispute fraudulent or low-quality transactions with your bank.
- Protect your privacy on Facebook, Twitter and Instagram. Sue big tech companies for every data breach.
- Make money on your airline and hotel bookings with price protection.
- Track your packages and earn refunds (or free Amazon Prime) for late package deliveries.

This decision had other impacts on the design of the chatbot. First, the chatbot was turned into a mobile app. After the increase of functions, the problem for users was to find the right chatbot. After gaining further funding for his project, Browder started to employ search machine technologies in order to allow finding the right service for people. Furthermore, the modes of interaction are to be improved through AI technologies. He is currently working on those functions after receiving substantial funds from investors and access to commercial AI technology.

b. Takeaways

This is a clear example of the employment of automation and AI technologies in order to further access to justice. DoNotPay aimed explicitly at helping people to claim their rights that would in other circumstances not be pursued by making it easier to produce legal documents or to have very easy guidance on how to act before a court. It is a good example of how technology can further an SDG. Another important aspect is how scaling such a technology is dependent on innovations and information on different levels. In the first phase, Browder understood that a problem he faced himself would be relevant to others. Later, he remained open for active input from people. They outlined their problems to him, and he took them up by including new functions. In this phase he worked together with legal experts, public administrations and others. In a third phase, he has provided others with technical building blocks to create their own chatbots. In a way, DoNotPay has almost become a technology platform for others.

If one were to look for the decisive innovation, many things had to do with social awareness and taking people's needs seriously. The underlying technology of the chatbot is comparatively simple. It was only in the later stages of the project that more refined AI technologies played a larger role. On the technical layer, it is interesting to see that the bot is able to have an impact without, at least for now, using state of the art machine learning technologies. Despite the fact that everything was based on rule-based systems, Browder managed to scale the system. As regarding the social layer, the major point here is that he managed to be responsive to new problems and questions from the public. The RoboLawyer extended to areas in which it could have the greatest impacts. Looking at the perspective of a governance layer, it is significant how Browder managed to collaborate with public administration and with lawyers supporting his idea. It is a good example of civic technology, which is technology that is created by civil society to empower individuals in relation to civil society.

II. The Centrelink Issue

a. Description

Australia may be one of the countries which is most advanced when it comes to digitisation. Government and public administrations have been integral to this process. Notably, Australia managed to deal with a problematic application of digital administration in an open and transparent manner.

This concerned the so-called 'online compliance intervention' (OCI). The online compliance intervention consisted in further automating the processes of the Australian Tax Office (ATO) and taking civil servants out of the loop also to save costs (Belot 2017). Whereas previously only 20,000 cases a year were started, the projection was that automation would produce 783,000 interventions. It was aimed at raising and collecting debts, but ultimately resulted in a political scandal. An algorithm matched various tax-relevant data from two authorities. In order to achieve the right results, it used, among other things, fuzzy logic and techniques of data cleansing. The system found alleged contradictions between different data. Previously, those contradictions were taken up by civil servants dealing with cases. In a process of further automation, humans were taken out of the loop. After the changes, the system notified citizens automatically via SMS or letter about the alleged contradictions and asked them to make corrections in an online portal. If the citizens did not object, a payment notice was issued and the recipients had to object to it (Commonwealth Ombudsman 2017). This notice also contained a 10 per cent recovery fee as provided for by Australian law. The algorithm looked for mismatches in the data. But the data is very error prone, mismatches can happen easily. The full automation meant that there were no civil servants involved in order to look for obvious or hidden errors before citizens were contacted. This, however, also limited the number of cases that could be dealt with. While the hope was to deal with more cases using less resources, there were many challenges to the system on different levels and a rising need for information. Because it was no longer possible to answer citizens' enquiries, temporary workers were hired and telephone contact with citizens was outsourced to a private call centre (Knaus 2017). People from weaker societal strata were particularly negatively affected as well as especially vulnerable or disadvantaged population groups, who could not defend themselves against the decision. The actual number of wrongfully issued notifications remains controversial.

b. Takeaways

Due to the open, thorough and transparent way Australian authorities dealt with the issue, it is possible to learn many things about how the implementation of AI systems relates to access to justice on different levels.

On the governance level, it is a good example of a governance system that has enough watchdogs in place that can require improvements of the system and actually have done so. Firstly, Australian and international media engaged in the issue and highlighted problems continuously (Knaus 2016a; Martin 2017; McIlroy 2017; Medhora 2017; Towell 2017; Whyte). There were also watchdogs within the government that made suggestions to improve or to halt the system. One was the Commonwealth Ombudsman, an impartial and independent institution responding to complaints of the public and aiming at improving public service. The Commonwealth Ombudsman filed a report with many suggestions to improve the system (Commonwealth Ombudsman 2017). Another report was filed by a senate committee (Community Affairs References Committee 2017). What is striking in the case of both reports is that they deeply engaged with technological and social issues and made specific recommendations. Government replied to both reports and reacted specifically to the report of the Ombudsman (Australian Government 2017). While the Australian government was very well equipped for external review of such an incident, the same could not be said for its organisational governance within the respective agencies. The entities responsible for explaining and reviewing decisions were obviously not well trained for the job. A media report suggests that critical employees even lost their job. Another general omission was that there was no random testing in order to improve the system. In comparison, the German tax administration is obliged to do some random testing according to § 88 of the German Fiscal Code.

The striking feature on the technical layer is that there have been hardly any technical changes to the matching algorithm. The same technology was used for the matching algorithm, but instead of making recommendations, the system decided automatically. While the affected citizens had the possibility to correct data, it was the system issuing the final decision. A technical problem was that the system continued to make many assumptions that led to wrong results. The following mistakes were mentioned in one report:

- 'income averaged over twenty-six fortnights in equal portions when the income was earned in a shorter time period;
- difference in employer's name (for example, where a business name is provided to Centrelink and the ATO record includes company name) which resulted in the same income being duplicated; and
- non-assessable income considered assessable income such as a lump sum termination payment, paid parental leave and meal, laundry and uniform allowances'. (Community Affairs References Committee 2017)

Previously, these problems were compensated by humans overseeing the process and correcting some of the flaws of the system. Discrepancies were resolved through the human correction of the data or by contacting the respective employers. In the new iteration of the system, there was no feature of the system providing for an adequate quality. The system also relied on computing averages of certain values. This was sometimes favourable for the subjects of the decision, sometimes the debt was stated too high. Both reports criticised that there was no model that allowed to project what errors this averaging would produce. It was unclear what the relation of people with less and more money would be. With this feature, it would have been possible to change the process of averaging or to understand its risks better.

As regarding the social layer, it is interesting that there have been general problems of communication. The Ombudsman states:

'Our investigation revealed DHS' initial messaging to customers through its letters and in the system itself, was unclear and did not include crucial information such as a contact phone number for the DHS compliance team. Many complainants did not realise their income would be averaged across the employment period if they did not enter their income against each fortnight.' (Commonwealth Ombudsman 2017: 2)

These communicative problems were in no way grounded in any feature of the technology, but in the face of the error rate of the system, they had huge effects. There was a lot of room for misunderstandings. Consequently, people missed the opportunity to correct their data. This is a good example of the facets of the transparency of a decision. It is far more than the ability to understand the basis of an automated decision. There has to be much more information. This communicative social aspect is all the more important if one considers the context. When considering social payments, the people affected are most likely not very skilled in accounting and correcting data. Therefore, there needs to be adequate communication for the social group to be addressed. One example for that would be to use 'Simple Language', that is an easy way to express which can be understood by people with different needs (Community Affairs References Committee 2017: 54ff).

One very interesting point about the discourse surrounding the OCI is the argument about what the error rate would be. The error rate of a hypothesis is defined 'as the proportion of mistakes it makes – the proportion of times that h(x) ≠ y for an (x,y) example' (Russell et al. 2016: 708). One disagreement during the discussions about the OCI was what an error would constitute. Some assumed that an initial notification by the system in cases in which there was only seemingly a debt due to incomplete or incorrect data was to be considered as an error of the system (Martin 2017; Pett and Crosier 2017). Others argued that in the initial stage, the system explicitly asked for more information and concluded that there was no error if the data was successfully corrected (Commonwealth Ombudsman 2017: 1). This disagreement relates to several questions such as who would be responsible to correct data in the system and how such a notice to correct the data is to be understood. Both views are viable, the difference maybe stems from a general shift in responsibility that is implicit in the further automation of the OCI. The further automation relied on the assumption that citizens are now solely responsible for their data management and public administration can merely rely on the data they provide. This shift in responsibility also means that citizens are ultimately responsible for correcting inconsistencies in their data. To ask them to correct the records in cases in which they have no debts is then not to be considered as an error. From the perspective of the citizens receiving the notice, this looks quite different. From their perspective, the hypothesis in the notice is that there is a debt and this is wrong (Knaus 2016b). A teacher receiving a letter because the system had mistakenly averaged his income in an incorrect manner, described his perception as follows: 'I was livid, absolutely livid. What really got me was the fact that the mentality behind it. It was like I was getting asked to pay back a loan.'(Whyte 2016). The fact that there has been such a profound misunderstanding and disagreement about questions of responsibility and error rates once again shows how important social factors are in setting up a technology.

E. Conclusion

Artificial intelligence is a general research question defining a field that deals with the independent solution of complex problems by machines. Under this umbrella, many technologies have been developed. When discussing these technologies, they are often framed in a particular way. We then talk about the ethics of AI or AI and human rights. Each frame highlights certain aspects and omits others. Therefore, I propose to aggregate different views about pursuing sustainability goals or designing digital technology in a sustainable way and to establish sustainable development as a frame for artificial intelligence. This allows to incorporate many learnings that have been made in the discourses surrounding sustainable development, but also to update these discourses and to include new learnings from the field of artificial intelligence.

Another advantage is that the discourse around sustainable development is inclusive and pluralist while having an international range. Sustainable development also allows to analyse technology on different layers. On the technical layer, specific questions regarding the technology can be analysed. The social layer analyses the socio-technical surroundings of the technology that can be as important. Yet, sustainable development also looks at technological issues from a macro-perspective analysing the governance of the technology as a whole. The sustainable development goals have a double function. They are goals that should be supported by new technologies such as AI. They also give guidance on how AI should be developed generally and where developers should be careful. AI and access to justice are apt reflections of the aforementioned. The chatbot DoNotPay shows how technology can be used to give people access to justice. A simple chatbot allows people to formulate letters that they can send to public administration or to court. This system proliferated over a short period of time and now grants access in vastly different regards. The Australian Authorities used the online compliance intervention to collect debts from social benefits. In order to collect more debts, they turned an assistance system into a fully automated system. The burden to correct data was shifted from civil servants in public administration to citizens receiving social benefits. After several severe problems, two inquiries highlighted different issues with the system. Many of those remarks are hints on how to increase access to justice when drawing up a fully automated application with legal effects. An analysis structured by the different layers of SAID showed that many aspects have to be taken into consideration. These range from modelling the impacts of certain decisions and providing enough information on how to challenge the decision and who to ask for information to general governance questions about the organisation of public administration. This example also shows that access to justice in the system of public administration has many faces. On the one hand, there is taxpayers' justice and the need for all people to pay taxes according to the same rules and not to receive unjustified benefits. But there is also access to justice when debts are reclaimed, and citizens challenge them. As in so many cases, justice is only achieved if there is an equilibrium of several views and needs. The concept of sustainable development explicitly addresses the question how to find such an equilibrium and convergence in the face of conflicts and opposing needs. This might be one aspect where sustainable AI development might turn out to be a frame that is useful for the analysis and design of artificial intelligence.

Bibliography

Australian Government (2017), *Australian Government response to the Community Affairs References Committee Report: Design, scope, cost-benefit analysis, contracts awarded and implementation associated with the Better Management of the Social Welfare System initiative*, available at <https://www.aph.gov.au/Parliamentary_Business/Committees/Senate/Community_Affairs/SocialWelfareSystem/Government_Response> (last accessed 5 January 2018).

Belot, H. (2017), 'Centrelink debt recovery: Government knew of potential problems with automated program', *ABC News Australia*, 12 January 2017, available at <http://www.abc.net.au/news/2017-01-12/government-knew-of-potential-problems-with-centrelink-system/8177988> (last accessed 5 January 2018).

Commonwealth Ombudsman (2017), 'Centrelink's automated debt raising and recovery system', available at <http://www.ombudsman.gov.au/data/assets/pdf_file/0022/43528/Report-Centrelinks-automated-debt-raising-and-recovery-system-April-2017.pdf>.

Community Affairs References Committee (2017), *Design, scope, cost-benefit analysis, contracts awarded and implementation associated with the Better Management of the Social Welfare System initiative*.

Djeffal, C. (2018), 'Künstliche Intelligenz in der öffentlichen Verwaltung', *Berichte des NEGZ*, 3, pp. 1–32.

——— (2019a), 'Künstliche Intelligenz', in T. Klenk, F. Nullmeier and G. Wewer (eds.), *Handbuch Verwaltungsdigitialisierung*, Wien: Springer.

——— (2019b), 'Sustainable development of artificial intelligence (SAID)', *Global Solutions Journal*, 4, pp. 186–92.

Dyson, G. (2014), *Turings Kathedrale: Die Ursprünge des digitalen Zeitalters*, Berlin: Propyläen.

Fukuda-Parr, S. (2018), 'Sustainable Development Goals', in T. G. Weiss and S. Daws (eds.), *The Oxford handbook on the United Nations*, Oxford: Oxford University Press, pp. 766–77.

Gasser, U., R. Budish and A. Ashar (2018), 'Module on Setting the Stage for AI Governance: Interfaces, Infrastructures, and Institutions for Policymakers and Regulators', *Artificial Intelligence (AI) for Development Series*, available at <https://www.itu.int/en/ITU-D/Conferences/GSR/Documents/GSR2018/documents/AISeries_GovernanceModule_GSR18.pdf> (last accessed 24 September 2018).

Grudin, J. (2017), *From tool to partner: The evolution of human-computer interaction*, London: Morgan & Claypool, 35.

IEEE (2018), 'Ethically aligned design: Version 2', available at <https://ethicsinaction.ieee.org/> (last accessed 2 June 2017).

Ihde, D. (2012), *Experimental phenomenologies: Multistabilities*, Albany: SUNY Press.

Knaus, C. (2016a), 'Centrelink urged to stop collecting welfare debts after compliance system errors', *The Guardian – International Edition*, 14 December 2016, available at <https://www.theguardian.com/australia-news/2016/dec/14/cen-

trelink-urged-to-stop-collecting-welfare-debts-after-compliance-system-errors>
(last accessed 7 June 2019).

Knaus, C. (2016b), 'Government backs Centrelink debt system despite "incorrect" $24,000 demand', *The Guardian – International Edition*, 28 December 2016, available at <https://www.theguardian.com/australia-news/2016/dec/29/government-confident-in-centrelink-debt-compliance-system-despite-reported-errors> (last accessed 5 January 2018).

Knaus, C. (2017), 'Centrelink to use 1,000 labour-hire staff to help recover welfare debts', *The Guardian – International Edition*, 21 November 2017, available at <https://www.theguardian.com/australia-news/2017/nov/22/centrelink-to-use-1000-labour-hire-staff-to-help-recover-welfare-debts> (last accessed 5 January 2018).

Lowe, V. (2001), 'Sustainable Development and Unsustainable Arguments', in A. E. Boyle and D. A. Freestone (eds.), *International law and sustainable development: Past achievements and future challenges*, Oxford: Oxford Univ. Press, pp. 19–37.

Mainzer, K. (2019), *Künstliche Intelligenz – Wann übernehmen die Maschinen?*, Berlin, Heidelberg: Springer.

Martin, P. (2017), 'How the Centrelink debt debacle failure rate is much worse than we all thought', *The Sydney Morning Herald*, 25 January 2017, available at <http://www.smh.com.au/federal-politics/political-opinion/how-the-centrelink-debt-debacle-failure-rate-is-much-worse-than-we-all-thought-20170124-gtxh8q.html> (last accessed 5 January 2017).

McCarthy, J., M. Minsky and C. Shannon (1955), 'A Proposal for the Dartmouth Summer Research Project on Artificial Intelligence', available at <http://www-formal.stanford.edu/jmc/history/dartmouth/dartmouth.html> (last accessed 31 March 2017).

McIlroy, T. (2017), '20,000 people sent Centrelink "robo-debt" notices found to owe less or nothing', *The Canberra Times*, 13 September 2017, available at <http://www.canberratimes.com.au/national/public-service/20000-people-sent-centrelink-robodebt-notices-found-to-owe-less-or-nothing-20170912-gyg8mm.html> (last accessed 5 January 2018).

Medhora, S. (2017), '"This is a joke": fighting Centrelink's robo-debt, one year on', *ABC News Australia*, 22 December 2017, available at <http://www.abc.net.au/triplej/programs/hack/centrelink-debt-one-year-on/9283108> (last accessed 5 January 2018).

Mulder, K., D. Ferrer and H. van Lente (eds.) (2011), *What is sustainable technology?: Perceptions, paradoxes and possibilities*, Sheffield: Greenleaf Publishing.

Pett, H. and C. Crosier (2017), 'We're all talking about the Centrelink debt controversy, but what is "robodebt" anyway?', *ABC News Australia*, 2 March 2017, available at <http://www.abc.net.au/news/2017-03-03/centrelink-debt-controversy-what-is-robodebt/8317764> (last accessed 5 January 2018).

Poole, D. L. and A. K. Mackworth (2011), *Artificial intelligence: Foundations of computational agents*, Cambridge: Cambridge University Press.

Principles for Digital Development (2017), 'Principles for Digital Development', available at <https://digitalprinciples.org/principles/>, (last accessed 7 June 2019).

Riegner, Michael (2016), 'Implementing the "Data Revolution" for the Post-2015

Sustainable Development Goals: Toward a Global Administrative Law of Information', *The World Bank Legal Review*, 7, pp. 17–41.

Russell, S. J., P. Norvig and E. Davis (2016), *Artificial intelligence: A modern approach*.

Towell, N. (2017), 'Centrelink robo-debt: public servants removed for asking too many questions, says Andrew Wilkie', *The Canberra Times*, 16 January 2017, available at <http://www.canberratimes.com.au/national/public-service/centre-link-robodebt-public-servants-removed-for-asking-too-many-questions-says-andrew-wilkie-20170116-gts7na.html> (last accessed 5 January 2018).

Turing (1950), 'Computing Machinery and Intelligence', *Mind A Quarterly Review of Psychology and Philosophy*, 59, pp. 433–60.

Tutt, Andrew (2017), 'An FDA for Algorithms', *Administrative Law Review*, 69, pp. 83–123.

United Nations Development Group (2017), 'Data Privacy, Ethics and Protection: Guidance Note on Big Data for Achievement of the 2030 Agenda', available at <https://undg.org/wp-content/uploads/2017/11/UNDG_BigData_final_web.pdf>, (last accessed 7 June 2019).

WGBU – German Advisory Council on Global Change (2019), *Towards our Common Digital Future: Summary*, Berlin: WGBU.

Whyte, S., 'How to dispute a Centrelink debt', *Crikey*, available at <https://www.crikey.com.au/2016/12/21/how-to-dispute-a-centrelink-debt/> (last accessed 5 January 2018).

Whyte, S. (2016), '"You feel powerless": Centrelink bullies are welfare collection cheats', *Crikey*, 13 December 2016, available at <https://www.crikey.com.au/2016/12/13/you-feel-powerless-centrelink-bullies-are-welfare-collection-cheats/> (last accessed 5 January 2018).

World Commission on Environment and Development (1987), *Our Common Future*, New York: United Nations, available at <www.un-documents.net/our-common-future.pdf>.

8

Digital Justice:
Nice to Have but Hard to Achieve

Dory Reiling

Our imagination is struck only by what is great; but the lover of natural philosophy should reflect equally on little things. Alexander von Humboldt

A. Introduction: Courts and Information Technology

Digital justice has been a buzzword around the judicial reform community for quite a while (Susskind 1998). In practice, we see court systems struggle to digitalise their procedures. This article aims to provide some insights into digital justice from practical, historical and future-oriented perspectives. If we want to understand how information technology (IT) can work in courts, we first need to understand what it is that courts do. In the context of IT, we need to find out how courts process information. Whether they do so in criminal, administrative or civil cases is largely irrelevant for our question. Historically, it helps to trace the development of information technology and its uses. Finally, the article looks at ways to put information technology to good use in courts and judiciaries.

B. What Do Courts Do?

Courts decide disputes, they also have a shadow function when their decisions are a guideline for behaviour by others than parties to a case. Deciding disputes involves processing information.

How courts process information is relevant for the kind of IT that is useful for courts. Parties be they the prosecution, someone appealing an administrative decision, a couple requesting a divorce or a party to a civil case, bring information to court. In most cases, another party is involved. The court processes the information, and at the end of the process a result comes out that is new information. Courts transform information and turn it into new information that can be useful for the parties involved. It can also be useful for those who are not involved but take the information as a guideline for their behaviour.

How courts process information is largely determined by two factors:

1. how unpredictable is the outcome, and
2. what is the relation between the parties?

Below is first a description of the concept.

- As a package of information comes in, that information can be sufficient to decide the outcome of the case in question. Example: a money claim that remains undefended, or a one-sided request that does not involve a second party. Cases like that belong in group one. All the court does is provide a title for execution. For this outcome, no information exchange between the parties is necessary.
- In group two, parties bring a proposal to court, but the law requires that court to examine the request for legality. Here, parties do exchange information, and work together to put together their proposal. Most family cases come into this group, as do certain labour cases. The cases in this group have in common that they largely deal with long-term relationships and regulation is light. In this group, the court has a rather notarial role, checking whether all legal provisions have been complied with.

So far, cases largely had a predictable outcome. In more unpredictable cases, more activities are needed to transform the information and make the outcome more predictable. That can be requests for further information, another reaction from the other party, a hearing, a witness hearing or a visit to a location.

- Sometimes, parties still reach an agreement between themselves to settle their dispute during the procedure. This is group three. In this group, parties work together, that is, they exchange information, for a win-win outcome.
- If parties do not reach agreement, a decision by a judge is needed to bring the case to a conclusion. That is group four. In this group, whether the parties exchange information is not relevant for the outcome.

This give us a first impression of the way courts process information.

Next, it is helpful to find out how these groups are distributed across the total case load. In my research, I have found that for 1st instance civil cases in

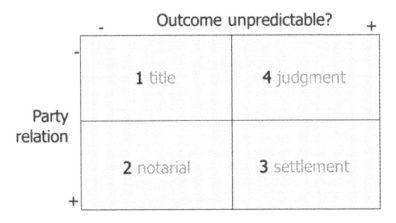

Figure 8.1   Courts process information

the Netherlands, group one is about 41 per cent of the total case load (Reiling 2009: pp. 120–22). Group two is about 36 per cent. Group three is about 12 per cent, and group four 11 per cent.

Group one lends itself to automation: digital case filing will remove the need to input data into the court systems. Because the outcome is largely predictable, automating parts of the process is an obvious use of IT for this group. Most courts already do some of this. There may be some use for artificial intelligence, for instance to triage cases, in this group.

For group two, that is largely the same, except that some form of Internet support may help parties put together a proposal that will comply with the criteria the court uses to examine it. For group three, an added benefit can come from negotiation software.

Group four is what we think of as the essence of what courts do. It makes up only 11 per cent of the total case load, but it is the majority of the judges' work load. Cases here can be somewhat to very complex. There is a lot of information in the case file, legal research needs to be undertaken to bring the case to a close. This is where digital case files, knowledge systems and search engines come in. Artificial intelligence may be helpful for structuring large case files and for research purposes.

Meanwhile, some courts in Europe and elsewhere have started to digitalise their procedures. The next section describes a model of a digital court procedure, based on my experience with building procedures for the Dutch courts.

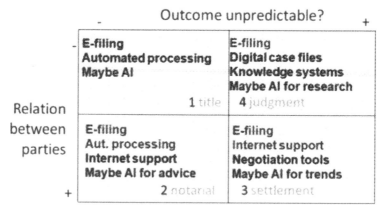

Figure 8.2   Information technology for each group

B. Digital Procedures

What can a fully digital court procedure look like? From the procedures we built for the Dutch courts, I can present the following picture. The court, or the court system, has a portal. There is a web interface, and there is also a systems interface. The web interface allows users to file cases through the Internet. The systems interface allows filing through a connection between – for instance – a lawyers' office system and the court system.

In criminal cases, the prosecution will file information with the court. The defendant in the case will need to be notified. In an administrative case, someone will lodge an appeal against an administrative decision. The court system can notify the system of the administration, for instance the social security service, the immigration service or the tax office, in question, which can send the case file to the court automatically. The description below focuses – by way of an example – on the civil procedure as designed and built for the Netherlands courts. Two assumptions: (1) this procedure is for civil cases with claims over €25,000, and compulsory legal representation by a lawyer, (2) filing is done by lawyers, not by others.

I. About E-filing and Case Details

Lawyers file cases either through the web portal of the systems interface. Information can be sent to the court in a structured way, in a form, or as a document. Filing a case will usually involve a combination of both: information in a form that will feed into the court case management system and information about the content of the case. The content information can either be laid down in a form with text fields, or in a document that is attached to the filing. Case details are, to a large extent, retrieved from the case management system. If necessary, an administrator can adjust details of the case in the case detail screen in the court work space. The case header in the case provides an overview of the most important information about the case, such as the parties' names, the court and the court date. The case history shows information about the course of the case.

II. The Procedure (1)

A lawyer can start a civil case in different ways: (1) the lawyer of the claiming party first submits the claim with grounds and evidence to the court; or (2) the lawyer first serves the claim on the defendant and then submits the claim to the court. Lawyers log in to the court system through the Netherlands Bar portal, with their lawyer's pass, a smart card. Their support staff can log in with their own pass. The system remembers which card was used for the login. E-filing is restricted to lawyers and their authorised support staff because authorisation to access the information in the case files requires a secure identification of the person accessing the court system (European Union 2018). This secure identification is in place in some countries, but in most countries it is not. The system calculates the court fees. The lawyer can pay the calculated court fee in the filing process via their current account with the court system, their bank account, or they can request an invoice and pay within twenty-eight days from filing.

Immediately upon filing, the court's case management system generates a case number, creates a digital file, gives feedback of the filing to the lawyer with the URL to the case file, and assigns the administrator the task: check process introduction, and also gives the administrator the task of checking court fees.

a. About Digital Case Management: Tasks and Activities

The backbone of the system is digital case management, balancing strict process control with flexibility in case management. The system assigns tasks that are required, the court can also, when needed, assign tasks to case-related persons if they are needed. Tasks comprise actions that have to be performed because they are prescribed by the law, by procedural rules or by a decision of the case judge. Tasks have a due date. Due dates, for example for lawyers, are usually regulated by law. If they are not, then the due date in our example is two weeks. Internal tasks for the courts have a due date of – in our example – five working days, unless the law provides otherwise. Distinct from tasks are activities. A court user can digitally start an activity when needed, for instance in exceptional situations in the procedure. An activity will then generate a task.

III. The Procedure (2)

The next step in a procedure is to involve the other party, in a civil case this will be the defending party. There are several ways in which this can be done: notification by the court, or by the claiming party's lawyer. Dutch civil procedural law allows informal notifications. The lawyer can also opt for formal service by a bailiff. In all cases, the summons notice is generated by the court system in a standard format. The system monitors whether the defending party joins the case. The defending party's lawyer can access the case file access code that is included in the summons notice. The defending party's lawyer can report that he will join the case for one or more parties. The lawyer of the defending party will also pay the court fee calculated in the filing process, using their current account with the court system, their bank account, or they can request an invoice and pay within twenty-eight days from filing.

The system sends a message to the claiming party's lawyer: defending party joined the case and assigns the defending party's lawyer a task to file a defence within six weeks from joining the case.

If the defending party did not join the case within the term specified in the summons, the system reports this in a message to the claiming party's lawyer. Generally, the system will the assign a task to check the claim, and then issue a default judgment (group one).

a. About Messages and Notifications

The lawyers, the judge and other parties involved in the case can communicate with each other via messages in the case. The messages are a simple way to exchange information quickly, for instance about procedural and hearing planning issues. The messages are part of the case file. With every event in the case, the system sends case-related lawyers a notification on a self-chosen email address. Notifications are meant to alert lawyers to new information in the file. In the systems interface, the notification is sent to the law firm's system. The law firm's system then retrieves that information from the attorney's file. As email is considered to be a non-secure way of transmitting information, there is only a minimal amount of information in the notification, since it is a way to alert the recipient to a change in the case. What the change is, is contained in the message that is in the case file itself.

The defending party's lawyer submits the statement of defence with a form. He can include evidence and possibly a counterclaim. In the event of a counterclaim, the system gives the claiming party's lawyer a task to file a defence to the counterclaim within two weeks. The system assigns two tasks to the administrator role: checking the statement of defence and checking the court fee.

b. About Roles

The judge, the clerk, the session planner, the administrator: they all fulfil different roles in the process. These roles determine which tasks and activities they need to be able to perform. The courts determine who has which role, and who can perform which tasks and activities. The administrator role, for example, can be performed by more than one person.

IV. The Procedure (3): The Case in Court

Now that the case file is complete with a claim, a defence, possibly a counterclaim and a counter-defence, the system assigns a task to assign a judge to the case. The court determines who can or may perform this task. Whoever performs this task will assign a judge or a panel to the case.

Assignment of judges to cases is also decided by the court itself.

The system then assigns the case judge the task of deciding whether a hearing should be held in the case or not. In the case of a hearing, the judge sets the agenda for the session, the time allotted to the hearing, and any details relevant for hearing planning. The hearing planner, using this information from the judge, plans the hearing. The hearing planner can request availability dates from the lawyers in an exchange of messages. As there is no standardised procedure to set hearing dates, the system allows courts to either request availability for hearing dates or not.

The administrator will finalise the hearing invitation. The agenda for the hearing is in the invitation. The system places the invitation in the digital case file and sends the lawyers a message and a notification. The lawyers can use message traffic to request a date change for the hearing. The administrator may change or cancel a session.

V. The Procedure (4): The Hearing

The hearing team can prepare their hearing in the case file viewer with a preparation form. In the case file viewer, they can: filter/sort documents, annotate, bookmark, include links in a preparation form. In the hearing, the judge can present a document to the parties and the audience on a large screen using the case file viewer. The registrar can create session notes in Word and add them to the internal part of the file.

At the end of the hearing, the judge determines the next step. The system has assigned him a task for this purpose. These are the options:

- if the case is settled (group three), the case can be closed. Someone will be assigned a task to close the case
- if more information is needed (group four), one party will be assigned the task of providing it, after which the other party gets the task of reacting to it
- if more discussion is needed (group four), a new session can be scheduled immediately in consultation with the parties
- if the information is sufficient for a decision (group four), the team member assigned with drafting a decision will get the task to do this within six weeks from the hearing date.

The hearing clerk can make an official report with an ordinary word processor. It will be saved as a pdf-A document and signed by the judge. It is part of the case file.

VI. The Procedure (5): Judgment

The judgment can be drafted either by the judge or by support staff. Information can be retrieved from the case data, and also inserted by cutting and pasting from the case file and from sources of law in the knowledge systems. The judge finalises the judgment with a digital signature. The administrator/registrar also signs the statement digitally. The administrator/registrar makes the decision ready to be shared with the parties and uploads it to the case file. The system sends the parties a message and a notification to signal the judgment has been issued.

The administrator registers additional information for accountability purposes and closes the case. Case information remains accessible for the parties at least until the term for appeal has expired.

VII. Improvements

The most important element of how a digital court may work is the combination of procedural rigor of tasks and due dates with flexible case management using message traffic and activities. The Dutch administrative courts use a very similar system that was built on the same platform for all *habeas corpus* procedures nationwide. They have processed more than 40,000 cases since the start.

The digital procedure has brought considerable improvements. Compliance with the right to a fair procedure in Article 6 of the European Convention on Human Rights increased:

- Easier court access through digital case filing.
- Equal access to information and increased transparency since parties' lawyers all have access to the digital case file.

- Less delay with instant messaging and automated case management. One full adversarial procedure, including a hearing, was completed in seven weeks.

There are also other improvements:

- The civil procedure was simplified.
- Information security: digital documents are kept in a persistent format with metadata on their status.
- Process information is now public.

Starting September 2016, two courts have piloted the system. Digital filing became compulsory for those two courts in September 2017. At the time of writing, the end of April 2019, in the Netherlands, more than 3,000 cases were filed in the two pilot courts that handle new commercial cases using this system. In June 2018, The Netherlands judicial council decided not to implement the commercial courts digital procedure in the other nine first instance courts. The next sections will try to explore some lessons that can be drawn from this unfortunate development.

D. Three Worlds of Information Technology

Before we try to understand what happened in The Netherlands, it is helpful to put the IT development in a broader perspective. Andrew McAfee, a professor at the Massachusetts Institute of Technology, distinguishes three worlds in information technology (McAfee 2006).

- *Function IT*, which supports the execution of a task, for example registering cases, document production or case law databases. This is the first world, the one we know from the 80s. This IT works stand-alone, it does not need a network to function.
- *Network IT*, such as the Internet, e-mail, more sophisticated case law databases or digital files needs a network to be able to work. This IT supports collaboration but does not enforce a specific working method. In this second world user takes a tool like you take a bucket from the kitchen cupboard, uses it and then puts it back again. The paper case file is still the main carrier of information. This world emerged with the arrival of the Internet for everyone. The simplest form is a website that provides information to the reader. In a next stage of development, the user can also perform an activity, for example download a form that he or she can print, fill in by hand and then send in by mail or email. A next step up is that the user can also fill in the form online. Still a step further, and the

user also receives the result of the transaction in digital form. But by then, we have already entered the third world of IT.

- *Enterprise IT.* That is what McAfee calls Enterprise IT. Examples include workflow and digital interaction with external users. Now we are no longer talking about a tool like my proverbial bucket, that we can choose to use or not. The system has become an environment, and the user can only work within this environment. This IT requires that work processes are predetermined and standardised. The work process only exists within the set rules, the rules and the process merge; they become one and the same.

As Lawrence Lessig already predicted: 'Code is law' (Lessig 1999). According to McAfee, who has studied the process of introducing Enterprise IT at many large companies, this is the most difficult transition there is. Only companies recognising this in advance and taking measures for it will successfully manage this transition. Decision rights about the process and about changes to the system must be established in advance.

I. Information Technology is Like PUR Foam

Spray polyurethane foam into a space, and it will extrude from all the weak spots. Just like PUR foam, developing and implementing IT will bring up all the weak spots in an organisation. And more specifically, court IT turns out to be particularly difficult. Why is court IT so difficult? Ten years ago, my fellow judges plagued me with this question when I was writing my book. So, I felt I had no choice but to investigate. The shortest answer to this question is that, in all IT projects, complexity is underestimated (Reiling 2009: pp. 60–80). In addition, participants tend to be overly optimistic about results. Risks, however, are usually underestimated. Governance is an issue: who decides what, and when? The amount of change needed for an organisation to use the IT effectively is also usually underestimated. In government IT projects, the political environment makes things even more complicated. Court culture is also a concern. Courts and judges are the guardians of the existing legal order. Their work is looking back and deciding who should get the blame for what went wrong. This means that looking ahead and envisioning how to innovate does not come naturally to them.

Nowadays, agile development is the standard for developing digital processes. Agile development is a strict methodology to design, develop, build and test technology in an integrated way. In order to be successful, all users need to be involved – one way or the other – in the development and implementation process from the start. Agile development requires experimentation. Legal culture tends to be quick to find someone to be blamed if something goes wrong. Blaming in retrospect does not help innovation. Concluding: court reform with IT is difficult.

E. Reforming Court Procedures with IT

So, the question to be answered is: how to effectively develop, build and implement court IT? The short answer is: Simplify, simplify, simplify. The longer answer depends on the type of procedure as described in the section about how courts work.

In the case of the Dutch civil commercial claim's procedure, all complexity and risks came together in a toxic conflagration. To make matters worse, funding ran out before the procedure could be implemented in all courts. Implementation, so much was clear, was going to be very complicated as well. Many changes were made to civil procedural legislation to speed cases up. These changes mostly had nothing to do with the digitalisation process. Translating the new digital procedure into work processes, something that should be done with the two pilot courts, was far from complete.

From my experience with court IT, there appear to be three models, and there are practical examples of each of them.

- **Replace existing processes in their entirety.** This can be an option for relatively short, simple procedures, like the ones in groups one and two. This can work if:
  - The legal basis for this procedure already exists.
  - Decision rights can also stay the same, because the work processes, although digitalised, basically stay the same as well.
  - Agile development is viable because the process can be piloted in a single case, on a voluntary basis.
  - Implementation, in these conditions, will still not be easy, but it can be successful.
- **Reform existing processes**. This may be an option for longer running procedures like group three and four cases, for instance large criminal cases or adversary civil proceedings. Replacing longer running existing processes in one operation is extremely complex and costly. Existing processes were designed for processing information on paper. They will need redesign if they should provide the full advantage of digital processing. They most likely will need changes to the legal basis, decision rights and work processes. Reforming existing processes gradually may be an option, either starting from the front, with e-filing, or from the back, starting with a digital case file. The court system in Austria is a very early example of e-filing; Austria is now developing a digital case file. After the decision not to implement the fully digital commercial claims procedure

any further, the Netherlands is now planning to develop simple e-filing as well as a digital case file.

- **Design a new process.** A model that appears to be successful is to design an entirely new process, or even a new institution, for processing cases. This seems an attractive option, since there are no constraints to be reckoned with. An early example is the United Kingdom's Money Claim Online (HM Courts and Tribunal Service 2019). This tool was designed for handling money claims only. Another, more recent, example is the Civil Resolution Tribunal in British Columbia, Canada. The Tribunal is a new institutional body set up to handle disputes between owners and tenants of subsidised housing. It gradually expanded into other areas of civil justice (British Columbia Civil Resolution 2019).

In each case, factors to be taken into account are the legal basis for the transition, decision rights and work processes, requirements of agile development and pilots, and implementation. The more change in the existing situation is needed, the more difficult the transition will be.

F. Conclusion

This article discussed information technology for courts. Experience is that introducing information technology to courts is difficult. The courts' primary process is processing information. Courts process information in different ways, depending on the cases in question. The main factors influencing the process are the level of predictability of the outcome of the case, and the relation between the parties. This is important to know because different processes are best served with different kinds of technology. Simple, predictable processes profit from e-filing and automation, complex processes involving research need search engines and knowledge systems.

The second step in understanding IT for courts is to envisage what a fully digital procedure can look like. By way of an example, the article described in general terms how a digital commercial claims procedure works. The most important element is digital case management combining procedural rigor with flexibility where needed.

Replacing a paper-based process with supporting IT tools by a fully digital process is a complex process. In order to understand the complexity of moving from a paper-based process using IT tools to a fully digital process, the article applies findings from some of such transitions to court systems. Finally, the article identified three models for developing and implementing IT for courts, based on the known factors involved. And here as well, the choice is determined by the type of procedure. As more change to the existing organisation is needed implementation will be more difficult.

Bibliography

British Columbia Civil Resolution Tribunal (2019), *The Civil Resolution Tribunal*, available at <https://civilresolutionbc.ca/> (last accessed 26 April 2019).

European Union (2018), *Regulation 2016/679 European Union General Data Protection Regulation*, Art, 5, 1f., 27 May 2018.

Lessig, L. (1999), *Code: And Other Laws of Cyberspace*, New York: Basic Books.

McAfee, A. (2006), 'Mastering the Three Worlds of Information Technology', *Harvard Business Review*, November 2006.

HM Courts and Tribunal Service (2019), Money Claim Online, available at <www.moneyclaim.gov.uk> (last accessed 26 April 2019).

Reiling, D. (2009), *Technology for Justice: How information technology can support judicial reform*, Amsterdam: Leiden University Press, also available at <www.dory.reiling.com>.

Susskind, R. (1998), *The Future of Law*, Oxford: Oxford University Press.

9

Improving Access to Justice Through Social Media Service of Process in Germany: Thinking Outside the (In)Box

Cedric Vanleenhove

A. Introduction

Access to justice in its purest form relates to a person's ability to have his case heard in court. As a basic principle of the rule of law this fundamental right ensures that one can enforce his legal rights and seek redress. Access to justice is, however, a two-way street. Allowing a legal subject to litigate also implies affording his opponent the right to defend. In that regard, it is crucial that the other party be warned about the claim that has been filed against him. The rules of procedural law lay down how the defendant should be notified about the commencement of the lawsuit. Service of process on the defendant safeguards the latter's right to access to justice.

In most instances service of process in civil matters is uncontroversial. The bailiff hands the service papers to the defendant or a family member at his residence, leaves it in his letterbox or effectuates service via post. These traditional methods are widely accepted as valid procedures for informing the defendant. When there is no address for the defendant in Germany or abroad, the situation is more complicated and fragile. In such cases the law specifies that service by publication acts as the last resort (Section 185, 1 ZPO). Such service is implemented by hanging a notification on the court's bulletin board or by publishing the notification in an electronic information system that is publicly accessible in the court. Additionally, the notification may be published in an electronic information and communications system established by the court for such notifications (Section 186(2) ZPO). The court may also order the notification to be published once, or several times, in the Bundesanzeiger (Official Gazette) or in other publications (Section 187 ZPO). These means of service amount to a large extent to fictitious service of process as it is extremely unlikely that the defendant will actually see the notice.

This paper contends that access of justice (on the side of the defendant) is encroached upon by the use of the current last resort service methods. Fictitious service guarantees the plaintiff access to justice as it ensures that his lawsuit can continue, despite the fact that the defendant is untraceable. On the other hand, the methods are not the most appropriate ones to achieve the ultimate purpose of service: notification of the defendant. It is argued that serving the defendant via one or more of his social media accounts may be a viable addition to the existing last resort service techniques. This idea should not be dismissed out of hand because, as noted by an American court at the end of the previous century,

> 'any unspecified form of alternative service usually has its genesis in untried or formerly unapproved methodology ... It would be akin to hiding one's head in the sand to ignore such realities and the positives of such advancements' (United States Bankruptcy Court for the Northern District of Georgia, Broadfoot v. Diaz, 15 February 2000, 245 B.R. 719 (2000)).

Social media are ubiquitous in today's society. They can be defined as 'a group of Internet-based applications that build on the ideological and technological foundations of Web 2.0, and that allow the creation and exchange of user-generated content' (Kaplan and Haenlein 2010: 61). The term Web 2.0 was first used by Darcy DiNucci (DiNucci 1999: 32). The Web 2.0 model stands for the transition the Internet has made from users who passively view websites to users as creators of content. The list of social media is long but the most important ones for the topic of this paper are: Facebook, Twitter, LinkedIn and Instagram.

In addition to penetrating our daily lives, the platforms are starting to intersect with the law as well. Citizens' social media accounts are a rich source of information which leads to them being used for evidence-mining (Mark Howitson, in his capacity of Deputy General Counsel at Facebook, reportedly said that Facebook receives almost daily requests for user information from law enforcement and legal counsel: http://eddblogonline.blogspot. ch/2010/02/facebook-gc-tells-lawyers-hes-looking.html). It is questioned whether the existence of a Facebook 'friendship' between a judge and a lawyer is sufficient to disqualify the judge (Supreme Court of Florida, Law Offices of Herssein and Herssein, P.A., etc., et al. v. United Services Automobile Association). Defamatory statements on social media, referred to as "Twibel" (a combination of the words "Twitter" and "libel"), are prevalent. In Germany there was a case before the Kammergericht of Berlin about whether a Facebook account is inheritable (Zimmermann 2017). The International

Criminal Court in the Hague issued the first ever arrest warrant based largely on evidence collected via social media (Irving 2017). Courts around the world have a social media presence: the European Court of Justice and the UK Supreme Court, for instance, are active on Twitter. Different fields of law are wrestling with how social media should be handled (Finke 2016: 139). One – for the topic of this paper – notable field in which social media are used for legal purposes is the area of class action notification. Especially in the United States courts increasingly consider using social media websites to inform potential class members (on this issue see *inter alia* Piché 2018; Aiken 2017: 967–1018; Bartholomew 2018: 217–274; Wyman 2014: 103).

The unusual and remarkable idea to rely on social media for service of process (outside the class action sphere) is inspired by a relatively recent practice observed in the common law world. In this paper we, therefore, first outline this trend of employing social media networks to bring notice to defendants (part B). Subsequently, we set out the benefits of this type of service (part C). Lastly, we put forward some initial reflections about the concrete implementation of such service (part D). In the concluding part we wrap up our thoughts (part E). This paper uses the methodology of traditional legal research. It builds in particular on foreign case law and doctrinal literature in order to give advice as to how the (German) legal system may be enhanced.

B. Fragmented Common Law Endorsement of Social Media Service

I. Examples

In various common law nations around the world the possibility of serving the defendant via their social media profile(s) has emerged. In multiple cases the plaintiff has petitioned the court for approval to send notice to the defending party over social media platforms. A few examples will illustrate this new development.

In the Canadian case of *Knott v. Sutherland*, for instance, Byron Knott, as administrator of the estate of Carol Dianne Knott, sued several people and organisations for medical negligence. As to one of the defendants, Abdulmutalib Al-Masloom, he obtained permission to serve by publication of the notice in the Edmonton Journal, by forwarding it to the Human Resources department of the hospital where the defendant had previously worked and by sending notice of the action to the Facebook profile of the defendant (Court of Queen's Bench of Alberta Judicial District of Edmonton, Knott v. Sutherland, 5 February 2009, AJ No 1539).

In a shareholder dispute the New Zealand High Court also had to consider the acceptability of using social media networks as avenues for service of process. The matter of *Axe Market Gardens v. Craig Axe* dealt with a corporation suing one of its minority shareholders for misappropriation of funds. The company Axe Market Gardens was represented by Mr. Axe and its claim was directed at Craig Axe, Mr. Axe's son. According to the plaintiff the defendant had electronically accessed the plaintiff's bank account and had transferred a large sum of money out of it. The defendant was resident in England but his exact whereabouts were unknown, therefore rendering publication in a newspaper impractical. As the conventional methods of service had failed, a more creative solution had to be sought. Father and son had communicated with one another via e-mail and Facebook. Under those circumstances the High Court allowed service via e-mail and Facebook (High Court of New Zealand, Axe Market Gardens v. Craig Axe, 16 March 2009, CIV: 2008-485-2676).

The American federal case of *Ferrarese v. Shaw* saw the plaintiff bring an action against his ex-wife, who he alleged had absconded with their daughter. He sought to secure the immediate return of his child and to ensure his rights of custody. His lawyers were unable to locate his ex-wife. The latter took active measures to avoid being located and to evade service. Service at her last known address proved unsuccessful as the house was occupied by the defendant's sister who refused to cooperate. Judge Pollak agreed that it would be impracticable to serve the defendant using traditional methods and ordered service via e-mail, Facebook message and certified mail on defendant's last known address and on defendant's sister (United States District Court, Eastern District of New York, Giovanni Ferrarese v. Vinda Shaw, 19 January 2016, 164 F.Supp.3d 361).

In *Graves v. West* before the Supreme Court of New South Wales in Australia the victim of an assault on a football pitch sued the offender, a player of the other team. The defendant had moved to England. At first a lawyer appeared for him, but this legal representation did not last. The lawyer did not have a street address for the defendant, only an e-mail address. The Australian court ruled that service via the defendant's LinkedIn account, along with service via a personal e-mail account (as well as service on the defendant's lawyer), was sufficient to bring documents to the attention of the defendant (New South Wales Supreme Court, Graves v. West, 24 May 2013, NSWSC 641).

Closer to home, the English High Court was confronted with a request for service via Facebook in *AKO Capital LLP v. TFS Derivatives*. The plaintiffs were investment managers who brought suit against their broker for overcharged commission. The defendant contested the claim and asserted that any liability should be shifted to – among others – Mr. Fabio de Biase, a former employee of the broker. It, therefore, sought to implead Mr. De Biase in the proceedings. The defendant served the claim at his last known address but sought judicial approval to serve via Facebook message as well because there was doubt over whether he still lived there. For the first time the High Court allowed service of process via Facebook (High Court of Justice, 17 February 2012, AKO Capital LLP & another v. TFS Derivatives & others, unreported but the case is *inter alia* discussed in the press and in Browning 2012: 175).

In another litigation in the United States, *WhosHere v. Orun*, the court ordered service via Facebook, LinkedIn and e-mail. The plaintiff had sued the Turkish defendant for trademark infringement. Service via the Turkish Ministry of Justice under the Hague Service Convention did not work out because the defendant could not be located at the Turkish address provided by the plaintiff. Judge Thomas Rawles Jones Jr. subsequently approved service via the social networks Facebook and LinkedIn as well as via e-mail (United States District Court for the Eastern District of Virginia, Alexandria Division, WhosHere, Inc. v. Gokhan Orun, 20 February 2014, 2014 WL 670817, *5).

II. Common Conditions

From the available case law two recurring requirements for this type of service can be distilled. First, the plaintiff must provide convincing evidence that the social media account marked for service actually belongs to the defendant. Second, the court must be satisfied that the defendant is regularly using this account. The judicial insistence on these safeguards is logical because it is essential in the interest of due process that the right person is notified, and that this person views his account regularly enough to discover the notice in time for him to prepare a defence. Access to justice would be distorted if service of process were to be effected on an account that is not controlled by the defendant or on an account that he seldom looks at or has abandoned.

As to the former condition, the English High Court in *AKO Capital LLP v. TFS Derivatives* found support in the fact that Mr. De Biase was Facebook friends with employees at the defendant company TFS Derivatives (High Court of Justice, 17 February 2012, AKO Capital LLP & another v. TFS Derivatives & others, unreported but the case is *inter alia* discussed in the press and in Browning 2012: 175). In *Axe Market Gardens v. Craig Axe* the authentication of the Facebook profile of the defendant was relatively easy to establish because there was a communication trail between the defendant and his father (the head of the plaintiff company) on the social medium platform. Many forms of proof could be useful to convince the court. In an effort to link the defendant to the social media profile the plaintiff could point to various information contained in the profile, such as education, occupation, hobbies, friends, interests, age, hometown, and possibly general location, to match this to information known about the defendant sought to be served (Knapp 2014: 576).

As to the latter condition, the United States District Court for the Eastern District of Virginia in *WhosHere v. Orun* noted that the parties had already exchanged e-mails with regard to the alleged trademark infringement. In this conversation the defendant had provided the plaintiff with an alternative e-mail address and had indicated that he was present on all social networks under that e-mail address. The plaintiff indeed found a Facebook and a LinkedIn account under the defendant's name. The District Court derived from the defendant's announcement that those channels were his preferred methods of communication which he used on a regular basis (United States District Court, for the Eastern District of Virginia, Alexandria Division, WhosHere, Inc. v. Gokhan Orun, 20 February 2014, 2014 WL 670817, *4). In *AKO Capital LLP v. TFS Derivatives* the English High Court concluded that the account was in use because Mr. De Biase had accepted a few recent friend requests (High Court of Justice, 17 February 2012, AKO Capital LLP & another v. TFS Derivatives & others, unreported but the case is *inter alia* discussed in the press and in Browning 2012: 175). Verification as to whether the defendant is the one in control of the social media account targeted for service can take place through a wide range of factors. Naturally, prior conversations between plaintiff and defendant on the platform take the crown but other actions of the defendant may serve the same purpose. Activities on social media are usually time-stamped and the plaintiff may avail himself of them to demonstrate that the defendant engages with his profile. Written posts, the changing of one's profile picture, the posting of pictures, comments on other users' posts, checking into an event, updated job titles and the "last active" feature on the chat function are but a few examples. Similar to the first requirement, the privacy settings enacted by the defendant will dictate the depth of the investigation that can be carried out.

C. Why Social Media Service Deserves a Friend Request: Advantages Over Other Forms of Service

As argued, the administration of justice would benefit if last resort service in Germany were to be supplemented by sending the notice to the defendant's social media account(s). The current methods employed in those situations fail to achieve the core purpose of service, namely actually informing the defendant of the claim filed against him. Very few citizens are looking for these published legal notices.

It might come as a surprise to nominate this novel type of service as the saviour among the last resort methods. However, social medial service has a number of benefits and outshines other service techniques in many respects. An important advantage of this means of service is that it has a high likelihood of actually reaching the person for whom it is intended. This is caused by the fact that users regularly access their accounts. Figures relating to the social network Facebook confirm this. In a quarterly report, the company announced that as of 30 September 2018 there were 2.27 billion monthly active users (Facebook 2018). Instagram reached 1 billion monthly active users in June of 2018 (Statista 2019a). In the third quarter of 2018 Twitter had 326 million monthly active users worldwide (Statista 2019b). A large number of people are thus active on social media. Besides, the platforms themselves reach out to their users on a continuous basis, for example by the applications on the users' mobile devices that push notifications to the account holders (Upchurch 2016: 601). Under Facebook's default settings the account holder will receive a notification through e-mail of received messages (See for instance the District Court for the Southern District of New York in *FTC v. PCCare 247 Inc*: '*Defendants would be able to view these messages when they next log on to their Facebook accounts (and, depending on their settings, might even receive email alerts upon receipt of such messages).*') ('FTC v. PCCare247 Inc.': 7 March 2013, WL 841037, *5). Social media platforms represent a direct and instantaneous pathway to the defendant. Even the passive defendant who makes no effort to look for legal notices containing his name either in newspapers or on Internet sites, could be informed of the litigation in this manner. The existence of the digital divides thwarts the usefulness of service via social media to some degree. Due to socio-economic deprivation and/or a lack of digital literacy citizens might not have access to the Internet and social media platforms. Their online absence prevents them from receiving notice of the upcoming litigation through social media accounts. For these people the current last resort mechanisms, as prescribed by the law as it stands today, would remain the default, thus lowering the likelihood of providing actual awareness.

Furthermore, social media service outperforms other (potential) last resort methods in terms of achieving actual notice (Beazley 2013: 18). Service by publication is not very effective at informing the defendant about the impending lawsuit. The number of copies of newspapers circulated in Germany is dropping every year (Statista 2019c). In contrast, social media usage penetration is on the rise (Statista 2019d). To give but one example: out of a world population of 7.7 billion people (Worldometers 2019) over 2 billion people are to be classified as monthly active Facebook users (Facebook 2018). The inadequacy of publication was noted in the United States as well. In *Baidoo v. Blood-Dzraku* the Supreme Court of New York County rejected this service technique, calling it 'a form of service that, while neither novel nor unorthodox, is essentially statutorily authorized non-service' ('Baidoo v. Blood-Dzraku': 27 March 2015, 48 Misc 3d 316). It found that even for publications in more widely circulated newspapers 'the chances of it being seen by defendant, buried in an obscure section of the paper and printed in small type, are still infinitesimal' ('Baidoo v. Blood-Dzraku': 27 March 2015, 48 Misc 3d 317; in the same vein the court in *Mpafe v. Mpafe* considered service via publication in a legal newspaper but argued that it would be unlikely that the defendant would ever see it: 'Mpafe v. Mpafe': 10 May 2011, No. 27-FA-11-3453). A further advantage of social media as a channel for service lies in the costs attached to performing the service. Whereas publication in newspapers is relatively expensive (this is no different in the United States: in *Mpafe v. Mpafe* service by publication was called 'antiquated and prohibitively expensive' ('Mpafe v. Mpafe': 10 May 2011, No. 27-FA-11-3453)), social media service is free (Eisenberg 2014: 814). Social media service is generally less expensive than traditional service methods (Upchurch 2016: 606).

When seeking an appropriate service method for the digital age in which we live in, the natural reflex could be to look at e-mail. The problem with e-mail is that the sender cannot be sure if the account actually belongs to the intended recipient, unless the recipient explicitly acknowledges so (Knapp 2014: 569). A social media profile, on the other hand, can be examined, depending on its privacy settings, to verify whether the defendant and the account owner are one and the same. To that end, confirmed information about the defendant can be compared to information found on the social media profile (see supra part B.II). Social media networks are also less spam-infested than e-mail (Wolber 2016–2017: 450, footnote 1; Shultz 2008–2009: 1525, footnote 205 (in the context of Facebook)). This is relevant because all forms of electronic service lack the ritual function that only paper-based, in-hand service can provide (Hedges, et al. 2009: 73). They do not create the same ritualistic formality and finality as the hardcopy traditional methods of service (Specht 2012: 1955–1956). Formality is crucial to warn the defendant about the seriousness and legal implications of the act of service. If the recipient's inbox is not swamped by spam attacks, there is more chance he will not doubt the believability and authenticity of the notice.

The idea to rely on social media networks for subsidiary service finds support in the ELI-UNIDROIT Draft European Rules of Civil Procedure (UNIDROIT 2017). UNIDROIT and the European Law Institute (ELI) cooperate towards the development of European Rules of Civil Procedure. In light of the emergence of an expansion of rules at the European level in the field of procedural law, they aim to create a tool to avoid a fragmentary and haphazard growth of European civil procedural law. Completion of the instrument was expected in 2019 (UNIDROIT 2019). Rule 13 of the Draft deals with service methods of last resort. It provides that when the defendant's address is unknown, service of documents may be effected by publication of a notice to the addressee in a form provided for by the law of the forum state, including publication in electronic registers accessible to the public, and by sending a notice to the addressee's last known address or e-mail address. The comments accompanying Rule 13 state that:

> 'The wording of the rule is also broad enough to cover giving notice via text message, "Facebook" or other social media if appropriate and accepted in the forum state, although it is not a "publication" in a narrow sense' (UNIDROIT 2017).

Reference can also be made to the service of process rules in the country of Estonia. The tiny Baltic republic is one of the most technologically advanced nations in the world, aptly called E-stonia for its competences and knowledge in technology. In Estonia a court may notify the defendant of the existence of procedural documents using social network accounts belonging to the recipient. § 311, paragraph 2 of the Code of Civil Procedure states:

> "The court may also send a notice on making the document available to the phone number or e-mail address found in the public computer network, on the presumed user account page of a virtual social network or on a page of another virtual communication environment which the addressee may be presumed to use according to the information made available in the public computer network or where, upon sending, such information may be presumed to reach the addressee. If possible, the court makes the notice available on the presumed user account page of a virtual social network or on a page of another virtual communication environment in such a manner that the notice cannot be seen by any other persons than the addressee" (own emphasis) (English translation of the Estonian Code of Civil Procedure))

When the defendant has not retrieved the file from his personal e-toimik account (e-toimik is the country's e-File procedural information system), Estonian courts sometimes notify him through social media. A court clerk will perform an Internet search for the defendant and will reach out to him through, for example, the court's official Facebook Page to inform him and to encourage him to visit his e-toimik account. Although this practice does not amount to official service, it shows a willingness to embrace social media platforms as viable portals to the defendant.

D. Precursory Considerations

The introduction of social media service as an additional *ultimum remedium* in Germany gives rise to a number of fundamental and practical questions. One of these relates to whether the notice should be sent via a private message or through a public communication. A Facebook message or a Direct Message on Instagram are examples of private messages. These are only viewable by the recipient. Public communications are, for instance, a post on the defendant's Facebook Timeline or a public Tweet. They are visible by more people than just the addressee, such as his digital friends or the general public. In the common law cases the issue of privacy is very rarely addressed.

There is, however, one decision that explicitly touches upon the defendant's right to privacy. In a case before the Kwazulu-Natal High Court of Durban in South Africa Judge Steyn argued that the privacy of the defendant would not be infringed upon because the notice would be transferred via a personal Facebook message, to which no other person than the defendant would have access ('CMC Woodworking Machinery (Pty) Ltd v. Pieter Odendaal Kitchens': 3 August 2012, case no. 6846/2006, para. 13). The overwhelming majority of courts have subscribed to the position that the defendant should be informed via an individualised method of communication ('MKM v. Corbo & Poyser': 16 December 2008, case no. SC 608; 'Blaney v. Persons Unknown': 1 October 2009, IHQ/12/0653 (Ch.); 'Byrne v. Howard': 21 April 2010, FMCAfam 509; AKO Capital LLP & another v. TFS Derivatives & others: 17 February 2017, unreported but the case is *inter alia* discussed in the press and in Browning 2012: 175; 'CMC Woodworking Machinery (Pty) Ltd v. Pieter Odendaal Kitchens': 3 August 2012, case no. 6846/2006; 'FTC v. PCCare247 Inc.': 7 March 2013, 2013 WL 841037; 'Biscocho v. Antigua': 12 September 2014, docket no. F-00787-13/14B; 'Baidoo v. Blood-Dzraku': 27 March 2015, 48 Misc 3d 310 (although not entirely clear whether a private message was sanctioned); 'K.A. & K.I.A. v. J.L.': 11 April 2016, docket no. C-157-15). Only one judgment approves of a public communication (a public Tweet) as the avenue for service of process on the defendant ('St. Francis Assisi v. Kuwait Finance House, et al.': 30 September 2016, 2016 WL 5725002).

Reliance on public pathways of communication, such as the Facebook Timeline of the defendant, arguably augments the chances of actually notifying him about the matter in which he is expected to defend himself. If the latter's social media connections can view the communication, they are likely to inform him of the existence of the service (Wagner and Castillo 2013: 275, footnote 114; Grové and Papadopolous 2013: 434). In our estimation this purported increase in likelihood of actual notice is too limited to justify the infringement of the defendant's privacy. Social media service ought to remain as discreet as possible: a private message should be the norm (Finke 2016: 162; Knapp 2014: 576; McEwen & Robertson 2010: 8). In that regard the Estonian Code of Civil Procedure takes the same stance as its § 311, paragraph 2 reads in relevant part:

> 'If possible, the court makes the notice available on the presumed user account page of a virtual social network or on a page of another virtual communication environment in such a manner that the notice cannot be seen by any other persons than the addressee'.

The informal nature of social media platforms (as already noted supra part C) is another issue that needs advanced thought. For many people social media networks form sources of entertainment. On social media users chat with their friends and family, watch funny videos, follow pages of companies or celebrities they like and participate in groups. Most, if not all, citizens do not associate these networks with official legal communication. If service of process is suddenly effected through social media, it is conceivable that the receiver will not give the notice the attention it deserves. He might not take the notice seriously or he might deem it to be a fraudulent message seeking to trick him. In such circumstances, the objective at the heart of service has not been fulfilled.

One possible solution could be to include a unique case identification number in the private message to the defendant, a suggestion already formulated in the context of e-mail service (Wolber 2016–2017: 468). The defendant can subsequently visit an official website where he can find the documents of the service by entering the number provided in the message. This approach is to be preferred over providing a link to the documents because Internet users are – with good reason – wary of clicking on links to unknown websites.

E. Conclusion

It is by no means time to write an obituary for the traditional methods of service of process. The arrival of social media in the toolbox of service methods will not send shockwaves through the legal system. Service via social media networks will not become the new gold standard, replacing personal service or service by post. It is suggested that the current means of service in cases where there is no known address for the defendant are ineffective at actually reaching him, which negatively impacts his right to access to justice. Social media can act as a backstop because they open a direct line of communication to the defendant, provided it can be shown that the account indeed belongs to the defendant and he regularly accesses it.

If the German legislator decides to incorporate this form of service, the use of social media in the everyday life of citizens may undergo a significant transformation. At the moment, members of social media do not perceive their participation as capable of producing legal consequences. In the future they could be surprised to find notice of a lawsuit in their social media inbox. Once it becomes common knowledge that one is able to be sued through one's social media account(s), some users may decide to delete their profiles (McEwen & Robertson 2010: 7). After an Australian court's pioneering approval of Facebook service (Supreme Court of Australian Capital Territory, MKM v. Corbo & Poyser, 16 December 2008, case no. SC 608), Facebook warmly welcomed the ruling, expressing in a statement:

> 'We're pleased to see the Australian court validate Facebook as a reliable, secure and private medium for communication. The ruling is also an interesting indication of the increasing role that Facebook is playing in people's lives'(The Associated Press 2008).

Faced with an exodus, however, social media giants like Facebook may decide to rethink their initial delight at the new trend.

Bibliography

Aiken, A. W. (2017), 'Class Action Notice in the Digital Age', *University of Pennsylvania Law Review*, 165, pp. 967–1018.

'AKO Capital LLP & another v. TFS Derivatives & others' (17 February 2012) *High Court of Justice*.

Associated Press, The (16 December 2008), 'Australian Court approves Facebook for serving lien notice' available at <https://www.cbc.ca/news/technology/australian-court-approves-facebook-for-serving-lien-notice-1.731597> (last accessed 14 May 2019).

'Baidoo v. Blood-Dzraku' (27 March 2015) *Supreme Court of New York County*.

Bartholomew, C. P. (2018), 'E-Notice', *Duke Law Journal*, 68: 2, pp. 217–74.

Beazley, M. J. (2013), 'Social Media and the Courts: Service of Process', Address at the Fourth Judicial Seminar on Commercial Litigation, Singapore, 16–18 May 2013, pp. 1–21.

'Biscocho v. Antigua' (12 September 2014) *Family Court of the State of New York, Richmond County*.

'Blaney v. Persons Unknown' (1 October 2009) *High Court of Justice*.

Browning, J. G. (2012), 'Your Facebook Status – "Served": Service of Process Using Social Networking Sites', *Reynolds Courts & Media Law Journal*, 2:2, pp. 159–84.

'Byrne v. Howard' (21 April 2010) *Federal Magistrates Court of Australia*

'CMC Woodworking Machinery (Pty) Ltd v. Pieter Odendaal Kitchens' (3 August 2012) *Kwazulu-Natal High Court of Durban*.

DiNucci, D. (1999), 'Fragmented Future', *Print*, 53:4, pp. 32 & 221–22.

Eisenberg, A. L. (2014), 'Keep Your Facebook Friends Close and Your Process Server

Closer: The Expansion of Social Media Service of Process to Cases Involving Domestic Defendants', *San Diego Law Review*, 51:3, pp. 779–822.

Estonian Code of Civil Procedure, English Translation, available at <https://www.riigiteataja.ee/en/eli/513122013001/consolide>, (last accessed 29 July 2020).

Facebook (2018), 'Facebook Reports First Quarter 2018 Results', available at <https://investor.fb.com/investor-news/press-release-details/2018/Facebook-Reports-Third-Quarter-2018-Results/default.aspx> (last accessed 14 May 2019).

Finke, C. M. (2016), 'Friends, Followers, Connections, Lend Me Your Ears: A New Test for Determining the Sufficiency of Service of Process Via Social Media', *University of Baltimore Law Review*, 46:1, pp. 139–68.

'FTC v. PCCare247 Inc.' (7 March 2013) *District Court for the Southern District of New York*.

Grové, L. B. and S. M. Papadopoulos (2013), 'You Have Been Served . . . On Facebook!', *Journal of Contemporary Roman-Dutch Law*, 76, pp. 424–36.

Hedges, R. J., K. N. Rashbaum, A. C. Losey (2009), 'Electronic Service of Process at Home and Abroad: Allowing Domestic Electronic Service of Process in the Federal Courts', *The Federal Courts Law Review*, 4:1, pp. 55–77.

Irving, E. (2017), 'And So It Begins . . . Social Media Evidence In An ICC Arrest Warrant', *OpinioJuris,* available at <http://opiniojuris.org/2017/08/17/and-so-it-begins-social-media-evidence-in-an-icc-arrest-warrant> (last accessed 14 May 2019).

'K.A. & K.I.A. v. J.L.' (11 April 2016) *Superior Court of New Jersey, Chancery Division, Morris County*, available at <https://www.njcourts.gov/attorneys/assets/opinions/trial/ka.pdf>, (last accessed 29 July 2020).

Kaplan, A. M. and M. Haenlein (2010), 'Users of the world, unite! The challenges and opportunities of social media', *Business Horizons*, 53:1, pp. 59–68.

Knapp, K. (2014), '#serviceofprocess@socialmedia: Accepting Social Media for Service of Process in the 21st Century', *Louisiana Law Review*, 74:2, pp. 547–79.

McEwen, A. and C. Robertson (2010), 'At Your Substituted Electronic Service', Kingston and the 1000 Islands Legal Conference, 1 October 2010, pp. 1–10.

'MKM v. Corbo & Poyser' (16 December 2008) *Supreme Court of Australian Capital Territory*.

'Mpafe v. Mpafe' (10 May 2011) *Fourth District Family Court of Minnesota (Hennepin County)*.

Piché, C. (2018), 'The Coming Revolution in Class Action Notices: Reaching the Universe of Claimants Through Technologies', available at <https://papers.ssrn.com/sol3/papers.cfm?abstract_id=3167510>, (last accessed 29 July 2020).

Shultz, A. L. (2008–2009), 'Superpoked and Served: Service of Process via Social Networking Sites', *University of Richmond Law Review*, 43:4, pp. 1497–528.

Specht, C. M. (2012), 'Text Message Service of Process – No LOL Matter: Does Text Message Service of Process Comport with Due Process', *Boston College Law Review*, 53:5, pp. 1929–965.

Statista (2019a), 'Number of monthly active Instagram Users from January 2013 to June 2018', available at <https://www.statista.com/statistics/253577/number-of-monthly-active-instagram-users/> (last accessed at 14 May 2019).

Statista (2019b), 'Number of monthly active Twitter users worldwide from 1st quarter 2010 to first quarter 2019' available at <https://www.statista.com/staistics/282087/number-of-monthly-active-twitter-users/> (last accessed 14 May 2019).

Statista (2019c), 'Total circulation of newspapers in Germany from 2003 to 2019' available at <https://www.statista.com/statistics/386743/newspapers-circulation-germany/> (last accessed 14 May 2019).

Statista (2019d), 'Number of social media users worldwide from 2010 to 2021' available at <https://ec.europa.eu/knowledge4policy/visualisation/number-social-media-users-worldwide-2010-17-forecasts-2021_en> (last accessed 14 May 2019).

'St. Francis Assisi v. Kuwait Finance House, et al.' (30 September 2016) *United States District Court for the Northern District of California.*

Supreme Court of Florida, Law Offices of Herssein And Herssein, P.A., etc., et al. v. United Services Automobile Association, 15 November 2018, no. SC17-1848, available at <http://www.floridasupremecourt.org/decisions/2018/sc17-1848.pdf>, (last accessed 29 July 2020).

UNIDROIT (May 2017), 'Consolidated Draft European Rules of Civil Procedure' available at https://www.unidroit.org/english/governments/councildocuments/2017session/cd-96-07-e.pdf (last accessed 14 May 2019).

UNIDROIT (2019), 'European Rules of Civil Procedure' available at <https://www.unidroit.org/civil-procedure#EuropeanRulesofCivilProcedure> (last accessed 14 May 2019).

Upchurch, A. (2016), '"Hacking Service of Process": Using Social Media to Provide Constitutionally Sufficient Notice of Process', *University of Arkansas at Little Rock Law Review*, 38: 4, pp. 559–625.

Wagner, W. and J. R. Castillo (2013), 'Friending Due Process: Facebook as a Fair Method of Alternative Service', *Widener Law Review*, 19:2, pp. 259–79.

Wolber, J. (2016–2017), 'Opening a Can of Worms and Viruses: The Impact of E-Service on E-Mail Users Everywhere', *New York Law School Law Review*, 61:4, pp. 449–70.

Worldometers (2019) 'Current World Population' available at <http://www.worldometers.info/world-population/> (last accessed 14 May 2019).

Wyman, T. Z. (2014), 'Sufficiency of Legal Notice Provided by Online Publication or Electronic Mail in Class Action Suits', 84 American Law Reports Fed. 2d 103.

Zimmermann, K. (2017), 'Is a Facebook account inheritable under German Law?', available at <http://www.mepli.eu/2017/07/is-a-facebook-account-inheritable-under-german-law/> (last accessed 14 May 2019).

Part III

Civil Society:
Realising the Implications of
Technology Change

10

Gamified Digital Advocacy and the Future of Law

Gianluca Sgueo

A. Digital Pets, Awards and Interactive Documentaries

You might remember the Tamagotchi. Released in 1996, the keychain-sized digital pets became one of the biggest toy fads of the 1990s. With over forty-four versions released since its inception, by 2017 around 82 million Tamagotchi had been sold worldwide (Bandai-Namco Group 2017). The original game mechanics of the Tamagotchi were pretty basic. Once the toy was activated, an egg would appear on the screen. Players would set the unit's clock, and then the egg would wiggle for a few minutes before hatching into a small pet. Players could care for their digital pet as much or as little as they chose. Pets would go through stages of development, and could 'die' from neglect, old age, sickness, or be killed by predators. Recent models of Tamagotchi have included infrared connectivity among users, the possibility for the pets to fall in love and get married with other pets, and a virtual currency – the "Gotchy Points", to be used within the in-game shop to buy new accessories.

In 2010, Depaul – a youth homelessness charity headquartered in Britain (Depaul 2019), launched iHobo, an app with a similar concept to the Tamagotchi. But instead of a fun pet, it generated a virtual homeless person. After installing the app, players were asked to take care of the needs of this iHobo for three (real time) days. Like in the case of the Tamagotchi, if players failed to properly care for their 'virtual dependent', the homeless person would deplete his/her resources and, eventually, die. At the end of the three days, users were asked to make a donation, via mobile, of £3, £5 or £10 to Dupal.

In 2017 *The Good Lobby* (TGL), a civic start-up committed to equalising political power and influence in Europe, was established in Brussels (The Good Lobby 2019). In order to achieve its goals, TGL promotes skill-sharing and cooperation among citizens with different professional backgrounds.[1] TGL ideated the *TGL Awards* to recognise the most successful citizen-driven projects and advocacy collaborations between citizens – be they professionals or volunteers – companies, civil society organisations, political representatives, and universities. There are eight different awards, rewarding – inter alia – the citizen-lobbyist of the year, the most civically committed academic, the most civically engaged political representative, and the most impactful non-governmental organisation (NGO) campaign. Nominees are crowdsourced through the website of TGL, and then elected by a jury. The winners for each category are announced during an official ceremony.

Similar in scope is an initiative promoted by the Women's Link Worldwide (WLW), an international non-profit organisation advocating the human rights of women and girls, especially those facing multiple inequalities (women's link worldwide 2019). Every year, the WLW holds the *Gender Justice Uncovered Awards* to recognise the influence of the judiciary in the daily lives of people. There are two award categories. The 'Gavel award' is allocated to judicial decisions that promote gender equality. The 'Bludgeon award', instead, is allocated to judicial decisions that are retrograde and discriminatory.[2] In both cases there are a gold, silver and bronze winners. An independent jury of three members, composed of women and men from different parts of the world, is nominated every year and tasked with the responsibility of selecting the winners of the categories. In addition to these two awards, there is a 'People's Choice Award'. As the name suggests, this is decided by the number of votes received online – with the person with

---

[1] In terms of educational offer, formats may range from the "advocacy schools" (young advocates are trained on EU legal and political advocacy and pro bono collaboration) to the "EU pro bono master classes" (aimed at instilling a culture of pro bono collaboration into non-profit advocates, lawyers and business professionals) and the "Lobbying Summer Academy" (an international event running for a week in Bilbao that combines skilled-based, theoretical insights and other forms of experiential learning on lobbying and advocacy). In 2018 the Academy hosted a session dedicated to the use of game-design elements to support advocacy strategies. Interestingly, the simulation exercise was itself based on game dynamics. The aim was to provide participants with practical insights about the complexity of developing a gamified strategy (Alemanno 2019).

[2] The awards recognise either sentences or decisions issued in the context of a judicial process – be it national, regional or international – by judges, members of committees or commissions that monitor human rights treaties through individual cases, or members of asylum and refugee boards or offices, or sentences or decisions that have had a positive or negative effect on gender equality (for example, decisions regarding sexual and reproductive rights or gender discrimination).

the most online votes winning the award. Some of the cases nominated for Awards may also become part of the Gender Justice Observatory of WLW. The Gender Justice Observatory is a programme that maintains a free online database of jurisprudence with case summaries, as well as the complete texts of judicial decisions that have established a significant precedent on gender issues, in both English and Spanish.

The storytelling adopted by *Fort McMoney* is less playful compared to the TGL and WLW awards. *Fort McMoney* is an interactive game and documentary launched in 2013 by the filmmaker David Dufresne.[3] Divided into three episodes, *Fort McMoney* let players to virtually walk around Fort McMurray, the largest industrial site in Canada, meet residents and interact with them. The game is designed to be played in real-time over a four-week period, with the aim of acquainting the audience with the social, economic and environmental problems of that industrial region. Players are also asked to vote in referendums and surveys at the end of each week of game. Through the website hosting the documentary, players could engage in debates, and gather consensus about their proposals on the future of the city.[4]

One last case before moving to the comparative analysis is that of *Empaville*. Launched in 2016 by an international research consortium, *Empaville* is a role-playing game on participatory budgeting (Empatia 2019). Albeit not the first in this genre (Gordon 2017) it has been one of the most successful. The project tests the skills of participants in an experience of participatory budgeting in the fictitious city of Empaville. Citizens/players must identify and point out the needs of the main districts of the city (Downtown, Midtown and Uptown), engaging as equal partners on issues of public significance and arriving from individual preferences to collective decisions.

B. The Evolution of Gamified Advocacy

The six cases described above share three common traits. First: all these initiatives are run by civil society actors, who operate individually – such as

---

[3] The documentary involved over two years of research and cost of $870,000 (Canadian dollars). It incorporated sixty days of filming in twenty-two locations in the city, with 2,000 hours of footage shot (office national du film de Canada 2019).

[4] David Dufresne was not new to this kind of interactive documentary. In 2009 he directed an interactive road-movie called *Prison Valley* (Prison Valley 2019). Viewers of this interactive documentary were asked to impersonate a journalist investigating the prison industry in Fremont County, Colorado – home to 36,000 residents, thirteen prisons, and 7,735 convicts. As in the case of *Fort McMoney*, players can virtually explore the area and interact with local characters. At key moments, all the site's visitors and those affiliated with the industry can join in live online debates and exchange emails with characters on the issues raised in the story.

in the case of *Fort McMoney* – or in a more structured form, typically a NGO. Second: they incorporate game-elements (points, badges, levels, challenges, rewards). These are woven into digital applications or websites, for a variety of purposes, from gaining attention on a specific issue, to raising awareness of the public or fundraising. Third, and fundamentally, all cases presented above offer insights to assess the evolving role of law and access to justice in contemporary societies.

In the following paragraphs we introduce the use of game-design elements for advocacy purposes, and then analyse the three pillars of gamification in civic advocacy. We then move to assessing the rationale behind the use of gamification, and to discussing the impact on the evolution of law.

In scholarly parlance, the use of game-elements into non-game contexts, with the former aimed at making the latter more enjoyable, is described as 'gamification' (S. Deterding, et al. 2011; Burke 2014). It is important to distinguish gamification from 'mere games' – since the use of game mechanics does not necessarily make a product a (video-) game (Chorney 2012). While the main scope of games is pure entertainment, gamification is aimed at transmitting a sense of gamefulness (McGonigal 2011). According to some authors (Landers, et al. 2018) this happens under three conditions: first, the perception of a non-trivial goal that can be reasonably pursued; second, the desire to pursue that goal under behavioural rules that differ from the behavioural rules that one would normally apply; third, the voluntariness of the decision to pursue that goal. Other scholars (Yohannis, et al. 2014) claim that a gameful system must contain at least some of the nine key features of games – namely: player, environment, rule, challenge, interaction, goal, emotional experience, quantifiable outcome, negotiable consequence.

The idea that specific techniques used in games to influence player motivation could be extracted, tested, and incorporated into non-game systems dates back as the 1980s (Carroll and Thomas 1988). Yet the use of gamified elements for problem-solving beyond the traditional connotation of games as entertainment has reached new prominence in recent years with the rise of digital platforms, and especially with the near-universal adoption of social media.

Civil society actors are no exception to this trend. The use of game-design elements has developed quickly in the civic sector and has become increasingly common in advocacy strategies. But be warned on this point: the use of games with the aim of producing social change dates back decades. Art is a case in point. In the early Seventies, for instance, the futurist Buckminster Fuller (Buckminster Fuller 1971) designed what he called 'The World Game: Integrative Resource Utilization Planning Tool'. The installation consisted of a map illustrating world resources. Players were asked to propose solutions to global problems by matching human needs with available resources. The New Games Movement is also a well-known example. The Movement, which took off in the San Francisco Bay Area and quickly expanded worldwide, started as a protest against the Vietnam War, against a backdrop of dramatic social and economic change, fuelled by civil rights, feminism, and a looming energy crisis (Fluegelman 1976). The first multi-player game created by the New Games Movement was called *Slaughter*. The game consisted of forty players competing with each other on a large wrestling mat over four moving balls and two moving baskets. Anyone could be arbitrarily eliminated from the game by being jarred over the mat by the other players. Over the years, The New Games Movement has inspired many scholars and activists around the world (Fullerton, et al. 2007).

In recent years, games have been used to support ideologically driven campaigns. Corporate multinationals are typical targets of these campaigns. Ian Bogost (Bogost 2008) defines this type of games 'anti-advergames': games created to censure or disparage a company rather than support it. Take the case of *The McDonald's Videogame*, developed by the Italian collective MolleIndustria (McDonald's 2019). Players impersonate business managers at McDonald's and are required to make difficult business choices in different sectors. When not directly targeting multinationals, games have been used in campaigns against politicians and policy-makers. One example of this is *Dodgy Deals* (Corporate Europe Observatory 2019). Developed by the Brussels-based non-profit Corporate Europe Observatory, this game aims to raise awareness of the lack of transparency of the EU-Canada treaty Comprehensive Economic and Trade Agreement (CETA). *Dodgy Deals* casts players as politicians, journalists or activists in a post-CETA world. Each character is assigned a mission – whether it is to pass a law for the prevention of toxic gold-mining or write a newspaper article about weed killers – and navigate the formidable new obstacles that, according to the authors of the game, CETA will introduce via 'regulatory cooperation'.

C. Technology

I. Mechanics: Technology

Let's return to our five case studies. Clearly, the projects differ in length, target audience and overall objectives. Yet they all implement game-design elements. This gives us the opportunity to introduce and discuss the three pillars of gamification in civic advocacy. The first is concerned with the mechanics of gamified advocacy strategies. The second is related to the rationale of gamification. The third has to do with its goals.

Mechanics first. All cases described at the outset of this chapter are based on technological features, be it an app, an interactive website, a social network, or a combination thereof. This is an important clue. Technologies have altered the way citizens and civic groups locate and access information, communicate and learn from each other, and interact with public powers. Thanks to the spread of electronic devices, social interaction costs have lowered radically, and audience numbers have become potentially unlimited. A communication technology such as the Internet – explained Manuel Castells (Castells 1996) – allows anyone to communicate information from any location simultaneously and has scaled up the social pressure to participate in social networks (Lupia and Sin 2013). Drawing on Castells' ideas, it has been argued that the growing connectedness of the world is among the most important social facts of our times (Mulgan 1997).

Look at data on smartphones, instant messaging apps, and social media. The number of smartphone users is forecast to grow from 2.1 billion in 2016 to around 2.5 billion in 2019, with smartphone penetration rates also on the rise. Over 36 per cent of the world's population is projected to use a smartphone by 2018, up from about 10 per cent in 2011 (Newzoo 2018). By 2017, WhatsApp reached 1.3 billion monthly active users, becoming the world's most popular messaging app alongside Facebook Messenger. On 31 December 2017 – in India alone – 14 billion messages were reportedly exchanged through the app (Singh 2017). As of the third quarter of 2017, Facebook had 2.07 billion monthly active users, and the micro-blogging service Twitter averaged 330 million monthly active users.

The pervasiveness of digital technologies has fostered a culture of convergence, with key consequences for civil society actors. Many of us live our lives as much online as off. This means that anyone with an Internet connection is potentially allowed to participate in matters that, in the past, were reserved to an elite few (Jenkins 2009). Technological progress has allowed citizens to interact via networks, reciprocate favours, build trust, engage in 'connective action' (Crouzet 2007; Bennett and Segerberg 2013), and eventually turn into 'communities of practice' or 'trust communities' (Wu 2015). When considering how we interact online, argues Trevor Smith (Smith 2017), it becomes clear that 'the Internet is not just a technological object or tool, but a new form of space'. Smith distinguishes three layers to this space: a physical layer, corresponding to the physical infrastructure of the Internet; a software layer, composed of the websites and programs that run on the Internet; and, finally, a layer that he calls 'wetware'. This is composed of the people that use the Internet and determine the entire structure. Other scholars have used the word 'materiality' to define the online platforms and the devices that people rely upon for interpersonal communication or organising (Milan 2015). Proof of this is that digitally coordinated activism campaigns have become the norm (Lovejoy, et al. 2012; Ober, et al. 2012). Cases like the 'Ice Bucket Challenge', 'BlackLivesMatter' or '#Metoo' remind us that technology matters to the way we live together socially (MacKenzie and Wajcman 1999).

II. Technological Determinism

Obviously, technology is not without risks. We should avoid falling into the pitfall of technological determinism – also known as the 'Borg complex' (Sacasas 2018) – by presuming that the most advanced technological solution is inherently the best one to address contemporary issues.

Technology may actually be a source of risk for civic actors experimenting with gamification. Biases in availability may limit participation only to those with appropriate technologies, while leaving those without access powerless – a problem that scholars describe in terms of a 'digital divide' (Norris 2003). Admittedly, only a few of the many cases of gamified advocacy are designed to engage both online and offline communities. Concerns about the digital divide will become less pressing while Internet penetration will improve worldwide. For the time being, however, access to the Internet is still far from being universal. The case of India is telling. We mentioned before the rapid spread of instant messaging apps such as WhatsApp and social media among Indians. In spite of this data, there are still more than a billion Indians offline. According to the latest figures, over 30 per cent of rural Indians are illiterate and 90 per cent of CSOs operating in the country do not have a web presence and barely know how to operate a computer (Silberfeld 2017).

Secondly, and relatedly, blind trust in technology may exacerbate the under-representation (or exclusion) of social groups that are already marginalised in online political and social discourses – the LGBT community or indigenous people, for instance (Barabas, et al. 2017). The case of Turkey is telling. In the aftermath of the failed coup d'etat of July 2016, thousands of smartphone owners were arrested for downloading the encrypted communication app *ByLock* (available publicly through Apple and Google app stores) amid allegations that they could be among the organisers of the putsch.

Third, digital technologies may not necessarily be the best medium to reach a wide and diversified audience, because of algorithmic biases. This is typically the case with social media: the feedback loops contained by the algorithms that govern most common social media may involuntarily drown the outreach of certain messages (Tufekci 2017).

Fourth, and finally, technology may undermine privacy. Digital technologies, with no exception, rely extensively on user data. Users decrease the control on their privacy by sharing large amount of personal information. As levels of engagement increase, a larger amount of personal information is required to be shared with administrators. Verification processes also become important because in most of cases are privacy intrusive. According to Bruce Schneier (Schneier 2013), the relationship we establish with social media providers make us comparable to a new feudal society.

D. Rationale: Social Impact and Access to Justice

Let us move to the second common trait among the cases illustrated at the outset of this chapter: the rationale behind the use of gamification. What motivates civic actors to implement game-design elements into their advocacy strategies?

To answer this question, we need to look into the numbers. With an estimated 40,000 NGOs – most of which are small organisations that may count on considerably, less membership, funding opportunities and political leverage – effective strategies for mobilising the public are essential. Small civil society organisations may have problems as simple as being unable to update their websites. They might have been provided with initial grants to build their sites, but not to pay for their upkeep and maintenance. There is often a high turnover of volunteer staff, which can lead to the abandonment of certain projects considered beyond the capability of the organisation. Small organisations may not be able to employ personnel with a good knowledge of English or French, and thus give up on engaging a wide international audience. Small civic organisations may also lack the resources to send delegates to conferences and other networking opportunities.

In sum, many organisations find it a constant struggle to raise enough funds not only to keep their advocacy projects running, but also to improve and widen their reach. Hence, the rationale of using gamification: to amplify social impact. Civic actors seek to combine digital technologies and game-design elements to develop inexpensive, yet potentially highly remunerative, ways of engaging audiences while maintaining high levels of trust from donors and relevant stakeholders. At this point, we can try to clarify the relationship between social impact and access to justice. Having framed access to justice as a matter of exclusion of segments of population from legal protection, due to lack of security or opportunity to redress legal problems to the judiciary, can we assume that innovative approaches to advocacy may indirectly help to reduce such exclusion? In other words, does the gamification of advocacy contribute to solve the issue of access to justice?

The numbers seem to confirm this hypothesis. iHobo shot to the top of the iTunes download chart. At the end of the first week of its release, it had collected 210,000 downloads. Most importantly, the app generated 4,956 new one-off donors for Depaul, who received an average donation of £2 (Civil Society 2011). Both the *TGL Awards* and the *Gender Justice Uncovered Awards* attracted impressive media coverage and generated a significant response from stakeholders. The first edition of the *TGL Awards* received fifty submissions and had 250 participants. The second edition (held on November 2018) received over 100 submissions. From November 2013 to July 2014, when the game was live, *Fort McMoney* attracted approximately 412,000 players, 21,000 of whom were 'hard-core' players who spent a considerable amount of time with the project. Around 2,000 players left 6,477 comments, and the project was mentioned 7,300 times on Twitter (Uricchio, et al. 2015). In 2015 the documentary was named 'Best Original Interactive Production Produced for Digital Media' at the Canadian Screen Awards. It also obtained distribution partnerships with three major newspapers and online media partners, in three countries: The Globe and Mail and ICI Radio Canada, in Canada; Süddeutsche Zeitung in Germany; and Le Monde in France. Finally, sessions of *Empaville* have been hosted by several municipalities in Portugal, as well as in the rest of Europe, to test the implementation of participatory budgeting and to assess the receptivity of local communities. The final report of EMPATIA (EMPATIA 2018) – the project that incorporated *Empaville* – reports a total of thirty publications, a collection of behavioural and demographic data of more than 27,000 participants, out of more than 33,000 visitors that attended four primary pilots. The webpage of *Empaville* received 1.2 million views by 200,000 unique visitors.

E. Effectiveness of Gamified Advocacy

I. Thin vs. Thick Engagement

With these numbers in mind, someone might hastily conclude that gamification provides an effective leverage of social impact. Does gamified advocacy always work? Most importantly: are game-design elements incorporated into civic-driven initiatives encouraging low-risk/low-cost engagement, or are they being a driver of social change online and offline?

On the one hand, there is a solid body of scholarship demonstrating that approaches that are 'fun' can be a powerful trigger for individual motivation, especially for democratic participation. In 2009, for instance, a study published by the MacArthur Foundation investigated the correlation between video games and their capacity to stimulate civic and political engagement. The report identified a direct correlation between the civic potential of video games and further engagement in civic life, especially by young citizens (Kahne 2009). Empirical evidence suggesting that adding game characteristics to a system results in enhanced engagement exists in the field of public policy (Sgueo 2015; Lerner 2014), college students' engagement (Barata, et al. 2017), user activity with online services (Hamari 2017), and physical exercise (Koivisto and Hamari 2017).

Similar conclusions have been reached by studies focused on civic advocacy. Pokémon Go, a location-based media game, is a case in point. Albeit
the popularity of this game plummeted after 2016, it is estimated that there
are still 5 million players daily. In 2017 Niantic, the company that created
Pokémon Go, teamed with the Knight Foundation in a multi-year commitment to promote civic engagement in local communities. The first experiment
was run in Charlotte, North Carolina: residents could explore sixteen spots
across the city and, while playing, engage in civic activities and connect with
other players. A study published in 2018 (Evans and Sacker 2018) examined
whether the intermingling of play and ordinary life might encourage players
to spend more time outside in public spaces, and how this mode of play is
experienced. The research explored whether the game mechanics of Pokémon
Go might lead players to traverse their environment using modified routes,
as well as frequent new places, and might enable new forms of sociability
to emerge. The authors found that for many players Pokémon Go worked
as a powerful incentive to be more physically active. Some players reported
that they had decided to take longer walks to work instead of using public
transportation or had decided to vary their commuting routines with a view
to extending travel, rather than reducing it. Interestingly, the research found
that many players had started to use Pokémon Go not due to an interest in
the game per se, but rather as a way to bond with their children, and thus
expand their familial relationships.

Another study led by the University of Massachusetts Lowell Climate
Change Initiative, identified a promising approach in gamified simula-
tions on climate change (Rooney-Varga, et al. 2008; Synclair 2018). The
authors of the study examined a game called the *World Climate Simulation*,
originally developed by the non-profit organisation Climate Interactive, in
which participants play delegates at international climate change negotia-
tions. Participants assume the roles of delegates from different countries or
regions and are charged with reaching an agreement to limit global warming
to no more than 3.6 degrees Fahrenheit. Each delegation offers policies to
manage its own greenhouse gas emissions. They also pledge either to support
or request money from the Green Climate Fund, which was created to help
developing countries cut their emissions and adapt to the impacts of climate
change. Since the middle of 2015, 'World Climate' has been played by more
than 46,000 people in 85 countries, including students, community groups,
executives, policymakers and military leaders. More than 80 per cent of
participants reported increased motivation to combat climate change, regardless of their political orientation or prior engagement with the issue. Across
this diverse population, people who participated in 'World Climate' deepened
their understanding of climate change and became emotionally engaged in

the issue. These emotional responses, explains the study, were linked to a stronger desire to learn and do more, from reducing the personal carbon footprints to taking political action.

II. Is Gamification Always Successful?

Can we conclude that gamification is always successful? Not always, not necessarily. Here it is useful to look at Hahrie Han's distinction between mobilising and organising (Han 2014) to assess the effectiveness of gamified advocacy. Mobilisation – explains Han – is obtained through e-mail lists or online petitions, and it normally leverages powers that already exist. Organising, in contrast, consists of capacity-building activities that create new power by bringing people to take action as a community. Organising can lock in sustained support in ways that commitment to a single issue – the type of motivation on which tend to rely the mobilising approaches – may not. Gamified advocacy seems to work well with mobilising citizens. The 'attentive public' – that is the portion of the broader general public that shares similar issue-perspectives and values, as in the case of the environmentalists (Lowe and Goyder 1983) – is an ideal target of gamification.

On occasions, the attentive public could be organised into a convergent strong public – this is a committed public, formally committed to objectives and values, usually via provision of membership fees or donations. In this respect, however, gamification seems to be less effective. With the sole exception of the *Gender Justice Uncovered Awards*, which has now reached its tenth anniversary, all cases discussed in this chapter have been unsuccessful in nurturing long-term engagement and commitment. This may indeed depend on the young age of the initiatives (think about the *TGL Awards*), or on the fact that these were one-time, non-replicable, initiatives (as for *iHobo* and *Fort McMoney*). Yet the feeling is that gamification is more effective with encouraging 'thin' engagement rather than 'thick' engagement. Thin engagement is faster, easier and potentially viral – it encompasses mainly online activities that allow people to express opinions and affiliate themselves with a particular cause. Thick engagement, on the other hand, is more intensive, informed and deliberative – it relies on small-group settings, either online or offline, in which people decide how they want to help to solve problems (Zuckerman 2013).

F. Goals

I. Gamification for Information

Having defined the mechanics and the rationale of the use of gamification for advocacy, we can now move to the analysis of the goals. There are three broad types. The first can be described as 'informative' and will be analysed in the present paragraph; the second and third (to be discussed in following paragraphs) are 'networking' and 'fundraising', respectively.

What is informative gamification? Informative types of gamified advocacy aim at raising awareness and spreading ideas about topics of interest to civic actors. Cases falling within this type of gamified advocacy are designed to provide the largest possible number of users with (direct) knowledge of a given problem as well as (indirect) knowledge of the activity of the civic actor who is responsible for the initiative. *Fort McMoney* is illustrative of this type of gamified advocacy strategy. The aim was to raise the public's awareness of a broad topic such as climate change. *Empaville* is also a case of informative gamification – the aim was to spread across local communities the values of participatory budgeting.

Examples of informative gamified advocacy abound. Take the *Get Loud Challenge*. This was launched in 2016 by two American non-profits: the Alliance for Climate Education and NextGen Climate America. The programme challenged teenagers to talk to family members about climate change and then post some kind of proof of the conversation online (for example a video, a Facebook post, an Instagram photo) (SocialToaster 2019). For each post, challenge participants received points. At the end of the 15-week challenge, those with the highest score were awarded with prizes like a college scholarship or an educational trip (Smith 2016). As the authors of the *Get Loud Challenge* explained, the game was focused on engaging teenagers in serious conversation on climate change with their relatives, ideally their parents. In fact, almost in concomitance with the challenge, the Alliance for Climate Education launched a curriculum to explain climate change to young generations.

II. Gamification for Networking

Can the *TGL Awards* and the WLW's *Gender Justice Uncovered* also be classified as examples of gamified advocacy with an informative goal? Yes and no. Both the awards are aimed at spreading knowledge about important topics. The final aim of such initiatives, however, goes beyond the simple act of sharing information with citizens, and embraces networking goals. Through the respective awards, TGL and WLW aim at creating 'engagement networks' – communities connected by a common purpose and distributed in both leadership and infrastructures. It is no coincidence that the organisations and individuals that are awarded by TGL are later engaged in the activities of the organisation, either as speakers in workshops, or as sponsors and supporters of the initiatives and events organised by TGL. According to Anne-Marie Slaughter' taxonomy (Slaughter 2017), this should be described as a 'collaboration networks', consisting of a linked group of individuals figuring out together the best ways to carry out a prescribed task that itself may evolve. In the case of WLW, the networking objective is even more evident. The Gender Justice Observatory is not only a repository of over 400 legal decisions of gender-related issues; it actually serves the scope to encourage the use of creative and innovative legal arguments by activists and advocates for the implementation of human rights standards. This, in Slaughter's terminology, would make of the Observatory an 'innovation network' – that is a linked group of individuals tasked with generating new ideas, processes, and products in the service of a prescribed general goal.

There are several more meaningful examples of gamified advocacy for networking. Look at *Recyclebank* and *Crowdrise*, for instance. The former was created in 2004 to encourage recycling of disposable waste. Users of *Recyclebank* are invited to recycle through gamified strategies (for example points redeemable for goods at local shops). The initiative has expanded over the years. It now liaises with 300 local communities, employs 180 workers, and has almost four million members. *Crowdrise*, an online platform dedicated to charitable giving, differs from other crowdfunding platforms in one essential aspect: it aims at gamifying charity. Users of the platform create their pages and profiles and compete against other users on a board based on how much they can fundraise. Since its creation, *Crowdrise* has attracted over 33 million users and raised hundreds of millions of dollars for non-profits worldwide.

III. Gamification for Fundraising

Gamified advocacy strategies that are aimed at raising funds are described in this chapter as 'fundraising'. This is obviously a vital goal for any civic actor, regardless of size and outreach. Available research shows that digital technologies may boost the success of campaigns for raising funds on social issues (Flannery, et al.: 2009), and that online and offline donors have different motivations, the former being more impulsive than the latter (Saxton and Wang 2014). *iHobo* is a good example of gamification being harnessed for fundraising. But other examples can be found, too. Since 2004, for instance, Games for Change has worked to create 'social impact games' (games that allow players to engage in civic actions with impact in the real world). The most successful case is the Facebook-game *Half the Sky*. The game resembles the aesthetics of Farmville, with the difference that players are challenged to reflect on women's precarious situations all over the world. The game gathered 800,000 players in the first three months after its launch and collected more than $300,000 in donations or sponsorships.

G. Gamification and Crowdsourcing

Admittedly, the boundaries between information/networking/fundraising types of gamification are not watertight. To begin, both networking and fundraising types of gamification are also aimed at informing communities and stakeholders. At the same time, we can safely assume that networking initiatives are also designed to attract donors, and that fundraising is already the result of a networking strategy. These divergences notwithstanding, we believe that all types of gamified advocacy share a common aim, and this concerns crowdsourcing resources – be these material or immaterial.

What do crowdsourcing and gamification have in common? The former is a relatively recent term (Howe 2006), used to describe a model of distributed problem-solving and production that leverages the collective efforts of online communities for specific purposes set forth by a crowdsourcing organisation, be it public or private (Brabham 2008). The primary general goals of crowdsourcing are cost saving and efficiency: organisations are capable of handling tasks that would be difficult to perform without collective support. Experiments with crowdsourcing, as well as experimenting with gamification, rely on the expected benefits that collective participation can produce (Morschheuser 2017). From a material point of view, both crowdsourcing and gamification may potentially enhance crowd magnitude and boost fundraising. From a more general perspective, they provide a further chance to civic actors to respond to their respective challenges and become alternative sources of power.

H. Concluding Remarks

The evidence examined in this chapter suggests that, taken alone, gamification is not a game changer for civic advocacy. The moment we combine the thin and short-term engagement nurtured by most of the cases of gamified advocacy with the drawbacks stemming from the use of digital technologies, we should conclude that gamified tools are not advancing civic advocacy much further.

On the other side, the increased use of gamified nudges into advocacy strategies from civic actors is having an impact on a number of legal issues. First and foremost is the access to justice. As we explained before, technology-driven strategies have important implications for the outreach of civic actors and may potentially help to reduce the margins of exclusion of individuals and communities. Second, the combination of digital technologies and game-design elements to foster social change is still at the outset, and many of the processes described in this chapter are still unfolding, but its legal implications are crucial. Two are particularly important.

The first concerns privacy-protections. We explained how the issue of privacy is pervasive across gamified forms of advocacy. Civic actors have started to develop early responses to this problem, by using blockchain technology. The Californian non-profit organisation Democracy Earth, for instance, has developed a project called Sovereign. This is based on existing blockchain software platforms, but instead of producing units of cryptocurrency, it creates tokens called 'votes'. These units are assigned to registered users, who can vote as part of organisations (political parties, municipalities or governments) who set themselves up on the network. Unlike conventional voting systems, users of Sovereign can debate with each other before voting, and are allowed to assign more votes to a single issue. In order to protect users' anonymity (transactions on blockchain platforms are typically free to view to anyone), Sovereign proposes to partner with providers (ZCash for instance) specialised in anonymous transactions.

The second key legal issue that is currently at stake is equal access. On this point an interesting example is the People-Led Innovation project, ideated by the NYU GovLab, in partnership with the Bertelsmann Foundation. This is a methodology that city officials can use to determine how to become more empowered and effective by placing citizens and interest groups at the centre of problem-solving processes. Several of the best practices reported by the GovLab incorporate gamified elements.

Bibliography

Alemanno, A. (2019), 'The Lobbying Summer Academy', available at <http://albertoalemanno.eu/the-lobbying-summer-academy/> (last accessed 24 May 2019).

Bandai-Namco Group (2017), *Tamagotchi 20th Anniversary Edition!*, available at <https://www.bandainamco.co.jp/cgi-bin/releases/index.cgi/file/view/5986?entry_id=5435> (last accessed 23 May 2019).

Barabas, C., N. Narula and E. Zuckermann (2017), *Defending Internet Freedom Through Decentralization: Back to the Future?*, MIT Media Lab, available at <https://static1.squarespace.com/static/59aae5e9a803bb10bedeb03e/t/59ae908a46c3c480db42326f/1504612494894/decentralized_web.pdf> (last accessed 21 May 2019).

Barata, G., S. Gama, J. Jorge, D. Gonçalves (2017) 'Studying different differentiation in gamified education: a long-term study', *Computational Human Behaviour* 71: 550.

Bennett, L. W. and A. Segerberg (2013), *The Logic of Connective Action Digital Media and the Personalization of Contentious Politics*, Cambridge: Cambridge University Press.

Bogost, I. (2008), 'The Rhetoric of Video Games', in K. Salen (ed.), *The Ecology of Games: Connecting Youth, Games, and Learning*, Cambridge, MA: MIT Press.

Brabham, D. C., 2008. 'Crowdsourcing as a model for problem-solving: An introduction and cases'. *Convergence: The International Journal of Research into New Media Technologies*, 14: 75.

Buckminster Fuller, R. (1971), *The world game: integrative resource utilization planning tool, World Resource Inventory*, Carbondale, IL: Southern Illinois University.

Burke, B. (2014), *Gamify: How Gamification Motivates People to Do Extraordinary Things*, New York: Routledge.

Carroll, J. M. and J. C. Thomas (1988), FUN, *ACM SIGCHI Bulletin* 19:3, p. 21.

Castells, M. (1996), *The Rise of the Network Society*, Oxford: Blackwell.

Chorney, A. I. (2012), 'Taking the game out of gamification', *Dalhousie Journal of Interdisciplinary Management*, 8:1.

Corporate European Observatory (2019), *Dodgy Deals*, available at <https://corporateeurope.org/en/international-trade/2017/12/dodgy-deals> (last accessed 23 May 2019).

Civil Society (2011), 'iHobo iPhone app tops 600,000 downloads', available at <https://www.civilsociety.co.uk/news/ihobo-iphone-app-tops-600-000-downloads.html> (last accessed 24 May 2019).

Crouzet, T. (2007), *Le cinquieme pouvoir: Comment internet bouleverse la politique*, Paris: François Bourin Éditeur.

Depaul (2019), available at <https://uk.depaulcharity.org> (last accessed 23 May 2019).

Deterding, S., D. Dixon, R. Khaled and L. Nacke (2011) *From Game Design Elements to Gamefulness: Defining Gamification*, Proceedings of the 15th International Academic MindTrek Conference: Envisioning Future Media Environments, New York: ACM.

Empatia (2018), Enabling multichannel participation through ICT adaptations, available at <https://cordis.europa.eu/project/rcn/199845/factsheet/fr> (last accessed 21 May 2019).

Empatia (2019), *Empaville,* available at <https://empatia-project.eu/empaville/> (last accessed 23 May 2019).

Evans, L. and M. Saker, M. (2018), 'The Playeur and Pokémon Go: Examining the effects of locative play on spatiality and sociability', *Mobile Media and Communication.*

Flannery, H., C. Rhine and R. Harris (2009), *2008 DonorCentrics Internet Giving Benchmarking Analysis*, Blackbaud.

Fluegelman, F. (1976), *The New Games Book*, Garden City, NY: Dolphin Books.

Fullerton, T., J. Fron and J. Morie (2007), 'Sustainable Play: Towards a New Games Movement for the Digital Age', *Games and Culture* 2:3, p. 261.

Fung, A., J. Shkabatur and H. Russon (2013), 'Six models for the internet + politics', *International Studies Review*, 15: 30.

Gordon, E., J. Haas and B. Michelson (2017), 'Civic creativity: Role-playing games in deliberative process', *International Journal of Communication*, 11: 3789.

The Good Lobby (2019), available at <http://thegoodlobby.eu> (last accessed 23 May 2019).

Hamari, J. (2017), 'Do badges increase user activity? A field experiment on the effects of gamification', Computational Human Behaviour 71: 469.

Hamari, J. and J. Koivisto (2014), 'Measuring flow in gamification: dispositional flow scale', *Computational Human Behaviour*, 40: 133.

Han, H. (2014), *How Organisations Develop Activists*, Oxford: Oxford University Press. HOWE, J. (2006), 'The rise of crowdsourcing', *Wired Magazine* June 2006.

Jenkins, H., K. Clinton, R. Purushotma, A. Robinson and M. Weigel (2009), *Confronting the Challenges of Participatory Culture: Media Education for the Twenty-First Century*, Chicago, IL: MacArthur Foundation.

Kahne, J. et al. (2009), *The Civic Potential of Video Games*.

Krasodomski-Jones, A. et al., (2018), *Plugged In*.

Landers, R. N., G. F. Tondello, D. Kappen, A. Collmus, L. Nacke and E. Mekler (2018), 'Defining gameful experience as a psychological state caused by gameplay: Replacing the term 'Gamefulness' with three distinct constructs', *International Journal of Human-Computer Studies*, 1:1.

Lerner, J. (2015), *Making Democracy Fun: How Game Design Can Empower Citizens and Transform Politics*, Cambridge, MA: MIT Press.

Lovejoy, K. and Saxon, G. D., (2012), 'Information, Community, and Action: How Nonprofit Organizations Use Social Media', *Journal of Computer-Mediated Communication*, 17: 3, p. 337.

Lowe, P. and G. Goyder (1983), *Environmental Groups in Politics*, London: George Allen & Unwin.

Lupia, A. and G. Sin (2003), 'Which public goods are endangered? How evolving communication technologies affect the logic of collective action', *Public Choice*, 117: 315.

McDonald's (2019), *McVideogames*, available at <http://www.mcvideogame.com> (last accessed 23 May 2019).

McGonigal, J. (2015), *Super Better: A Revolutionary Approach to Getting Stronger, Happier, Braver and More Resilient*, London: Harper Collins.

MacKenzie, D. and J. Wajcman (1999), *The social shaping of technology*, Buckingham: Open University Press.

Milan, S. (2015), 'From social movements to cloud protesting: the evolution of collective identity', *Information, Communication & Society*, 18: 887.

Morschheuser, M., J. Hamari, J. Koivisto and A. Maeche (2017), 'Gamified crowdsourcing: Conceptualization literature review, and future agenda', *International Journal of Human- Computer Studies*, 106: 26.

Mulgan, G. (1997), *Connexity: How to Live in a Connected World*, London: Chatto & Windus.

Newzoo (2018), 'Global Mobile Market Report', available at <https://newzoo. com/insights/trend-reports/newzoo-global-mobile-market-report-2018-light-version/> (last accessed 21 May 2019).

Norris, P. (2003), *Democratic Phoenix: Reinventing Political Activism*, Cambridge: Cambridge University Press.

Obar, J., P. Zube and C. Lampe (2012), 'Advocacy 2.0: An Analysis of How Advocacy Groups in the United States Perceive and Use Social Media as Tool for Facilitating Civic Engagement and Collective Action', *Journal of Information Policy*, 2: 1.

Office national de film du Canada (2017), available at <https://www.onf.ca/interactif-sans-flash/> (last accessed 23 May 2019).

Prison Valley (2009), available at <http://prisonvalley.arte.tv/?lang=en> (last accessed 23 May 2019).

Rooney-Varga, J. N., J. D. Sterman, E. Fracassi, T. Franck, F. Kapmeier, V. Kurker, E. Johnston, A. P. Jones and K. Rath (2008), 'Combining role-play with interactive simulation to motivate informed climate action: Evidence from the World Climate simulation', *PLOS ONE* 13: 8.

Sacasas, M. (2013), 'Borg Complex: A Primer', The Frailest Thing Blog, available at <https://thefrailestthing.com/2013/03/01/borg-complex-a-primer/> (last accessed 21 May 2019).

Saxton, G. D. and L. Wang (2014), 'The Social Network Effect: The Determinants of Giving Through Social Media', *Nonprofit and Voluntary Sector Quarterly* 43: 5, p. 850.

Schneier, B., (2013), 'You Have no Control over Security on the Feudal Internet', *Harvard Business Review,* 6 June 2013.

Sgueo, G. (2015), 'Web-based participatory democracy', in G. Reddick and L. Anthopoulos (eds.), *Information and Communication Technologies in Public Administration: Innovations from Developed Countries*, New York: Routledge.

Silberfeld, A. T. (2017), *Disrupting Democracy: Point, Click, Transform,* Bertelsmann Foundation.

Singh, M., (2017), 'WhatsApp hits 200 million active users in India', *Mashable*, February 2017.

Slaughter, A. M. (2017), *The Chessboard and the Web: Strategies of Connection in a Networked World*, New Haven, CT: Yale University Press.

Smith, H., (2016), 'Can You Turn Climate Change Activism into a Game? Here's How To Find Out', *Grist*, February 2016.

Smith, T. G. (2017), 'Politicizing Digital Space: Theory, the Internet and Renewing Democracy', *SocialToaster* (2019), available at <https://my.socialtoaster.com//st/campaign_geoblocked/?source=iframe&key=ace> (last accessed 24 May 2019).

Synclair, M. (2018), 'How a game can move people from climate apathy to action', *The conversation*, 22 October 2018, available at <http://theconversation.com/how-a-game-can-move-people-from-climate-apathy-to-action-103822> (last accessed 21 May 2019).

Taeihagh, A. (2017), 'Crowdsourcing: a new tool for policy-making?', *Policy Sciences Journal*, 50: 629.

Tufekci, Z. (2017), *Twitter and Tear Gas: The Power and Fragility of Networked Protests*, New Haven, CT: Yale University Press.

Uricchio, W., S. Wolozin, S. Flynn and D. Tortum (2015), *Mapping the Intersection of Two Cultures: Interactive Documentary and Digital Journalism*, Chicago, IL: McArthur Foundation.

Women's Link Worldwide. (2019), available at <http://thegoodlobby.eu> (last accessed 23 May 2019).

Wu, I. (2015), Forging Trust Communities: How Technology Changes Politics, Baltimore, MD: John Hopkins University Press.

Yohannis, A. R., R. N. Landers and L. Nacke (2014), 'Defining gamification: from lexical meaning and process viewpoint towards a gameful reality', *International Journal of Human-Computer Studies*, 127, pp. 81–94, Paper presented at the 2014 International Conference on Information Technology Systems and Innovation, Indonesia.

Zuckerman, E. (2013), 'Beyond the "Crisis in Civics"', *My Earth's in Accra Blog*, 26

March 2013, available at <http://www.ethanzuckerman.com/blog/2013/03/26/beyond-the-crisis-in-civics-notes-from-my-2013-dml-talk/> (last accessed 21 May 2019).

11

Communicating the Law: Thinking through Design, Visuals and Presentation of Legal Content

Siddharth Peter de Souza

A. Introduction[1]

With the creation of Agenda 2030 and the Sustainable Development Goals, an attempt was made to embed questions of justice in Goal 16 into building inclusive institutions and societies. This is to be achieved by addressing challenges including on matters of violence, exploitation, corruption, identity and access to information while also increasing efforts to increase transparency and participatory decision-making (United Nations Sustainable Development Goals 2015). The remit with the goals is large and multi-layered, and the challenge going forward is how to develop a roadmap to address these changes.

Technology and innovation has often been mooted as a solution to challenges of access to justice for example through the use of online courts, case management techniques, different forms for automation review, crowd funding platforms and legal information and literacy apps. These technologies can deliver access by making it more inexpensive, efficient and open. There is a need, however, to examine how these technologies are designed and importantly who they are designed for in order to determine their successes (Walker and Verhaert 2019)(HiiL 2019).

One of the challenges of making technologies work is how they communicate to different audiences of users in terms of language, mediums, and designs. Unpacking the design in legal content to make it understandable,

---

[1] An earlier version of this paper was published on the Justice Innovation Blog of the Winkler Institute of Dispute Resolution available here: – <https://winklerinstitute.ca/vernacularizing-the-law-can-it-be-made-more-accessible/>

assumes importance if we are to think of the scale and usefulness of the content. It also helps to identify what gaps exist between the development of the content and the use of it.

B. The Justice Gap

Measuring a justice gap is oftentimes subject to different conceptualisations. What these interpretations can tell us is that whether on matters related to knowledge, finance, custom, identities or capabilities, there are deeply entrenched barriers that prevent the development of processes to ensure access to justice. The justice gap offers a metaphor to locate the challenges that constrain or hamper what Amartya Sen has called the distinction between *Niti* and *Nyaya*. While in the former he speaks of the justice in the form of institutions and organisational correctness, in the latter he speaks of the lived reality of the law (Sen 2011). He argues that focusing on how law manifests and is realised helps us to take cognisance of the injustices around us, rather than if we just focus on an abstract idea of equality.

In a recent study by a Task Force consisting of international organisations, an attempt was made to calculate the justice gap based on addressing questions of unmet legal needs and systematising it on the basis of whether people could obtain justice for everyday legal problems. The numbers ascertained that over 5.1 billion people lived without meaningful access to justice of which 4.5 billion did not have social, economic and political opportunities to use the law such as in terms of proof of housing or legal identity, 1.5 billion did not have the capacity to resolve their disputes for reasons including that it was expensive, unfair or complex, while over 253 million lived in situations of injustice including slavery, statelessness and conflict (Pathfinders 2019). The Task Force goes on to call for people-centred justice solutions, which focuses on understanding people's justice needs and thereafter designing solutions that are reflective of it. It also calls for a more open and collaborative way of working that also engages with other sectors like health and education, and argues that to make justice work for all, it is necessary to work towards preventing injustices, while also creating opportunities for people to participate more openly and fully in different processes (Pathfinders 2019). Arguing for a people-centred approach to justice is welcome because it acknowledges the importance of understanding the material realities, diversities and contexts of people who engage with the justice system across the world. It also reinforces the importance of a realisation-focused approach to justice because it identifies matters of agency which is whether people can use particular justice systems, it raises questions of capacity which whether people can resolve disputes and it examines questions of security which is whether people have the confidence and freedom to find resolutions to their legal problems. These aspects of agency, capacity and security in turn raise three questions: How accessible are justice solutions? How understandable are justice solutions to people who use them? How usable and useful are these solutions?

From these general discussions on the gap, this chapter aims to focus on one element that has been a barrier to access to justice, the question of communication and the ways in which legal information and knowledge is transmitted from those that develop and produce it to those that consume it. It seeks to investigate the design with which legal content is written, the language that is used, and finally how it is presented. In turn, it argues whether legal content creates structures of alienation that prevent the everyday use of such information and further what are the different ways to remedy it.

In the next section of this chapter, we will investigate the nature of legal content, how and why it is written the way it is and what are the implications of such content. Thereafter, we focus on questions of access, translation and use of legal content and emphasise the need to investigate the design of the legal content and inquire into what needs and problems the content seeks to address. Through reflection of use-cases from the authors' own work, and other projects around the world, this chapter tries to propose different ways of developing and communicating legal content to make the law accessible and useful for everyday use and consumption.

C. The Complexity of Legal Content and Its Cycle of Reinforcement

Can the language and medium commonly used to communicate the law be challenged? When laws are framed, written and published, who is the audience that they aim to address and who is being considered? If laws are meant to govern citizens and ignorance is no excuse, then is it up to these citizens to understand the language of the law in the manner in which it is written, or is it a function of law to be able to communicate its nuance and complexity in the most clear and accessible manner? These questions raise arguments for the ways in which law is communicated, and for the way in which legal information is shared. It further allows us to investigate whether there is a strategy in terms of why legal content is communicated the way it is, to whom it aims to be communicated, who the primary audience is, how it is communicated in terms of the medium that is being used and what is being communicated, in terms of content and style.

The production of legal documents, texts, and judgments are part of an industry that is designed to demand technical know-how, command over language, and knowledge of nuance to be able to meander through the intricacies of resolving disputes. David Mellinkoff in his indictment of legal language calls law, 'a profession of words' and spoke of how lawyers and judges engaged in 'contagious verbosity' (Mellinkoff 2004). He also argued how the language of the law thrived on an 'uncommon touch', where commonly used words appeared with unfamiliar meanings such as 'action' to mean 'law suit' or 'alien' to mean 'transfer' – and by doing so created legalese that became difficult for non-lawyers to follow (Mellinkoff 2004).

Take lease agreements for example, these documents need to be drafted in a manner that includes several protections for both landlord and tenant, sometimes to foresee situations that may or may not arise. They are required to convey both the rights and the obligations of both parties but at the same time also draft provisions based on particular scenarios in case of unexpected contingencies. Do standard lease agreements need to reflect just the key principles of a contract including an offer, acceptance, and consideration, and are the additional protections that are included meant to safeguard the client or are they examples of the lawyers justifying their fees, time, and knowledge. Are parties asked what is central to facilitate their intention and willingness to contract or are the conditions pre-decided for them?

Unpacking the informational density that is promoted in legal documentation and communication is challenging because it is a system that continues to reinforce itself. It requires a high degree of expertise from experts who create legal contracts or similar documents, and then it requires similar expertise and knowledge to be able to make sense of these documents. Sometimes as David Graeber argues this complexity and the creation of documentation is done in order for certain jobs just to be able to justify their roles (Graeber 2018).

It is a similar challenge when reading a judgment: is the language used by a judge meant to speak to the parties to the dispute? Is it to the public at large? Is it rather to an academic community or to further a legacy? These are all legitimate readers, and consumers of the judgment and it is often impossible to please all audiences. However, do the parties of the dispute not have the most pressing need to understand the implications of a decision? As Vicki Waye argues in her analysis of Australian judges, given the length and complexity of judgments, it is often that the judges write for each other or for each other's legal advisers than for the general public (Waye 2009). She explains how oftentimes the need to be transparent, rigorous and fair result in judges providing detailed thesis that then becomes of use only to the legal community and less to the everyday consumer of the justice sector.

Through constructing complexity, different legal instruments create power structures where only those vested with the capacity to read the law are competent enough to use it and apply it. And yet the law is very much designed to order and impact the everyday life of citizens, who have to understand the intricacies of these instruments to safeguard themselves whether with respect to the buying and selling property or leaving a will or even in understanding what a particular court is propounding on a daily basis. Providing legal content that can be useful and usable for a citizen is fundamental to enable their participation and involvement in the legal system. This is also a core component of access to justice.

With document automation systems, contract review systems and other process-related systems, there is now a real fear that particular types of jobs among lawyers will be made redundant. While technology has shown how to synthesise and analyse patterns of legal documents, it is also worth investigating how we can make the design of such content more meaningful and usable for people. (Ross Davis 2017)

In the ensuing sections, this chapter will draw from the author's own work with Justice Adda, a legal design social venture in India, as well as other use cases where design has been used to make the communication of law more engaging and understandable. The chapter builds on three main arguments. The first is to argue that accessibility in legal content does not mean 'dumbing' down the law; the second is to argue that the medium through which the law is communicated does not have to be constrained to only textual solutions but can engage in other mediums that speak to the constituencies that are most affected by it, and the third is to argue that when legal content is created it needs to be more clear about who it is speaking to.

This chapter argues that when we think of communicating the law, we must find ways to vernacularise its content. This means that the method of presenting the law must be in a manner that considers whether those that are impacted by it will find it understandable and impactful. It seeks to embed arguments for accessibility in the construction of the legal instrument by introducing reflections on the user and the medium that they will require in order to be able to use it and make sense of legal content in practice.

D. Accessibility Does Not Mean Losing Nuance

One of the misconceptions of building accessibility into legal instruments is that you can only do so by 'simplifying' or 'dumbing' down the complexity of the legal document. However, I would argue that the challenge is different. It is instead the process of identifying the need of a particular legal document or text, the value that such a text has for a particular group of people, and finding how they will use it in their everyday practice. If the purpose of a legal text is only to provide explanation or knowledge for lawyers or academics that study the law, then this is inherently problematic. This is because lawyers are not the end users of such content. They instead use this content to then exercise a function to customise it to a client's needs. Constructing content with an end user's (client's) interest in mind does not devalue or eliminate

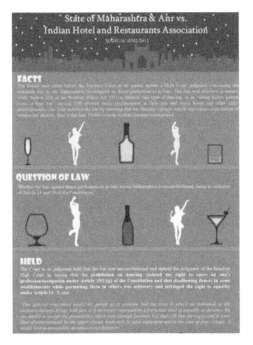

Figure 11.1 Sample from 'Illustrated Cases from the Supreme Court of India' by Justice Adda and Manupatra (Justice Adda, 2018)

the role of a lawyer – it just makes the process and the relationship between client and lawyer more transparent. This is because in this case, in addition to understanding the density or complexity of content, other aspects like understanding the application and use of content assume importance. The entangling of different aspects of inaccessibility whether knowledge related or financial or symbolic are what must be considered when understanding the impacts of legal content.

In a project designed to unpack judgments of the Supreme Court of India, which had a public interest value, Justice Adda attempted to understand what were the key elements that needed to be communicated in a case to make the knowledge around the case useful and usable for an end user, in this case a lay citizen (Justice Adda 2018). Through studying projects that focused on communicating the law and what information was essential for everyday practice, the project focused on reframing the language, visual representation, and brevity while trying to represent the case. An example from the project is shown above, and highlights three key aspects, the facts of the case, the questions of law and what the court ruled as being significant to be communicated.

While the project does attempt to communicate the law in a more accessible manner, among the feedback received for the project was that the language could still be simplified further. One of the challenges of approaching accessibility through a process of 'simplification' is that the starting point of such as process is the original document and judgment, one that is riddled with complexity and legal verbosity. As a result, any content that is produced is seen in comparison with the original content. This could be seen favourably as it communicates the content more clearly and accessibly or it can be seen unfavourably and accused of losing nuance.

The process advocated above of thinking of accessibility of communication while drafting legal content ensures that accessibility is not seen as a process of distillation or interpretation but rather very much part of the construction of the content in the first place. Doing so, will ensure the content creators – whether lawyers, judges or policymakers, are forced to confront the end user while producing such content (Passera 2018).

E. More than Text

Most legal content in the official legal system (state law) is produced in the form of text. However, if we are to reflect on how people consume legal content, text is just one of many options. With the advent of technology, the mediums through which we can consume content has increased exponentially. If law is meant to be used and understood, can the medium through which it is communicated be chosen based on user preferences of convenience, opportunity and need. A common feature of most of the textual mediums is that they are synonymous with detail and technicality.

In fact back in 1992, Joseph Kimble, a law professor, wrote a charter for plain language writing where he highlighted the importance of design and advocated the use of diagrams, table and charts to help explain the legal text (Kimble 1992). In their work on developing Self Help legal material, Greiner et al. offer a new way to think through building legal content by identifying what is seen as a legal problem, breaking it down into its parts which maybe cognitive, psychological or mental and then measuring how far these parts have to do with law, and then drawing influences from other disciplines (Greiner, Jiménez, and Lupica 2017). They further show by using visuals and plain language, that complex legal jargon can be broken down to make it more accessible for a non-legal audience.

The Comic Contracts project in South Africa is one powerful example where contracts are built using illustrations. In such contracts the parties are represented by characters, the terms of the agreement are in the form of pictures and the parties then sign it based on the illustrations. As Robert de Rooy mentions in an article to Forbes

'We produce illustrated contracts for people who are illiterate, people who are not literate in the language of the contract, employers with multicultural workplaces or companies that wish to transact with people who suffer from reading or intellectual disabilities. We want to enable people to be able to independently understand the contracts they are expected to sign' (Vitasek 2017)

A key idea of the comic contracts besides its simplicity and transparency is that it places agency in the hands of the user to be able to not only make sense of the terms of agreement, but also, decide whether it is able to meet its needs and demands. Comic Contracts now has different kinds of contracts including Fruit Picker agreements, General Farm Workers Agreement, Kitchen Staff contracts for hotel etcetera. In this case, the information that is being developed is specifically for the purpose of enabling business transactions, and meant to ensure that it could be used in place of a legal document. Visualisation techniques as Helena Haapio has argued help promote greater understanding and use of contracts while also reducing transaction costs and reducing the risks of disputes (Haapio 2013)(Barton, Berger-Walliser, and Haapio 2013).

When the idea is to create legal awareness and literacy, then the content can also take different mediums and forms. For knowing more about rights, the Stanford Legal Design Lab, and a pioneer of the Legal Design movement, Margaret Hagan developed an application called Law Dojo, which allows different kinds of audiences to know more about their rights through gamification. (Hagan 2012) These apps are on a variety of aspects from criminal law, to how to figure your way through law school. While they do use text, what is clear is that the medium to communicate legal content is interactive and engaging. Hagan also provides strategies for how to communicate visually including thinking through why the visual is important, what format to use and how to execute it, depending upon the target audience (Hagan 2014).

In my work with Justice Adda, for a project on the Sustainable Development Goals, we attempted to find out what these ideas actually mean for children. One of our challenges was to communicate technical frameworks of targets and indicators into knowledge that could be contextually significant for a younger audience. It was also relevant to emphasise that children were not just consumers of content, but they could also drive it. To do so, we asked children from ten countries including India, Brazil, and Russia to record on a short mobile video what they felt about goals and why they were important and relevant to their everyday lives. The result was that rather than distil these responses into a paper or blog, and offer a narrative, we put together a short film, where the children drove the narrative. As a result, the nature of the content was not technical as may have been the case if we had written about it. It was rather in a language of the user, but also in a medium (film) that children would be more interested in following.

Another example of trying to use mediums beyond text that Justice Adda used was to create a series of playlists around common social justice issues. The challenge here was while we are all confronting challenges of climate change, gun violence, crackdowns on dissent, these are debates that affect everybody, and yet the arena through which they are discussed is often limited to largely technical debates. In this project, we attempted to blend text with existing music that has already reflected on such issues, in an attempt to draw those who want to engage with contemporary challenges but feel left out by technical discourses.

With both projects while the mediums chosen were meant to introduce different ways of presenting and speaking about law and justice issues, there was also an acknowledgement that such content is still not seen as mainstreamed, but rather as interpretation of other discourses. A takeaway from the project is that while we presented the content as being 'different', it was important not to showcase this work as 'alternatives' but rather as equally useful 'options' to engaging with everyday legal issues. Only then would the reluctance of moving beyond text be confronted.

F. Who Are We Talking to?

A common theme in this paper has been to identify whom the end user and audience is when generating, producing and consuming legal content. As has been demonstrated in the paper, thinking about mediums and questions of accessibility stem from changing the way we approach producing legal content. It requires a change from a supply-oriented approach where the providers speak a language that is convenient to them, or represents their interests, whether institutional, political or personal, to rather a demand oriented one where they think more in terms of the audience.

Helena Haapio has also argued for a similar approach in her work on contracts. She introduces the model of proactive contracts as one where the contract 'is crafted for the parties, especially for the people in charge of its implementation in the field, not for a judge who is supposed to decide about the parties failures' (Haapio 2013). She often cites the example of Elizabeth Warren who said, 'I teach contract law at Harvard Law School and I can't understand my credit card contract. It is not designed to read' (Haapio 2013) (Warren 2009).

The idea of the end user/audience is thus critical when producing legal content. Drawing ideas from human-centred design in order to develop legal documents that serve the needs of people can be helpful. Don Norman argues how this approach puts 'human needs, capabilities, and behaviour first, then designs to accommodate those needs, capabilities, and ways of behaving' (Norman 1990). He argues that for good design, what is essential is that there must be 'discoverability', which means that it is possible to figure out what actions are suitable to make use of a particular design, and second 'understanding', which means to be able to make sense of what the particular product is all about (Norman 1990). These factors are currently not seen as a critical aspect of building legal content where the use and service of legal content is part of a complex network of intermediaries or experts whether judges, lawyers, or mediators. The end user who is required to be able to understand and discover the details of particular legal findings, is compelled to do so through seeking assistance from one of these intermediaries or experts, rather than resolve it on their own.

G. Conclusion

From the previous analysis of examining the complexity of legal documents, exploring the challenges of making documents accessible, unpacking models beyond text and then testing it with different audiences, this chapter has attempted to show how through changing the ways in which legal content is produced it is possible to increase the consumption and awareness of the law, and in the process demystify it.

This chapter advocates for a vernacularisation of legal content that is attentive to the needs of the people most impacted by it, and most vulnerable to disinformation and lack of information. Using avenues for interpretation by lawyers or translations by other experts is not enough because then the content is designed to facilitate that industry, and not the needs of lay citizens. It would be completely contradictory to propound principles of access to justice when such principles are offered in a language that is inherently exclusionary and in mediums that require translation and interpretation.

In sum what is needed is firstly that the production of the legal content must emerge from responding to user needs for particular kinds of documentation. It should then do so by observing how particular disputes play out, and what are the barriers to access to justice. Based on this understanding, those producing legal content should then prototype different kinds of legal documentation but before finalising it, should test whether such content works. The nature of legal documentation and content, must take on a more iterative approach, wherein, it is not built for perpetuity but rather responds and is reflexive of the needs and behaviours of the users.

Bibliography

Barton, Thomas D., G. Berger-Walliser, and H. Haapio (2013), 'Visualization: Seeing Contracts for What They Are, and What They Could Become', *Journal of Law, Business & Ethics* 19: 47.

Graeber, D. (2018), *Bullshit Jobs: A Theory*, Simon and Schuster.

Greiner, D. James, Dalié Jiménez, and Lois R. Lupica. 2017. 'Self-Help, Reimagined', *Indiana Law Journal* 92 (3), available at <https://papers.ssrn.com/abstract= 2633032>, (last accessed on 12th March 2020).

Haapio, H. (2013), *Next Generation Contracts: A Paradigm Shift*, Lexpert.

Hagan, M. (2012), 'Law Dojo', *Margaret Hagan* (blog), 2012, available at <http:// www.margarethagan.com/apps-games/law-dojo/>, (last accessed on 12th March 2020).

——— 2014, 'Legal Communication Design Toolbox', Legal Design Toolbox, 16 March 2014. <http://www.legaltechdesign.com/LegalDesignToolbox/commu nicate-info-in-a-better-way/>, (last accessed on 12th March 2020).

HiiL (2019), 'Innovating Justice: Needed and Possible. The Report of the Innovation Working Group of the Task Force on Justice.', available at <https://www.hiil. org/news/innovating-justice-needed-and-possible-report-of-the-innovation- working-group-of-the-task-force-on-justice/>, (last accessed on 12th March 2020).

Justice Adda (2018), 'Illustrated Cases of the Supreme Court of India', 2018, avail- able at <https://www.justiceadda.com>, (last accessed on 12th March 2020).

Kimble, J. (1992), *Plain English: A Charter for Clear Writing*. Thomas M. Cooley Law School.

Mellinkoff, D. (2004), *The Language of the Law*, Wipf and Stock Publishers.

Norman, D. A. (1990), *The Design of Everyday Things*, Doubleday.

Passera, S. (2018), 'Flowcharts, Swimlanes, and Timelines: Alternatives to Prose in Communicating Legal–Bureaucratic Instructions to Civil Servants', *Journal of Business and Technical Communication* 32 (2): 229–72.

Pathfinders (2019), 'Task Force on Justice ¦ Justice for All Report', available at <https://www.justice.sdg16.plus/report>, (last accessed on 12th March 2020).

Ross Davis, A. (2017), 'Plain Language Law Shaping the Way Legal Solutions Are Delivered', *Legal Insight* (blog). 7 November 2017. <http://insight.thomsonreu ters.com.au/posts/plain-language-law-shaping-way-legal-solutions-delivered>, (last accessed on 12th March 2020).

Sen, A. (2011), *The Idea of Justice*. Harvard University Press.

United Nations Sustainable Development Goals (2015), 'Peace, Justice and Strong Institutions – SDG 16', available at <https://www.un.org/sustainabledevelop ment/peace-justice/>, (last accessed on 12th March 2020).

Vitasek, K. (2017), 'Comic Contracts: A Novel Approach To Contract Clarity And Accessibility', *Forbes* <https://www.forbes.com/sites/katevitasek/2017/02/14/ comic-contracts-a-novel-approach-to-contract-clarity-and-accessibility/>, (last accessed on 12th March 2020).

Walker, T., and P. Verhaert (2019), 'Technology and Legal Empowerment around the World', *The Engine Room*, available at <https://www.theengineroom.org/ tech-and-legal-empowerment-around-the-world/>, (last accessed on 12th March 2020).

Warren, E. (2009), 'Elizabeth Warren on Credit Card "Tricks and Traps"'. *NOW on PBS*, available at <https://www.pbs.org/now/shows/501/credit-traps.html>, (last accessed on 12th March 2020).

Waye, V. C. (2009), 'Who Are Judges Writing For?' *UWA Law Review* 34 (December), available at <https://papers.ssrn.com/abstract=2354845>, (last accessed on 12th March 2020).

12

Digital Rights, Design and Data Protection

Alistair Alexander and Mira Suleimenova

A. Introduction

In recent years the sheer scale and growth of the tech sector has caused unbridled optimism over digital platforms to become a growing public anxiety about the power of Silicon Valley.

In 2019, seven of the ten largest companies in the world by market capitalisation were tech companies. The five largest US tech companies, the so-called 'GAFAM –' Google (now Alphabet), Amazon, Facebook, Apple, Microsoft – have a combined value of four trillion US dollars, (Wikipedia 2019) whereas the world's ten largest oil companies are worth a mere 1.37 trillion US dollars in comparison (Coleman 2017).

The rapid rise of the tech industry has been based on technology platforms' inherent tendency for market dominance. Google maintains a staggering 89.9 per cent share of all web searches worldwide. 75.4 per cent of all desktop operating systems still run on Microsoft Windows. Indeed, Microsoft recently eclipsed Amazon and Apple as the world's most valuable company. With its rapidly growing cloud services Amazon accounts for 52.7 per cent of all e-commerce sales in the US (Statista 2019). Amazon Web Services provides 34 per cent of Internet 'cloud' infrastructure (Meyer 2019). Facebook's market share for social media, although decreased in recent months, remains an astounding 66 per cent (Meyer 2019). Google and Facebook (McNair 2018) combined pull in 52 per cent of the global digital advertising market of 327 billion US dollars.

This extraordinary dominance of global economy by a handful technology services is highly dependent on the extraction, processing and commodification of personal data.

This business model has far-reaching implications for all societies, as was starkly revealed by the 2018 scandal over Cambridge Analytica, whereby data surreptitiously acquired from Facebook was being extensively used to influence the outcome of political campaigns.

This business model was described by Shoshana Zuboff in her book *The Age of Surveillance Capitalism* as follows:

> 'Surveillance capitalism unilaterally claims human experience as free raw material for translation into behavioural data . . . Today . . . rights to privacy, knowledge, and application have been usurped by a bold market venture powered by unilateral claims to others' experience and the knowledge that flows from it.' (Zuboff 2019)

Zuboff identifies the core purpose of social media and communication platforms as the extraction of intimate personal data to create what she calls 'behavioral surplus'. This data is increasingly being used not only to market to us precisely what we want – but actually to shape our choices not just as consumers, but also as citizens:

> 'Surveillance capitalists discovered that the most-predictive behavioral data come from intervening in the state of play in order to nudge, coax, tune, and herd behaviour toward profitable outcomes . . . [so] automated machine processes not only know our behavior but also shape our behavior at scale . . . In this phase of surveillance capitalism's evolution, the means of production are subordinated to an increasingly complex and comprehensive "means of behavioural modification."' (Zuboff 2019)

In the corporate sector, a steady stream of data breaches has further eroded public confidence. In 2018 alone it was revealed that 327 million guests of the Marriott Hotel group had their names, addresses, passport numbers and check-in dates compromised (Cook 2018). Cathay Pacific revealed that data relating to names, passport numbers and credit card details of 9.4 million customers were affected (The Guardian 2018). British Airways also disclosed that data was stolen from them, which revealed financial information on over 360,000 customers.

The tech sector is also vulnerable to data breaches. Google acknowledged that external developers could access personal data on Google+ between 2015 and March 2018 (Wong 2018). Last year Facebook also admitted that intruders could access profile data on up to 50 million users.

The right to privacy is a fundamental human right, equivalent to right to life, liberty and security. It is documented in the Universal Declaration of Human Rights (United Nations General Assembly 1948). In Europe, similarly, right to private life is guaranteed by the European Convention of Human Rights (European Council 1950) and the European Charter of Fundamental Rights (European Union 2012). The right to protection of personal data, per Article 8 of EU Charter (European Union 2012), was implemented and put to action with General Data Protection Regulation (GDPR) (European Union 2018).

Adopted in 2016 and enforced in 2018, GDPR is the product of harmonisation of fragmented national laws of EU member states into one binding normative framework. It would be fair to say that GDPR is the only current normative framework laying ground rules for EU consumers to actually exercise the rights in relation to processing of personal data in any jurisdiction. This makes GDPR a unique example of regional legislation impacting organisations globally. Since becoming law GDPR has become a major argument in the discourse about digital privacy and data protection world-wide. Under GDPR, the 2018 Facebook data breach may well lead to a fine of up to 1.6 billion US dollars (Techworld 2019).

For lawyers, these issues present a new and challenging terrain that will – at the very least – need to be effectively navigated in order to maintain the trust and confidence of their clients. Lawyers who cannot persuade their clients that their data and communications are secure will surely struggle to survive in this environment.

For most in the legal sector, this will require a far more comprehensive understanding of data and privacy regulations, as well as the principles underlying it. In the meantime, these issues also present significant opportunities for lawyers who recognise the critical importance of digital privacy in their work.

In this article, we aim to reflect the key challenges relating to data security and privacy in the legal sector and suggest how lawyers can address them. We will first discuss general public approach and then explore how issues of data and privacy relate to legal profession. We then examine main aspects of GDPR and what effect they have on the day-to-day work of legal professionals. We also look at various approaches law firms may explore to review their own business practices and internal processes, to achieve a 'privacy first 'culture, as well as to implement the principles of 'privacy by design'.

This article then covers The Glass Room project, which presents an immersive exhibition to raise awareness about issues around data and privacy. This project has been highly successful in engaging staff in large companies as well as lawyers.

B. Public Discourse about Privacy and Data Protection

In over fifteen years of work in this field, Tactical Tech has collected thousands of opinions about digital privacy and data security from members of general public and professionals of different industries. When trying to reach and engage professionals in the legal sector, we face many of the same barriers that we see when talking to the wider public.

A very common response from members of the public is that they have 'nothing to hide' online. Lawyers, mindful of their client confidentiality, are less likely to make this argument. Indeed, the relationship between lawyer and client actually presents one of the strongest arguments against that thinking, namely, that there must be confidential areas of communication in order for civic structures to function effectively.

Many others suggest that no one would be interested in their data; but of course, no one needs to be – the main processes behind data extraction are algorithmically automated to match our profiles and online histories with highly targeted advertising.

Legal professionals, as many members of the wider public, will often believe there is nothing they can do; the 'genie' of their personal data is already out of the bottle. Of course there is some truth to that, as so much of our data is shared online – there are plenty of practical measures people can take to moderate the amount of data they share and reclaim their agency over the data extraction process.

Many see no alternatives to the common online tools and services, which invasively collect up our most intimate thoughts and behaviours and then turn them into marketable data, but there are plenty of privacy-respecting alternatives out there, from secure email services (posteo.de or runbox.org), to secure messaging (Signal for iPhone and Android), to easy video calls (meet.jit.si) – that is, if you know where to look.

The other key issue we find is the 'connection problem': there is really no point in people having secure apps and tools if none of their colleagues or friends use them. Here an organisation such as a law firm can help, by fostering a culture where privacy is not just considered but placed at the core of all activities and communications.

These barriers are important to understand in the context of legal practice where, with GDPR and other legal regulations, lawyers are finding a comprehensive understanding of data and privacy is increasingly central to their work.

C. Privacy and Data Protection in the Context of Legal Profession

The increasing complexity of the economy and the rapid growth of technology require modern law firms to make their services more sophisticated, in terms of scope and content of the services provided, as well as in relation to the tools lawyers rely on to increase the efficiency of these services. Also, many law firms worldwide and in Europe have begun developing legal technology addressing the three main paradigm shifts happening in the legal industry: automation, cost pressure and liberalisation of legal services (Susskind 2013).

Against this background, privacy and data protection plays a very important role in the legal profession. The legislation and ethical considerations relating to privacy and data protection concerns individual lawyers, law firms, legal technology and the law profession as a whole. Dealing with the dichotomy between societal and individual interests is the essence of legal work. Awareness about existing privacy and data protection issues becomes an indispensable tool enhancing legal practice.

GDPR introduced a number of novelties that changed the approach to processing of personal data in many organisations across the world. Below we set out the main changes in regulatory approach that in our opinion affect the legal industry.

I. Extraterritorial Scope of GDPR and Broad Definition of 'Personal Data'

Extraterritorial scope of GDPR signifies a major shift in the normative regulation of privacy and data protection in Europe. This approach aims at providing 'a level playing field for companies active on the EU markets, in a context of worldwide data flows' (European Data Protection Board 2018). Basically, two types of entities must comply with the rules laid down in the GDPR: (1) those that are established in the EU; and (2) those that directly or indirectly process personal data of the EU residents.

The last two decades have seen rapid growth of corporate law firms and internationalisation of legal practices (Empson 2007). Clifford Chance, Baker McKenzie, DLA Piper, to name just a few, are headquartered in the US, but represent clients globally. It goes without saying, that international law firms, due to their offices (establishments) in the EU, will automatically fall under the jurisdiction of GDPR.

Take another example: a Canadian law firm representing a local company in a merger deal with a German company. Most likely, due to the international nature of the project, the law firm would process data of European residents and therefore will be subject to GDPR.

GDPR does not cover information relating to legal persons (European Union 2018: Recital 14). However, definition of 'personal data' is very broad – 'any information relating to an identified or identifiable natural person' (European Union 2018: Art. 4). Although often representing legal entities, lawyers inevitably collect a significant amount of various personal information. Starting from contact details of employees of a given client, following with various data items relating to natural persons directly or indirectly connected to the client's projects.

II. Accountability Principle

GDPR introduced the principle of accountability, meaning that an organisation is under an obligation to demonstrate compliance with GDPR. In the context of a law firm, trustworthiness plays a vital part in its success. Therefore, a strong compliance programme would be directed at maintaining trust of the clients.

A strong GDPR compliance programme should start with the understanding of personal data 'flows' within a law firm. One should look into the types of personal information collected from different categories of persons: the clients and third parties (witnesses, opponents, transactional counterparts), representatives of partner firms and collaborators (experts, auditors, researchers), as well as the law firm's own employees. A data flow map should take into account how the data 'travels' into and through an organisation by tracing the specific types of personal data throughout its life cycle up to deletion.

Detailed data flow map will assist in drafting internal documentation required for demonstrating compliance, such as technical and organisational measures adopted by the organisation, overview of processing activities, documentation reflecting specific actions in case of data subjects' requests, data breach, guidelines for employees, etc.

All existing documentation should also be updated – engagement letters, employment contracts, privacy policies, and notices must comply with GDPR. Lawyers constantly share data with various vendors and tools, such as case management software companies, billing systems, emails, information storage, e-discovery solutions, and so on. All third-party tools need to be reviewed for compliance with the GDPR and Data Processing Agreements should be concluded with every vendor and service provider.

Another important aspect of a GDPR compliance programme is setting up internal systems to ensure data subjects' rights. Such rights include rights of access and right to information, right to rectification and erasure, right to restriction of processing and data portability, right to object to processing (European Union 2018: Chapter 3). The GDPR stipulates a number of exceptions to the exercising of data subjects' rights (The European Union 2018: Art. 23).

III. Data Protection by Design and Default

The former Information and Privacy Commissioner for the Canadian province of Ontario, Ann Cavoukian, introduced the concept of privacy by design during her tenure. The concept has been adopted as an essential component of the personal data protection legislation in Europe. Privacy by design (PbD)

198 | ALISTAIR ALEXANDER AND MIRA SULEIMENOVA

is a 'broad concept of technological measures for ensuring privacy' (European Data Protection Supervisor 2018).

In the EU legislation it was implemented as 'data protection by design and default' (European Union 2018: Art. 25) and became a specific legal requirement under the GDPR. It obliges data controllers and technology providers to implement data protection measures 'at the planning stage of information-technological procedures and systems.' (Data Protection Working Party and Working Party on Police and Justice 2009).

Specifically, data protection by design and default requirement calls for privacy and security to be considered at the early stages of designing products and services or setting up business practices, as well as at the time of processing the data itself. The GDPR Article 25 places emphasis on technical and organisational measures, security safeguards and data minimisation principle.

Although, there is no clear official GDPR-based methodology of implementation of data protection by design and default, the older cousin of the GDPR Article 23, PbD may provide a good basis for creating business processes, services and products with a privacy first approach in mind. PbD framework is based on seven foundational principles. A service, a product or a business practice has achieved 'privacy by design' if it has the following characteristics:

1. It is proactive, not reactive, preventative, not remedial;
2. It is private by default;
3. It embeds privacy into design;
4. It is fully functional – positive sum, not zero sum;
5. It is end-to-end secure;
6. It is visible and transparent; and
7. It respects user privacy by user-centric.

In 2018, the International Organization for Standardization (ISO) formed a proposal for a new ISO standard: Consumer Protection: Privacy by Design for Consumer Goods and Services (ISO/PC317), to be developed by 2021 (International Organization for Standardization 2018). Privacy by design, therefore, will become an official standard for those goods and services that guarantee privacy as their integral part.

Internal compliance programmes and business practices in law firms, as well as legal tech solutions may significantly benefit from implementing the Privacy by Design framework.

IV. Increased Liability and Reputational Risk for Failing to Provide Adequate Data Protection

From the perspective of the market in general, trust is the central element of any business. It goes hand in hand with the ability of a business to protect personal information and privacy of clients. Trustworthiness of a company became one of the main drivers for revenue and profitability. Based on 2018 research from Gartner, by 2020 digitally trustworthy companies are expected to generate 20 per cent more online profit than those that are not (Panetta 2018). In the meantime, according to 2017 survey by PwC, out of 2,000 adult Americans, 87 per cent will seek for an alternative service if they do not trust that a company is handling their data responsibly, while only 25 per cent of the surveyed believe that most companies handle their data responsibly (PwC 2017).

In the context of a legal profession, the trust of the client may become a major competitive advantage. Clients trust that law firms will protect their data. Client's relationships, trust and client's data are the most important assets law firms have. Protection of privacy and security has become an ongoing concern for many law firms. According to UK National Cyber Security Centre, 60 per cent of UK law firms reported information security incidents in 2017 (National Cyber Security Centre 2018). It is a known fact that confidential information held by law firms is a lucrative target for hackers. Inability of a law firm to provide adequate data protection may result not only in financial damages and loss of clients' trust, but now it is a GDPR violation sanctioned with huge fines.[1]

In June 2017, one of the industry's major players, DLA Piper, was under threat of losing all of the company's data as a result of the 'Petya' (a.k.a. 'NotPetya') ransomware cyber-attack (Janofsky 2017). For three consecutive days, the firm's management shut down all communication systems, including emails and phone. Before reconnecting the firm's intranet, all computers and devices were inspected and cleared (Salvo and Middlebrook 2018).

As a result of the cyber-attack, all of the firm's data centres and Windows-based servers on its network in forty countries were affected. The firm reported that it had to pay 15,000 hours of overtime to its IT staff. Recently, DLA Piper filed a claim against the insurance company for damages and costs arising from the attack, which may amount to several million UK pounds (Cluley 2019). If this incident were to have happened after May 2018, the

---

[1] potentially up to 4 per cent of global revenue or €20 million depending on severity of violations (European Union 2018: Art. 83).

law firm most likely would have been investigated by a responsible data protection authority and probably would pay a huge fine.

This incident also highlights that the scope of cyber security is not limited to an assigned IT specialist. Petya infected computer systems when a single employee of a company downloaded a file that was disguised as a software update. After installation, the ransomware encrypted file system structures and locked users out of their computers. Thus, it was human error that played the main role in disruption caused by Petya, not only to DLA Piper, but to many other international businesses.

Many law firms still rely on paper-based processes, specifically in the course of dispute settlement and large multinational transactions. Lawyers regularly scan or print confidential contracts and personal documents, however such devices in the office are quite often overlooked when it comes to security threats. Storage and transfers of printed materials may also present a significant risk for privacy and protection of data processed by law firms. Also, legal professionals often work remotely, for example, during a business trip, using free unsecured WiFi connections, which are easy to hack. These are only a few areas of concern relating to security and data protection.

The safety of the socio-technical environment and the security of a company's systems play an important role in protecting privacy. The protection of privacy in the context of the digital environment is defined as 'the ability of an individual (or organisation) to decide whether, when, and to whom personal (or organisational) information is released.'(Saltzer and Schroeder 1975). Again, the technical aspect of privacy protection cannot be confined only to the scope of work of duties of an IT-specialist. Management and employee practices, as well as company culture, must be also included in the basic considerations of security and safety. Both the understanding of risks stemming out of security and the ability to minimise such risks should be part of a law firm's culture and an ongoing concern.

V. Personal Data in the Context of Rules of Professional Privilege

At the centre of the legal profession lies the representation and defence of rights of clients. Rules of professional conduct prescribe that a lawyer must 'always act in the best interests of his client and must put those interests before his own interests or those of fellow members of the legal profession' (Council of the Bars Law Societies of the European Union 1988). Acting in the best interests of their clients, legal professionals often have to deal with personal information, including sensitive data.

Provisions of the GDPR do not cover professional privilege rules inherent to the legal profession, specific rules of professional privilege and confidentiality will depend on the applicable jurisdiction.

For example, if a data subject, a client or a third party whose data has been collected by the law firm, requests to exercise his or her rights under the GDPR, lawyers have an obligation to respond to the data subject's request. On the other hand, lawyers have a confidentiality obligation to their clients and are subject to legal professional privilege.

Both in general terms and in specific relation to the GDPR, legal professional privilege rules do not apply to all personal data collected and processed over the course of the work of a law firm or an individual lawyer. It covers only specific personal data, which would normally fall under attorney-client communications in the process of obtaining legal advice or materials used in preparation for potential litigation (Cane, et al. 2018).

In practice, this would usually mean that a law firm would still have to provide access to personal data based on a data subject access request from a client on whose behalf it maintains a claim to legal professional privilege, but it may not be required to do so in response to the client's opponent or a third party.

D. Public Engagement to Address Data Protection and Privacy Issues

For the legal sector, data protection and privacy are then multi-dimensional challenges in which firms must ensure their staff are sufficiently informed and engaged in the key issues. This may also extend to informing their client base. These are dauntingly difficult topics in which to generate interest, much less change professional behaviour.

Public exhibitions and education campaigns have been effective ways to engage the public and can show how to overcome widespread reluctance of people to critically examine challenging issues.

One such project, *The Glass Room*, is a pop-up 'tech store with a twist' that, at first glance, seems to offer the latest in shiny digital consumer products, such as the newest tablet or fitness tracker. But as you go inside, you find there's nothing for sale. Instead, as you explore, you'll find a selection of art works exploring who is collecting our data and why, and what we can do about it.

Whereas *The Glass Room* was designed and conceived as a project to engage the wider public, the project is increasingly focused on organisations, businesses and professionals, and some pilot interventions have shown how this approach could be used effectively at law firms and also professional law associations.

Over the last four years, Tactical Tech with partners like Mozilla, have opened Glass Room exhibitions in Berlin, New York and, most recently, San Francisco in 2019.

The exhibitions have attracted over 40,000 visitors, widespread media coverage including articles in The New York Times (Wortham 2016), Channel 4 News (Manji 2017) and even Vogue (Garcia 2017). In addition, it has sparked social media activity, such as a Facebook Live event with over 40,000 viewers.

Even more striking was that *The Glass Room* reached far beyond the usual audience for a campaign on data and privacy. The people coming through the door were tourists, hipsters on the way to the cinema, families on a day out or simply people wandering in while shopping.

Furthermore, the exhibit sparked a depth of engagement in those people rarely seen in awareness raising campaigns. Many visitors stayed for at least two hours, some stayed for an entire day to attend free workshops. Others came back after their first visit, bringing with them a group of friends.

For all cities, Tactical Tech recruited and trained a local group of 'Ingeniuses' (named after the 'Geniuses' at the Apple Store) from diverse backgrounds and communities. Many had no experience in technology or privacy but after a four-day training camp, had enough knowledge to give privacy help and advice. Our Ingeniuses also led our free Ingenius workshops, such as 'WTF – What the Facebook,' 'Mastering your Mobile 'and 'DeGooglize your Life'.

Critical to the objectives of the project was finding out how people felt about the issues raised.

In New York and London visitors filled out over 840 feedback cards, which showed their appreciation. When asked 'After visiting The Glass Room I feel:', answers included;

> 'as if I'm finally accessing the vault control room. Shocked, enlightened, provoked', 'happy someone is showing us how our data is being used.', and 'interested in technology and data. I want to study technology and data.' (Logan, 8 years old).

For the project Tactical Tech also commissioned an external evaluator, who conducted in-depth interviews with visitors – this showed about half interviewees 'spontaneously reported changes that are best interpreted as attitudinal shifts, or changes in awareness'.

From the report, examples included:

• One person said she 'never forgets the experience' of going through the exhibit each time she turns her phone on.
• One person is 'definitely more aware' and is thinking about the key issue more; while another said he is 'a lot more conscious' and thinks about changes he needs to make 'at every step' when he is online.
• Another person finds herself questioning more now when she is asked for

some of her personal information: 'why is this being asked for?'

Nearly half the people interviewed said they would tell family and friends about the exhibit.

- Furthermore, the evaluation found significant changes in behaviour from visitors:
- Four people said they now shut their location services when they do not explicitly need them
- A senior IT/privacy lead at a major UK company, who is teaching privacy needs and techniques to company staff, has adapted her pedagogical approach based on what she saw at Glass Room London.
- One IT security expert from a high-profile company said she was 'astonished' at how good the Glass Room London explanations were; Glass Room London was 'one of the best things I've seen on information security.'

More recently the concept has been developed further with a smaller version – *The Glass Room Community Edition*. This smaller version is designed to be produced in large numbers with a series of printed posters and visualisations than can be set up on a set of tables and wall space just about anywhere. The posters are complimented with a set of video animations displayed on large screens as well as tablet apps, such as the game 'Fake of Real', where visitors are presented with a random selection of 'smart' devices, such as Fitbits for cows, Smart underwear, or self-driving prams – and have to guess whether they really exist (spoiler alert: all those examples do actually exist).

So far, over 120 Glass Room Experience sets have been produced and sent to libraries, schools, events and other organisations who want to host their own exhibitions around Europe and the US, reaching a further 80,000 people.

Alongside the exhibits, a key element of The Glass Room project is the *Data Detox Kit* – an eight-day easy self-learning guide to Data and Privacy. The *Data Detox Kit* is normally handed out as a print format guide but can also be read online (The Glass Room Project 2017).

The Glass Room shows that by creating an engaging and compelling experience in a public space, it is possible to reach a genuinely mainstream audience on difficult issues, change their attitudes and even their behaviours. This approach certainly has challenges and limitations, but it could be applied to many campaign topics and issues with equally dramatic results.

This approach with smaller installations is highly effective with companies. For the legal sector it has two unique benefits: firstly, to present the issues in a clear and engaging way that all lawyers will fully understand; secondly, to present a set of tools and resources that show how to easily explain these issues to other people, such as clients.

So, what have we learnt from *The Glass Room* project?

By setting up an exhibition in prime shopping locations, we were taking the issue of data and privacy to where people are, rather than hoping they'd come to us.

By using art to explore these topics, we were challenging peoples' assumptions in ways a conventional narrative will never achieve and opening avenues for further enquiry.

By mirroring the design cues of tech stores, we were using a visual language that everyone understands, so attracting people who might well be put off by an art exhibition.

We also found that those core elements could be adapted and could work in any kind of space, that people in organisations and events, companies and professional associations found the smaller exhibition a perfect format for talking to the people they work with about data and privacy.

Perhaps most critically, we found that taking this issue offline and creating an immersive physical space that was free and open to everyone, we created a public spectacle; an inclusive space where the experience of discovering these curious objects was shared with others, making the whole experience far less intimidating, more memorable and impactful.

Crucially, by having people host the large and small exhibition, we made the intervention a vibrant, warm and human space – where visitors always had someone they could talk to.

In 2020 a new version, *The Glass Room Misinformation Edition*, has been released, exploring social media influence, so-called fake news and deep fakes. Although the coronavirus pandemic has inevitably disrupted the project, an online and a hybrid online/offline format ensure dozens more Glass Room events will take place in 2020 across the world.

A smaller version of *The Glass Room Community Edition* has also been tested within several corporate organisations. These pilot projects have shown a significant shift in raising awareness of companies' employees to address and deal with privacy online as well as data security. As part of these pilot interventions within companies, Tactical Tech provided interactive workshops, Data Detox trainings and immersive *Glass Room* exhibits. We believe that introducing such interventions within legal sector may significantly contribute to 'privacy first' culture within law firms and foster development of larger number of legal tech solutions based on the privacy by design concept.

E. Conclusion

Today, many profitable businesses are increasingly dependent on the extraction, processing and commodification of our personal data. However, digital privacy and issues relating to protection of personal data are gaining momentum. Bringing awareness to the ongoing public discourse on the topic of privacy is an important safeguard against potential breaches of security.

Specifically, for the legal sector, privacy plays an important role. Law firms should tackle the issue of privacy on all levels: organisational, managerial, cultural and individual. Addressing privacy on organisational and managerial levels may be achieved by implementing strong compliance programmes and through staff training. At the company culture level, legal teams should work together on general awareness about privacy concerns. *The Glass Room* experience, *Data Detox Kit* and privacy by design methodology may be a good way for law firms to approach this necessary cultural shift.

Unfortunately, many individuals believe that personal data collection and processing in the age of surveillance capitalism is inevitable. It is often assumed that nothing may be done to protect or manage the data we share online. Lawyers are uniquely placed to challenge these assumptions and to shape the rapidly-evolving relationship society has with the technology platforms on which it increasingly depends.

Bibliography

Cane, P., J. Conaghan and D. M. Walker (2018), *The New Oxford Companion to Law*, Oxford: Oxford University Press.

Cook, J. (2013), 'Private date of 500 million Marriott guests exposed in massive breach', *The Daily Telegraph*, 30 November 2018, available at <https://www.telegraph.co.uk/technology/2018/11/30/private-data-500-million-marriott-guests-exposed-massive-breach/> (last accessed 1 June 2019).

Cluley, G. (2019), 'DLA Piper and its insurers clash over multi-million NotPetya payout', available at <https://www.grahamcluley.com/dla-piper-and-its-insurers-clash-over-multi-million-notpetya-payout/> (last accessed 7 May 2019).

Coleman, P. (2017), 'Top 10 Oil and Gas Companies in the World', *Energy Digital*, 17 March, available at <https://www.energydigital.com/utilities/top-10-oil-and-gas-companies-world> (last accessed 18 April 2019).

Council of Europe (1950), *European Convention for the Protection of Human Rights and Fundamental Freedoms, as amended by Protocols Nos. 11 and 14*, Art. 8, available at <https://www.echr.coe.int/Documents/Convention_ENG.pdf> (last accessed 18 April 2019).

Council of the Bars Law Societies of the European Union (1988), *Code of Conduct for Lawyers in the European Union*, Section 2.7, available at <https://www.idhae.org/pdf/code2002_en.pdf> (last accessed 18 April 2019), Section 2.7.

Data Protection Working Party and Working Party on Police and Justice (2009), 'Future of Privacy. Joint contribution to the Consultation of the European

Commission on the Legal Framework for the Fundamental Right to Protection of Personal Data', Art. 29, Doc. No. 02356/09/EN, WP 168, paragraph 46, available at <https://ec.europa.eu/justice/article-29/documentation/opinion-recommendation/files/2009/wp168_en.pdf> (last accessed 18 April 2019).

Empson, L. (2007), *Managing the Modern Law Firm: New Challenges New Perspectives*, Oxford: Oxford University Press.

European Data Protection Board (2018), *Guidelines 3/2018 on the territorial scope of the GDPR (Article 3)*, 16 November 2018, available at <https://edpb.europa.eu/sites/edpb/files/consultation/edpb_guidelines_3_2018_territorial_scope_en.pdf> (last accessed 7 May 2019).

European Data Protection Supervisor (2018), 'Opinion 5/2018. Preliminary Opinion on privacy by design', paragraph 4, 31 May 2018, available at <https://edps.europa.eu/sites/edp/files/publication/18-05-31_preliminary_opinion_on_privacy_by_design_en_0.pdf> (last accessed 18 April 2019).

European Union (2012), 'Charta of Fundamental Rights of the European Union', *Official Journal of the European Union*, C326/391, Art. 7.

European Union (2018), 'Regulation (EU) 2016/679 of the European Parliament and of the Council of 27 April 2016 on the protection of natural persons with regard to the processing of personal data and on the free movement of such data, and repealing Directive 95/46/EC (General Data Protection Regulation)', *Journal of the European Union,* L119/1.

Garcia, P. (2017), 'Forget about cleanse – do a Data Detox instead', 5 January 2017, available at <https://www.vogue.com/article/digital-data-detox-how-to> (last accessed 1 June 2019).

International Organization for Standardization (2018), 'Consumer Protection: Privacy by Design for Consumer Goods and Services', ISO/PC 317, available at <https://www.iso.org/committee/6935430.html> (last accessed 18 April 2019).

Janofsky, A. (2017), 'DLA Piper CIO on 'Petya' Attack: 'The Future of the Entire Business Was At Stake', *The Wall Street Journal*, 13 December 2017, available at <https://blogs.wsj.com/cio/2017/12/13/dla-piper-cio-on-petya-attack-the-future-of-the-entire-business-was-at-stake/> (last accessed 18 April 2019).

Manji, F. (2017), 'The darker side on data privacy', 24 October 2017, available at <https://www.channel4.com/news/the-darker-side-of-data-privacy> (last accessed 1 June 2019).

McNair, C. (2018), 'Global Digital Ad Spending Update', *eMarketer*, 20 November 2018, available at <https://www.emarketer.com/content/global-ad-spending-update> (last accessed 18 April 2019).

Meyer, D. (2019), 'AWS Remains Dominant Player in Growing Cloud Market, SRG Report', *SDxCentral,* 5 February 2019, available at <https://www.sdxcentral.com/articles/news/aws-remains-dominant-player-in-growing-cloud-market-srg-reports/2019/02> (last accessed 18 April 2019).

National Cyber Security Centre (2018), *The cyber threat to UK legal sector*, 9 July 2018, available at <https://www.ncsc.gov.uk/report/-the-cyber-threat-to-uk-legal-sector--2018-report> (last accessed 7 May 2019).

Panetta, K. (2018), 'Gartner Top 10 Strategic Technology Trends for 2019', *Gartner*, 15 October 2019, available at <https://www.gartner.com/smarterwithgartner/gartner-top-10-strategic-technology-trends-for-2019> (last accessed 18 April 2019).

PwC (2017), 'Consumer Intelligence Series: Protect.me', *PwC*, available at <https://www.pwc.com/us/en/advisory-services/publications/consumer-intelligence-series/protect-me/cis-protect-me-findings.pdf> (last accessed 18 April 2019).

Salvo, J. and B. Middlebrook (2018), 'Cybersecurity and the Lawyer's Standard of Care', *American Bar Association*, 22 May 2018, available at <https://www.americanbar.org/groups/litigation/committees/commercial-business/articles/2018/spring2018-cybersecurity-and-the-lawyers-standard-of-care/> (last accessed 18 April 2019).

Saltzer, J. and M. D. Schroeder (1975), 'The protection of information in computer systems', in *Proceedings of the IEEE*, September 1975, 63:9, pp. 1278–1308.

Statista (2019), 'Global Retail E-Commerce Market Share of Amazon from 2016 to 2019', available at <https://www.statista.com/statistics/955796/global-amazon-e-commerce-market-share/> (last accessed 18 April 2019).

Susskind, R. (2013), *Tomorrow's Lawyers: An Introduction to your Future*, Oxford: Oxford University Press.

Techworld Staff (2019), 'The most infamous data breaches', *Techworld*, 16 April 2019, available at <https://www.techworld.com/security/uks-most-infamous-data-breaches-3604586/#r3z-addoor> (last accessed 18 April 2019).

The Glass Room Project (2017), 'The Data Detox Kit', available at <https://datadetoxkit.org/en/home> (last accessed 1 June 2019).

The Guardian (2018), 'Cathay Pacific hit by data leak affecting up to 9.4 m passengers', *The Guardian*, 24 October 2018, available at <https://www.theguardian.com/technology/2018/oct/24/cathay-pacific-hit-by-data-leak-affecting-up-to-94m-passengers> (last accessed 1 June 2019).

Wikipedia (2019), *The List of Public corporations by market capitalization*, available at <https://en.wikipedia.org/w/index.php?title=List_of_public_corporations_by_market_capitalization&oldid=892984893> (last accessed 18 April 2019).

Wong, J. C. (2018), 'Google shut down Google+ after failing to disclosure user data leak', *The Guardian*, 13 October 2018, available at <https://www.theguardian.com/technology/2018/oct/08/google-plus-security-breach-wall-street-journal> (last accessed 1 June 2019).

Wortham, J. (2016), 'Finding Inspiration for Art in the Betrayal of Privacy', *The New York Times Magazine*, 27 December 2016, available at <https://www.nytimes.com/2016/12/27/magazine/finding-inspiration-for-art-in-the-betrayal-of-privacy.html> (1 June 2019).

United Nations General Assembly (1948), *Universal Declaration of Human Rights*, Article 12, available at <https://www.un.org/en/universal-declaration-human-rights> (last accessed 18 April 2019).

Zuboff, S. (2019), *The Age of Surveillance Capitalism: The Fight for a Human Future at the new Frontier of Power*, London: Profile Books Ltd.

13

Friend or Foe? Examining the Potential and Pitfalls of ICTs in Improving Access to Justice in Post-conflict Countries

Astrid Wiik

A. Introduction

Access to justice forms a standard pillar in rule of law assistance in post-conflict states. Its importance for social and economic development has since 2015 been formally recognised in Goal 16.3 of the Sustainable Development Goals (SDGs). Nonetheless, access to justice remains one of the most challenging elements in rule of law assistance portfolios not least, because progress hinges on various, including citizen- or user-dependent factors. Effective access to justice initiatives thus require deviating from the still dominant top-down institution-building focus of rule of law assistance. Donors and implementing organisations ('development actors') increasingly realise the importance of mobilising citizens and communities in ensuring access to justice, but often struggle to fully gauge and address their justice needs, especially regarding vulnerable groups.

This paper examines to what extent information and communication technologies (ICTs) can bridge access to justice gaps in post-conflict states using Afghanistan as a case study. It argues that ICTs possess characteristics that have the potential to amplify community- and citizen-focused access to justice initiatives. At the same time, ICTs might aggravate access to justice barriers. The paper suggests a framework to evaluate the potential benefits and risks of ICT-based access to justice initiatives in a post-conflict setting. The first part of the paper sets out the theoretical case for the employment of ICTs in access to justice programming followed by a case study of ICT-based access to justice initiatives in Afghanistan.

B. Towards User-based Access to Justice Approaches

User-centric concepts of access to justice are relatively new within law and development. Governance and law reform re-emerged as a development priority of development actors in the 1990s in light of evidence highlighting the importance of strong institutions for economic (and social) development (Garth 2003: 385–7). Formal justice sector reform (courts, police, prisons) became the focal point for state-building initiatives in post-conflict and fragile states, particularly after the UN started to deploy peacekeeping missions to support institutional reform in 2003 (Marshall 2014: 86; Trebilcock, et al. 2014: 33, 61). The assumption was (and is) that the state should be the primary provider and mediator of conflict because a justice system that is functional and accessible to the general population secures peace and prevents further conflict (UN Secretary-General 2004: 3).

Access to justice, a concept that emerged in domestic scholarly discourses in the 1970s, features in these reform agendas as an instrument to facilitate resort to the state court system in addition to typical justice reform components, such as law reform, independence of the judiciary, capacity training of justice personnel, anti-corruption and legal education reform.

In light of evidence that up to 60 per cent of institutional reform programmes in developing countries fail to show a lasting improvement in justice sector functionality despite billions spent, critics have called for a departure from the state-centric, top-down and broad rule of law reform agenda (UN Secretary-General 2004: 6–7; Trebilcock, et al. 2014: 61–2). Reformers argue that rule of law and accordingly access to justice reforms are ends in themselves under the umbrella of a rights-based approach to development and not solely means to achieve economic well-being (Sen 1999: 3; UNDP 2004: 3). This rights-based approach accords with calls for bottom-up initiatives to justice sector reform in which the needs of civil society and local communities as users of the justice system determine the reform agenda (UNDP 2004: 5–6; Golub 2003). The approach correlates with observations that up to 80 per cent of citizens in post-conflict states rely on informal justice mechanisms, partly due to deep mistrust in the state (justice system) (Wojkowska 2006: 5; Golub 2007: 53).

Although state-centric reforms still form the heart of rule of law reform programmes in post-conflict states, development actors have increasingly attempted to devise programmes that address the justice needs and preferences of civil society. This development has affected a surge in access to justice programmes over the past decade, most notably legal empowerment and awareness raising among vulnerable groups, especially the poor, women and marginalised minorities (UNDP 2004: 4–5, 182–183; Kötter 2018:

12). Further, development actors have started to explore means to engage with non-state or informal justice mechanisms in recognition of the pivotal role they play particularly for poor and disadvantaged communities (UN Secretary-General 2004: 12). The term informal justice mechanism denotes mechanisms outside the formal state court system that may rest in customary or tribunal social structures, religion, local authorities or community forums that are trained in conflict settlement (UNDP, et al. 2009: 9).

Three main access to justice strategies can be distinguished within the current portfolio of initiatives: legal empowerment and awareness raising regarding legal needs and how to enforce them; individualised legal aid or advice; and improving accessibility and functionality of formal and/or informal justice mechanisms, including through legal reform or public oversight (Barendrecht 2011: 1; UNDP 2004: 7; World Bank 2019a).

These changes impinge on the concept of access to justice itself. The concept is inherently fluid and no general definition exists. International human rights law instruments address access to justice with a view to guaranteeing equal access to and functionality of the state court system, through fair and public trial rights, judicial independence and impartiality (Art. 10 UDHR; Art. 14 ICCPR), the right to counsel and free legal aid (Art. 14 ICPCR) and a right to effective remedy (Art. 8 UDHR). There is agreement that access to justice covers not only access to a forum, but also a just, equitable and enforceable outcome (Kötter 2018: 8). Some further include formal and informal justice systems. The following definition by UNDP, on which this paper relies, has gained considerable relevance in practice and mirrors the broader concept: access to justice is 'the ability of people . . . to seek and obtain a remedy through the formal or informal justice system, and in accordance with human rights principles and standards' (UNDP 2004).

These conceptual changes are not exclusive to the law and development discourse. Access to justice has re-emerged as an issue in several developed countries following realisation that low income and rural groups face significant hurdles to access to justice not least because of cuts to state-funded legal aid. Many scholars and politicians regard ICTs – understood here in the broadest sense possible as all devices and equipment that facilitate the storage, transmission, processing, retrieving and use of knowledge and information electronically and/or that enable communication, such as personal computers, television, emails, radio and (smart) phones – as a means to alleviate, if not tackle, the access to justice crisis. The following section will provide an overview of ICT-based access to justice initiatives and explore if these experiences could improve access to justice in post-conflict states. The hypothesis is that ICTs are innately user-focused and thus align with modern access to justice approaches that target justice system users and seek to address their actual justice needs.

C. The Potential of ICTs in Post-conflict Settings

I. Sketching ICT-based Access to Justice Initiatives

Scholars, especially in the UK, the USA and Canada, have analysed ICTs seeking to improve access to justice for underserved parts of the population, particularly low-income households who might not recognise the importance of their legal problem and are unaware of ways to address it without costly legal representation (Rhode 2013: 531; Brescia, et al. 2014/15: 591). ICTs are considered a potential solution. User-centric access to justice measures concern especially legal empowerment and awareness raising as well as individualised legal aid and advice, two classic access to justice strategies. ICT-based initiatives include explanatory websites or mobile applications as well as educational and information videos facilitating access to general legal information, databases for online legal research, case repositories, legal encyclopaedias and lawyer or service-support directories (Brescia, et al. 2014/15: 567–8, 595). Some view social media, including Facebook, as a tool to promote access to justice and for individuals to seek legal advice from 'lay advocates' (Robertson 2012: 80–84). ICT-based programmes that individualise legal aid and advice complement these initiatives with legal communications tools, smart/interactive or analytical software to assist self-represented individuals, for instance through online interviews or intelligent questionnaires, legal aid eligibility assessments, legal document preparation and assembly tools, and evidence collection programs (Staudt 2009: 1120; Brescia, et al. 2014/15: 577).

The main market for ICT-based access to justice initiatives are programmes improving the accessibility and functionality of courts or providing services for legal professionals. An array of programmes exist covering the initiation of proceedings to the enforcement of judgments. They include case management and filing systems; video and teleconferencing systems for remote court appearances; digital storage systems to improve transparency and user-access to case information; legal databases; and predictive systems to assist adjudication or, for lawyers, gauge courts' decision patterns. US legal aid providers endorse mobile technologies as part of their strategy to meet legal needs of justice seekers (Flagg 2015: 581). Efforts are underway to create artificial intelligence-based online dispute resolution mechanisms that combine intelligent questionnaires, problem analysis, legal information and solutions (Thompson 2016: 16). Several corporations already work with software-facilitated dispute resolution processes replacing the need for third party involvement (Thompson 2016: 33).

In short, the portfolio of initiatives ranges from the digitisation of offline or conventional initiatives to the creation of 'disruptive' innovative digital programmes. Their common goal is to reduce the need for individualised legal advice and/or to support legal professionals (McGill, et al. 2017: 238–40). Target users of these programmes are the public and/ or legal professionals and the initiatives are mostly developed in, and for, the Western hemisphere driven largely by the private sector and thus commercial (McGill. et al. 2017: 237). Still, technological advances hold great potential also for underserved citizens. Machine learning and recording systems are adaptive to users' verbal and legal skills and some programmes are now able to respond to users' emotional needs via emotional intelligence features (Thompson 2016: 45).

II. The Promises of ICTs in a Post-conflict Setting

Development actors and governments through ICT-based access to justice programmes could reach more citizens directly (and vice versa) than conventional access to justice programmes given the exponential growth of mobile and smart devices in low-income post-conflict states (UN Secretary-General 2017) and the growth of Internet users by annual rates above 5 per cent globally (Broadband Commission 2018: 8). ICTs because of their general accessibility could somewhat democratise the typical top-down centralised state-building process. Citizens and thus civil society could easily be involved in access to justice initiatives and convey their needs in real time in accordance with the above-described human-rights-based approaches to rule of law. ICTs thus could help to mobilise civil society to secure the effectiveness of access to justice initiatives and to restore and build trust in the governing system even where conflict and migration have destroyed social structures and where conventional governance reforms have consolidated available resources and power in the hands of powerful elites. ICTs could mitigate some of these burdens, even skip standard steps in access to justice strategies that take years to build or stagger due to the unavailability of human or financial resources, especially in areas that are difficult to reach.

Further, ICTs have the potential to transcend socio-cultural barriers. Marginalised groups with limited access to public spaces and discourse can be addressed within their spheres and call attention to their needs through ICTs. Thus, ICTs might alleviate the problem that despite numerous advances in fragile states concerning access to justice, vulnerable groups, including the poor, remain largely excluded from progress. Equally, ICTs can help to overcome geographical barriers to justice, which often are impenetrable due to direct and indirect costs. In addition, ICTs are less vulnerable to security incidents. System operators can work in a decentralised manner from safe locations. ICTs therefore could secure access to justice in challenging security environments as well as record and possibly alleviate access to justice deficits caused by power inequalities and corruption. Equally, ICTs can facilitate communication between various justice system actors, including between formal and informal dispute settlement mechanisms.

III. Measuring ICT Solutions

ICTs are an evolving strategy in access to justice programming. Informatics and social sciences scholars debate the general advantages and disadvantages of ICTs in development (Dey, et al. 2016), but so far there appears to be no study on what the implications of ICTs are in improving access to justice in post-conflict states. This section suggests a framework to determine whether to employ ICTs or not. The framework combines law and development assessment tools with ICT-specific parameters.

Human rights are the primary law and development assessment parameters. Foreign state donors are bound to them as contracting parties to international human rights treaties and various international organisations have pledged adherence (Dann 2013: 275). Human rights are also enclosed in the 'do-no-harm' framework (Anderson 1999), which requires aid workers to avoid conflict-exacerbating (or aggravating) impacts of development assistance. A tenet of both frameworks has become the carrying out of human rights impact assessments to determine a project's human rights risks prior to its funding. However, human rights assessments are carried out on a voluntary basis (Dann 2013: 277).

It is suggested to add two parameters: First, the human rights assessments should be expanded to an assessment of the general legal environment with a view to identifying potential legal hurdles to the use of ICTs for access to justice. This is because ICTs might violate domestic laws, including commercial, privacy and data protection laws, as well as ethical duties.

The legal assessment should be complemented by a four-pronged test developed by Tongia, Subrahmanian and Arunachalam to determine the value of ICTs from a user perspective. The element awareness measures whether people know and are open to the use of ICTs. Availability assesses the proximity of ICTs, whereas accessibility addresses the ability to use them, including (e-)literacy and navigability of interfaces. Affordability measures the complete expenses incurred by ICT use (Tongia, et al. 2005: 29). Access to justice literature relies on similar considerations when stressing the need for individuals to have not only physical access to legal information but also that the information is adjusted to the cognitive and literacy levels of users. The latter is often a challenge with regard to text-based ICT access to justice solutions (Hughes 2013: 13). ICT tools must be tailored to the needs of the target audiences to not increase access to justice barriers, for example, through plain language or reading tools, provision of human assistance via local intermediaries or interactive formats, and measures to ensure privacy in public Internet points (Bailey, et al. 2013: 198).

Having established the existing possibilities and the framework to assess their usefulness in the post-conflict context, the paper now turns to the case study.

D. Case Study Afghanistan

The successes and challenges of the international actors in Afghanistan are well-documented. This paper thus only briefly retraces access to justice barriers in Afghanistan as an empirical reference point to measure ICT initiatives in access to justice programmes to then explore current ICT-based access to justice initiatives and assess them based on the above framework.

I. Access to Justice Barriers in Afghanistan

Access to justice barriers in Afghanistan fall into three basic inter-related groups: infrastructural or institutional, socio-cultural and conflict-related.

As in other post-conflict states, reconstruction of the justice system after the overthrow of the Taleban regime focused on the creation (including building and furnishing) of state civil and criminal courts, law reforms to comply with international human rights law and capacity building of judges and other justice system personnel (Wardak 2016: 7). To facilitate access to justice, legal aid departments were created in Kabul and some provinces and an Independent Bar Association was established to bolster the legal profession.

Significant geographical and institutional hurdles to access justice remain. Reconstruction focused on urban centres. Remote areas that were deemed unsafe or difficult to access were often left without courts. The deterioration of the security situation has led to the additional closing of courts, including in urbanised areas, thereby increasing barriers to justice due to financial, security and, for women, social reasons (NRC 2014: 31–2). Capacity shortages in the justice system, including lack of access to adequate legal support increases the problem. Only 3,700 lawyers are registered with the Afghan Bar Association and legal aid providers total at 300 for criminal cases nationwide (Asia Foundation 2017: 3, 64). An additional severe challenge is endemic and widespread corruption, which is reported to be particularly high in the judiciary due to a lack of institutional and external oversight as well as illegitimate influence of strongmen over the conduct and outcome of proceedings (Stahlmann 2016: 18, 40). Overly bureaucratic and lengthy proceedings provide strong incentives for corruption, as does the continued predominant manual operation of court filing systems. Judges regularly extract bribes in exchange for processing a case, significantly increasing litigation costs, to the detriment of the poor (Stahlmann 2016: 24).

Given these institutional shortcomings, the majority of Afghan citizens seek justice through informal justice systems, if at all. The World Justice Project reports that only 23 per cent of Afghan citizens use the formal justice system to settle disputes (World Justice Project 2016: 7). Informal mechanisms mainly are customary *jirgas* and *shuras*, but also include Taleban courts and mediation and other services offered by non-governmental and non-judicial government entities (Wardak 2016: 11). Particularly traditional mechanisms are perceived as more legitimate than the state judiciary and seem to have fewer difficulties concerning enforcement (New York Times 2015). While generalisations are difficult given the heterogeneity of informal dispute resolution mechanisms, many raise fundamental access to justice concerns, such as insufficient recording of disputes, allegations of corruption and disrespect for basic human rights regarding the process and outcome, particularly the rights of women in family and property disputes (Stahlmann 2016: 55, 79). Further, the relationship between formal and informal justice systems is unclear and contested, prompting forum shopping and parallel proceedings (Wardak 2016: 16–7). Since around 2009, donors have started to acknowledge the importance of informal justice mechanisms as dispute resolution providers (Gaston, et al. 2009: 73), even though the local formal framework, including the Afghan Constitution, do not recognise the informal justice system and several justice officials in conversations expressed hesitation towards integration of the informal dispute resolution systems. The aim of the Afghan government's National Development Strategy remains to expand and improve the state justice system.

Socio-cultural barriers add to the difficulties in accessing justice. This is particularly noticeable with respect to the lagging operationalisation of laws and institutional structures. Socio-cultural barriers include vulnerabilities such as poverty and illiteracy, which affect the awareness of rights and ways to enforce them, as well as limit access to dispute resolution mechanisms and legal representation given the direct and indirect costs of participation (Beqiraj, et al. 2014). According to UNESCO, an estimated 69 per cent of the Afghan population is illiterate, with female illiteracy at 83 per cent.

Though legislative reforms have largely tackled legal discrimination, women, particularly outside urban areas, face systemic and endemic discrimination. Women report difficulties in accessing dispute resolution forums, as well as suffering discriminatory actions by justice providers during the process. Barriers include shaming by the community and family for laying bare private issues up to the point of shunning (Luccaro, et al. 2014: 29–30), the regular denial of personal agency in court and informal justice mechanisms and stigmatisation. Apart from often lacking awareness about basic rights, women regularly choose to forego them to protect themselves (Luccaro, et al. 2014: 43). If they seek to enforce them, they prefer the informal justice system viewing it as less damaging to their personal and family reputation (Luccaro, et al. 2014: 35).

These access-to-justice-barriers are aggravated by the volatile security situation, which increases physical barriers to justice and entails delays. The state judiciary's reach remains limited and in many areas, the conflict has eroded social and informal governance structures affecting the operation of traditional conflict resolution mechanisms.

II. ICT-based Access to Justice Initiatives in Afghanistan

Numerous programmes since 2001 have sought to address these barriers to justice, particularly through institution- and capacity-building. A review of central development actors' Afghanistan rule of law programmes during the past five to ten years (UN, USAID, World Bank, GIZ, IDLO) as well as the Afghan Ministry of Justice, and the Afghan Supreme Court's websites indicate a nascent trend towards inclusion of ICT-based initiatives. Focus was held on projects with an access to justice component. All actors that were surveyed run programmes within the above-referred main access to justice strategies.

Legal empowerment and awareness account for the largest share of ICT-related access to justice initiatives. Legal empowerment interventions primarily seek to improve legal literacy work, increase access to legal information, laws, decisions and judgments, provide access to legal and other support and, finally, to build the capacity of individuals to enforce their rights. The Afghan Supreme Court and the Ministry of Justice on their websites provide a free-of-charge repository of select important cases, as well as access to laws, Afghanistan's official gazette and a description of available services and how to access the formal court and state dispute resolution, including legal aid. The websites are available in three languages: Dari, Farsi and English. Interventions by development actors include websites explaining legal rights and the constitution, e-learning programmes for public officials and awareness campaigns via traditional mass communication tools, such as the radio and television, using case scenarios to explain basic rights and how to enforce them, such as USAID's Rule of Law Stabilization Program (RLS) or the World Bank's Justice Service Delivery Project (Vapnek, et al. 2016: 34; World Bank 2018: 21). Through radio programmes and a Facebook page IDLO within its Supporting Access to Justice in Afghanistan project (SAJA) has sought to raise awareness of the Afghanistan Legal Aid and Advocates

Network (ALAAN) to inform citizens of their rights and encourage them to enforce them. Equally, it has relied on TV, Internet and radio to raise the profile of the Afghanistan Bar Association (IDLO 2017: 3). The Ministry of Justice as part of the RLS programme has broadcast two TV dramas across thirteen provinces in local languages addressing violence against women and child labour (Vapnek, et al. 2016: 34).

While community- and citizen-based use of ICTs, especially via social media, has played an important role in securing accountability, inducing reforms and in promoting access to information in various countries, including Rwanda, Ukraine and Pakistan, social media studies in Afghanistan show that there ICTs are mainly used as a private social networking tool. Its information value is secondary. Social media-run public debates on certain topics remain isolated (Altai 2017: 56–7) despite intentions expressed otherwise by UNAMA and some civil society organisations.

ICT projects seeking to improve the accessibility and functionality of the justice system mostly fall into two categories: first, IT-infrastructure projects and management tools. IT infrastructure projects are essential given lack of access by many courts and ministries to modern technology or the inability to store information adequately (cf. Vapnek, et al. 2016: 8, 43). Until 2023, the World Bank is implementing the Digital Central Asia South Asia project (Digital CASA). Its objectives, among other, are to secure more affordable Internet through better regional and domestic connectivity, including establishing broadband connections to public institutions and Internet exchange points, and to improve the government's ability to deliver e-government services – including via mobile devices – by installing the critical technical foundations (World Bank 2019b). Digital CASA builds on the preceding Afghanistan ICT Sector Development Project, which ended in 2017 and sought to expand connectivity, create an enabling environment for the mainstream use of mobile applications in strategic government sectors to improve public service delivery and kick-start the development of the Afghan IT industry (World Bank 2019b). Smaller previous projects furnished select justice institutions with better Internet and telephone access and videoconferencing facilities (World Bank 2018: 18).

The second category of ICT projects concern case management in courts and for legal aid delivery. Case management tools are essential to improve transparency, accountability and the quality of service delivery. Projects include the building of an internal case management system called CMS by foreign contractors. CMS' objective is to track and record cases in Afghanistan's criminal justice system covering the entire process from the investigation of a person up until release from their prison. The system converges data from eight justice institutions in one central database, including the Supreme Court, the Attorney General's office, the Anti-Corruption Agency and several line ministries (SIGAR 2014). Further, the ALAAN in cooperation with the Legal Aid Department of the Ministry of Justice and supported by IDLO's SAJA project has created standardised systems for filing and case management and has built a central digital database to manage cases and optimise service delivery by all legal aid organisations (Asia Foundation 2017: 9). Lawyers document case events and steps and the database assists them in complying with minimum practice standards (Asia Foundation 2017: 11). There appear to be no ICT-based efforts to tackle reported shortcomings in the registration, publication and enforcement of decisions systematically – possibly, because registration is effected mostly through provincial sub-units of the Ministry of Justice. No ICT projects addressing the informal justice sector were found.

As regards individualised legal aid and advice, an important ICT-related development is the launch of the World Bank-funded Legal Services Call Center in the Ministry of Justice in 2017. Four employees provide free legal advice during business hours to citizens in criminal, civil and family law through a hotline (MoJ 2018). The MoJ recently announced plans to expand legal advice services to cable networks. More sophisticated ICT-based systems, for example interactive or 'smart' assistance systems, including chatbots or communication tools to establish access to remote legal advisers, do not seem to be employed. An exception is a Facebook webpage by ALAAN detailing the availability of legal aid offices throughout Afghanistan. Finally, USAID recently awarded a grant to a consulting firm to improve access to justice and transparency, which includes, among other, a call for locally-rooted civil society organisations to apply for innovative solutions to improve access to justice.

Overall, ICT based measures are still at a nascent stage. ICT measures address institutions, but also citizens. The following section examines these initiatives based on the suggested framework.

III. Assessment: Challenges and Risks in the Use of ICTs

The nascent use of ICTs in access to justice programmes in Afghanistan faces several challenges. One main concern is the availability of ICTs. Remote and urban areas struggle with poor technical infrastructure, including lack of sufficient broadband capacity, and the financial and human resources to maintain IT systems (UNESCAP 2015: 8). From the earliest planning stage programmes need to be designed so that the competent institution can eventually run them. As noted, projects are underway to improve IT infrastructure, create a domestic Internet provider market and build IT expertise in line with Goal 9C of the SDGs to significantly increase access to ICTs and provide universal and affordable Internet access in least developed countries. However, currently, Internet-based content remains largely unavailable to rural and poor populations, also because of electricity shortages for the majority of the country (UNESCAP 2015: 25). The above-mentioned CMS was supposed to cover courts nationwide, but due to geographic and logistical difficulties, ultimately it was set up in only seven out of thirty-four provinces (SIGAR 2014). It is difficult to provide concrete numbers on connectivity as estimates range from an 8 per cent to a 50 per cent Internet penetration rate (UNESCAP 2015: 10). Community-based Internet access points or local or telephone-based human assistance could partially overcome the limitations (Cabral et al. 2012: 249, 270).

Current efforts focus on increasing public access points (UNESCAP 2015: 12). The low Internet use contrasts with an estimated 80 per cent mobile-phone penetration in 2016 (Guo 2018). Broader studies indicate that generally access by vulnerable groups to mobile phones and the Internet is significantly lower than for other groups. In South Asia, for example, in 2015, women were 38 per cent less likely to own a mobile phone than males (Hussain, et al. 2018: 253). In addition, mobile network availability is an issue. Only few areas have 4G/LTE services and most users rely on GSM (UNESCAP 2015: 12). Still, it is surprising that access to justice initiatives have largely focused on web-based programmes.

Availability also entails institutional and political challenges such as creating the conditions necessary for the long-term sustainability of IT systems. Reports on the CMS indicate that incorrect data was entered into the management system on a significant scale. This prompted the foreign contractor to announce in late 2018 that it would carry out large-scale data cleaning and retrain personnel, as well as take steps for the system to identify missing court data and return to parallel paper court files indicating that the difficulties concerned court staff responsible for maintaining the system. Similarly, IDLO reports the need to ensure regular use of the legal aid databases (IDLO 2017: 4). These examples illustrate that training and change management must complement any technical innovations.

Accessibility and awareness relate to fundamental socio-cultural challenges. There is a serious risk that the introduction of ICT solutions will further disenfranchise vulnerable groups, because they lack the requisite technical or (e-)literacy skills to navigate ICTs. End-user design and accessibility of systems need to be tailored to the needs and skill-sets of vulnerable groups. The mentioned government websites as well as the case and law databases do not cater to the illiterate majority of the population. Visual tools and text to speech voice reading programmes should be introduced to increase accessibility. In addition, development actors should acknowledge that placing the onus on learning how to navigate digital systems on the justice seeker might further alienate users from accessing justice. This might also be a reason for the limited use of the above-mentioned databases. Similarly, development actors have found large media and awareness campaigns to be ineffective in increasing access to justice (IDLO 2017: 3). Field studies show that awareness training, though highly important, is insufficient to empower people to seek enforcement of their rights (Stahlmann 2016: 57–65). Active support, for instance, in the form of legal representation or negotiation assistance is necessary, particularly for people with low legal and literacy competency levels. Thus, initiatives need not only be affordable, available and accessible, but also transfer agency on target groups (Hussain, et al. 2018: 254). Further, development actors should acknowledge that citizens might face significant backlash in their personal or social environment over online activities (Hussain, et al. 2018: 258–9).

Finally, affordability is also a major concern. UNESCAP evaluates the current costs for connectivity and equipment in Afghanistan as prohibitive especially for high-volume bandwidth connections. In 2015, they amounted to about 118 per cent of the per capita GDP (UNESCAP 2015: 13).

The use of ICTs to address access to justice gaps is also problematic with respect to do-no-harm. The expansion of ICT-based access to justice tools, particularly those seeking to assist self-represented litigants, might create a two-class legal system, in which only those with means have access to legal representation whereas all others are relegated to computer-mediated support. In relation to the US and Canadian legal markets, the prevailing view seems to be that ICT-assisted support is better than no support at all (Brescia, et al. 2014/15: 610; Schindler 2012: 191). However, the usefulness of a programme ultimately depends on the quality of information and its user-appropriate delivery, including the risk of misinterpretation of information.

An added risk in the post-conflict context is that the nascent legal market might be stymied as development funds are redirected to ICT-based assistance given their scaling potential. It is further questionable to what extent ICTs should be operationalised to bridge access to justice gaps. There are so far no studies as to whether the use of ICTs can replace the establishment of physical court and justice infrastructure from a legitimacy perspective in a post-conflict or fragile environment. Empirical studies from the USA show that the forum is irrelevant as long as the process is perceived as fair (Tyler 2018). However, these studies might not be transferable to post-conflict societies. Especially in a communication-based society like Afghanistan where trust in justice institutions is fragile, a physical demonstration and experience of justice being done might be necessary to rebuild peace and trust in the justice system.

The use of ICT-based access to justice systems finally raises numerous legal challenges, which can only be grazed here. One key issue is data protection, which is particularly vulnerable to breaches if users access legal apps or websites through public networks or computers. Further, no information is available on how personal data is protected for justice seekers calling the Legal Services Call Centre. Personal data must be protected and saved against unwarranted government uses and against misuse by third parties (Cabral, et al. 2012: 265). This concerns the use of private data and documents that justice seekers convey, as well as the use of meta data and data storage (McGill, et al. 2017: 244). While the harvesting of meta data might help to improve ICT based access to justice systems, it is important that the process is accompanied by a sound regulatory framework that places privacy rights at the centre.

A prospective digitalisation of court proceedings might violate human rights guarantees, especially the publicity of hearings and the right to an independent and impartial judge. The Human Rights Committee has strongly rejected the concept of anonymous or faceless judges for contravening basic standards of fair trial (HRC 2007). The publicity exceptions of Art. 14 (1) ICCPR do not include videoconferencing or virtual courtrooms, limiting the extent to which (criminal) court hearings can be transferred to the digital sphere in view of the transparency and individual dimensions of the right (HRC 2007).

Thirdly, like many legal systems, Afghanistan in its Advocates Law prohibits the unauthorised practice of law and place special professional, including ethical and fiduciary duties on legal professionals, mostly, to ensure the accuracy and reliability of legal advice (Cabral, et al. 2012: 317–22). These duties generally are triggered once a client receives personalised information on a specific case as opposed to general legal information (Brescia, et al. 2014/15: 587). There is a risk that smart ICT systems that individualise legal information based on user input constitute (illegal) legal advice. Calls to create exemptions for software to assist legal aid providers have so far not been successful in the USA (Cabral, et al. 2012: 321–22).

E. Conclusion

This paper intends to contribute to the discussion of the role of ICTs for access to justice programmes in post-conflict states. While, theoretically, access to justice can be addressed through ICTs and a number of innovative solutions can secure that more citizens obtain the support needed to enforce their rights, the usefulness of ICTs can be decided on a case-by-case basis only, taking into account the specific local context and situation. The paper proposes a framework for this decision that combines established law and development evaluation parameters with specific ICT evaluation parameters. Applied to Afghanistan, it shows that Afghanistan's nascent experience with ICTs to improve access to justice could be improved to better meet the needs of justice seekers. Currently, efforts focus largely on digitisation of conventional access to justice strategies, such as building case management systems or media-driven legal empowerment and awareness campaigns, such as website-based plain text explanations of how to enforce rights or legal databases. As shown, these measures are accessible only to the literate minority. The need to engage and empower civil society as amplifiers and guardians of development initiatives has been recognised over the past decades (Banks, et al. 2012). However, in Afghanistan this recognition has not translated into ICT-based initiatives with the exception of the new Legal Services Call Centre (though information on its performance is not yet available). The current dominating ICT-based access to justice strategy risks cementing existing barriers and increasing inequalities in the justice system. The innate user focus of ICTs has yet to be harnessed in Afghanistan. Whatever the solutions are to address access to justice gaps and barriers, they need to be based on a firm understanding of how law and technology operate in the specific sociocultural context of the target community. Development actors should engage with communities directly to devise holistic solutions to access justice within and outside the formal justice system.

Bibliography

Ahmed, A. (2015), 'Taliban Justice Gains Favor as Official Afghan Courts Fail', *New York Times*, 1 February, available at <https://www.nytimes.com/2015/02/01/world/asia/taliban-justice-gains-favor-as-official-afghan-courts-fail.html> (last accessed 26 April 2019).

Altai Consulting (2017), *Social Media in Afghanistan: Users and Engagement*.

Anderson, M. (1999), *Do No Harm: How Aid Can Support Peace – or War*, Boulder/London: Lynne Rienner Publishers.

Asia Foundation (Day, D. and S. Rahbari) (2017), *Legal Aid Assessment and Roadmap submitted to the Ministry of Justice of Afghanistan and the World Bank*.

Bailey, J., J. Burkell and G. Reynolds (2013), 'Access to Justice for All: Towards an "Expansive Vision" of Justice and Technology', *Windsor Yearbook of Access to Justice*, 31:2, pp. 181–207.

Banks, N. and D. Hulme (2012), 'The role of NGOs and civil society in development and poverty reduction', *Brooks World Poverty Institute Working Paper*, p. 171.

Barendrecht, M. (2011), 'Legal aid, accessible courts or legal information?', *Global Jurist*, 11:1, pp. 1–26.

Beqiraj, J. and L. McNamara (2014), *International Access to Justice: Barriers and Solutions*, London: Bingham Centre for the Rule of Law.

Brescia, R., W. McCarthy, K. Potts, C. Rivals and A. McDonald (2014/15), 'Embracing Disruption: How Technological Change in the Delivery of Legal Services Can Improve Access to Justice', *Albany Law Review*, 78:2, pp. 553–621.

Broadband Commission for Sustainable Development (2018), *The State of Broadband: Broadband Catalyzing Sustainable Development*.

Cabral, J., A. Chavan, T. Clarke and J. Greacen (2012), 'Using Technology to Enhance Access to Justice', *Harvard Journal of Law & Technology*, 26:1, pp. 241–324.

Dann, P. (2013), *The Law of Development Cooperation*, Cambridge: Cambridge University Press.

Dey, B. and F. Ali (2016), 'A Critical Review of the ICT for Development Research', in B. Dey, K. Sorour and R. Filieri (eds.), *ICTs in Developing Countries – Research, Practices and Policy Implications*, Heidelberg: Springer.

Flagg, R. (2015), 'Access to Justice: Keeping America's Promise', *Kansas Journal of Law and Public Policy*, 24, pp. 571–83.

Garth, B. (2003), 'Building Strong and independent judiciaries through the new law and development: behind the paradox of consensus programs and perpetually disappointing results', *DePaul Law Review*, 52:2, pp. 383–400.

Golub, S. (2003), 'Beyond the Rule of Law Orthodoxy: The Legal Empowerment Alternative', *Carnegie Endowment for International Peace Rule of Law Series*, p. 41.

––––––– (2007), 'The Rule of Law and the UN Peacebuilding Commission: a Social Development Approach', *Cambridge Review of International Affairs*, 20:1, pp. 47–67.

Guo, E. (2018), 'Afghanistan's Real Internet Lives on Its Streets', *New York Magazine*, 31 October, available at <http://nymag.com/developing/2018/10/afghani stan-sneakernet-internet-physical-file-sharing.html> (last accessed 29 April 2019).

Hughes, P. (2013), 'Advancing Access to Justice Through Generic Solutions: The Risk of Perpetuating Exclusion', *Windsor Yearbook of Access to Justice*, 31:1, pp. 1–22.

Human Rights Committee (2007), 'General Comment No. 32', *Article 14 International Covenant on Civil and Political Rights: Right to equality before courts and tribunals and to a fair trial*, UN Doc. CCPR/C/GC/32, 23 August.

Hussain, F. and S. Amin (2018), '"I don't care about their reactions": agency and ICTs in women's empowerment in Afghanistan', *Gender & Development* 26:2, pp. 249–265.

IDLO (2017), *IDLO Evaluation Brief, Final Evaluation 'Supporting Access to Justice in Afghanistan'*.

Kötter, M. (2018), 'Besserer Zugang zum Recht (Access to Justice) durch staatliche Anerkennung informeller Justizsysteme?', *SFB-Governance Working Paper Series*, p. 74.

Luccaro, T. and E. Gaston (2014), 'Women's Access to Justice in Afghanistan, Individual versus Community Barriers to Justice', *Peaceworks*, p. 98.

Marshall, D. (2014), 'Reboot required: The United Nation's engagement in rule of law reform in postconflict and fragile states', in D. Marshall (ed.), *The International Rule of Law Movement*, Harvard: Harvard Law School Human Rights Program Series, pp. 85–133.

McGill, J., S. Bouclin and A. Salyzyn (2017), 'Mobile and Web-based Legal Apps: Opportunities, Risks and Information Gaps', *Canadian Journal of Law and Technology*, 15:2, pp. 229–63.

Ministry of Justice (2018), 'Ministry of Justice to Publicize its Legal Services Call Center', 24 July, available at <http://moj.gov.af/en/news/337930> (last accessed 12 April 2019).

Norwegian Refugee Council (NRC) (J. Madzarevic and S. Rao) (2014), *Strengthening Displaced Women's Housing, Land and Property Rights in Afghanistan.*

Rhode, D. (2013), 'Access to Justice: An Agenda For Legal Education and Research', *Journal of Legal Education*, 62, pp. 531–50.

Robertson, C. (2012), 'The Facebook Disruption: How Social Media May Transform Civil Litigation and Facilitate Access to Justice', *Arkansas Law Review*, 65, pp. 75–102.

Schindler, L. (2012), 'Skirting the Ethical Line: The Quandary of Online Legal Forms', *Chapman Law Review*, 16:1, pp. 164–86.

Sen, A. (1999), *Development as Freedom*, New York: Anchor Books.

Special Inspector General for Afghanistan Reconstruction (2014), *Support for Afghanistan's Justice Sector: State Department Programs Need Better Management and Stronger Oversight*, SIGAR 14-26 Audit Report.

Stahlmann, F. (2016), *Exploring Primary Justice in Afghanistan: Challenges, concerns, and elements that work*, Leiden: Vollenhoven Institute.

Staudt, R. (2009), 'All the Wild Possibilities: Technology that Attacks Barriers to Access to Justice', *Loyola Los Angeles Law Review*, 42, pp. 1117–46.

Thompson, D. (2016), 'Creating New Pathways to Justice Using Simple Artificial Intelligence and Online Dispute Resolution', *International Journal of Dispute Resolution*, 1:2, reprinted as *Osgoode Hall Law School Legal Studies Research Paper Series*, 12:6, Research Paper 27.

Tongia, R., E. Subrahmanian and V. Arunachalam (2005), *Information and Communications Technology for Sustainable Development: Defining A Global Research Agenda*, Bangalore: Allied Publishers.

Trebilcock, M. and M. Mota Prado. (2014), *Law and Development*, Cheltenham: Edward Elgar.

Tyler, T. (2018), 'The influence of citizen experiences on trust and confidence in the courts, Presentation Notes', *Symposium on the Future of Justice*, 14–15 May, University College London, available at <https://www.ucl.ac.uk/laws/events/2018/may/future-justice-harnessing-power-empirical-research> (last accessed: 26 April 2019).

UNESCAP (2015), *An In-Depth Study on the Broadband Infrastructure in Afghanistan and Mongolia.*

UN Secretary-General (2004), *Report of the Secretary-General on The Rule of Law and Transitional Justice in Conflict and Post-Conflict Societies*, UN Doc. S/2004/616.

UN Secretary-General (2017), *Progress Towards the Sustainable Development Goals*, UN Doc. E/2017/66.

UNDP (2004), *Practice Note on Access to Justice.*

UNDP, UN Women, UNICEF (2009), *Informal Justice Systems – Charting a Course for Human Rights-Based Engagement.*

Vapnek, J., P. Boaz and H. Turku (2016), 'Improving Access to Justice in Developing and Post-Conflict Countries: Practical Examples from the Field', *Duke Forum for Law and Social Change*, 8, pp. 27–44.

Wardak, A. (2016), *A Decade and a Half Rebuilding Afghanistan's Justice System: An Overview*, Leiden: Van Vollenhoven Institute.

Wojkowska, E. (2006), *Doing Justice: How Informal Justice Systems Can Contribute*, Oslo: UNDP, Oslo Governance Centre.

World Bank (2018), *Implementation Completion and Results Report For the Justice Service Delivery Report*, Report No. ICR00004475.

World Bank (2019a), 'Justice and Development', available at <http://www.world bank.org/en/topic/governance/brief/justice-rights-and-public-safety> (last accessed: 26 April 2019).

World Bank (2019b), Afghanistan Digital Casa Project, <http://projects.worldbank. org/P156894/?lang=en&tab=overview> (last accessed: 26 April 2019).

World Justice Project (2016), *The Rule of Law in Afghanistan*.

Part IV:

Reflecting on Legal Education in the Future

14

Elements of a Strategic Roadmap to Legal Education and Accreditation in the Digital Environment

Ana Paula Camelo and Cláudio Lucena

A. Introduction

When Valentina announced in the middle of 2018 through her Facebook profile (Valentina 2019) that, although she was not a lawyer, she could help Brazilian employees fight for their rights and bear the costs of the litigation, all for a small fee, an immediate wave of protest and outcry came from various lawyers' associations in the country, including the federal branch of the Brazilian Bar Association, the institution which is officially responsible for the organisation of lawyers and the regulation of their activities, and of those of the legal profession in Brazil. Whatever was to happen, though, Valentina herself could not be sued. Valentina is a chatbot.

The role of artificial intelligence (AI) tools and techniques, and their impact expected in very different areas in terms of the potentialities and related risks, have been one of the main discussions globally in the last few years. This excitement is connected to the broader development and adoption of solutions that incorporate artificial intelligence powered algorithms such as digital and intelligent assistants, chatbots, or even autonomous intelligence and machine learning used to make determinations and predictions in health, education, consumer routines, and communication activities. They have been rapidly developed and explored for different purposes, changing the way people live and work. However, it is important to pay attention to how all these transformations have happened, since 'The AI revolution is not in its infancy, but most of its economic impact is yet to come' (McKinsey 2018). Many concerns are also related to the nature of employment and working conditions in multiple sectors and the future of labour market considering the potential impacts the increasing adoption of new technologies and digital devices everywhere. This complex scenario forces some institutions to engage 'social scientists, economists, labour organizers, and others to better understand AI's implications for labour and work – examining who benefits and who bears the cost of these rapid changes' (AI Now Institute 2019).

I. Artificial Intelligence and the Future of Legal Practice

This scenario has not been so different regarding law activities and legal professionals. The applications and impact of AI are growing inside the law firms and institutions and it is undoubtedly affecting the legal profession practices in different ways. These technical solutions can help or do the complete job of conducting legal research, eliminate routine tasks in legal practice, execute tasks faster and, with more efficiency than humans, review contracts and calculate risks automatically, make predictions about the outcomes of legal proceedings, just to mention few examples. In other words, these technologies are helping lawyers to improve their work, providing additional insights through analytics and automating processes addressing internal and external demands of law firms. At the same time, the markets for legal start-ups are going through a process of expansion on a global scale and it seems there is a general interest of entrepreneurs, law and academic operators in this segment.

In turn, the expectations are that AI-powered software increases the efficiency, cost-effectiveness, productivity, develop stronger business strategies, minimise contract risks and better deliver legal services.

However, the real impacts of these processes are not clear. According to Deloitte, 100,000 legal roles will be automated by 2036, which will imply new strategies, business models and services offered and demanded (Deloitte 2016). In the same sense, the American Bar association argues 'These initial applications of AI to legal practice are just the early beginnings of what will be a radical technology-based disruption to the practice of law. AI "represents both the biggest opportunity and potentially the greatest threat to the legal profession since its formation"' (Marchant 2017).

One of the biggest fears legal professionals have is that rapid technological progress and innovation, such as AI, can have a displacement effect, threatening employment and substitute workers in traditional tasks. Besides this, the ongoing revolution based on automation and advanced machine-learning techniques indicate a shift in terms of demand for high-skilled labour. The complexity of this scenario is all the more enhanced by the fact that all of this is taking place in the scope of profound intergenerational clash, where the future digital professionals are being prepared to develop the necessary skills and solve the problems of their age by an essentially analogue generation, one that grew up, learnt develop values and became active under significantly different circumstances.

Based on this, it looks urgent to discuss, based on empirical evidence and experiences, how AI has been affecting the competitiveness among law firms and services; whether legal companies will develop their own technologies or explore strategic partnerships with lawtechs or other technical experts; how legal training and law schools need to rethink and transform also their realities considering the education of the future professionals and what the market expects regarding AI-driven legal routines.

In this paper, we aim at addressing how law schools and professional associations are dealing with this complex transformations based on technological innovation, especially in the Global South, considering the debates and the coproduction of legal education and digitalisation phenomenon. In other words, we will discuss the role and the challenges of these institutions to follow all the transformations in course and to be proactive, preparing themselves according to the demands of the market. To do this, we start exploring some experiences that have been occurring in different places and contexts, based on the acknowledgment that the digital revolution is already there and old and young professionals must still struggle for their careers.

The selection of the cases that are presented here was based on three complementary fronts: (1) initiatives in which we participate directly, (2) initiatives from other institutions in which we had the opportunity to observe and interact through contact with fellow institutions in academic conferences, and/or (3) initiatives that stood out from desk research. Our main goal is to bring to the discussion the most possible diverse actions and teaching dynamics that could illustrate the transformations going on and how the educational institutions are addressing them.

B. Incorporating Digital Competences into the New Skillset

I. CEPI – FGV DIREITO SP

Since 2017, the Center for Teaching and Research in Innovation (CEPI) from São Paulo Law School of the Getulio Vargas Foundation (FGV DIREITO SP) has been conducting research addressing the future of legal professions considering the digital and intelligent transformations already acknowledged. Besides this academic approach, which is dedicated to identifying new technologies (e.g. learning algorithms, expert systems, etc.) that have changed the legal activities and professions in the country, it also reflects on how this process can impact the legal training in Brazil, regarding skills, knowledge, competences and abilities required to deal with these new technologies in their jobs. The project has been developed based on three specific approaches: (1) a quantitative research, which intends to evaluate the degree of technological adoption of law firms in Brazil; (2) a qualitative research that performs specific case studies of technological application in the public and private sectors; and (3) the elaboration and application of legal technology laboratories at FGV Law courses. One of the main outcomes of these initiatives was the Labtech course (2017), designed to familiarise law undergraduate students with basic programming concepts and allow them to produce their own legal document automation algorithms.

CEPI initiatives are based on the idea that, in view of this scenario of changes in the legal profession, a reorientation of objectives and methods of legal teaching would be necessary in order to provide an educational experience that is relevant and meaningful for all those involved. In this sense, a more participative legal education is favoured, in which the student becomes the protagonist of the education process, creating the capacity not only to know something, but to apply this knowledge in a practical way, from a critical perspective of the context.

With the aim of improving the reflection on the interface of law and technology, in 2017, immersion laboratories were created. These new courses aimed at testing innovations in legal teaching that would help to train students to be better adapted to the use of new technologies in the scope of their future professional activity.

The experiments were diversified, divided into two fronts with specific objectives: (1) the Technology Laboratories (Labtech), optional courses that focus on the production of a technology project by the students that would impact legal services, all elaborated with a partner company; and (2) immersion courses in which, for a whole week, students immerse themselves in practical questions that lead them to an intense reflection on the challenges of their future profession and instigate them to propose solutions based on the contact with several agents involved in the theme. Each of the teaching fronts has already had two editions, with a different theme, and different partners.

In order to meet the challenge of seeking a new way of training law students regarding technological changes in the legal professions, Labtech (the optional course created) is taught along ninety hours, in fifteen weekly meetings, focused to provide students with the experience of working together with a partner company to develop a technology project that could change the way legal activities are being performed. The idea is also to expose the students, not only to know, but to experience the relationship between law and technology, through the use of tools that needed programming language skills and the development of logical-legal reasoning. In the first edition, the technology project that guided the initiative's focus was the automation of legal documents. The students learnt about automation of legal briefings and contracts, and, at the end, two automated contracts were delivered as product. In the second edition, the project developed aimed to build a chatbot that would help the general public to know about the feasibility of pursuing their rights in the judicial scope before even seeking help from a lawyer. The two courses were developed in partnership with lawtechs and legaltechs.

Simultaneously with the laboratories, immersion courses addressing law and technology issues were carried out. This teaching activity differs from the technology lab because they lasted for a concentrated period of time, a whole week, in which the students dedicate themselves to understand a legal challenge coming out of these technological changes, and to propose a solution based on real challenges that can be brought even by companies. The role of these immersions are also to enable students to leave the classroom environment, bringing them closer to the actual reality of companies and public agencies, allowing them to broaden their perception of different perspectives and challenges associated to the use of new technologies.

II. Rede INNOVATE – Paraíba State Bar Association (OAB-PB), Brazil

Still in the Brazilian context, a group of young lawyers have gathered, initially in a rather informal way, but currently in an initiative which is supported by the Brazilian Bar Association, Paraíba Branch (OAB-PB), through the New Higher School of Advocacy (ESA), which culminated in the INNOVATE social start-up. The idea is to identify how the digital realm has brought opportunities, difficulties, challenges, professional barrier entries to young lawyers, and collectively discuss and address them. The operating channel is mostly the Internet itself. Activities are usually conducted through webinars, online courses on these issues, like a webinars dedicated to themes such as "Advocacy 4.0", blockchain, digital legal marketing and client prospection. Recently, the group has also started to organise presential events to address those issues. At OABTalks, pitch presentations are given in digital-related themes such as smart cities, data protection, digital client prospection, followed by a debate in which the audience interactively engages in search of solutions and alternatives. These events are being held out of the Bar premises, in co-working spaces or universities, so as to engage these other audiences as well, in an attempt to call their attention to the issues that are relevant to the Bar and to tap into other competences, skills and even mindsets. The Federal Council of the Bar Association has acknowledged the initiative and it is considering expanding it on a national level.

III. Master in Law and Informatics – Minho University, Portugal

The master's degree in Law and Informatics which has been offered for over a decade by the University of Minho, in Portugal, is evidently not the only one that develops around the relationship between Information Technology and Law. It aims to give students a perspective on how law and informatics influence each other. But there are some characteristics that are peculiar considering that the programme's scientifically predominant area is Law. To start with, admission to the programme is open to students from other backgrounds. Moreover, mandatory courses cover highly technical areas such as Data Transfer and Telecommunications Services, Cryptography, Electronic Identification and Documents, apart from more legally-related issues such as Legal Logic, Argumentation and Representation of Knowledge, and Intellectual Property in the Information Society and Privacy and Protection of Personal Data, Commerce Electronic and Electronic Contracting. Students are expected to be able to identify legal issues regarding the use of information technology from both a technical and a legal point of view by familiarising students with the latest technological developments in this area. To ensure that aim will be achieved, the programme has a longstanding tradition of incentivising co-supervisions of the final course dissertation by faculty members from both academic units that are directly involved in the programme, namely, Law and Computer Sciences. This means that when designing and preparing the dissertation, students will have access to and interact with both a faculty member who will direct him/her about the legal issue which he or she has decided to address, but also with a faculty member who understands and who is able to guide him/her through the technical aspects of the problem under evaluation, describing scenarios or models and highlighting constraints. It is possible that in a near future, where technology is growingly pervasive in more aspects of life, these skills will be more embedded into the profile of any graduate student. But for now, in a transition phase, where we face legal issues which are derived from technical arrangements that we do not necessarily understand, this approach seems insightful, adequate, and could point out to an alternative in tackling interdisciplinary research initiatives.

IV. Michigan State University, USA

At Michigan State University College of Law, Centre for Legal Services Innovation, it offered interdisciplinary classes such as LegalRnD, which addresses legal-service delivery and access across the legal industry. Some of the themes converged in this course are: artificial intelligence and law, quantitative analysis for lawyers, information privacy and security law, and entrepreneurial lawyering. They also have courses addressing artificial intelligence and law connections, or lawyer ethics and regulation in a technology-driven world, highlighting the need of new regulations and new ways of understanding how laws and code interact.

V. Georgetown University, USA

Last, but not least, it's worth mentioning an interdisciplinary initiative, called 'Privacy Legislation in Practice: Law and Technology', a course which is taught jointly by faculty from the Massachusetts Institute of Technology (MIT) and Georgetown University Law School. One (of a number of others) initiative promoted by the law faculty in integrating law and technology knowledge and capacity-building development among its students, the course takes place simultaneously at both institutions, relying on robust and efficient videoconferencing equipment that allow full and seamless interaction, just as if the course were taking place in one place. Law students at Georgetown and engineering students at the MIT sit once a week in well-equipped classrooms in their respective universities, where initial discussions about emerging technologies and their effects and consequences are carried out jointly by law and technology faculty members from both institutions, in an interactive way. After a couple of introductory sessions, the students are divided into necessarily mixed groups from which they will explore in-depth privacy policy issues concerning an emerging technology. Students are also expected to discuss these issues from their multidisciplinary perspectives, and finally develop and propose policy solutions that could possibly be adopted by state governments. Along the course, they present checkpoints of the work which receive comments from the faculty and other fellow students. At the end of the course, they present their final proposals in an open public session, and the proposals are evaluated by jury members who are invited by the faculty among tech-industry public policy executives, administration officials, legislators and faculty from other academic and research institutions, who bring their real life experiences and perspectives into the comments they make when judging the proposals. In other courses, such as Georgetown Law's Technology, Innovation and Law Practice students have the chance to design and develop apps addressing technical and legal dimensions of their area.

A noteworthy aspect of the experiences at FGV and Georgetown is that they are offered to and carried out with undergraduate students. It has usually been very hard for universities to find a way to incorporate these issues and to help students develop those skills in their undergraduate courses. Proposing and effecting change in the legal curricula is often a difficult, time-consuming, complicated task in most countries, and this dynamic does not seem appropriate to address the pace in which innovation is happening. As a result, the current scenario is that undergraduate students normally end up having little or no exposure to structured knowledge in this intersection of technology and law. The ones who will have that initial, more systematic contact will be those who take on graduate studies or some form of extension course, or, alternatively, through a professional association. These issues are too pressing, too present and too necessary for the current lawyer to be left as a further graduate alternative, and not to be addressed during undergraduate studies. This is not to say, by any means, that fundamental legal thinking, basic national and international legal standards, as well as national and international legislation and norms should be taken for granted in formal legal education. But it is certainly a way of reflecting if courses should not also grant some institutional space for a more dynamic experimentation, where cutting-edge issues could be brought to the attention and knowledge of undergraduates.

These examples come from a continuous process of universities and other related institutions initiatives to connect to a market that currently demands specialised and technical knowledge from the lawyer, so she or he can offer more value added to new services.

An interesting aspect that was possible to observe from the particular selection of cases that are reported in this work is that this process is felt as a need in different geographic regions, however different may the circumstances, access to technology and other human and technical resources be. Initiatives in Brazil, as it will eventually be the case with many similar ones in the Global South, often lack the use of highly advanced technology, include students and professional who are not always in a position to follow cutting-edge debates and techniques, and also address companies in a market that many times still does not fully grasp the value and the depth of the transformations that are going on. Yet, the more digital society goes and the more convergence it promotes, the more legal challenges tend to become global and legal professionals in every part of the world will need to develop this view of the world through digital lenses. Profound regional differences aside, this is already being felt by students and professionals in the Global South, and both faculties and professional associations are making significant efforts trying to address these issues with the tools they have at hand, but in the end of the day, serious efforts to bring legal education to the next level in a networked society will have to acknowledge and address this regional gap.

This scenario has been well described by Bernard Hibbitts (2002),

> Law students can enroll in "Computer Law," "E-commerce Law," "Cyberspace Law," "Information Technology and Law" and a plethora of other tech-law courses where law professors explore the bewildering array of regulatory and constitutional issues posed by the explosion of the Internet. But in a few law schools, some new courses are entering the curriculum:

courses that focus not on the law of technology, but rather the technology of law.

To the domain of the programming language adds the need for a professional who understands quantitative and statistical methods that are increasingly used to price the legal assets and liabilities. And law schools need to adapt to this new environment if they are to continue to train professionals connected to the reality and market nowadays. This requires both a methodological readjustment to introduce new tools and new teaching models into the classroom as well as a readjustment of the course's pedagogical project.

C. Reflecting Deeper About the Future of Legal Activities

A number of initiatives and studies that have been recently carried out, reported and observed are worth mentioning and analysing if our aim is to ultimately contribute to identify common elements and strategies that will help legal higher learning institutions and professional associations to incorporate the digital dimension and related skills into the training they offer.

It is true that innovation brings a number of opportunities and alternatives, even creating job positions that are absolutely new or at least that have never been needed in such a scale. This is also true for the legal scenario. A good example is the new data protection legal wave, that comprises the EU data protection reform, but also a global movement of reasonably aligned laws, provisions, regulations, tools and ideas in many countries around the General Data Protection Regulation (GDPR). By 2016, the International Association of Privacy Professionals (IAPP) had estimated that around 28,00 new workers would be needed in Europe, and later in the same year that as much as 75,000 new professionals throughout the world would have to be found to fill the position of data protection officer (DPO), a role which already existed to some extent in certain organisational and corporate structures, but which has now been redesigned by the mentioned data protection legal wave, with strengthened importance and also with much higher expectations about the skills that candidates that will fill that role should possess. Those figures were based on numbers provided by Eurostat and excluded micro, small, and medium-sized companies (Heimes; Pfeifle 2016). A DPO, according to articles 37–39 of the GDPR (European Union 2018), should have legal knowledge regarding data protection law, serve as an internal auditor in the institution as well as a point of contact with external authorities, understand, advise and assist in the management of risks in which the core activities of the organisation could possibly incur. Besides that, it is evidently necessary for the person taking this role to have fair understanding of information security practices, including technical certifications, to be able to coordinate the internal communication to make sure awareness of data protection reaches out to all relevant collaborators, and to have a feeling of which capacity building initiatives would fit best to ensure that not only all these relevant collaborators are ready and possess the necessary skills to deal with the issue, but also that hey continuously and constantly update those skills. Not all data protection reform and implementation movements go that far in entrusting so many powers and thus demanding so many skills from the function that corresponds to the DPO in their frameworks, but all of them, to some extent, recognise, acknowledge and demand a set of skills for such a task that will not be easy to find among professionals with conventional education in any area. This was already patent in the European data protection reform, and now it is also becoming very visible in data protection reform processes in other parts of the world, including in the Global South, as it is the case of Brazil and other Latin American countries that are moving in the same direction.

The explosion of digital content production and the exponential increase in traffic and audience in social media digital platforms are other examples of activities that have expanded professional legal opportunities. More and more legally relevant situations take place within these environments, and although a large extent of content moderation and analysis is already being automated by the larger players in the digital platform industry (Keller 2018), a lot of legal work concerning intellectual property violation, privacy and data protection breaches, hate speech, contractual compliance, cybercrime and many others remains to be done in the scope of digital environments. To perform professionally in all these circumstances, lawyers are required to have at least basic technical working knowledge of how things happen within these platforms, and how they are organised. More than that, as already mentioned, local differences and the diversity of circumstantial, technical and human realities across various regions of the world are also increasingly important in an interconnected world. To build interesting opportunities, it is essential that this range of realities is highlighted instead of made invisible, and that the skills to understand and interact in this multifaceted environment are developed and encouraged.

If we consider automation techniques, more strictly speaking artificial intelligence, that seems to be in the core of the automation revolution that is about to come, some other concrete experiences and developments deserve careful attention and consideration.

Still in 2016, a joint research by University College London (UCL), the University of Sheffield and the University of Pennsylvania developed a method based on artificial intelligence[1] techniques that managed to predict judgments from the European Court of Human Rights (ECtHR) to a 79 per cent accuracy. These judgments are regarded as highly semantically-charged, since they assess human rights issues, they involve a significant level of abstraction, and they are subject to a considerable margin of appreciation. The study is the first systematic approach that attempts to predict an international court's judgments using only textual information from the court's own database, although extracted from relevant sections of the decisions themselves, since the original text of lodged applications was not available (Aletras et al. 2016). It analysed a dataset consisting of judgments that addressed Articles 3, 6, and 8 of the European Convention on Human Rights (ECHR) through a binary classification mechanism whose inputs were taken out a textual structure organised into the sections full case, procedure, circumstances, relevant law, facts, law, and topics, which are arrangements organised according to the structured suggestion that similar words will appear in similar contexts.. The researchers concluded that the combination of the analysis from the circumstances subsection with the topics one reaches the highest level of accuracy in predictions. The authors propose that the work could be improved to become a tool that would reliably identify cases with similar patterns that will potentially point to similar outcomes and to improve the development of prior indicators of potential violations that could be identified from the applications, allowing the court to give priority processing to more violations that appear as more likely.

In another study in 2018 (LawGeex 2018), twenty lawyers trained in the United States with extensive legal corporate practice and substantial experience in contract review were required to identify legal issues in five Non-Disclosure Agreements (NDAs). The same NDAs were also submitted to an artificial intelligence algorithm developed by LawGeex, a legal tech company which has created a specific language and a learning model for the task over three years while training it with tens of thousands of contracts. Whereas the lawyers achieved an average rate of 85 per cent of accuracy, going through the five NDAs in an average time of ninety-two minutes, the algorithm completed the same task in an average of twenty-six seconds, with a 95 per

---

[1] We would rather refer to the use of analytics over big data, which is the capacity to make inferences over an extremely vast amount of information. A stage of the development of the area in which general artificial intelligence becomes viable, which is currently not envisaged by experts in the field, could justify the use of the expression, although we acknowledge the fact that its use has been extensively consolidated, including in business strategies for marketing purposes and, more broadly, in everyday life. Yet, we believe the terminological distinction is relevant and should be emphasised.

cent of accuracy rate. The lawyers that took part in the experiment expressed a positive view of the tool and of the results, understanding the outcome as a sign that automation can be an important ally in improving the efficiency and accuracy of their work. They highlight, however, that they should retain strategic importance in performing legal activities, that artificial intelligence should not be thought of as a standalone tool, and that it is a combination of human excellence and technology that will enhance competitiveness, consistency and impact of legal services, strengthening the role of a lawyer as a trusted advisor.

The scenario is not less thriving in Brazil for lawtechs (AB2l 2019) and similar automation initiatives. For the first time, on 7 November 2018, The High Court of the States of Minas Gerais deployed the *Radar* tool, developed by the court's IT Department, and tried 280 cases in a matter of seconds (Tribunal de Justica 2018). The tool identifies and separates appeals whose claims present similar characteristics and elements, drafts an opinion based on higher court rulings on the matter, offers the rapporteur an opportunity to customise, amend or add any argument to the opinion, and rules on all of the selected appeal at the same time.

On the corporate side, Urbano Vitalino, a Brazilian legal office with more than eighty years of existence and over 100,000 litigation cases to manage, has pioneered a customisation of IBM Watson and established a plan to implement in its operations (Müller 2017). In the first phase, which has already been completed, *Carol* – which is the name the system has received – has been trained to input client information into the office's record and internal management system, extracting them from documents, including legal briefings and evidence provided by clients. The work of around eighty administrative employees within the office was already replaced in this phase. The firm decided to keep all these employees and re-assigned them other functions and responsibilities, but that is a strong evidence that a certain amount of job positions in the legal industry, depending on the context, on their nature, on the degree of specialisation, will not resist when a wider wave of automation comes. Carol is currently being trained for Phase 2, where it will assist lawyers in a more specifically legal task, by drafting legal documents, indicating useful evidence, relevant precedents, updated legislation which is applicable to the case, and the position of courts or judges on specific issues. Phase 3 will comprise the analysis of non-structured data in order to provide strategic advice both to the firm, as the level of complexity of the case, and to the clients, concerning, for instance, their corporate practices and the suggestion of measures to reduce litigation.

As to Valentina, the chatbot referred to in the introduction, the institutional outcry triggered by the professional associations with the view of preserving the corporate interests at stake argued that the bot was proposing a private, alternative mechanism for the solution of legal conflicts, and that the initiative was an offense to federal legislation that ensures professional exclusivity over those activities to registered lawyers. The head of Hurst Capital, the company behind Valentina, issued a public note, through which he clarified that Valentina merely uses artificial intelligence to identify and negotiate patrimonial rights via a kind of legal cession expressly provided by national law, and directly with their holders. He stated that any litigation or other procedure covered by the legal exclusivity of lawyers in Brazil were strictly observed by the company, in which case they hire specialised legal service. The episode led to the institution of an 'artificial intelligence coordination' (OAB 2018) group by the Brazilian Bar Association. While announcing the creation of the group, the President acknowledged the impact and effects of technical progress, the potential it has to contribute to the efficiency of legal services, the fact that evolution is unavoidable, the importance of addressing this issue at an early stage, when a good balance is more likely to be found, but also that the group would put all its efforts in preventing massive and disorderly technical development from pushing the legal professional to a marginal role in the country.

It is true that apart from crypto actives (Fenwick, Vermeulen 2019) and of an experience in humanitarian use that consists in identifying Syrian refugees in Jordan refugee camps (UNHCR 2015), concrete Blockchain implementations are still scarce, either due to technical constraints or to a general lack of knowledge of how to implement. In spite of that, the idea of substituting or simply eliminating the intermediary, third party of an operation – the very party that through the centuries happened to be the guardian of an element as important as trust – will not go away any time soon. Whole industries have thrived over the performance of those various intermediary functions, such as notary services, land records, central banks, Internet domain names and identifiers coordination (Cartwright 2018), certification bodies and authorities, and other centralisation services in general. Once technical restrictions are overcome, computing power becomes feasible, awareness of the environments and tools to build blockchain applications evolve, or even when another similar technology comes with similar or improved features, providing the same capacity to overcome the intermediary and to redesign trust, only with better performance and viable enough to start being deployed more easily and more frequently, not only will those mentioned services experience complete disruption, it will also unleash other possibilities. It will be the time to implement services for which an intermediary would be too costly or whose operations demand an amount of trust which is unrealistic given current circumstances. And all this scenario comes with concerns around regulatory, contractual and liability issues, intellectual property, privacy and data protection rights, among a number of other legal aspects that need to be considered, defined, and monitored for eventual enforcement.

D. Analogue Professors to Address a Digital Generation

A final word on a very important aspect of incorporating a technology view-point in legal education, about the teachers and instructors who are to be involved in the process.

Because we are dealing not only with ground-breaking advancements, but at times with the first significant change in decades in the particular legal field, it should not come as a surprise that this is often unknown territory for legal education professionals as well. Up until now initiatives of integrating law and technology have usually been conducted by one individual in an institution who happens to be somewhat more connected to this dialogue, or a specific department or centre that is dedicated to the area, but which comprises a limited number of the members of a faculty. Taken from a wider institutional perspective, this is the first generation of professionals to collectively face this kind of challenges from an educational standpoint – and they are enormous. Concepts are not yet totally clear, the impact of the tech-nologies at the table is not yet totally clear, what is to be addressed and what is not is not yet totally clear, there is not even – and there could not be yet – a consensus around the right approach to explaining how a certain technology plays in the legal field, because, again, that is also not totally clear. At times even convincing colleagues in legal departments and centres that addressing the issues mentioned here bears legal relevance – and is not just a trendy topic that will eventually fade away and as such it is to be avoided by a serious law faculty – is a hard task.

Add that to the fact that most of the times the technology that becomes a component of the work of these educational professionals was not even there when they were preparing themselves to perform legal and legal teaching activities; they did not grow up knowing those tools, they were not immersed in the digital environment, and they did not have a reason to consider them while getting ready to teach. Now this generation of teachers who are at best digital immigrants have to guide students who are digital natives (Palfrey and Gasser 2010). They have to transpose their legal experience from the analogue world to help students build a critical legal thinking of a digital environment with which these students happen to be much more familiarised than the teacher himself. This is not a simple obstacle to be considered as of less importance or even disregarded. It needs a structured reconciliation, that will just not happen as an evident outcome of teaching skills and legal knowledge and will not develop seamlessly, without special attention and efforts to the preparation of professionals in legal education to overcome this gap. As if these were not enough challenges, transforming education in this domain means calling for subsequent and deep change in an area, structures and institutions that are among the most traditional ones in a society. That is not something which is easy to push.

More, these are institutions that have been delivering access to justice, a value that should be extremely dear to any human society, in a very similar way across centuries, a way that is clearly not the most adequate one for the current kind of human interplay throughout the world. We must be able to redesign legal education and leverage the potential that technology offers to improve access to justice in a way that it becomes more effective, more transparent, convergent and human-centred by design. If we manage to incorporate these features into the mechanisms through which societies have been delivering justice over the last centuries, while finding ways to keep the necessary human control and oversight over the automation measures that are deployed, that can mean that access to justice will undergo its most major shift so far, coming closer to the tool that solves human conflicts in an appropriate, fair and timely manner, which it is supposed to be. And the further the society is from that horizon nowadays, the more it could benefit from the shift. This means that regions such as the Global South, as mentioned earlier in this text, could benefit even more from a movement which is structured and considers local differences as important variables in the global debate, and reduce the inequality gap in this area in a more significant way.

The generational clash between analogue x digital people, as proposed, is already a relevant element of this final reflection. But another generational clash stems from it, one between an analogue x a digital model of access to justice. Rethinking access to justice in these terms might carry an even larger potential for positive transformation.

E. Strategic Elements to a Roadmap in Legal Education and Accreditation

Legal branches and other spaces of legal work in many countries are already on their way to a degree of automation that will render paperwork virtually non-existent in the coming years. Thus, apart from legal knowledge, lawyers must already have the most basic digital skills that will allow them to deal confidently with the electronic files that will represent a great deal of the evidence and working material with which courts, clients and firms will handle in a short term. This is evidently not a problem in most developed countries, where lawyers that are being admitted into professional associations are digital natives, with those skills embedded into their life experiences, but it can be an issue to the legal profession around the world, where technology has not been equally accessible.

Moreover, from the experiences that were analysed, and from the concrete initiatives that were mentioned and observed in the course of this work, the following relevant skills and steps stand out as possible elements for a roadmap that addresses the incorporation of a technology view within current legal education:

1. **Interdisciplinarity:** All the teaching and professional capacity-building experiences referred to along this work strongly resort to an approach that comprises tackling problems from the perspectives of different areas of knowledge. For recent data protection issues, for example, there is no way one single domain will cover all the skills that are demanded from the new individuals who will be filling the roles. That is the main reason why the University of Minho works with a supervisor from each area in the programme described above. It is evident that a solid, formal education in related areas is very welcome, but shorter, introductory courses that give a bird's eye view on another field, or even self-learning initiatives are also a way to start looking out of the legal discussion alone. The important thing is to bear in mind that purely legal approaches are unlikely to successfully address new problems that were not perceived as such before because the technology that creates the conditions for them to surface was not available back then;

2. **Interaction:** Considering the knowledge and perspectives of other areas is important, but no longer enough. Professionals of the future in legal practice will not adequately incorporate a technology view in their experience if they do not actually interact, exchange, get in touch with professionals from other domains – and the sooner, the better. This kind of exchange is not a frequent teaching practice in undergraduate courses around the world, but it tends to be worse in legal teaching environments, where purely legal assessments tend to predominate along the education and preparation of professionals. Experiences like the ones at Georgetown and FGV, as described, demonstrate the richness and the value of learning how to work together, how to think and solve problems in actual collaboration and how to tap into each other's best, sharing material, opinions and insights from the remote tools and alternatives that are already becoming part of the working scenario of the coming years;

3. **Coding skills:** The initiatives from the Center for Legal Services Innovation at Michigan State University College of Law, as well as others which are mentioned along this work highlight a controversy

around the question whether lawyers – it happens with other professionals too – should be trained in coding skills. The experiences show that there is added value for lawyers in learning how to code, but also that this is not a necessary skill to work in the legal technology scenario. What is undoubtedly necessary to train a lawyer whose career will be influenced by technology is to understand basic data structures and the underlying logic of basic algorithmic operations, rather than programming language as syntax per se. Through time, evidence started coming into law from areas such as engineering, finance, accounting and health without demanding the lawyer to become an engineer, a financier, an accountant or a doctor, but only that he can reasonably understand the language so as to interact and collaborate with the experts who will be called into action for each case. Technology-related evidence will also come to be part of the lawyers' work, and he will not have to be a computer scientist to develop his work, provided he can reasonably understand the jargon, basic structures, interact and collaborate with experts, when need be;

4. **Continuous education and training:** Lifelong learning opportunities for all are one of the United Nations Sustainable Development Goal for a good reason. Less inequality concerning the sharing of the wealth that digital industries provide depends on ensuring a more equitable education and training. This is particularly necessary in the legal field. A number of good opportunities will be available in the coming years for lawyers that are ready to perform in that domain, and it is essential that they are aware of this need from early career stages, and make efforts and take concrete steps towards actual and constant improvement. The space for that improvement, however, does not necessarily have to be formal education spaces. Rede INNOVATE is a good example of that;

5. **Economic and innovation standpoints:** Finally, it is essential that this new professional has a wider view about how innovation economically impacts institutions and corporations that play a role in the scope of his activities. This stems from the need of an interdisciplinary approach, but it constitutes a specific call to go out of the mere legal mindset and devote more attention to actually understand the business models, needs and institutional missions, and how technical developments are playing in. Law itself has been an intermediary function with the exclusive right to manage the tools of legitimate enforcement along time. This power many times leads legal professionals to overrate the importance of law, and neglect the demands, the concrete needs, the reality of the scenario they are called to assist in. Failing to understand those corporate needs, those institutional features, and that reality in the current scenario, where technology constantly offers creative and innovative options

to circumvent intermediaries, might represent a risk to the profession itself.

F. Conclusions

No tradition or professional licensing model can isolate the legal activities from the huge impacts and the consequences of recent technological development. In light of that impending shock it is obvious that the institutions which are responsible for the education, preparation and accreditation of legal operators in each society must consider that incorporating the digital dimension into the vision of world which they convey to their students is key. It is essential to have a strategy to embed an appropriate view of the digital environment into the education of current law students, and to identify which initiatives could constitute a possible roadmap. This work suggests that at least two paths must be pursued in the direction of such roadmap. The first one is incorporating digital competences into the skills which institutions convey and demand from their law students/candidates. The second one is a deeper reflexion about the future of the profession itself in different contexts and professional realities.

Concerning the first path, the work looked at initiatives that either add coding skills to the legal education, as it is the case of the experience at The Center for Legal Services Innovation, Michigan State University College of Law, or that build truly interdisciplinary, collaborative knowledge through an actual exchange among students/professors/researchers from different backgrounds in order to enhance perspectives and solve common problems, as it is the case with the Privacy Legislation in Practice course, offered by the Massachusetts Institute of Technology (MIT) to their students in conjunction with law students from Georgetown Law School, and the double supervision scheme from Minho University in Portugal, in its Masters in Law and Informatics. Apart from those skills, the ability to actually interact and work collaboratively, the need for constant training and education and for a broader view of the business and of how innovation can impact it can be highlighted among the elements that will offer the roadmap searched for in the scope if this work.

Regarding the second aspect, law schools and associations need to discuss seriously the impact of a combination of technologies that will redefine legal services as they have been offered along the centuries, which are blockchain, with its capacity to revolutionise trust and eliminate intermediaries, and artificial intelligence, with its current potential to scale highly semantically charged tasks.

The challenge is considerable, since what conventionally worked well so far in this educational realm might not work henceforth while delivering education and providing accreditation to a very different digital native generation. Also, the challenge of delivering this education is to be faced by a generation of professors who are themselves, if anything, digital immigrants.

The elements which were pointed out along this work contribute to an approach that tackles key issues and suggests strategic steps to a roadmap in legal education and accreditation that envisages sustainable development goals, not only offering continuous learning opportunities (United Nations Sustainable Development Goal 4 – Ensure inclusive and equitable quality education and promote lifelong learning opportunities for all), but which is also, to the extent that a lawyer that understands and makes full and adequate use of the tools that are available in his activity is in a position to offer better solutions to the conflicts he manages, driven in the direction of the achievement of a better justice service and a better justice ideal (United Nations Sustainable Development Goal 16 – Promote peaceful and inclusive societies for sustainable development, provide access to justice for all and build effective, accountable and inclusive institutions at all levels).

Bibliography

AB2l (2019), 'Radar de Lawtechs e Legaltechs Versão 4.6', available at: <https://www.ab2l.org.br/radar-lawtechs/> (last accessed: 05 August 2019).

AI Now Institute (2019), available at <https://ainowinstitute.org/> (last accessed: 30 July 2019).

Aletras, N., D. Tsarapatsanis, D. Preoțiuc-Pietro and V. Lampos (2016), 'Predicting judicial decisions of the European Court of Human Rights: a Natural Language Processing perspective', *PeerJ Computer Science* 2:93.

Brin, S. and L. Page (1998), The Anatomy of a Large-Scale Hypertextual Web Search Engine. In: *Seventh International World-Wide Web Conference* (WWW 1998), April 14–18, 1998, Brisbane, Australia.

Cartwright, M. (2018), 'Could a Blockchain replace DNS?', available at: <https://medium.com/blockchain-city/could-a-blockchain-replace-dns-7a53c5607d4a> (last accessed: 05 August 2019).

Deloitte (2019), 'Developing legal talent Stepping into the future law firm', available at <https://www2.deloitte.com/content/dam/Deloitte/uk/Documents/audit/deloitte-uk-developing-legal-talent-2016.pdf> (last accessed: 05 August 2019).

European Union (2018), 'Regulation (EU) 2016/679 of the European Parliament and of the Council of 27 April 2016 on the protection of natural persons with regard to the processing of personal data and on the free movement of such data, and repealing Directive 95/46/EC (General Data Protection Regulation)', *Journal of the European Union*, L119/1.

Feferbaum, M., E. R. Fabiani and A. P. da Silva (Org.) (2018) 'O futuro das profissões jurídicas: você está preparad@? Sumário executivo da pesquisa quantitativa "Tecnologia, Profissões e Ensino Jurídico"' São Paulo: CEPI – Centro de Ensino e Pesquisa em Inovação (FGV Direito SP), 2018, available at <https://www.academia.edu/39575688/Sum%C3%A1rio_Executivo_da_Pesquisa_

Quantitativa_TECNOLOGIA_PROFISS%C3%95ES_E_ENSINO_JUR%
C3%8DDICO_> (last accessed 30 September 2019).

———— (2018) 'Iniciativas de ensino inteligência artificial e profissões jurídicas.' São
Paulo: CEPI – Centro de Ensino e Pesquisa em Inovação (FGV Direito SP),
2018. available at <https://www.academia.edu/39307191/Relat%C3%B3rio_
das_Iniciativas_de_Ensino_-Projeto_TECNOLOGIA_PROFISS%C3%
95ES_E_ENSINO_JUR%C3%8DDICO> (last accessed 30 September 2019).

Fenwick, M. and E. Vermeulen, (2019), 'A Primer on Blockchain, Smart Contracts
& Crypto-Assets', *Lex Research Topics in Corporate Law & Economics Working
Paper No. 2019- 3*, 29 April, available at <https://papers.ssrn.com/sol3/papers.
cfm?abstract_id=3379443> (last accessed: 05 August 2019).

Floridi, L. (2014), *The 4th revolution: how the infosphere is reshaping human reality*,
Oxford; New York: Oxford University Press.

Heimes, R. and S. Pfeifle (2016), 'GDPR's global reach to require at least 75,000
DPOs worldwide', 19 April, available at <https://iapp.org/news/a/study-gdprs-
global-reach-to-require-at-least-75000-dpos-worldwide/> (last accessed: 05
August 2019).

Hinton, G. E. (2007), 'Learning multiple layers of representation', *Trends in cognitive sciences*, 11:10, pp. 428–434.

Keller, D. (2018), 'Internet Platforms: Observations on Speech, Danger, and Money'
Hoover Institution's Aegis Paper Series, 13 June, available at <https://ssrn.com/
abstract=3262936> (last accessed: 05 August 2019).

LawGeex (2018), 'Comparing the Performance of Artificial Intelligence to Human
Lawyers in the Review of Standard Business Contracts', available at <https://
images.law.com/contrib/content/uploads/documents/397/5408/lawgeex.pdf>
(last accessed: 05 August 2019).

Marchant, G. (2017), 'Artificial Intelligence and The Future of Legal Practice', *The
SciTechLawyer*, 1 November, <https://www.americanbar.org/groups/science_
technology/publications/scitech_lawyer/2017/fall/artificial-intelligence-and-
future-legal-practice/> (last accessed 05 August 2019).

Müller, L. (2017), '"Advogada robô" facilita trabalho de humanos em escritório bra-
sileiro', *tecmundo*, 12 April, available at: <https://www.tecmundo.com.br/soft
ware/125166-advogada-robo-facilita-trabalho-humanos-escritorio-brasileiro.
htm> (last accessed: 05 August 2019).

Ordem dos Advogados do Brasil (OAB) (2018), 'OAB cria coordenação para discutir
regulamentação do uso de inteligência artificial', available at: <https://www.oab.
org.br/noticia/56480/oab-cria-coordenacao-para-discutir-regulamentacao-do-
uso-de-inteligencia-artificial> (last accessed: 05 August 2019).

Pagallo, U. (2013), *The Laws of Robots: Crimes, Contracts, and Torts,* Torino: Springer.

Pagallo, U. and M. Durante (2016), 'The Pros and Cons of Legal Automation and its
Governance', *European Journal of Risk Regulation*, 7:2, pp. 323–334.

Palfrey, J. and U. Gasser (2010), *Born Digital – Understanding the First Generation of
Digital Natives*, New York: B. Books ed.

Pasquale, F. (2015), *The Black Box Society: The Secret Algorithms That Control Money
and Information*, Cambridge, Massachusetts: Harvard University Press.

Pasquale, F. and G. Cashwell (2015), 'Four Futures of Legal Automation', *UCLA
Law Review Discourse*, 63, pp. 26–48.

Tribunal de Justica do Estado de Minas Gerais (2018), 'TJMG utiliza inteligência artificial em julgamento virtual', available at <https://www.tjmg.jus.br/portal-tjmg/noticias/tjmg-utiliza-inteligencia-artificial-em-julgamento-virtual.htm#.XyG99PhKhsM> (last accessed 29 July 2020).

Tutt, A., (2016), 'An FDA for Algorithms', *Administrative Law Review*, 15 March, available at: <http://ssrn.com/abstract=2747994> (last accessed 05 August 2019).

United Nations High-Commissioner for Refugees (UNHCR) (2015), 'Blockchain digital identity to deliver international aid to Syrian refugees', available at: <https://www.unhcr.org/withrefugees/map-location/blockchain-digital-identity-deliver-international-aid-syrian-refugees/?mpfy_map=885> (last accessed: 05 August 2019).

Valentina – Robô do Trabalhador (2019), *Social Media Account*, available at <https://www.facebook.com/ValentinaRoboDoTrabalhador/> (last accessed: 27 July 2019).

15

Challenges and Opportunities: Engaging a Reluctant Profession in Its Own Future

Aviva Rotenberg

A. Introduction: Lawyers (and Penguins) and Change

John Kotter's management fable, *Our Iceberg is Melting* (2006), is the story of a colony of penguins whose iceberg is, well, melting. The iceberg has sustained the community for a very long time, and the penguins have never questioned the permanency and safety of their home. But times are changing, and one of the more observant penguins realises that the iceberg is becoming unstable, making the penguins increasingly vulnerable. He tries to warn the other penguins; some believe him, many do not. Those who do believe that the iceberg is melting argue about how long it will take to melt, whether and how the penguins need to move, and to where. In the meantime, the iceberg continues to destabilise beneath them. Kotter's book goes on to outline a framework for dealing with change but underlying all of this is the truism that change is hard for people (and penguins!), even when the alternative threatens their very existence.

There is an obvious parallel here to how the legal profession has and could deal with necessary change. We have seen how practitioners of historically successful and lucrative professions can be unmotivated to do business differently. 'If it ain't broke, don't fix it' is a common mantra with a comfortably common-sense rationale to it. But, as the CBA Futures Report (CBA 2018a) details, this kind of thinking belies some demonstrable transformations to the profession that will necessitate new approaches.

For the first time, the legal market is a buyer's market. Business leaders are heading the charge for internal teams to do more with less, and this challenge is being passed on to outside counsel. New technologies have given clients unprecedented bargaining power in determining the limits of their legal representatives' functions, methods, and rates, and this will only continue to develop with the use of artificial intelligence. Between technological shortcuts, increasing competition, and growing financial anxiety resulting in part from the 2008 recession, clients are searching for the best value for their money and will look for alternatives when faced with high legal bills unless there is an accompanying perception of value that goes beyond basic service.

In Canada, legal professionals are facing the further challenge of limited growth capacity as a result of greater competition and downward pressure on prices for legal services. Worldwide, publicly traded firms and alternate business structures (ABS) with non-lawyer ownership are gaining ground. As these competitors introduce aggressive business practices and greater capacity for 'value-added' service, many larger firms may be forced to follow suit with more economical and efficient processes at all levels of management and hiring. Compounding the problem of competition are changing demographics and accompanying sets of values. Young lawyers are more numerous, but they are also seeking a different kind of work/life balance than previous generations. These changing priorities reflect similar shifts in client bases. The legal profession will be forced to understand the needs of a changing marketplace, where clients have easier access to legal knowledge and tools, transforming their perception of the function of lawyers in many cases. Naturally, these shifts also present opportunities for lawyers attuned to the needs of the market and ready to embrace technological solutions and progressive business practices.

And yet, we are seeing globally strong resistance to taking steps to revitalise the way lawyers conduct their businesses. In the face of an obvious need to do law differently and the glacial pace at which professionals are doing so, we must ask if there is more to the legal profession's reluctance to change than merely a commitment to an historically profitable business model. Is there a reason why lawyers struggle to see that their iceberg is melting? And is there a reason they struggle even harder to do something about it? American psychologist and lawyer Dr. Larry Richard (Richard 2002), tells us that yes, lawyers are usually resistant to change. Certainly, there are institutional, organisational, regulatory, economic and other elements confounding the evolution of legal service delivery, but lawyers themselves are also not naturally positioned well for change. Understanding this phenomenon and the reasons behind it can be very helpful when determining strategy and tactics.

B. Why Are Lawyers More Resistant to Change?

To understand lawyerly resistance to change, it is important to examine some of the personality traits common to most lawyers. Although Dr. Richard's work uncovers many valuable insights, the focus here will be on those qualities that speak directly to the struggle to make change.

The first trait to consider is skepticism. People who score highly in this trait on personality tests also tend to be self protective, analytical, argumentative, and questioning. The research indicates that this is the highest-ranking trait in lawyers – averaging in the 90th percentile, relative to the 50th percentile in the general public. Although skepticism may not have the most positive connotation, it should be obvious that a critical and disputatious mindset could be considered assets to lawyers, particularly litigators.

The second relevant trait is resilience. In this context, resilience refers to whether or not an individual is able to take feedback, whether they tend to react defensively, and whether or not they can accept critique. It is also understood that resilience relates strongly to how a person responds to 'stress, change, and adversity' (Daavis-Lack, Richard and Shearon 2014). On average, lawyers scored 30 per cent on this trait, relative to the general population, which sits at 50 per cent. The low score suggests that although lawyers have a reputation for confidence, this may belie more sensitive personalities underneath. This may ring true for anyone who has ever participated in a performance review process in a law firm!

In Stanford Magazine, Marina Krakovsky (Krakovsky 2007) refers to well-known American psychologist Carol Dweck, who describes these types of attitudes and responses as a 'fixed mindset', explained as the belief that success relates more to natural intelligence than it does to effort. People with a fixed mindset are motivated mainly by appearing smart, and much less so on whether they are learning anything in the process. 'For them, each task is a challenge to their self-image, and each setback becomes a personal threat. So, they pursue only activities at which they're sure to shine—and avoid lots of experiences necessary to grow and flourish in any endeavor." (Krakovsky 2007). This mindset, which is reinforced through law school (Socratic method, anyone?), precedent based practice, the huge emphasis on risk management, and in a hundred other ways, has fostered fear, an aversion to experimentation, and the lack of resilience described above.

The third trait identified by Dr. Richard is that of autonomy. This relates to a desire for independence, resistance to being managed, and reaction to being told what to do. Unsurprisingly, lawyers ranked high on this trait, scoring 89 per cent relative to the general population's score of 50 per cent. Psychologist Ron Friedman (Friedman 2015) describes autonomy as a 'basic psychological need,' but lawyers appear to be needier than most.

To summarise (and generalise), Dr. Richard's research suggests that lawyers do not like being told what to do, do not like hearing that they could be doing it better or differently, and are more than likely to argue about these (and other) points. These traits have serious implications: the lack of resilience and sensitivity to feedback (also known as the need to be right all the time) means that lawyers are afraid to take risks, get things wrong, and try new things. Such resistance impedes growth and change. One wonders if there had been lawyers on the iceberg, would they have made it, or would they have gone down arguing.

The analogy of the penguins tells us that even when professionals agree that a change is needed, they may not agree on how to respond. Given lawyerly resistance to risk, error, and change, we cannot expect the profession to respond to new challenges organically; practitioners need to be guided by clear evidence of what sorts of change are required, why they will be successful, and how such change can be integrated into existing practice. Thus, the kinds of decisions that need to be made right now require an objective analysis to assess the conditions and to implement a programmatic response with the weight of past success behind it. The Canadian Bar Association conducted just such an intervention in 2012 when it launched the CBA Legal Futures Initiative (CBA 2014) (hereafter referred to as 'Futures') to 'identify the factors likely to change the market for and work of practicing lawyers in the future, to assess the likely shifts in client demands, and to make related recommendations' (CBA 2014, p. 9).

As in most large organisations, there were many steps to take to properly set up, resource, and frame the project. One of these critical steps was the development of Futures' Terms of Reference. The clarity provided by the Terms of Reference at the very early stages of the project helped facilitate a well thought out structure going forward. Futures was to work with this mission in mind:

- To identify and consider the factors (economic, social, legal, technological) that are likely to change the market for and the work of practising lawyers in 2020 and beyond.
- To assess the likely shifts in demands of clients – from major companies to consumers – in the coming decade.
- To make recommendations on the organisation and structure of the profession and of legal businesses to ensure that legal services are fit for purpose in the long-term.
- To make recommendations on the training and education of the next generation of lawyers (in law firms and in-house).
- To make recommendations on the regulation of the legal profession in the future (including consideration of liberalisation).

In 2014, the CBA released *Futures: Transforming the Delivery of Legal Services in Canada*, the product of a huge amount of work, supported by extensive consultations within the industry as well as commissioned research and expert analysis.

CBA Futures had its own momentum and energy, propelled by the belief that changing market forces bring opportunities for lawyers to survive and thrive. Finding those opportunities represents a way for lawyers to maintain or enhance relevance and value, improve on legal service delivery, and meet the needs of those who should be, but are not, being served. According to the Futures report (CBA 2014), there was no question who needs to take the lead. Underlying CBA Futures was, and is, the understanding that if lawyers themselves do not take responsibility for shaping the future of legal services in Canada, others, from outside the profession, will: 'Major change is coming to the legal profession – in many respects the seeds have already been planted. The legal profession must adapt to that change or be forced to do so by others – or risk being marginalized' (CBA, p. 14).

Given these stakes, lawyers ought to understand the urgency and importance of changing their mindsets, evolving their practices, and considering new ways to serve clients. Unfortunately, it was not (and is not) that easy. Despite the undisputed integrity of the Futures Report, many members of the profession have yet failed to take its recommendations seriously as the impetus to re-evaluate their own practice. In the meantime, the profession continues to evolve rapidly.

When CBA Legal Futures was originally launched in 2012, many still needed to be convinced of the changes facing the industry. After consulting with well known legal futurist and Special Advisor to Futures, Professor Richard Susskind, the CBA embarked on an exploration of the major trends and issues affecting the profession resulting in seven research papers and a summary report called 'The Future of Legal Services in Canada: Trends and Issues'. This work included:

- a report on the state of research;
- a round up of relevant social media discourse;
- an examination of economic trends;
- a set of case studies in innovation;
- an overview of changing legal market patterns; and
- a body of original client research.

Regarding the original client research, the objective of this part of the study was to gain insight into the shift that seemed to be taking place with respect to client expectations. It was not meant to be statistically valid research, and extremely tight timelines constrained the process. Using online forums created and managed by a third-party provider, the CBA invited a range of legal service users to participate in the process. The groups were arranged into users with more and less experience using legal services, and into groups of individuals and organisations (with in-house counsel). The individual groups were further divided into anglophone and francophone participants to ensure that language was not a barrier to gaining representation from across the country. The groups were asked for their reactions to various themes and ideas drawn from Professor Susskind's work, notably *The End of Lawyers?* (Susskind 2010), including those related to accessing legal help online, alternative sourcing, and market conditions.

Perhaps unsurprisingly, this part of the project gained a considerable amount of attention in conversations with members of the bar on the subject of change. Whether the research is statistically relevant or not, the exercise is worthwhile both for gaining directional insight into the market, as well as for starting (and continuing) meaningful conversations about changes in the profession. In retrospect, this aspect of the project may have been undervalued. There is a true absence of information and understanding of how the public perceives the legal profession. Without greater knowledge of perception, we cannot understand what sorts of change will be productive for the spheres of innovation and access to justice. Futures (CBA 2014) did not go as far as it could have, had it allocated more time and resources and developed a more specific orientation to how the work could interact with access to justice initiatives.

The 'Trends and Issues' paper served as a springboard for the next phase of the work, which involved three sub teams examining different critical issues: (1) Education and Training, (2) Ethics and Regulatory Issues, and (3) Business Structures and Innovation. Each of these teams was populated with legal community experts and had distinct mandates. Ultimately, the work of these teams, along with the feedback gleaned from a variety of consultation vehicles, formed the basis for the Futures Report's twenty-two recommendations (CBA 2014, p. 84). Among these are four key initiatives that have been identified for their direct and indirect benefits among Canada's leaders in the profession:

1. Take a leadership role in promoting innovation
2. Establish a Centre of Expertise and Information on the Legal Profession in Canada
3. Champion Access to Justice and Diversity
4. Update/Create Tools and Resources to Help Members Adapt

I. Take a Leadership Role in Promoting Innovation

Any lesson to be learnt from the Futures Report (CBA 2014) derives from its status as an innovation-driven initiative designed to advance the legal profession in general. The CBA preaches what it has practiced in conducting this study: lawyers and firms must take a proactive role in getting to know their clients, their needs and expectations, and how to deliver better service. In effect, necessary productive change will only come from those willing to take charge, to make informed and creative decisions about how to take advantage of new opportunities while discarding dated practices. This mindset guided the Futures research as we first set out to understand what kinds of innovation were needed.

Hoping to engage the broader innovation community, Futures (CBA 2014) hosted twenty-two Twitter chats (a public Twitter conversation around one unique hashtag), reaching as many as 71,000 Twitter accounts per session, with one notable exception being a Twitter chat with Richard Susskind that reached almost 260,000 accounts. The chats were hosted by members of the legal innovation community. Topics included:

- Lawyer as adviser: where are the ethical boundaries?
- Innovative forms of employment for lawyers
- How can legal services be changed to increase access to justice?
- Law and design
- Why should new and young lawyers care about ABS?
- How to achieve equitable representation of under-represented groups
- Doing less law: why lawyers should adopt preventative lawyering practices

The first year following the publication of the report focused on the intensive communications strategy outlined here, not just to establish a leadership role for the organisation, but because

> 'the constraints on achieving change, and on advancing Futures' recommendation, are as true today as in 2014. Lawyers are risk averse, there is a lack of diversity in the profession, there is an absence of good data on the Canadian legal profession . . . [and] the absence of a collective culture of innovation.' (CBA 2018a, p. 20)

Although it may have been tempting to immediately allocate resources to some of the more concrete Futures recommendations, the effort spent on connecting with the profession, garnering support, interest, and engagement, was critical.

Ensuring that various parts of the profession 'saw themselves' in Futures, was especially important given that many of the recommendations outlined in the report would require participation or leadership of other stakeholders such as law schools and regulatory bodies. As a voluntary association, the CBA was and is limited in effecting some of the kind of changes that are needed. That said, Futures still contained an action plan highlighting some of the most pressing priorities.

Despite not having the mandate to make regulatory change, for example, Futures served a critical role in providing the 'heads up' firms needed to do their own strategic thinking about how they wanted to be positioned. One leader of a large national firm commented:

> 'The Futures report has focused our firm on the changing competitive landscape. We can see more clearly the case for multi-disciplinary practices and alternate business models. We must ready ourselves immediately for the real prospect of such changes. While some of [the changes we've made] have been a natural evolution of a growing national firm, the work of the CBA has been instrumental in our assessing the competitive landscape and in critically analyzing our direction. The Futures Report has been the catalyst for a long overdue dialogue about change in our profession. In doing the important work it did, the CBA has reasserted its relevance as a body of 'thought leadership.' Its presentation was thoroughly researched, reflective, provocative, and informative. It has undeniably moved the profession forward.' (CBA 2018a, p. 15)

As this one example demonstrates, through its many Futures related events and writing, the CBA facilitated a national dialogue on innovation in the legal profession. Futures inspired significant debate and commentary, but it remains an open question, however, just how broadly the Futures message penetrated beyond those already alive to changes in the industry and innovation. Yet, convincing the sceptics will only be possible once the innovators have achieved a certain degree of success, and so industry efforts ought naturally to be directed toward encouraging necessary experimentation.

One notable instance of Futures' influence was a high-profile innovative effort launched in response to this question of audience. This took the form of 'The Pitch', the first national legal innovation competition in Canada, held in partnership with a legal incubator, and with sponsorship from a legal publisher. In brief, the competition ran as follows: Canadian legal tech innovators were invited to submit slide decks showcasing their products/services for consideration by a roster of experts. The top five submissions were invited to participate in the live presentation of 'The Pitch', held alongside another large CBA conference, and judged by a panel made up of innovators and venture capitalists.

The presentation was also webcast in its inaugural year, inviting participation from the broader community, and the live audience used a voting tool to choose a fan favourite. This event represented a stylistic departure for the CBA, but the high production value, calibre of contestants, and professional execution resulted in a very successful event. 'The Pitch' has been held twice, once alongside the CBA's Canadian Legal Conference, and once in conjunction with the Canadian Corporate Counsel Association and In-House Counsel Worldwide (ICW). The second iteration was open to international start-ups as well, resulting in an exciting final round with three Canadian participants, one Russian, and one American. The companies who have participated in 'The Pitch' have gone on to notable success, and the events have helped the CBA clearly address the objective of encouraging innovation in the legal community, among others. As Frédéric Pérodeau, Directeur principal des enquêtes à l'Autorité des Marchés Financiers put it:

> 'The CBA Legal Futures Initiatives is a major contributor in making the CBA a more technologically savvy organization and in positioning it as the voice of the legal profession in Canada. It created a momentum that lead to the presentation of 'The Pitch' in 2016. I am proud to be a member of the association that has decided to lead the charge in finding and showcasing legal innovation in Canada' (Pérodeau 2017).

The enthusiasm and creativity that 'The Pitch' encouraged tells us that many in the legal profession are eager to try new things. By encouraging such opportunities, Futures models an approach to innovative leadership that has already inspired firms and individuals, with tangible results. Another way that the CBA continues to lead the conversation about innovation and legal services is through professional development opportunities. Over the years, Futures material has been the focus of a number of high-profile events other than 'The Pitch', such as:

- Inclusion of topics on artificial intelligence, design theory, working with other professions, and ABS within more general legal conferences.
- Hosting of the Canadian launch of Richard Susskind and Daniel Susskind's book *The Future of the Professions* (Susskind and Susskind 2015).
- Presentations by thought leaders like Richard Susskind, Bruce MacEwan (from *Adam Smith, Esq.*), and the Chair of the CBA Legal Futures Initiative, Fred Headon, at round table discussions with managing partners of law firms across the country.
- Annual law firm leadership conferences geared towards 'making and managing progress.' The 2018 iteration of this conference included panels on

how to measure innovation, a legal tech innovation showcase, a design principles session, a debate on the procurement of legal services, meeting client expectations, and more.

It is important to acknowledge that, as Dr. Richard taught us, there will always be lawyers who are skeptical of new approaches and who would never register for an 'innovation conference'. Employing standard adult education principles, particularly related to the learning process, may assist in sidestepping this challenge. Consistently relating the material back to delivering better client service, ultimately every lawyer's objective and day-to-day challenge, and adopting a multi-modal delivery strategy may underscore the message's relevance and maintain interest (Palis and Quiros 2014, p. 19). Just as the way forward in the legal profession requires greater sensitivity to client needs, so too must reluctant lawyers be persuaded by appealing to the language and values they already hold dear. Change, regarded in this way, is merely a matter of enabling continuity, rather than a disruptive force reinventing the profession.

II. Establish a Centre of Expertise and Information on the Legal Profession in Canada

In order to advocate for change, or rather productive growth, Futures (CBA 2014) identified a corollary need to understand the current state of things – any effort toward something new is blind without solid understanding of the current state of things. And yet, as legal industry analyst and commentator Jordan Furlong, among many others, has observed, 'it is extremely difficult to find reliable data on the legal profession in Canada. Without it, our decisions are based on anecdote, observation and gut instinct', (CBA 2018a, p. 37 footnote). The limited amount of information available in the areas of services offered, pricing, profitability, incomes, cost structures, and global trends challenged the Futures work throughout. The data gap extends to information related to demographics and diversity, longitudinal data on progression through the practice, comparative effectiveness of different education and training models, and more. The potential for centralised, accessible information is only one of the more obvious opportunities available for the growth of the profession.

The Futures report reflects on a recommendation made in 2005 to establish a 'professional centre of expertise and information on the legal profession in Canada' (CBA 2014, p. 38 footnote). The idea was that the Centre of Expertise would be a locus for the profession to collect, analyse and distribute relevant data, with one of its objectives being to develop and maintain competitive information on the profession. Despite the recommendation in

2005 being met with enthusiasm, no work was done to act on it by the time the Futures report was published nine years later. The report adopted the recommendation as one of its own, and again, the organisation adopted the report and its recommendations, including this one, in 2014. Unfortunately, to date there has been no progress on the Centre for Expertise, and there are no plans in the immediate future that will change this.

The creation of a Centre for Expertise and Information would 'allow the profession to see and understand macro changes, to reflect on its relationship with the public, and to contemplate transformations in ways that have not yet been envisioned,' all of which is critical to maintaining relevance (CBA 2014, p. 38). Beyond that, though, the absence of this and other data is an obstacle in making more progress on access to justice initiatives in Canada. As Malcolm Mercer, a Canadian lawyer and expert on legal ethics and professional responsibility put it, 'we cannot effectively address serious systemic issues like access to justice and unmet legal needs by intuitive responses that reflect our own limited perspectives. We need solid research and analysis' (Mercer 2017). Futures made the important step of identifying this issue and proposing a way to address it through the Centre of Expertise, but unfortunately has not progressed beyond that.

III. Champion Access to Justice and Diversity

Access to information is one promise of the modern age that the legal profession has failed so far to fully exploit. But its greatest failure as a service to the public in recent years has been its hesitance to address contemporary understandings of how to provide access to justice for everyone. Through its many presentations, CBA's Futures has highlighted the critical importance of inclusion and diversity to the future of the profession. Elsewhere in the organisation, various projects and initiatives bolster this view, such as through the CBA's *Measuring Diversity in Law Firms* guide, prepared by what was then called the CBA Equality Committee and advocacy work undertaken to amend the Canadian government's judicial appointments process to promote diversity on the bench (CBA 2018a, p. 29).

In keeping with its commitment to leadership, the CBA launched the Equal Justice Initiative in 2012, which 'studies access to justice issues in Canada and advocates for their improvement. [Our] vision is an inclusive justice system that is equally accessible to all, regardless of means, capacity or social situation' (CBA 2018b). Equal Justice issued an important and extensive report in 2013, which is seen as complementary and symbiotic to CBA Futures. The CBA has taken steps to integrate the work of these two initiatives, including collaboration and consultation on a number of projects including:

- Transforming Legal Education and Training in Canada: Learning Across Life Stages workshop (mentioned above)
- A paper exploring economic models featuring an intersect between accessibility, quality, and profitability jointly produced by CBA Futures and Professor Noel Semple from the University of Windsor Law School
- Equal Justice's soon to be released Experiential Learning Guide for Law Students

IV. Update/Create Tools and Resources to Help Members Adapt

Part and parcel of achieving greater access to justice is giving lawyers better tools for delivering it. The objective of providing tools to members of the profession to assist in adapting to change and preparing for the future is probably the easiest recommendation to implement, and indeed, the CBA has been successful in this area. Some of the tools that have been developed to encourage members to integrate Futures' findings into their own work include:

- How to Innovate: Futures for Small and Solo Firms (paper and accompanying workbook)
- A Guide to Strategy for Lawyers by Richard Susskind
- Futures Readiness and Self Assessment Tool
- Guidelines for Practicing Ethically with Information Technologies
- 14 Case Studies on Canadian Legal Innovation
- Available Business Models in Canada, by Jurisdiction
- Business Innovation Accelerators and Incubators in Canada

Another of the tools that has gained significant attention is a guide called *Do Law Differently: Futures for Young Lawyers* (DLD), which features 'new law' opportunities. This tool includes two sets of helpful resources.[1]

The bulk of the guide is made up of first-person stories from twenty-six new law practitioners and innovators outlining their experience with the innovation community, with a particular accent on advice for young lawyers going forward. Some highlights:

'Your greatest strengths are youth, energy, adaptability and a willingness to learn – use these strengths to create a competitive advantage for yourself and to add value first to your clients, then your colleagues and finally

[1] The tools mentioned here are available to CBA members only. Other than maintaining this exclusivity, the CBA has not done much to monetise Futures products, but of course, selling tools and resources would be one obvious way to do this.

to your firm, in that order.' (Peter Carayiannis, President and Founder, Conduit Law Professional Corporation)

'If you got into law because of the safety, certainty and ability to control success by putting in time, you're unfortunately too late – that party is over – but fresh opportunity is positively correlated with uncertainty and disruption.' (Joe Milstone, Founder, Axiom Cognition and Co-Founder and Owner, Caravel Law)

'Young Lawyers should focus on forming their own points of view – knowing why they are in the world of legal work, and what problems they want to be solving.' [They should be] literate in technology, information science, design, business management, and beyond. (Margaret Hagan, Legal Designer, Stanford Law School's Center on the Legal Profession)

Do Law Differently: Futures for Young Lawyers (DLD) also includes '109 New Ways to Do Law,' showcasing remarkably different approaches to the creation or provision of legal services. This included law firms, new legal service providers, and legal tech start-ups. Bite-size examples are broken down into 'aligning human talent with legal tasks' and 'applying technology to the performance of legal tasks.' Two years have passed since this guide's publication, so what seemed very cutting edge at the time is, in many cases, regular business today (which is good! Progress!). The ideas, though, remain transportable and relevant. There is a pressing need to make new model law firms, legal talent providers, and managed legal support services accessible; to point the way to tools that help lawyers do legal work differently; to help clients resolve disputes directly; and to help clients conduct their own legal matters.

It is worth noting that DLD was of great interest to career services professionals in law schools across Canada (Mackenzie 2016). Students are looking for help in accessing the 'hidden job market' and in acquiring the skills needed for emerging careers, suggesting all kinds of opportunities for educational providers, and not necessarily only legal ones. The conversation continues (slowly) on a 1,250 member Do Law Differently Facebook page, which is a forum for:

'a group of forward-looking law students and young lawyers building careers in the new legal market. We are re-thinking all aspects of the industry, from education to entrepreneurship and everything in between. We are innovating ways to better serve our clients and our communities. We are bringing attention to the people who do law differently. We are building Canada's new legal profession.' (Doing Law Differently 2017).

C. Building Engagement with the Futures Report

As these initial researches make clear, there is a pressing need for the legal profession to adapt; and, despite lawyerly resistance to change, the legal community in Canada in fact responded enthusiastically to the publishing of the CBA Legal Futures Report. The reflections below are taken from the *CBA Legal Futures Initiative Final Report* (CBA 2018a), but many more positive messages came to the CBA from all corners of the profession.

> 'The report is one of the most potent recipes for a New Legal Universe that has come from any legal association or governing body in this country, or even in North America.' (Gail Cohen, former editor in chief of Canadian Lawyer, InHouse, 4Students and Law Times and their associated websites and digital initiatives.)

> 'The CBA's report constitutes a watershed moment for the legal market-place in Canada, and possibly in North America.' (Jordan Furlong, leading Canadian analyst of the global legal market and forecaster of its future development.)

> 'What Futures did was allow for a different kind of dialogue within the profession. It legitimised many of the things that futures thinkers were talking about and made it mainstream. Talking about innovation, ABS, and changes in practices for legal services delivery was no longer fringe. CBA was early on this work and came to with a huge amount of credibility. It gave support to following futures work. Also, as law societies are all operating from the inside, CBA brought an external perspective to their work that is really important.' (Darrel Pink, former Executive Director of the Nova Scotia Barristers Society.)

These enthusiastic responses were not limited only to Canadian stakeholders. In short order, there was considerable interest internationally. Over the period of October 2014 to March 2017, the substance of Futures was presented to the American, Australian, International Bar Associations, Harvard, Yale, and Georgetown Law Schools, L'Incubateur in Paris, and the Law Society of New South Wales, among others. Within Canada, meetings were held to share the report's findings with firms across the country, government organisations like the Department of Justice and the Canadian Council of Chief Judges, and law society regulators. Within the CBA, every opportunity was embraced to spread the message at the local, regional, and national level. Today, Futures is part of the curriculum at several Canadian law schools and has inspired programming like Queen's University's Graduate Diploma in Legal Services Management.

The CBA also sought collaboration and partnerships to further Futures work. For example, Futures partnered with the *Canadian Bar Review*, a 95-year-old peer reviewed legal journal, to collaborate on a one-day workshop entitled 'Transforming Legal Education and Training in Canada: Learning Across Life Stages.' The event hosted a representative group of stakeholders – law students and young lawyers, legal educators, and legal employers. Through a highly facilitated process, the workshop allowed authors of proposed *Canadian Bar Review* articles to engage with key stakeholders for new insights. The intention was to launch an enduring dialogue and create a blueprint for the CBA and other stakeholders in their advocacy, strategies, and programming to support lawyers through the life cycle of their careers. A peer-reviewed selection of articles arising from the workshop was published in a special issue of the journal. Clearly, the Futures report spoke to matters and ideas that many have been eager to discuss, and it represents what for some represents an industry shift toward meaningful progress.

D. Conclusion

Futures has made significant progress in the last few years, especially in the areas of raising awareness and normalising the conversation about positioning the legal profession to better meet current needs. Indeed, Futures' most valuable contribution to date may be its role as a catalyst for discussion about changes in the profession and the practice of law. The CBA entrenched the importance of Futures by making 'Preparing the Profession for the Future' one of its five strategic directions. The direction is as follows:

> 'Building on a strong Futures foundation, further elevate CBA's leadership thinking to guide the profession toward a future that is in-step with emerging trends, needs and opportunities. See things before others see them, and inspire Members to lean into the future.' (CBA 2016).

Despite this mandate, the CBA has lost some momentum for a variety of organisational reasons. The goal now is for a forward-looking, innovative mindset to be integrated into everyday business at the CBA, with a focus on inspiring lawyers to resist their own reluctance to experiment and on building the skills needed for practice that are not necessarily being taught in law school. The CBA continues to look for ways to drive home the message of Futures, and this requires creativity, leadership, and courage. Yet, until the profession further advances the idea that their awareness must turn into action, progress will be limited.

If legal professionals expect to remain successful and relevant in the coming years, there are many obstacles to overcome, not least of which is a professional aversion to trying new things. The CBA has made strides to produce a body of knowledge and precedent that can provide a clear path for future success. At the end of *Our Iceberg is Melting* (Kotter 2006), the penguins thoughtfully relocate to another iceberg, escaping the one that was melting. But the story does not end there:

> 'The next season, the scouts found a still better iceberg, larger and with richer fishing grounds. And though it was tempting to declare that the colony had been subjected to enough change, and should stay forever on their new home, they didn't. They moved again. It was a critical step: not becoming complacent again and not letting up' (Kotter 2006, p. 117)

If penguins can find the key to their own survival, can't we?

Acknowledgement

These findings are a reflection on some of the things that I personally, and the Canadian Bar Association (CBA) organizationally, observed during our quest to orient the Canadian legal profession more decidedly toward its own future. This paper is in no way exhaustive; rather, the intention here is to share the CBA's approach, some examples of successful engagement strategies, tools and resources, and initiatives, as well as some of the areas where we might have been able to do more, gone further, and explored more deeply. I hope that these insights inspire meaningful progress and forward motion for others. Every jurisdiction has its nuances, but ultimately, *all* lawyers should be assessing their relevance and preparing themselves for the ongoing, ever changing future. This process has been described by Richard Susskind (2009) as 'changing the tires on a moving vehicle'. To extend the metaphor a bit further, either change now or get struck with a flat tire and go nowhere at all.

All comments are my own, although there were hundreds of extraordinary people involved in the CBA Legal Futures Initiative in professional, volunteer, and expert capacities. I would like to particularly recognize and dedicate this paper to Joan Bercovitch, the CBA's former Deputy CEO, the heart and soul of the Futures Initiative, and the best boss, mentor, and friend that anyone could ever ask for. Thanks for everything, Joan.

Aviva Rotenberg
Ottawa, Canada, November 1, 2018

Bibliography

Canadian Bar Association (2014), *Futures: Transforming the Delivery of Legal Services in Canada*, Ottawa.

Canadian Bar Association (February 2016) *Strategic direction for CBA amended by Board of Directors*, available at <https://www.cba.org/CBAMediaLibrary/cba_na/SecurePDF/Rethink/STRATEGIC-DIRECTIONS.pdf>, (last accessed 1 November 2018).

Canadian Bar Association (2018a), *CBA Legal Futures Initiative Final Report*, Unpublished report, Ottawa.

Canadian Bar Association (2018b) – *Equal Justice*, available at <https://www.cba. org/CBA-Equal-Justice/Home> (last accessed 14 November 2018).

Davis-Laack, P., L. Richard and D. N. Shearon (2016), 'Four Things Resilient Lawyers Do Differently', *Law Practice Today*, June.

Doing Law Differently (2017) available at <https://www.facebook.com/groups/dola wdifferently/> (last accessed 25 October 2018).

Friedman, R. (2015), *The Best Place to Work: The Art and Science of Creating an Extraordinary Workplace*, New York, NY: Penguin.

Kotter, J. (2006), *Our Iceberg Is Melting: Changing and Succeeding Under Any Conditions*, New York, NY: Portfolio/Penguin.

Krakovsky, M. (2007), 'The Effort Effect', *Stanfordmag.org*, available at <https:// stanfordmag.org/contents/the-effort-effect> (last accessed 7 April 2019).

Mackenzie, S. (8 December 2016), 'Memo to Aviva Rotenberg regarding CBA Connect content development: report on preliminary consultations'.

Mercer, M. (15 October 2017), 'Cost disease, the practice of law and access to justice', *Malcolm Mercer*, available at <https://malcolmmercer.ca/category/a2j/> (last accessed 7 November 2018).

Palis, A. G. and P. A. Quiros (2014), 'Adult learning principles and presentation pearls', *MEAJO*, 21:2, pp. 114–22.

Pérodeau, F. (2017), *Futures*.

Richard, L. (2002), 'Herding cats: the lawyer personality revealed', *AltmanWeil.com*, available at <http://www.managingpartnerforum.org/tasks/sites/mpf/assets/ image/MPF%20-%20WEBSITE%20-%20ARTICLE%20-%20Herding% 20Cats%20-%20Richards1.pdf> (last accessed 7 November 2018).

Susskind, R. (2009) Speech, Canadian Legal Conference, Dublin. 16 August 2009.

Susskind, R. (2010), *The End of Lawyers? Rethinking the Nature of Legal Services*, Oxford: Oxford University Press.Susskind, R. und D. Susskind (2015), *The Future of the Professions*, Oxford: Oxford University Press.

16

The Long and Short of It:
How Legal Education can Help Solve the
Profession's Identity Crisis

Maeve Lavelle

A. The Legal Profession Is Having an Identity Crisis.

Unavoidable change has finally come to the legal profession and it has brought with it a crisis of being for those who were historically assured of their place in the profession and in society. Momentum has been gathering for the past decade, and now the convergence of several important factors will make it difficult for legal professionals, law firms and law schools to make the status quo work for them in the coming years. We have, it seems, avoided facing inconvenient truths for quite a while. The nature of the legal profession, and the way society expects it to operate, has allowed it to keep its proverbial head buried in the sand for longer than other industries. The accepted opacity within the legal system and associated services, protectionist professional bodies and the inaccessibility of legal education are to name but a few of the pillars that support the status quo being upheld. The unfortunate result of this deferred awakening is that the profession and its various stakeholders now find themselves in reaction, or, more hyperbolically, survival mode.

Survival necessitates short-term planning to achieve specific objectives in the near future. When not in survival mode, one can look forward, anticipate future states of being in the context of various external environments and proactively engage with potential behaviours that could be beneficial when those states manifest. However, despite the urgency of the circumstances we find ourselves in, we cannot afford to continue to neglect the important long-term planning or we run the risk of ending up in exactly the same position in another few years. In this paper, I propose a two-pronged approach to bring the legal profession into the 21st century and avoid potential obsolescence.

1. The Long Game: A framework for future-gazing, both inside universities and law schools and out, which will allow the profession to self-actualise once again.
2. The Short Game: A plan of action for legal educators to implement in the next one to two years, which will help us avoid a critical skills gap over the next five years.

In order to understand the foundations of this identity that have been swiped from underneath our leather brogues, we need to understand where the legal profession came from. From there, we can see what is left to be salvaged, then cut our losses and march forward, arm-in-arm with our machine counterparts, into a bright new dawn.

B. Identity Crisis 101: Changed Expectations

An identity crisis is typically caused by a change in an individual's expected aims or role in society. I have found this a useful lens through which to view the changing landscape of the legal profession, and it makes for a good lead-in to the solutions I propose.

I. Where Did Those Expectations Come from?

Let us begin in Ancient Rome. The practice of law evolved out of a need for advocates skilled in rhetoric to argue cases on behalf of others, who may not have had the same skills or knowledge to get the outcome they wanted. The first version of the legal profession, as we currently know it, dates back to the Byzantine Empire. Until that point in time, advocating on behalf of others in court had been the hobby of wealthy intellectuals. By the end of the fourth century, these amateur advocates had begun to study the law, and in the sixth century, a four-year course of study in rhetoric and the law was made a requirement to gain admission to the legal profession (Jones 1964: 512–513). Some of the work that we now associate with solicitors and civil notaries; drafting wills, conveyances and contracts, was carried out by their earliest equivalents in the late Roman Empire. There was a general pause in the development of the legal profession as it all collapsed in the onset of the Dark Ages before a return in the thirteenth century. Renewed regulation by church and state in both England and France created structure again, and other European states followed this trend of professionalisation (Brundage 1994).

Irish law is believed to be the oldest surviving codified legal system in Europe. It comes from Brehon law, which got its name from the title given to judges in Celtic times, and because the system was entirely made up of the accumulated decisions of these judges, passed on in an oral tradition (Courts

Service Ireland n.d.). Brehon law became the statutes which governed every-day life in early Medieval Ireland. It was a civil code rather than a criminal one and dealt mainly with the compensation to be paid for harm done, as well as regulating inheritance, property and contracts (Duffy 2004). This indigenous system of law survived until the seventeenth century when it was supplanted by English common law.

The first 'modern' law school arrived in the nineteenth century with the opening of Harvard Law School in the United States. The classic Ivy League law school curriculum as we know it was introduced in the latter half of that century (with a standardised first-year curriculum of classes and the case method of teaching). Much of this style and substance has since been exported to law schools and universities around the world. The first 'elite' American law firm followed Harvard Law, as the products of the Harvard system 'merged with the needs of newly industrialised and financialised America (Madison 2017a).

The resemblances between the historical development of the legal profession and current legal education and work practices are prominent. It is not merely the substance and function of legal practice and education that has not changed. The type of people typically practising law has, for the most part, remained the same. The first 'lawyers' were wealthy Roman amateurs (read: wealthy, white men) who dabbled in law as an intellectual hobby prior to the legalisation of practice, while women in Ancient Rome were not allowed to engage in public discourse which removed them entirely from any possibility of engagement in the early versions of the legal profession. (See Mary Beard's 'Women and Power' for a brief examination of women's exclusion from power in Ancient Greece and Rome). The protectionism is not modern either. When the practice of the law was legalised by Claudius, there was initially a ban and then a strict cap on the fees that could be charged, which meant that people without another significant source of income could not support themselves by practising law alone (Jones 1964). Unpaid or poorly paid apprenticeships have had a similarly exclusionary effect in more recent times.

In pulling together a rough outline of this identity that is now in crisis, it could be said to be comprised of:

1. A unique work function. Broadly: advocacy, a knowledge of the law and how to apply it to a set of facts, and an ability to craft legal documents; and
2. Social status based on the exclusivity and opacity of the profession (see also Burrage 2004 for further explanations for the professional choices of lawyers).

II. What Has Caused This Change in Expectation?

This change in the expectation that legal professionals have for their role in society has largely been brought about by technological advances which; (1) undermine a body of work that has always been the sole domain of the trained legal professional, and (2) break down the barriers to accessibility of the profession. Although the legal profession is extensively altered and forced to change by technological progress, the prophecy of a defeat of lawyers by robots would be amiss. The role of the legal professional in today's society has developed into a complex and nuanced one, and it is in that complexity and nuance that lawyers will continue to find purpose.

Each of the components, which are parts of a legal professional, have to be looked at individually. Even glancing at the work functions shows that two of the components are already getting replaced by software (Andreessen 2011). Advocacy remains, and will remain for the near future, a task that is better carried out by humans.

A knowledge of the law includes both substantive and procedural rules, which in turn gives lawyers a body of knowledge that can be thought of as legal processes. Robotic Process Automation (RPA) has been around for a while, but law firms have only recently begun to explore the full potential of these systems. The kinds of tasks that can be taken over by process automation technologies are typically administrative in nature and can sometimes form the bulk of what a secretary or paralegal would contribute to the work of a firm. In addition to automating legal processes, expert systems are now being developed which mimic the analysis that a lawyer would carry out on a set of facts with a given set of rules. These expert systems excel where the rules can be mapped out in a decision tree to reach a pre-set conclusion at the end of a logic 'branch'. The successful implementation of these two types of technology in the delivery of legal services makes it clear, that they are best applied to a work that is routine and frequent. The set-up costs of these systems are so high that the business case for a rare and complex matter would be hard to justify.

The creation of legal documents is completed by applying a set of substantive and procedural rules to pre-set blocks of text and adding the data particular to a given case or client.

Document automation is a combination of logic-based and workflow automation systems which allows for the assembly of a document using pre-existing segments of text and data entered by the user (Mountain 2007). Aside from practice management software, document automation tools are probably the most readily adopted in the legal industry. Given that much legal administration work is just the creation and review of documents, it makes sense that a business case is easy to find. Document assembly and review has traditionally been the work that the trainee corporate lawyer cut their teeth on and makes up a lot of the work done by lawyers in certain transactional practice areas. With document automation technology providers constantly iterating on their user interface and functionality, it is hard to see how law firms still allow their employees to do it manually. The proliferation of competitors to the incumbent vendors shows that there are plenty of digital documents to go around (See Avvoka). Natural language processing software is improving all the time and is being embraced for more than just e-discovery work. One need only look at the momentum of Kira Systems to get a sense of the rate of adoption (Insight Venture Partners 2018).

To put the upcoming changes into perspective, McKinsey Global Institute estimates that about 60 per cent of occupations could be automated up to 30 per cent. The legal profession falls neatly around this statistic, with further estimates of 22 per cent and 35 per cent automation potential for lawyers and law clerks, respectively (McKinsey Global Institute 2017).

Leaving aside the fact that legal professionals are now competing with machines for their jobs, there are more law graduates and trained lawyers emerging into the European marketplace now than even a decade ago. Since 2011, there has been a 20 per cent increase in the number of solicitors on the roll in England and Wales (Solicitors Regulation Authority 2018). What was once an exclusive club is now accessible to anyone with the grades and the still pretty significant, but definitely smaller, bundle of cash. The profession in the UK and Europe is decidedly more accessible than in the US, where law school tuition has continued to increase above the rate of inflation since 1985 (Law School Transparency Data Dashboard 2018). The number of law graduates from traditional law schools in the US has actually been falling for the last four years, with a 20 per cent decrease in the number of people graduating in 2017 as compared to 2012 (American Bar Association 2018). Across Europe, the number of registered lawyers has been rising steadily. In the period from 1999 to 2016, the number of lawyers across a section of countries in Europe rose by almost 95 per cent (Germany, Austria, Denmark, Spain, Finland, France, Liechtenstein, Luxembourg, Norway, Portugal, UK, Sweden, Poland. Numbers from The Council of Bars and Law Societies of Europe (CCBE) 2018).

This increase in the accessibility of the profession throughout history has been largely driven by the democratisation of the knowledge and skillset needed to practice law, facilitated by advances in technology ranging from the invention of the printing press to the digitisation of legal research. This technological overhaul allows for more people to have access to the same body of information, which leads to not only more transparency and accountability, but also more creativity as a diverse group of people do new things in new ways beyond what the original club of knowledge-holders would have thought acceptable.

Whereas once upon a time an individual would need to have access to a master in rhetoric in order to learn the craft, we can now read books and online resources, watch seminars on YouTube and get online coaching from halfway across the world. Legal rules that were once passed down by word of mouth or handwritten on papyrus scrolls are now available for everyone to read online. The direct access to a well-stocked library of hardcopy court reports is not needed anymore in order to craft the best legal opinion. These online legal research tools are already being taken for granted, even though they have only existed since the late 90s. However, it is unlikely that the digitisation of legal information and the drastic increase in the number of lawyers are correlated.

C. The Required Adaptation and Changes

By tracking historical trends and current projections in the automation and digitisation of work, the future role of legal professions can be figured out safely. There are very obvious gaps being left in the wake of the machines, and those are the places that should be targeted. By doubling down on those gaps that machines cannot adequately fill, the legal profession will flourish.

I. Automation: The Favourite Colleague

There have been two constants to human evolution of late; automation and reaction to this automation. Since the Agricultural Revolution, society has struggled with the pace of change and what this means to those it affects, with the same stages being seen in every industry. The initial denial that it is technically feasible, then the anger that someone would try, the worry over what it means and then final acceptance that their work is replaceable and the realisation that there is now new work to upskill for.

Over the past fifty years, automation has contributed to a 1.8 per cent growth in global productivity and 1.7 per cent growth in employment. Contrary to what many journalists or populists might have people believe; the outlook is pretty positive. The World Economic Forum has estimated that 75 million people could lose their job to automation by 2022. However, one 133 million jobs could be created *if* these workers are given 'significant' re-skilling (Centre for the New Economy and Society 2018). We can take solace from the massive shifts in developed countries' workforces away from agriculture in the twentieth century. These technology-enabled changes did not lead to long-term mass unemployment, because new work was created that could not be foreseen prior to the shift (McKinsey Global Institute 2017).

Looking at how the legal profession has fared recently, a decline in US law firm productivity (defined as the number of billable hours worked per lawyer) over the past decade is noticeable, to the tune of 74,000 dollars per lawyer per year (Jones et al. 2018). This is a result of increased headcount and stagnating demand for law firm services, as distinct from legal services more generally. In the UK, growth in the revenue generated per fee earner has been slow among the top 100 law firms (Deloitte 2016).

In the face of slowing demand for their services, law firms have been increasing client's fees and slowing hiring. Many larger law firms have also been keeping the ranks of their equity partners relatively static. We saw law firms employ these traditional methods of margin management when the last recession hit. If a similar economic contraction hits again, firms will have a significantly reduced capacity to take similar measures to stay afloat (Jones et al. 2018). Staff cuts, without automated systems in place to maintain output, will not be possible.

As detailed above, humans have been 'doing law' for a while. Without the aid of non-human systems, our productivity has reached its limit. The demand for legal services more generally is growing (Jones et al. 2018). Law firms just have not figured out how to tap into that new, more informed demand. People will need to continue working alongside machines to produce the growth in per capita GDP to which countries around the world aspire. Productivity estimates which show continued growth thanks to advances in automation technology assume that people displaced by automation will find other employment (McKinsey Global Institute 2017). In order to find that other employment, the spaces in between the machines must be looked at.

II. The Void

In formulating a short-term plan to fill an already growing skills gap, the wealth of literature available on the kinds of tasks that are currently being automated, and how those technologies are progressing need to be examined. It is at a task, rather than occupational, level that a manageable theory of how legal professionals can continue to be useful to society in the next five years can be created (McKinsey Global Institute 2017). The bigger, more holistic and integrated thinking is rather part of the long-term vision development.

An interesting window into the kinds of jobs that are winning in this new digital age is provided by LinkedIn. Tracking the growth in particular kinds of jobs, globally, over the past five years throws up a few surprises. The top job for growth is predictably that of a Software Engineer, but not far behind is Marketing Specialist and Human Resource Specialist. The job that has declined the most is Administrative Assistant (LinkedIn Economic Graph 2018). Even if we only extrapolate from this data, we can already start

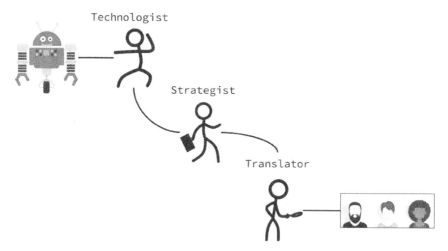

Figure 16.1   Categories of future work

to build an outline of the kinds of work that will remain for the legal professional when automation has been fully embraced.

The future of work and future roles, which will be available for humans
in the decades ahead can be categorised within the framework in Figure 16.1.

Broadly speaking, legal professionals can fall squarely into the Strategist
bucket, with some Translator responsibilities thrown in, if they so choose.
With this simplified view of the work that can be claimed, the kinds of skills
that would be most valuable can be identified.

Lawyers do not need to also be Software Engineers (or Technologists). In
fact, it makes absolutely no sense for them to try to be good at both (Hartman
2016). There are a few neglectable exceptions to this rule (for example, a
natural propensity for coding besides expertise in the legal profession). That
being said, legal professionals should know how to engage with the people
building the machines, as is the responsibility of the Strategist. Working well
with someone who is building software to optimise your business requires
a general knowledge of how that technology will work, and how to communicate what it is you want it to do. In other words, you need to be able to
give them your requirements in a format they understand, and then be able to
perform user acceptance testing (UAT) against those requirements.

Lawyers do need to understand what it is that their clients want and
need, and how to optimise their legal service experience. This is where the
responsibilities of a Translator come in, paired with those of the Strategist,
in the realm of customer service. Rarely is customer service spoken about in
the context of how a legal professional works. Taking a customer-centric,
or user-centric, approach will be crucial to the survival of law firms going

forward (Susskind 2018). Being able to communicate effectively and listen deeply are the hallmarks of a great Translator. This skill will be invaluable to any business. Large swathes of the population take these skills for granted. Being able to effectively gather information from a client will feed into the design and then implementation of a client-centric service strategy.

If lawyers are really listening to their clients and structuring their business around the information they receive, they will not need to listen to technology vendors to figure out what to do with their internal processes.

D. Legal Educators within the Technological Development of the Legal Profession

We are currently being carried along in a race between education and technology (Accenture 2018). Technology is in the lead, but this is a marathon, not a sprint, and with a bit of strategy, education and human workforce can pull ahead. Unless there is an immediate shift in the way that young lawyers are trained, the profession will end up with a critical skills gap in the next five to ten years. This is what this text aims to address within the short-term solution. Adopting a parallel long-term strategy for re-imagining the role of the lawyer will prevent the legal profession from arriving in the exact same spot in another ten years.

I. The Bandaid

This might not be a very appealing read. But this text tries to provide explicit advice on how to avoid further decrease in jobs in the legal profession and maximise the opportunities being created by automation. The way this solution is laid out is more directed towards universities and law schools, but the training in law firms is considered as well.

This is the short-term solution, which synthesises the work and research of many others, and draws from the experience of various technology vendors working in the legal industry. It is by no means the only solution but, based on the conversations with both students and educators, it is certainly not a bad one in the absence of any others. Furthermore, the lack of equivalent action in Europe shows that it has yet to be internalised by many people with the power to execute.

a. A Mandatory 'Soft Skills' Course in the Law Curriculum

This could be any of the soft skills typically associated with being a good project manager or senior executive: leadership, communication, planning, negotiation, or any of a number of others. Ideally, such a course would be created by someone who has experience working in a law firm, so that the skills can be taught in the context of how legal service providers are organised.

There are mountains of resources available that have already been distilled down. Law students could attend fitting courses and lectures at the business school, for example. As teaching resources are always in short supply, online courses in technological soft skills might be an option. There are many great courses available on edX, created by reputable universities. Taking an online course, in and of itself, would help students to see the value of these platforms as tools for self-led professional development, and might encourage them to do more online learning in their own time or later in life (a crucial mindset shift if this upskill imperative is to persist).

A follow-on course to be offered would be in project management, tailored to legal professionals. This would pull together those softer skills listed above and demonstrate their clear value in a business context.

b. Introduction of a 'Legal Tech Literacy' Course

This should include a full discussion, preferably in the first week or two, on the merits of automation and all the jobs that it will create, because law students seem to lack reaffirmation from lecturers and officials, as well as from potential employers. Many of the students question whether technology will impact job opportunities for people graduating in the next few years. Graduates are entering into employment with a fear that any day they will arrive in to see a robot sitting in their ergonomic office chair. Mistrust, caused by a lack of understanding can cause people to perceive a threat, which breeds fear. This attitude to technology is already pervasive in the profession. This fear of legal technology – without knowing how to use it or even trying to do so – prevents adaptation and lays at the root of the problem.

In the interest of pursuing an integrative curriculum, the material for the two courses above should really be brought in to the teaching of the substantive law modules. Being a good communicator is not a separate discipline to providing legal services. It is part of the package. Similarly, digital legal services are just that; a subset of legal services in general. Hopefully, this distinction will disappear soon. All that should matter is which method of delivery is judged to be best for the client, the lawyer and the firm, each considered with the appropriate weighting.

c. Informing and Advertising the New Career Opportunities

'Alternative Legal Careers' jobs fair or experience reports from legal professionals working with automation and digitisation to create an awareness of the advantages that technological development brings and to motivate students rather than create fear regarding the future. Attendance should be mandatory. Law students mostly do not tend to spend too much time on things that are not directly contributing to their final grade.

The same measures should be taken for law firms. Especially investing in re-skilling staff and adapting jobs to the new challenges in order to keep their employees at the pulse of technological development, is necessary (see also Madison 2015).

II. The Enduring Solution

This is a much more appealing read. Legal educators still shape and define the legal profession and will do so in the future. Grand plans usually come from very simple visions, as shown below.

The law is the framework that facilitates the peaceful and prosperous running of society. The law manifests in the actions and institutions of its agents; namely, the courts and their officers, legislators, lawyers and law firms, enforcement bodies and other agencies. If this framework, and those that make it real, cannot adapt with the changing society that it is supposed to serve, its purpose is void.

Put differently, the law should facilitate human flourishing. It should encourage and reward those activities that are beneficial to society and in line with its values at any given time, and it should punish, or similarly deter, those activities that cause hurt or destruction. In this way, the law must have the capacity to be as transient and adaptable as that society. This is similar to the 'outcome-thinking' that Susskind advocates, but on a more macro scale (Susskind 2018). It is here, in this specific question of relevance of the profession, that technology has shone a revelatory light on the way legal professionals work and serve (or fail to serve) society.

In light of the above, processes need to be put in place which force legal professionals to critically consider the direction the legal profession is heading, with broader societal trends and a unifying vision in mind. This should not just take place at a policy-making level, although there are no meaningful projects or changes discussed in most of Europe and the US.

A perfect forum where these processes can start is the university. Harvard Law's reputation was built on the beliefs of one of its earliest professors who saw a need for an elite law school based on merit and dedicated to the public service. This core value of preparing law students for service is echoed in Madison's 'Template for 21st Century Legal Education'.

a. Mandatory Semester-long Module on the History and Purpose of the Profession

A course which first explores the history of the legal profession, then discusses the philosophy of law, and finally invites students to contribute to the vision of what the profession should look like in the future should be mandatory at the beginning of a law degree or juris doctrine.

b. Regular University-wide Symposiums on the Role of the Law and the Legal Profession In Society

This foundation would then be built upon with formal symposiums that take place once or twice per semester, where any member of the university community could contribute to a broader conversation and debate about the role of the law and its agents in society. Such a discussion would be cross-disciplinary, involving students and teachers of business, philosophy, engineering, geography, for example. The content of these discussions would always be recorded and then distilled into a report. These symposiums could be broadcast online and could invite contribution from people in other institutions around the world via webcast.

c. Regional Symposiums

Selected representatives of those university discussion groups would then meet with an external industry and policy-focused group to present the ideas and issues raised and hear similar contributions from those others present. This wider group of stakeholders could be brought together by regional law societies or bar associations, or by the universities again, or a public authority. The discussions and any conclusions of this representative group would also be noted and published. Universities, and professional and regulatory bodies could then use the outputs of these sessions when reviewing their objectives in the short, medium and long term. Universities, specifically, could take insights from industry to keep their course material relevant.

d. Annual Review

After the first year of these processes being put in place, there could be time set aside at one symposium per year for representatives to present changes they have made on the basis of recommendations that were put forward in the year prior. All changes would be recognised, and there could be some kind of award given each year for the most ground-breaking change. Adaptations made by universities could be tied in with law faculty ranking on a national and international level.

In order to ensure commitment to these new processes, it could be made mandatory for law faculty students and staff to attend and contribute to at least one of the university symposiums per semester. Lawyers and legal professionals could be required to attend at least one symposium annually as part of their continued professional development or similar scheme. The Ministry/Department of Justice could have a team dedicated to the facilitation and formalisation of these symposiums on a national level, ensuring that all output from the sessions goes into a public repository, accessible to anyone around the world.

In the words of the Irish orator, John Philpot Curran, eternal vigilance is the price of freedom (Denning 1988). Constant re-evaluation is needed to leave old habits and past wisdom behind and be open towards new possibilities. The framework above is one way we could ensure systematic re-evaluation on an ongoing basis.

E. Conclusion

Everyone needs a good crisis of identity every now and again. Fear for the security of one's position in society can bring about amazing evolution if approached constructively. The legal profession has held a privileged position throughout history, and for good reason, but the privilege it afforded its members inevitably led to a complacency which brought us to where we are today. With a little work, the systems that have brought, and still bring, about a lot of good can be invigorated to ensure that both society and the profession itself continue to flourish. This work can and should begin with our legal educators; those who are best positioned to change mindsets and inspire the next generation of legal professionals.

Bibliography

Accenture (2018), 'Closing the Skills Gap in the Future Workforce', available at <https://www.accenture.com/us-en/insights/future-workforce/transforming-lea rning> (last accessed 22 November 2018).

American Bar Association (2018), *Statistics*, available at <https://www.americanbar. org/groups/legal_education/resources/statistics/> (last accessed 22 November 2018).

Andreessen, M. (2011), 'Why Software Is Eating: The World', *Wall Street Journal*, available at <https://www.wsj.com/articles/SB100014240531119034809045 76 512250915629460> (last accessed 22 November 2018).

Burrage, M. (2006), *Revolution and the Making of the Contemporary Legal Profession: England, France, and the United States*, Oxford: Oxford University Press.

Cohen, M. (2018), 'New Business Models – Not Technology – Will Transform the Legal Industry', *Forbes*, available at <https://www.forbes.com/sites/markco hen1/2018/11/08/new-business-models-not-technology-will-transform-the-leg al-industry/#51686a6918cc> (last accessed 16 November 2018).

Courts Service Ireland n.d., 'Brehon Law: HERITAGE', available at <http:// www.courts.ie/Courts.ie/Library3.nsf/pagecurrent/62421128B249FE94 80257FC3005C7C67?opendocument> (last accessed 24 November. 2018).

Darryl R. and M. Mountain (2007), 'Disrupting Conventional Law Firm Business Models using Document Assembly', *International Journal of Law and Information Technology*, 15: 2, 1 July 2007, available at <https://doi.org/10.1093/ijlit/ eal019> (last accessed 13 June 2019), pp. 170–91.

Law School Transparency Data Dashboard (2018), *Law School Tuition in the United States, 1985 – 2017 – LST Data Dashboard*, available at <https://data.lawschool transparency.com/costs/tuition/> (last accessed 22 November 2018).

Duffy, S. (ed.) (2004), 'Brehon Laws', *Medieval Ireland: An Encyclopaedia*, Oxford: Taylor & Francis.

Hartman, E. (2016), 'Counterpoint: No, Lawyers Should Not Learn to Code', *Lawyerist*, available at <https://lawyerist.com/counterpoint-no-lawyers-not-learn-code/> (last accessed 24 November, 2018).

Harvard (2016), 'Recommendation to the President and Fellows of Harvard College on the Shield Approved for the Law School', available at <https://hls.harvard.edu/content/uploads/2016/03/Shield-Committee-Report.pdf> (last accessed 21 November 2018).

Hekman, D. R., G. A. Bigley, H. K. Steensma, J. F. Hereford (2009), 'Combined Effects of Organizational and Professional Identification on the Reciprocity Dynamic for Professional Employees', *Academy of Management Journal*, 52:3.

Insight Venture Partners (2018), 'Kira Systems Receives $50M Series: An Investment from Insight Venture Partners', available at <https://www.insightpartners.com/about-us/news-press/kira-systems-receives-50m-series-a-investment-from-insight-venture-partners/> (last accessed 23 November. 2018).

Brundage, J. A. (1994), 'The Rise of the Professional Jurist in the Thirteenth Century', *Syracuse Journal of International Law and Commerce* 20, p. 185.

Jones, A. H. M. (1964), *The Later Roman Empire, 284–602: A Social, Economic, and Administrative Survey*, vol. 1, Norman, OK: University of Oklahoma Press.

Jones, J., M. Regan Jr., J. Hines, W. Josten and J. Blackwood (2018), '2018 Report on the State of the Legal Market', *Thomson Reuters*, available at <http://www.legalexecutiveinstitute.com/2018-legal-market-report/> (last accessed 19 November 2018).

LinkedIn Economic Graph, (2018), 'How artificial intelligence is already impacting today's jobs', available at <https://economicgraph.linkedin.com/blog/how-artificial-intelligence-is-already-impacting-todays-jobs> (last accessed 22 November 2018).

Madison, M. (2015), 'Preparing for Service: A Template for 21st Century Legal Education', *University of Pittsburgh Legal Studies Research*, 12 August 2015, Paper No. 2015–27., available at <https://ssrn.com/abstract=2646931> or <http://dx.doi.org/10.2139/ssrn.2646931> (last accessed 16 November. 2018).

——— (2017), 'For a New Year: An Invitation Regarding Law, Legal Education, and Imagining the Future, Part I', *Madisonian: Essays on law, leadership, culture, and technology*, available at <http://madisonian.net/2017/12/29/for-a-new-year-an-invitation-regarding-law-legal-education-and-imagining-the-future-part-i/> (last accessed 15 November 2018).

——— (2017a), 'For a New Year: An Invitation Regarding Law, Legal Education, and Imagining the Future, Part II', *Madisonian: Essays on law, leadership, culture, and technology*, available at <http://madisonian.net/2017/12/30/for-a-new-year-an-invitation-regarding-law-legal-education-and-imagining-the-future-part-ii/> (last accessed 15 November. 2018).

———. (2017b), 'For a New Year: An Invitation Regarding Law, Legal Education, and Imagining the Future, Part III', *Madisonian: Essays on law, leadership, culture, and technology*, available at <http://madisonian.net/2017/12/31/for-a-new-year-some-thoughts-on-law-law-schools-and-imagining-the-future-part-iii/> (last accessed 16 November. 2018).

———. (2018a), 'For a New Year: An Invitation Regarding Law, Legal Education, and Imagining the Future, Part IV', *Madisonian: Essays on law, leadership, culture, and technology*, available at <http://madisonian.net/2018/01/01/for-a-new-year-some-thoughts-on-law-law-schools-and-imagining-the-future-part-iv/> (last accessed 16 November. 2018).

———— (2018b), 'For a New Year: An Invitation Regarding Law, Legal Education, and Imagining the Future, Part V', *Madisonian: Essays on law, leadership, culture, and technology*, available at <http://madisonian.net/2018/01/02/for-a-new-year-some-thoughts-on-law-law-schools-and-imagining-the-future-part-v/> (last accessed 16 November. 2018).

Manyika, J., M. Chui, M. Miremadi, J. Bughin, K. George, P. Willmott and M. Dewhurst, (2017), 'Harnessing automation for a future that works', *McKinsey Global Institute*, available at <https://www.mckinsey.com/featured-insights/digital-disruption/harnessing-automation-for-a-future-that-works> (last accessed 12 November. 2018).

McKinsey & Company (2017), *A Future That Works: Automation, Employment, and Productivity*, McKinsey Global Institute.

McKinsey Global Institute (2017), *Technology, jobs, and the future of work*, McKinsey Global Institute, available at <https://www.mckinsey.com/featured-insights/employment-and-growth/technology-jobs-and-the-future-of-work>, <https://www.mckinsey.com/featured-insights/employment-and-growth/technology-jobs-and-the-future-of-work> (last accessed 12 May 2017).

Solicitors Regulation Authority (2018), *Regulated population statistics*, available at <https://www.sra.org.uk/sra/how-we-work/reports/data/population_solicitors.page> (last accessed 22 November 2018).

Statista (2018), *Barristers & Judges 2011–2018 | UK Statistic*, available at <https://www.statista.com/statistics/319217/number-of-barristers-and-judges-in-the-uk/> (last accessed 22 November 2018).

Susskind, R. (2018), 'AI, work and "outcome-thinking"', *British Academy Review*, available at <https://www.thebritishacademy.ac.uk/publications/british-academy-review/34/ai-work-and-outcome-thinking> last accessed 16 November 2018).

The Council of Bars and Law Societies of Europe (CCBE) (2018), *Statistics – CCBE*, available at <https://www.ccbe.eu/actions/statistics/> (last accessed 22 November. 2018).

The Future of Jobs Report (2018), 'Insight Report', World Economic Forum, available at <http://www3.weforum.org/docs/WEF_Future_of_Jobs_2018.pdf> (last accessed 23 November. 2018).

Thompson Denning, A. (1988), *The Road to Justice*, Fred B. Rothman & Company.

17

Teaching Law After the #feesmustfall Protests – How Technology Saved the Day at University of the Western Cape

Angelo Dube

A. Introduction

The struggle for academic inclusion and free education is much older than the #feesmustfall movement. For years students in historically black universities have been waging battles against academic exclusion and mounting student debt. The academic struggle for students has for a long time been closely intertwined with the struggle for freedom at the national level. South Africa's history is littered with attempts by white governments to subjugate the indigenes of the land to dehumanising treatment, such as linguistic assimilation. For example, when the apartheid government attempted to impose Afrikaans as a medium of instruction in the 1970s, this led to widespread student protests, with the epicentre being the Soweto student uprisings of 1976. Ndlovu asserts that this clandestine move was the brainchild of the Broederbond, the secret society that enabled the ascendance of the Afrikaners and their racist policies to government in South Africa (Ndlovu 2017).

Over the years racial policies had been adopted as a means to ensure that certain races only received poor quality education, and eventually could not take up certain trades. The 1950s saw this resort to racially segregationist policies intensify. Following the recommendations of the Commission of Inquiry on Native Education in the early 1950s, racial segregation was strengthened at South African institutions of higher learning. Part of the modus operandi was to tighten control over Bantu and Coloured education, by ensuring that only students of a particular skin colour could legally be enrolled at particular institutions.

Between 2015 and 2016, South Africa was again gripped by countrywide student protests, which saw a number of institutions of higher learning close down, and the academic calendar shifted. So dire was the situation that some institutions came to the brink of forfeiting the entire academic year to ensure the integrity of their degrees. The problem for most universities was compounded by the fact that round about the same time, the Department of Higher Education and Training (DHET) embarked on a review of the LLB degrees in all universities across South Africa. The DHET process involved three key steps, namely a national review process; institutional audits or reviews; and the accreditation or reaccreditation of LLB programmes at various institutions (Parliamentary Office 2017).

The protests which were carried out under the banner of the Fees Must Fall Movement (FMF), developed organically out of students' frustrations with many social ills and concerns about the lack of good governance in general. In some cases, these protests were levelled against the inefficiency of the student-funding scheme, the National Students Financial Aid Scheme (NSFAS) (Godsell and Chikane 2016). Popularised by the online hashtag #feesmustfall, the demands made by students began reverberating throughout South Africa. But the movement did not start off as the FMF movement calling for fee-free higher education; instead the first signs of commotion and student solidarity in South Africa's democratic era began to emerge after student activist, Chumani Maxwele adorned a statue of colonialist Cecil John Rhodes with human excrement at the Upper Campus of the previously white only University of Cape Town (UCT) in March 2015 (SA History 2018).

Despite media backlash and portrayal of the actions of Maxwele and company as nothing but hooliganism, the movement grew and added new demands to the initial one, which was the removal of the statue of Rhodes. The list now included the need to decolonise the UCT over and above the removal of the offending statue. At this stage, the movement was gaining popularity online with the hashtag #rhodesmustfall. The #rhodesmustfall movement finally had its victory a month later when the statute was brought down (Laing 2015). Slowly but surely, a fallist philosophy was beginning to emerge in South African student politics.

UCT's deeply entrenched colonial outlook on education goes beyond the simple matter of colonial symbols such as statues of Rhodes and other architects of African suffering, but permeates halls of learning and the pedagogical approaches that the university adopts in its teaching and learning. An illustrative case is that of Prof Mahmood Mamdani, who in 1999 resigned in protest after UCT refused to implement his proposed core course on Africa. He returned to the institution in 2017 (Omar 2017). When questioned on why he would return to an institution that rejected him for his attempts to decolonise the curriculum, he responded 'because Rhodes fell' (Davies 2017). In his 2017 public lecture, Mamdani also emphasised on the need to decolonise the curriculum and reiterated that 'to socialise education is to reduce fees' (Omoyele 2017). It is worth noting that the #rhodesmustfall movement was not only focused on removing the statute of Cecil John Rhodes, but tied to that demand was the disenchantment with the colonial culture at higher education institutions in general. These would later morph, by late 2015 and early 2016, into calls for decolonisation of universities and the appallingly low number of black South African scholars across South African universities (Costandius, et al. 2018).

Ndelu asserts that at the heart of the #feesmustfall protests, was the call for a radical reimagination of the higher education space, characterised by calls for decolonisation of the curriculum and transformation. The decolonisation call essentially demanded that the following elements be infused into the higher education sector, namely, to ensure that the academic space reflects South Africa's racial and gender demographics, the destabilisation of western epistemologies and pedagogies, as well as putting an end to outsourcing of services at universities (Ndelu 2017).

The FMF protests took place almost simultaneously at all institutions of higher learning in South Africa. Media coverage of these protests at historically black universities was very paltry, as most mainstream media houses focused on historically white-only universities (Langa 2017). This distortion is often influenced by the interests of economic power and desire to condemn protesting movements as mere hooliganism.

B. Understanding Fallism

Essentially, fallism is concerned about social justice and the exclusion that until recently characterised the South African higher education sector (Mabasa 2017). Developed on the back of a constitution that aspires to produce a transformed South Africa, eschewed of inequality, sexism, racism and other forms of prejudice, fallism brought to question the failures of the South African Government to transform the higher education sector two decades after it came into power. The movement highlighted that all that the government had done over the years was merely to pay lip service to the fight against inequality. Its growth was thus a response to the need to dismantle the exploitative socio-economic power configurations that appropriated social assets as a means of legitimising white economic and cultural dominance (Mabasa 2017). Fallism has been defined as an insistence on moving beyond the boundaries of civil discourse towards attacking the symbols of white supremacy through disruptive acts of rage (Headley and Kobe 2017).

C. Methodology

The study was carried within the Law Faculty of the University of the Western Cape (UWC), using two distinct questionnaires designed for students on the one hand, and academic staff on the other. These were administered through Google Forms. Random sampling was used. Each questionnaire was designed to elicit responses specific to each category of respondent, based on what their experiences were during the #feesmustfall protests. A total of twenty students responded to the questionnaire, while eight responses were received from staff members. The responses were then analysed and incorporated into the narrative on student and staff experiences during FMF movement.

D. An Overview of the South African Higher Education Sector

South African universities can largely be regarded as institutions that present higher education using the traditional teaching and learning methods. As such, the majority of institutions can be regarded as traditional contact universities, where the academic stands before a lecture hall full of students and presents his or her lectures to that class. With the exception of the University of South Africa (UNISA) which is an open distance learning (ODL) institution, the majority of South African universities require both the student and the lecturer to be physically present in the same venue for learning to take place. Blended learning, however, consists in the integration of online education technology together with traditional teaching and learning methodologies in legal teaching. Dzuiban et al. define blended learning as the integration of face-to-face and online instruction (Dzuiban, et al. 2018). They argue further, that this form of learning forces us to consider the characteristics of digital technology, in general, and information communication technologies (ICTs) more specifically. Sinclaire defines a blended or hybrid course as one in which a substantial portion of the content is delivered online (Sinclaire 2014).

As early as 2004, the South African Government was already engaging with the use of ICTs in the education sector. The 2004 Education White Paper highlights the centrality of ICTs in providing what the government terms 'e-Education'. E-Education is described as consisting in the connection of learners and teachers to each other and to professional support services, as well as providing platforms for learning. It effectively combines pedagogy and technology to bring about reforms within the education sector, resulting in improved assessments, and use of educational resources. In essence, ICTs are the main driver behind e-Education. ICTs are supposed to increase the quality and quantity of interactions between learners and teachers (Department of Basic Education 2004).

It is trite that ICTs enable e-learning. The White Paper defines e-learning as flexible learning using ICT resources, tools and applications. During this process, the main focus is on the following: (1) accessing information, (2) interaction among teachers, learners, and the online environment, (3) collaborative learning, as well as (4) production of materials, resources and learning experiences. While today the Internet is largely the most common platform via which e-learning occurs, it could also involve the use of CD-ROM, software, mobile apps, other media and telecommunications. E-learning is much more broader than the concept of online learning, which only relates more specifically to the use of the Internet and associated web-based applications as vehicles for facilitating the teaching and learning experience (Department of Basic Education 2004).

E. Technology in the South African Higher Education Sector

In South Africa, most universities adopt traditional, paper-based approaches to teaching and learning. Although this approach is from time to time augmented by online-based teaching tools, the uptake of newer technologies is not progressing at the desired rate. For a number of these institutions, this approach is part of their legacy, a historical fact that flows from the days of the segregationist apartheid regime (Ng'ambi, et al. 2016). For others, the prohibitive cost of technology prevents them from moving beyond the analogue format and embracing new educational tools. It has been said that teaching and learning in such environments is characterised by 'analogue professors in a digital world'.

Ng'ambi et al. opine that there has been a shift since 2006, in which more higher education institutions exhibited a shift towards emerging technologies in order to address challenges they faced. Some of the key catalysts for this move include the rising cost of education, diminishing governmental funding and increasing pressure to improve throughput and efficiency (Ng'ambi, et al. 2016).

The benefits of embracing educational technologies are manifold. For instance, Waghid and Waghid argue that technology can play a facilitative role in the improvement of and transformation in contemporary society (Waghid and Waghid 2016). Further benefits include encouraging students to engage in the process of teaching and learning more.

In 2016, there were 26 public higher education institutions, 123 registered private higher education institutions, 15 technical and vocational education and training (TVET) institutions, 279 registered private colleges and 9 community education and training (CET) colleges. Private colleges accounted for only 7 per cent of post-high school student enrolments in South Africa. The majority of enrolments (50 per cent) were enrolled in public higher education institutions. TVET colleges accounted for 31 per cent of enrolments, while CETs accounted for 12 per cent (DHET 2016). The rest were absorbed by various publicly funded higher education institutions.

The University of South Africa is the oldest open distance learning (ODL) university in South Africa, at more 145 years today. As such it was the pioneer in embracing technology in its teaching and learning activities. It thus remains far advanced in comparison to other South African universities. The fact that it serves students spread across the globe also adds to its preparedness to embrace any advancements in educational technology. The other institutions of higher learning, the University of the Western Cape included, trail behind in this regard. The #feesmustfall protests acted as a catalyst for most institutions to begin to look at innovative ways to deliver teaching and learning. While the uptake of new and emerging technologies might have spiked slightly after the protests, a majority of these institutions remain largely traditional contact universities.

I. The Discord in the Transition from Tertiary to the Workplace

While these advances in incorporating technology into legal training at university are commended, there remain real challenges when it comes to the other spheres of the law both inside and outside the classroom. Within the context of academia, the real challenge is that there remains a crop of professors who are slow to embrace these technologies. While students, and perhaps younger members of faculty may warm up to these technological interventions for teaching and learning, older professors, in the main, tend to want to have minimal contact with newer technologies. The academy is thus left with analogue professors in a digital world. This resistance to change can be explained in part as flowing from comfort with the status quo. Part of the problem, however, lies with institutions failing to provide adequate training for professors who are expected to adopt these technological changes (Nagel 2013). Howard and Mojesko assert that educators who are more confident in using technology are more likely to embrace it and integrate it in their teaching and learning (Howard and Mojesko 2015).

Apart from internal resistance to new technologies, there seems to be a disjuncture between the move by universities to embrace technology and the manner in which the world of work is designed. The legal sector is still a predominantly paper-based environment, which relies heavily on human presence or intervention. For instance, although firms globally have started to embrace articifical intelligence (AI) in the form of chatbots for offering advice to clients, South African firms still lag behind in that regard. Although the law firm Norton Rose announced its use of chatbots in 2018, it was doing so not necessarily as a South African firm, but as a spin-off of its European presence (Business Tech 2018).

F. Students as Rouble Rousers or Agents of Social Change? Understanding the Response of Universities to Student Demands

As more students gain access to higher education, classes grow larger, instructors have more students to teach and more classes become just lectures with little interaction time. The instructor student ratio increases exponentially (Bates 2015). UWC is characterised by very large class numbers in comparison to other universities. It is also characterised by a high number of students from very poor backgrounds, who struggle with tuition fees and mere subsistence throughout the academic year. Hence the call for free decolonised quality education resonated with them more than their counterparts in previously whites-only universities such as Stellenbosch University.

It is worth noting that the history of the South African higher education sector is replete with racial, class and gender inequities (Mabokela 2001). UWC classifies itself as a previously disadvantaged university. In other words, it developed as a response to the apartheid regime's policy of excluding black people from whites-only universities. The institution's history is steeped in active participation in the struggle against oppression, discrimination and disadvantage. It was created via an Act of Parliament by the then government, and it was classified as a 'coloured' university (UWC 2013). From its very inception, UWC has been an institution that housed the marginalised, and ensured that students who could not enrol either at Stellenbosch University or University of Cape Town on account of their skin colour, still had access to education. These two Western Cape universities, and others across South Africa, were initially reserved for whites only (Lueshcer 2009). Hence in the context of student protests aimed at decolonising the curriculum and pushing for fee free higher education, students at UWC had high expectations that university management would be sympathetic to their cause.

The protest action at UWC was led by student formations representing various political ideologies and affiliated to different political parties. These included the Pan-African Student Movement of Azania (PASMA), affiliated to the Pan African Congress; the South African Student Congress (SASCO), affiliated to the African National Congress (ANC); the Economic Freedom Fighters' EFF Student Command; the Democratic Alliance (DA) affiliated DA Student Organisation (DASO); and a group calling itself the 'feminist group', with no express affiliations (Maringira and Gukurume 2017). It should be noted, however, that the participation of members of these political groupings in the protests was not necessarily at the same level. For example, DASO members who mostly come from affluent suburbs largely did not participate in the FMF protests. SASCO members were also caught between a rock and a hard place due to their political ideology, as they did not want to be seen to be criticising the ANC, the very same ruling party that was refusing to deliver free higher education.

The response of the state and the university to the protracted, violent student protests was to send in heavily armed police officers, and private security personnel. The protests were characterised by the burning of buildings, the destruction of university infrastructure, looting of shops, and there were incidents of rapes of females within the residences on campus. Members of staff were violently thrown out of offices, had their cars toppled over, and some were kept hostage in their offices and could not leave campus. Those members of staff who insisted on continuing with their lectures on campus had their classes violently disrupted by toyi-toying students. The entire university scene became a very traumatic space for members of the faculty, and neither the state police nor the university could ensure the safety of both staff and their property. This was compounded by the fact that the university insisted that the campus remain open and it was business as usual, indicating that members of staff must still report for duty.

When it became apparent that the currency for the FMF protests was civil disobedience and violence, the university had to devise new strategies for coping with the unprecedented levels of violence and chaos. UWC's response to the disruption of classes and the threat posed for scheduled exams was the adoption of blended learning to convey teaching materials and ensure that all scheduled learning for the academic year was completed as planned. The survey conducted as part of this research indicates that this intervention was a novel one, and was highly appreciated by both learners and faculty staff. Wu and Liu posit that blended learning is sometimes referred to as mixed learning, hybrid learning and blended e-learning. Blended learning thus takes advantage of various delivery methods to perfectly achieve the course objectives (Wu and Liu 2013).

While some institutions of higher learning dismissed the protests as nothing more than criminal elements looking for a chance to disrupt, loot and vandalise property in the guise of protesting, others were beginning to slowly see the merit in the students' demands. For example, the Wits School of Governance at the University of Witwatersrand noted in its annual report that the FMF movement was legitimately calling for significant changes to the curriculum and how it is presented. The School's response consisted of various interventions, including developing a library of over 200 key words on governance by African scholars, while at the same time interrogating ways to decolonise the curriculum. For this, Wits had its academics squarely focused on devising ways and means to present a curriculum eschewed of colonial dogma, and instead to come up with one that takes into account current realities of the modern South African society (Wits School of Governance 2016).

The Wits School of Governance also acknowledged the positive spin-offs of the countrywide FMF protests. One of these outcomes was the open debate that ensued, which allowed universities to engage in some form of introspection. This led to a revision of the curriculum and pedagogy, and a reformation of the manner in which modules are presented and accessed by students. The University of South Africa also embraced transformation of the curriculum across various faculties. For instance, after the FMF protests, the teaching of the module International Law followed a decolonial approach as the module was taught from the perspective of the global south. This necessitated a complete revision of teaching material to include African epistemologies.

G. Specific Problems or Challenges Faced by UWC

Although the underlying problem that formed the thrust of the FMF protests resonated with a large majority of students across South Africa, different universities faced different challenges as a result of the violence and class disruptions. Much of these had to do with the history of each institution and the composition of the protestors. For UWC, as a historically black university, with a large proportion of the student body coming from extremely poor, gang-infested backgrounds, the problem was thus further compounded.

I. Educational Access

Dzuiban et al. argue that lack of access to educational technologies and innovations pose a challenge to institutions attempting to embrace blended learning. This is sometimes termed the digital divide (Dzuiban, et al. 2018). The digital divide is much more pronounced for previously disadvantaged universities such as UWC, and it got compounded even further with the onset of the FMF protests. The positive spin off though, was that the situation forced both staff and students to embrace technology, thereby breaching the digital divide. For example, 58 per cent of student respondents indicated that they had used technology to access education before, while 42 per cent had never done so. This is a higher threshold compared to only 37.5 per cent of staff who had used technology in their teaching prior to the protests. Among the interventions employed were: (1) the use of power point slides, (2) use of the online learning management system called iKamva, (3) use of online tests instead of traditional sit-in exams, as well as (4) use of videos in presenting materials to students.

Questioned on the use of technology by their lecturers during the protests, 79 per cent of the student respondents answered in the affirmative, while 21 per cent responded in the negative. For staff members, the uptake of technology in teaching and learning rose to 62.5 per cent during the FMF protests. The responses further indicate that lecturers became innovative as a result of the protests. For example, they provided 'consultation hot seats' where students met with faculty members in safer spaces away from campus. This was much more feasible for postgraduate modules where the class numbers are significantly lower. This intervention still required faculty members to get in touch with students via WhatsApp or Facebook to announce the venues for these hot seats, without triggering a violent response from the protest organisers. Despite the eagerness to embrace technology during the FMF protests, it is worth noting that 52 per cent of respondents (students) indicated that this use of blended learning was a one-off event, there was no continued usage by most members of faculty after the FMF protests. Faculty members also indicated that the disruptions brought about 'a greater chance to use technology', but 100 per cent of them reported that these interventions continued even after the FMF protests. Perhaps the disparity in opinion can be explained by conflicting understanding of what blended learning is.

II. Students' Perception of Their Learning Environment /of the Interventions

To ascertain the impact of these innovative interventions on the academy, it is imperative to look at student satisfaction with the measures adopted.

Underlying this is what is termed 'the construct of the student' and it involves the following parameters: students' demographic data, learning style and satisfaction with the course. Student satisfaction is a very amorphous term, and is extremely difficult to define. It has been defined as the perception of enjoyment and accomplishment in the learning environment. It has also been said to be the sum of a student's behavioural beliefs and attitudes that result from aggregating all the benefits that a student receives from using the blended system. Student satisfaction is pegged on five pillars, namely: learner-learner and learner-teacher interaction, online environment, technical support, printed materials and face to face environment (Wu and Liu 2013).

The results of the survey showed ambivalence with regards to students' satisfaction with the interventions introduced by UWC. Some felt that the university did nothing more than to continue to use the learning management platform, iKamva, which had been in use even before the FMF protests. Others pegged their satisfaction on the fact that they eventually passed their modules, and yet others found the interventions necessary and helpful. A handful indicated that they found these to be greatly received by students.

Student respondents also indicated that technology played a central role in ensuring that teaching and learning continued with minimal disruption during the FMF disturbances. They were able to carry on with their work in safer spaces away from the violence on campus. Meanwhile it also enabled them to get access to materials for exam preparation. The results showed a total of 90 per cent of respondents (students) who were satisfied with the use of technology. Others (up to 10 per cent) felt that even though notable overtures had been extended by the university, several factors militated against full enjoyment of those interventions. For instance, the dissatisfied students cited lack of Wi-Fi hotspots, smart phones or laptops to access those very same technologies. In fact, even those students who remained on campus during the protests, reported that Wi-Fi routers were offline. These are the factors that affected student satisfaction with the use of technology during the protests. The survey revealed that 47 per cent of those interviewed relied on free Wi-Fi provided by UWC, 42 per cent relied on Internet provided at their places of residence other than a UWC residence, and five per cent relied on data purchased by themselves or their families. These statistics demonstrate just how difficult, if not impossible, it was for students to continue with teaching and learning during the FMF protests.

While student satisfaction with overall use of new technologies in teaching and learning was extremely high, results showed a somewhat ambivalent result when assessing the role of social media in transmitting learning materials during the protests. A total of 53 per cent indicated that social media was much cheaper for them to utilise, and it offered real time updates as well as made it easy to interact with peers and share materials. Only 47 per cent indicated that either social media was not helpful at all, or that they had not used social media before and did not use it even during the FMF protests. Against the overarching drawback in responses to this question was the prohibitive cost of using WhatsApp and other social media platforms for students. The survey indicated that 53 per cent of students were affected by the prohibitive cost of buying data bundles, while 37 per cent cited lack of access to the Internet (insufficient Wi-Fi coverage) as the main stumbling block. As one faculty member responded, the introduction of blended learning 'made life hell for students'.

III. Technical Support

One of the critical determinants for improving educational quality is creating a supportive learning environment (Mavondo, Tsarenko and Gabott 2004). There was widespread apprehension and disillusionment when UWC decided to implement these interventions, and these could likely have influenced the perception of students vis-à-vis their satisfaction with the intervention. It could well be that indeed UWC had not sufficiently prepared students (and staff) for the interventions, since they were implemented as a response to a dire situation. The data indicates that 53 per cent of students felt unsupported by the university. The 47 per cent that responded affirmatively to the question of student support indicated that data bundles and USB storage devices with content were made available to those students without access to the Internet. Other student respondents highlighted that towards the end of the protests, students could visit the learning management site freely without being charged by the Internet service providers. However, this was in the second year of the FMF protests, indicating that universities were better prepared and much more responsive this time around.

IV. Learner-learner and Learner-teacher Interaction

The onset of the violent FMF protests disrupted normal schooling and introduced an environment which was not conducive for teaching and learning. Student perceptions about how FMF protests affected their ability to interact with each other and with their instructors drew varied responses. A total of 76 per cent of respondents indicated that email was the only functional mode of communication during the protests. The other 24 per cent used a combination of both email and WhatsApp to communicate with both their lecturers and their peers.

H. Conclusion

Although major gains were made as a result of the violent, protracted FMF protests, students and the UWC faculty members remain divided on whether such gains outweighed the losses. Some of the losses, they claim cannot be quantified, for example the trauma that was experienced by academic staff during the protests. While student trauma was widely covered in the media, and is generally acknowledged, members of faculty remain faceless victims, battling with their own trauma from that period. An illustrative case would be that of UCT professor Mayosi who committed suicide in the middle of 2018 (Cameron 2018). A number of possible causes were cited for his decision to untimely terminate his life. These included his battle with depression, which, some commentators argued, was worsened by students blockading his office and mocking him during the FMF protests.

The majority of student respondents (68 per cent), when questioned on whether the FMF protests were a negative or positive development in relation to teaching and learning, voted the protests overwhelmingly negative. Interestingly 50 per cent of faculty members were ambivalent, while only 12.5 per cent found it to be negative.

Bibliography

Bates, A. (2015), *Teaching in a Digital Age*, Vancouver: Tony Bates Associates.

Business Tech (2018), 'Legal chatbot will tell you whether new EU data laws apply to your South African business', <https://businesstech.co.za/news/technology/ 244249/legal-chatbot-will-tell-you-whether-new-eu-data-laws-apply-to-your-south-african-business/> (last accessed 16 April 2019).

Cameron, J. (2018), 'Reflections on suicide of Professor Bongani Mayosi, persecuted to death – Ed Herbst', *Biz News,* 7 August, <https://www.biznews.com/thought-leaders/2018/08/07/suicide-professor-bongani-mayosi-death-ed-herbst>   (last accessed 16 April 2019).

Costandius, E., M. Blackie, I. Nell, R. Malgas, N. Alexander, E. Setati, and M. McKay (2018), '#FeesMustFall and decolonising the curriculum: Stellenbosch University students' and lecturers' reactions', *South African Journal of Higher Education* 32:2, 65–85.

Davies, R. (2017), 'Mahmood Mamdani: Sixteen years on, UCT's old nemesis returns to talk decolonisation', 23 August, <https://www.dailymaverick.co.za/ article/2017-08-23-mahmood-mamdani-sixteen-years-on-ucts-old-nemesis-returns-to-talk-decolonisation/#.WzsKGtUzapo> (last accessed 2 July 2018).

Department of Basic Education (2004), *White Paper on e-Education – Transforming Learning and Teaching through Information and Communication Technologies (ICTs)*, White Paper, Department of Basic Education, Pretoria: Government Printers, <http://www.sahistory.org.za/archive/white-paper-e-education-2004> (last accessed 27 April 2018).

DHET (2016), *Statistics on post-school education and training in South Africa.* Pretoria: Department of Higher Education and Training.

Dzuiban, C., C. Graham, P. Moskal, A. Norberg and N. Sicilia (2018), 'Blended learning: the new normal and emerging technologies', *International Journal of Educational Technology in Higher Education* 15:3, 2–16.

Godsell, G and R. Chikane (2016), 'The roots of the revolution', in S. Booysen (ed.), *Fees Must Fall: Student Revolt, Decolonisation,* Johannesburg: Wits University Press.

Headley, S. and S. L. Kobe (2017), 'Christian activism and the fallists: What about reconciliation?' *Theological Studies* 73:3, 1–11.

Howard, S. and A. Mojesko (2015), 'Teachers: technology, change and resistance', in M. Henderson and G. Romeo (eds.), *Teaching and Digital Technologies: Big Issues and Critical Questions*, Port Melbourne: Cambridge University Press 1–10.

Laing, A. (2015), *The Telegraph*, 9 April, <https://www.telegraph.co.uk/news/world news/africaandindianocean/southafrica/11525938/Cecil-Rhodes-statue-pulled-down-in-Cape-Town.html> (last accessed 1 May 2018).

Langa, M. (2017), 'Researching the #feesmustfall movement', in M. Langa (ed.), *An Analysis of the #FeesMustFall Movement at South African Universities*, Cape Town: Centre for the Study of Violence and Reconciliation, pp. 6–12.

Lueshcer, T. (2009), 'Racial desegregation and the institutionalisation of "race" in university governance: The case of UCT', *Perspectives in Education* 27:4.

Mabasa, K. (2017), 'The rebellion of the born un-frees: Fallism and the neo-colonial corporate university', *Strategic Review for Southern Africa* 39:2, 94–116.

Mabokela, R. (2001), 'Student perceptions of institutional racial climate', *Equity and Excellence in Education* 34:3, 70–79.

Maringira, G. and S. Gukurume (2017), 'Being black in #feesmustfall and #freede-colonisededucation: Student protests at the University of the Western Cape', in M. Langa (ed.), *#Hashtag: An Analysis of the #FeesMustFall Movement at South African Universities*, Cape Town: Centre for the Study of Violence and Reconciliation, pp. 33–48.

Mavondo, F., Y. Tsarenko and M. Gabott (2004), 'International and local student satisfaction: resources and capabilities perspective', *Journal of Marketing for Higher Education* 14:1, 41–60.

Nagel, D. (2013), *Six technology challenges facing education*, <https://thejournal.com/articles/2013/06/04/6-technology-challenges-facing-education.aspx> (last accessed 16 April 2019).

Ndelu, S. (2017), 'A rebellion of the poor: Fallism at the Cape Peninsula University of Technology', in M. Langa (ed.), *#Hashtag: An Analysis of the #FeesMustFall Movement at South African Universities*, Cape Town: Centre for the Study of Violence and Reconciliation, pp. 13–32.

Ndlovu, S. (2017), *The Soweto Uprisings: Counter Memories of June 1976*, Hampshire: Pan MacMillan.

Ng'ambi, D., C. Brown, V. Bozalek, D. Gachago and D. Wood (2016), 'Technology enhanced teaching and learning in South African higher education – A rearview of a 20 year journey', *British Journal of Educational Technology* 47:5, 843–58.

Omar, Y. (2017), *Mamdani returns*, University of Cape Town, 24 August, <https://www.news.uct.ac.za/article/-2017-08-24-mamdani-returns> (last accessed 2 July 2018).

Omoyele, I. (2017), *Post-colonial universities are trapped by their past*, 17 August, <https://mg.co.za/article/2017-08-31-00-post-colonial-universities-are-trapped-by-their-past> (last accessed 2 July 2018).

Parliamentary Office (2017), *LLB Programme not meeting required standards*. Memorandum, Parliament of South Africa, Cape Town: National Council of Provinces, 1, <http://www.dhet.gov.za/Parliamentary%20Matters/PQ%202017/June/76%20LLB%20Institutions%20that%20does%20not%20meet%20requirements.pdf> (last accessed 6 November 2018).

SA History (2018), *University of Witwatersrand Student Protests 2015 Timeline*, 30 April, <http://www.sahistory.org.za/article/university-witwatersrand-student-protests-2015-timeline> (last accessed 30 April 2018).

Sinclaire, J. (2014), 'Student satisfaction with online learning: Lessons from organizational behaviour', *Research in Higher Education Journal* 11, 1–18.

University of the Western Cape (2013), *Welcome to UWC History*, <https://www.uwc.ac.za/Pages/History.aspx> (last accessed 26 July 2018).

Waghid, Z. and F. Waghid (2016), 'Examining digital technology for (higher) education through action research and critical discourse analysis', *South African Journal of Higher Education* 30:1, 265–84.

Wits School of Governance (2016), *Annual Report*. Johannesburg: Wits School of Governance, 3.

Wu, J. and W. Liu (2013), 'An empirical investigation of the critical factors affecting students' satisfaction in EFL blended learning', *Journal of Language Teaching and Research* 4:1, 176–85.

Index